LAWYERS' MEDICINE

The major theme of this book is the way the requirements, limitations and intellectual structure of the British legal process have shaped medicine and medical practice. The story of this inter-relationship is greatly under-researched, which is particularly concerning given that the legal system remains a significant and pervasive influence on medicine and its practice to this day. The question which unifies the series of historical studies presented here is whether legal consideration of medical practice and concepts has played a part in the construction of medical concepts and affected developments in medical practice—in other words how the external, legal gaze has shaped the way medicine itself conceptualises some of its practices and classifications. The majority of the papers consider this question in the context of the development and application of legislation, but the influence of court processes is also considered. Other themes which emerge from the book include the nature and exclusivity of medical expertise, the impact of public opinion on the development of medical legislation, and the difficulty the legal system has faced in dealing with new medical developments that existing legal mechanisms are inappropriate for or indeed incapable of regulating effectively. The chapters are arranged chronologically, with an introduction drawing out themes that emerge from the chapters as a whole.

Lawyers' Medicine

The Legislature, the Courts and Medical Practice, 1760–2000

Edited by
Imogen Goold
and
Catherine Kelly

•HART•
PUBLISHING
OXFORD AND PORTLAND, OREGON
2009

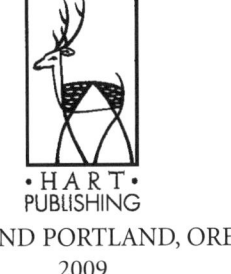

Published in North America (US and Canada) by
Hart Publishing
c/o International Specialized Book Services
920 NE 58th Avenue, Suite 300
Portland, OR 97213-3786
USA
Tel: +1 503 287 3093 or toll-free: (1) 800 944 6190
Fax: +1 503 280 8832
E-mail: orders@isbs.com
Website: http://www.isbs.com

© The editors and contributors severally, 2009

The editors and contributors have asserted their right under the Copyright, Designs and Patents Act 1988, to be identified as the authors of this work.

All rights reserved. No part of this publication may be reproduced, stored in a retrieval system, or transmitted, in any form or by any means, without the prior permission of Hart Publishing, or as expressly permitted by law or under the terms agreed with the appropriate reprographic rights organisation. Enquiries concerning reproduction which may not be covered by the above should be addressed to Hart Publishing at the address below.

Hart Publishing Ltd, 16C Worcester Place, Oxford, OX1 2JW
Telephone: +44 (0)1865 517530 Fax: +44 (0)1865 510710
E-mail: mail@hartpub.co.uk
Website: http://www.hartpub.co.uk

British Library Cataloguing in Publication Data
Data Available

ISBN: 978-1-84113-849-7

Typeset by Compuscript Ltd, Shannon
Printed and bound in Great Britain by
TJ International Ltd, Padstow, Cornwall

ACKNOWLEDGMENTS

This collection grew out of a seminar series held at the Wellcome Unit for the History of Medicine in Oxford between April and June 2007 entitled 'Medicine and the Law in History, 1760–1990', for which speakers were invited to present papers discussing the impact of legal regulation (in its various forms) on the development of medical practice and/or theory in different periods of history.

First and foremost, we would like to thank Professor Mark Harrison, the Unit's director, for giving us the opportunity to convene the series, and for all his subsequent support for the production of this collection. This book would not have been possible without the co-operation and enthusiasm of all the authors, and we thank them for both their support of the seminar series and their contributions to this collection. We are also very grateful to Carol Brady and Belinda Michaelides for their work in ensuring the seminar series ran smoothly and to Margaret Pelling for her wise advice along the way. Finally, we would like to express our sincere thanks to Richard Hart for having faith in our project and offering us a chance to bring these papers together in print.

Imogen Goold and Catherine Kelly
Oxford
November 2008

TABLE OF CONTENTS

Acknowledgments v
List of Contributors ix
Abbreviations xiii

1. Introduction: Lawyers' Medicine: The Interaction of the Medical
   Profession and the Law, 1760–2000 1
   Catherine Kelly and Imogen Goold

2. Parliamentary Inquiries and the Construction of Medical
   Argument in the Early 19th Century, 1793–1825 17
   Catherine Kelly

3. Bye Laws, the Environment, and Health before Chadwick,
   1835–1840 39
   James Hanley

4. Is a Burn a Wound? Vitriol-Throwing in Medico-Legal Context,
   1800–1900 61
   Katherine D Watson

5. Not Their Fathers' Sons: The Changing Trajectory in Psychiatric
   Testimony, 1760–1900 79
   Joel Peter Eigen

6. Speaking Out about Staying Silent: An Historical Examination of
   Medico-legal Debates over the Boundaries of Medical Confidentiality 99
   Angus H Ferguson

7. Law, Medicine and the Treatment of Homosexual Offenders
   in Scotland, 1950–1980 125
   Roger Davidson

8. The Medical Community and Abortion Law Reform: Scotland in
   National Context, c 1960–1980 143
   Gayle Davis

9. Regulating Reproduction in the United Kingdom: Doctors' Voices, 1978–1985 167
   Imogen Goold

10. Nobody's Thing? Human Tissue in Science, Ethics and the Law during the late 20th Century 197
    Duncan Wilson

Index 219

LIST OF CONTRIBUTORS

Roger Davidson is Emeritus Professor of Social History at the University of Edinburgh and a Leverhulme Emeritus Fellow. He read History at St Catharine's College, Cambridge and received his PhD at Cambridge in 1971. He was appointed to a Lectureship in Economic and Social History at the University of Edinburgh in 1970, and was subsequently promoted to Senior Lecturer in 1984, Reader in 1996 and to a Personal Chair in 2002. In collaboration with Dr Gayle Davis, he has recently completed a Wellcome-funded project on 'Health, Sexuality and the State in Scotland, 1950–80', that explored policy-making with respect to a range of issues relating to sexual health and sexual offences, including abortion, censorship, family planning, prostitution, homosexual law reform, prostitution, sex education and sexually transmitted diseases. He is a Fellow of both the Royal Historical Society and a former member of the Scottish Records Advisory Council. He co-edited *Social History of Medicine* from 2000 to 2004.

Gayle Davis is Wellcome Lecturer in the History of Medicine at the University of Edinburgh (School of History, Classics and Archaeology). She read history at the University of Glasgow, and in 2001 received her PhD from the University of Edinburgh. Between 2001 and 2004 she was a research associate of Professor Roger Davidson at the University of Edinburgh, and subsequently spent two years as a researcher in the Centre for the History of Medicine, University of Glasgow. She returned to the University of Edinburgh in 2007 as a Wellcome Trust University Award Holder. Her award funds her to conduct a three-year research project on 'The Social, Medical and Political Response to Infertility in Later Twentieth-Century Scotland'.

Joel Peter Eigen is the Charles A Dana Professor of Sociology at Franklin and Marshall College, Pennsylvania, where he teaches criminology, sociology of law, history of sociological theory and law and psychiatry. He completed his undergraduate studies at Ohio University, and later received both a Masters degree and PhD from the University of Pennsylvania. He is the author of *Witnessing Insanity: Madness and Mad-doctors in the English Court* (Yale, l995), and *Unconscious Crime: Mental Absence and Criminal Responsibility in Victorian London* (Johns Hopkins, 2003). In 2001–02, he was Visiting Scholar at Pembroke College, Cambridge University, and is currently Principal Fellow, Department of Philosophy, University of Melbourne.

List of Contributors

Angus H Ferguson is a Research Assistant in the Centre for the History of Medicine at the University of Glasgow. He received his PhD in the History of Medicine from the University of Glasgow for his thesis, entitled 'Should a Doctor Tell? Medical Confidentiality in Interwar England and Scotland'. He is currently working on two projects relating to the history of child health in Scotland. The first examines issues relating to infant health and nutrition in Glasgow in the early decades of the twentieth century. The second project examines the history of Sudden Infant Death Syndrome (SIDS).

Imogen Goold is Fellow and Tutor in Law at St Anne's College, University of Oxford. She studied Law and Modern History at the University of Tasmania, receiving her LLB in 1997 and her BA (Hons) in 1998. From 2002–04, she was a Legal Officer at the Australian Law Reform Commission, where she worked on the inquiries into Genetic Information Privacy and Gene Patenting. She received her PhD in Law in 2005 from the University of Tasmania, as well as a Masters degree in Bioethics from the University of Monash in the same year. She is currently completing her DPhil in the History of Medicine at Oxford University, and her research focuses on the historical development of laws to regulate reproduction.

James Hanley is an associate professor of history at the University of Winnipeg. He holds a BSc and an MA from the University of Toronto, and received his PhD from Yale. His research interest is in the history of 19th-century English public health and sanitary reform. His articles have analyzed Edwin Chadwick and medical statistics, the public response to national sanitary legislation, the development of nuisance law, and the significance of the judiciary in the evolution of public health. His current project is an examination of the legal dimension of local sanitary reform.

Catherine Kelly is a Research Officer at the Wellcome Unit for the History of Medicine at the University of Oxford. She studied Political Science and Law at the Australian National University, receiving her BA in 1995 and LLB (Hons) in 1997. She worked as a solicitor in private practice and in the policy section of the Australian Medical Association before commencing studies in the History of Medicine at Oxford. She received an MSc in 2003, and was awarded her DPhil in 2008.

Katherine D Watson is Lecturer in the History of Medicine since 1500 at Oxford Brookes University. She is author of *Poisoned Lives: English Poisoners and their Victims* (2004), and editor of a collection of essays on the history of violence. Her research focuses on topics where medicine, crime and the law intersect and she is currently working on a project, funded by the Wellcome Trust, which considers the history of medico-legal practice in England and Wales 1700–1914.

Duncan Wilson is a Wellcome Trust Research Associate at the Centre for the History of Science, Technology and Medicine at the University of Manchester who work centres on biological science and biomedical ethics in the 19th and 20th centuries. He holds a BSc and MA and was awarded his PhD in 2005. He has published articles on the cultural impact of tissue culture technologies in Britain, bioethical debates surrounding tissue research in the 1960s and 1970s, and on the conceptualisation of 'public' attitudes to tissue. He also works on the recent reorganisation of biology in UK universities. His book *Reconfiguring Biological Sciences* was published by the University of Manchester in 2008.

ABBREVIATIONS

ALRA	Abortion Law Reform Association
ART	assisted reproductive technologies
BL	British Library
BMA	British Medical Association
CEC	Central Ethical Committee
CCR	Commons Committee Reports
DNB	Oxford Dictionary of National Biography
ECT	electro-convulsive therapy
FRAME	Fund for Replacement of Animals in Medical Experiments
HC	House of Commons
HFEA	Human Fertilisation and Embryology Authority
HL	House of Lords
HO	Home Office
IVF	*in vitro* fertilisation
LRO	Liverpool Record Office
MH	Ministry of Health
MRC	Medical Research Council
NAS	National Archives of Scotland
NHS	National Health Service
OBSP	Old Bailey Sessions Papers
PRO	Public Record Office
PWC	Proceedings of the Wolfenden Committee on Homosexual Offences and Prostitution
RCOG	Royal College of Obstetricians and Gynaecologists
SHHD	Scottish Home and Health Department
SIDS	Sudden Infant Death Syndrome
SPUC	Society for the Protection of the Unborn Child
TNA	The National Archives, Kew
UCLA	University of California, Los Angeles
UKCCCR	UK Co-ordinating Committee on Cancer Research
VD	venereal disease
VLA	Voluntary Licensing Authority
WL	Wellcome Library
WRO	Worcester Record Office

1

Introduction: Lawyers' Medicine: The Interaction of the Medical Profession and the Law, 1760–2000

CATHERINE KELLY AND IMOGEN GOOLD

The 19th and 20th centuries were notable for two major and concurrent changes which have helped to shape modern Britain. It is the interplay of these processes which is the subject of this collected volume. One was the rapid development of medical science, which progressed through various stages allowing it increasingly to assert the 'scientific certainty' of medical conclusions or opinions. Over the same period, the role and regulatory activities of British government were significantly extended. Parliament began to pass legislation on a much broader range of issues than it had previously attempted. This wider sphere included medical practice. The increased 'scientific certainty' of medical conclusions gave those conclusions greater utility to the State when it engaged in fact-finding exercises and accounts, in part, for the increasing appearance of medical experts, opinion, and evaluation of medical practice in its law making bodies.

The papers in this volume explore the interactions between law and medicine that have occurred in the past 200 years as the legal arms of the State attempted to prescribe or describe medical practice. The volume was conceived during a seminar series held at the Wellcome Unit for the History of Medicine in Oxford between April and June 2007, titled 'Medicine and the Law in History, 1760–1990'. Papers were invited which discussed the impact of legal regulation on the development of medical practice and/or theory in different periods of history.

Legal regulation of medical practice can take many forms. The most prominent of these are the development and application of legislation and subordinate legislation, and the decisions of courts in the application of legislation and in the development and interpretation of precedent. The papers in this volume demonstrate that while such attempts often begin with prescription, in many instances, they also entail description of medical practices and indeed medical conceptualisations of disease and mental states. The majority of the papers discuss the issues which arise from those processes in the context of the development and application of legislation, but the influence of court processes is also considered.

The story of this inter-relationship is greatly under-researched, which is particularly concerning given that the legal system remains a significant and pervasive influence on medicine and its practice to this day. We consider a collected volume the best way to bring together the disparate pieces of research that are being undertaken by historians, who themselves do not necessarily perceive how this important theme links their work to those of other historians working on different topics and periods. Collected editions that focus particularly on the inter-relationship between legal regulation and medical practice itself, rather than a single area of law or medical practice, are extremely rare. The only major collection to be published in the past fifteen years is *Legal Medicine in History*, edited by Michael Clark and Catherine Crawford for the Cambridge Studies in the History of Medicine series in 1994. In contrast to this volume, Clark and Crawford's collection focuses on

> what the history of legal medicine stands to gain from new approaches to the social history of law and medicine', presenting 'studies of the place of legal medicine in the social, legal, administrative and political histories of societies in which it has been practised.[1]

Since that collection's publication, the research gap identified by Clark and Crawford has begun to be filled by numerous excellent contributions on the history of legal medicine in context. By drawing together studies of medical history grouped around the theme of medicine's interaction with the British legal system, our volume builds on this body of work, but more importantly brings the links between medical and legal history to the fore to focus attention on an area that remains under-researched, namely the relationship of medical professionals to development of laws and legislation. While discrete areas of research have touched on this relationship to some degree, there is not yet a body of scholarship that sufficiently draws out and explores its themes as they cut across the history legal medicine generally. In doing so, this collection sets an agenda for a new area of study defined by these links, which we hope will redress the absence of writing on these themes.

A range of legal problems require the courts to draw on medical knowledge to resolve them, with the application of such knowledge being broadly referred to as 'legal' or 'forensic' medicine.[2] Included within 'legal medicine' are the provision of a wide variety of medical evidence to courts, tribunals and coronial inquests; post-mortem examinations and testimony about cause of death; and the issuing of medical certificates and opinions in legal and semi-legal situations such as parole hearings. Legal medicine has been studied and taught for centuries; as Cyril Wecht points out 'it is known that Hippocrates and others discussed

---

[1] M Clark and C Crawford (eds), *Legal Medicine in History* (Cambridge, CUP, 1994) 1.
[2] For example, Cyril Wecht has defined 'legal medicine' as the study of 'the application of medical knowledge to the administration of justice'. See CH Wecht, 'The History of Legal Medicine' (2005) 33 *Journal of American Academy of Psychiatry and Law* 245.

many genuine medico-legal questions' such as the relative fatality of wounding different parts of the body.[3] The vast majority of medical historians who have considered interactions between law and medicine have written about 'legal medicine' in this sense, exploring, for example, the role of doctors in acting as expert witnesses in trials.

There are definite sites of strong interaction between law and medicine that have received significant attention from historians, and considerable work has been done on the history of legal medicine. Such work, as Elisabeth Cawthorn has noted, demonstrates how the medical profession participated in the legal process, and consequently 'the connections between medicine and the law at an important every day level'.[4] This work is strongly related to the papers in this collection, however the focus of 'legal medicine' as a discipline is on the role of the medical practitioner as a forensic expert in the courtroom. Very little of this work has considered the ways in which doctors have contributed to the creation of the laws and legal concepts which have been formulated to govern their activities. Neither has much attention been given to how those laws have affected the development of medical practice or the medical profession.

The historical considerations of medico-legal issues that are available are generally case studies of a single area, most often focused on contraception and abortion. The history of abortion and the law has been well-researched, but focuses less on the interaction between the medical profession and the law, and more on the history of women's rights. Many of these histories are essentially patients' histories, exploring changes that emerged when women pressed for the right to abortion. Leslie Reagan's *When Abortion Was a Crime: Women, Medicine, and Law in the United States, 1867–1973*,[5] is a good example of the genre. Other work has analysed changes in abortion law as an aspect of legislative changes in the 1960s more broadly, or has focused on the socio-political forces that shaped the creation of the Abortion Act in the United Kingdom.[6] Such works, while excellent contributions to the history of their subject, tend to be social or institutional histories with less to say about the developing relationship between law and medicine generally. Less work has been done on the evolution of that law and the influence on its development of the medical profession, with J Keown, *Abortion, Doctors and the Law: Some Aspects of the Legal Regulation of Abortion in England from 1803 to 1982* being a notable exception.[7]

---

[3] Wecht, above n 2, 245.
[4] EA Cawthorn, 'Legal Medicine in History (Book Review)' (1996) 14 *Law and History Review* 405, 407.
[5] RJ Reagan, *When Abortion Was a Crime: Women, Medicine, and Law in the United States, 1867–1973* (Berkley, University of California Press, 1997).
[6] Examples include LA Hall, *Sex, Gender and Social Change in Britain since 1880* (Basingstoke, Macmillan, 2000); J Lovenduski and J Outshoorn (eds), *The New Politics of Abortion* (London, Sage, 1986); and BL Brookes, *Abortion in England, 1900–1967* (London, Croom Helm, 1988).
[7] (Cambridge, CUP, 1988).

The development of legislation to regulate medical education and teaching, particularly the Anatomy Act 1832 and the Apothecaries Act 1815, has been a site of significant investigation and research. Elizabeth Hurren and others have produced significant scholarship on the implications of legislative measures to regulate the supply of bodies for medical study.[8] Hurren's work explores the various Poor Laws and their implications for anatomical teaching, while Ruth Richardson's *Death, Dissection and the Destitute* has become a seminal work on the interaction between the Anatomy Act and medical practice.[9]

Considerable research has also been done public health laws, poisoning, the defence of insanity, the coroner's court, forensic medicine, and the emergence of medical practitioners as expert witnesses.[10] In particular, much recent work has been done on the role of the medical practitioner as an expert witness in the courtroom, with some of the major work in the area of legal medicine being on medico-legal proof in the area of poisoning, such as that of Katherine Watson and Ian Burney.[11] Indeed, the coroner's court has been one of the major sites of investigation. Burney's research has also explored the role of medical practitioner in the context of the coroner's court.[12] While this collection touches on some related areas of medical testimony, its focus lies much more squarely on the interaction between the medical profession and the legal system, rather than the entry of doctors into the courtroom.

Conceptions of madness is an area where the interaction between the medical profession and the law has begun to be explored. The work of Joel Eigen, Tony Ward and others has teased out issues such as the definition of insanity in law and medicine, and how these definitions have operated together and often conflicted.[13]

---

[8] ET Hurren, 'The Pauper Dead-House: The Expansion of Cambridge Anatomical Teaching School under the Late-Victorian Poor Law, 1870–1914' (2004) 48 *Medical History* 69; ET Hurren, *Dying for Victorian Medicine: English Anatomy and its Trade in the Dead Poor, 1870 to 1929*, (London, Palgrave Macmillan, forthcoming 2009); and on the United States experience M Sappol, *A Traffic of Dead Bodies: Anatomy and Embodied Social Identity in Nineteenth-Century America*, (Princeton, Princeton University Press, 2002). See also I Loudin's *Medical Care and the General Practitioner 1750–1850* (Oxford, Clarendon Press, 1986).

[9] (London, Penguin, 1988). Another related work is DG Jones, *Speaking for the Dead: Cadavers in Biology and Medicine* (Aldershot, Ashgate, 2000), while Lori Andrews and Dorothy Nelkin have produced a wide-ranging and thoughtful study of the recent use and acquisition of human tissue for research. See L Andrews and D Nelkin, *Body Bazaar: The Market for Human Tissue in the Biotechnology Age* (New York, Crown, 2001).

[10] See, variously M Pelling, *Cholera, Fever and English Medicine 1825–1865* (Oxford, OUP, 1978); CAG Jones, *Expert Witnesses: Science, Medicine, and the Practice of Law* (Oxford, Clarendon Press, 1994); JC Mohr, *Doctors and the Law: Medical Jurisprudence in Nineteenth-Century America* (New York, OUP, 1993); B Rich, *Strange Bedfellows: How Medical Jurisprudence Has Influenced Medical Ethics and Medical Practice* (New York, Kluwer Academic/Plenum Publishers, 2001).

[11] See, eg I Burney, *Poison, Detection and the Victorian Imagination* (Manchester, Manchester University Press, 2006); K Watson, *Poisoned Lives: English Poisoners and Their Victims* (London, Hambledon and London 2004).

[12] I Burney, *Bodies of Evidence: Medicine and the Politics of the English Inquest, 1830–1926* (Baltimore, Johns Hopkins University Press, 2000).

[13] See, eg T Ward, 'Law, Common Sense and the Authority of Science: Expert Witnesses and Criminal Insanity in England, Ca 1840–1940' (1997) 6 *Social and Legal Studies* 343.

Recent research of writers such as Danuta Mendelson has also examined medical and legal conceptions of nervous shock in the law.[14]

Crawford and Clark have made the point that 'much of the history of legal medicine has been written in terms of the gradual emergence and increasing recognition of medico-legal expertise',[15] and it is evident from the foregoing that the absence of writing on 'forensic medicine' they identified in 1994 has begun to be addressed by historians. But what also emerges from this work, and which is an area for study we consider requires research, is the demonstrable influence medical practitioners have had the development of the law. While Clark and Crawford rightly highlighted what the history of legal medicine had to gain from more contextual studies drawing on social and political history, the next step is to explore how medical practitioners played a role in shaping the laws to which they were subject. Although it is not possible to examine the impact of the legal system's influence on the development of medicine without also considering the reverse relationship, it was hoped that the papers in this collection would address the comparative lack of historical investigation of the first question and begin to explore how the requirements, limitations, and intellectual structure of the British legal process shaped medicine and medical practice.

Over the past two centuries, both the British medical profession and the institutions of legal regulation in Britain underwent significant change. Not least, both have expanded dramatically in size and experienced a rapid process of professionalisation.[16] Medical practitioners consolidated from the diverse 'medical marketplace' of the 18th century into a regulated and relatively homogenous professional group, whilst also increasing opportunities for specialisation. Additionally, they began to enjoy the fruits of ever more developed tools of investigation, diagnosis, and cure. The reach of the British Parliament also extended over this period and increasingly came to regulate more and more aspects of British society.[17] The consequent increased utility of medical testimony to courts and medical expertise to legislators is reflected in the variety of interactions between those groups

---

[14] D Mendelson, 'English Medical Experts and the Claims for Shock Occasioned by Railway Collisions in the 1860s' (2002) 25 *International Journal of Law and Psychiatry* 303; D Mendelson, *The Interfaces of Medicine and Law: The History of the Liability for Negligently Caused Psychiatric Injury (Nervous Shock)* (Aldershot, Ashgate, 1998) and A Young, '*The Interfaces of Medicine and Law: The History of the Liability for Negligently Caused Psychiatric Injury (Nervous Shock)*' (Book Review) (2000) 74 *Bulletin of History of Medicine* 172.

[15] Clark and Crawford, above n 1, 9.

[16] HJ Perkin, *The Rise of Professional Society: England since 1880* (London, Routledge, 1989); PJ Corfield, *Power and the Professions in Britain, 1700–1850*, (London, Routledge, 1995).

[17] On the development of Parliament's role, the growth of the State, and the role of the 'expert' see, generally AC Dicey, *Lectures on the Relation between Law and Public Opinion in England during the Nineteenth Century*, 2nd edn (London, Macmillan, 1914); O MacDonagh, *A Pattern of Government growth, 1800–60: the Passenger Acts and Their Enforcement* (London, MacGibbon and Key, 1961); O MacDonagh, *Early Victorian Government, 1830–1870* (London, Weidenfeld and Nicolson, 1977); R MacLeod, 'Introduction' in R Macleod (ed), *Government and Expertise: Specialists, Administrators and Professionals 1860–1919* (Cambridge, CUP, 1988); and G Sutherland (ed), *Studies in the Growth of Nineteenth-Century Government* (London, Routledge and Kegan Paul, 1972).

considered in the following chapters. Those investigations highlight two overriding themes in which conclusions about the central question posed by the volume can begin to be formed: the attempts of medical professionals to influence the legislative process of the State in its attempts to create regulatory structures for medical practice; and, more fundamentally, the tensions inherent in any dialogue between the medical and legal professions resulting from the incompatibility of their underpinning intellectual frameworks, vocabulary, and assumptions.

The first of those themes is explored in the chapters written by Kelly, Davis, Ferguson, Goold and Wilson. Each of those chapters examines the efforts of medical practitioners to influence the development of government policy on matters directly affecting the regulation of medical practice and/or research. They demonstrate that while practitioners sometimes resented the intrusion of Parliament and the Courts into medical matters, the very interest of those bodies gave medical practitioners a forum to promote their perspectives. It is also apparent that medical practitioners became adept at pursuing medical goals through lobbying and discussions outside the formal processes of government inquiry. However, a necessary consequence of this process was also that divisions or disputes which could be seen (and often were seen by medical professionals) as internal to medicine and requiring expert training to be properly understood were decided by a non-medically expert body (Parliament) or fact-finder (judge). A direct result of these fact-finding exercises by the State was that laws and precedents which stipulated what was permissible or legal medical practice were created. The participation of medical practitioners in these processes, indeed which were often instigated by medical professionals themselves, is manifest. However, the quandary faced by medical professionals when engaging in those processes was that they were bound by conventions and processes which could limit, or disregard, the priorities of the medical profession.

This brings us to the second of the major themes to emerge from the chapters in this collection—the inability of medical and legal intellectual structures to communicate with each other. As is demonstrated in the majority of the chapters in this volume, the needs of the legal and medical systems were and are not always the same. Attempts by the legal system—especially the courts—to fit medicine and medical concepts into its discourses and intellectual structures produced serious problems. Problems also arose when medical practitioners were unaware of legal requirements which had been placed on them, or rights which they held. These incompatibilities are particularly evident in cases, such as those highlighted by Ferguson, where the interests of efficient legal process were set against the medical ethics or traditional practices of the medical profession. In most cases the resulting conflict was won by the legal system leading to the conclusion that medicine's increased utility to that system caused its own subjugation.

At its most basic this conflict can be perceived in the different understandings held by medical practitioners and the State about what constituted binding regulation. While within the legal system the definition of a regulatory instrument is clear—legislation, delegated legislation or judicially set precedent—throughout history doctors have believed themselves to be subject to another range of binding guidelines. In the chapters written by Ferguson, Wilson, and Goold the obligations of medical practitioners to statements of professional ethics, confidentiality and consent guidelines, and accepted professional practice have put them in conflict with the demands placed upon them by legislative and court processes.

These simple conflicts form part of a larger incompatibility between the two professional groups resulting from their distinct intellectual frameworks. As shown by Hanley, the two different systems of language and intellectual structures could inform each other and come together to achieve a mutually desired result. However, the outcome of their interaction was not always positive. The difficulties encountered when the two systems attempted to work together are most clearly seen when attempts to communicate resulted in struggles over definitions and vocabularies. In her chapter Watson shows how differing legal and medical understandings of the word 'wound', informed by the objectives of each group in seeking to define the word, proved difficult to resolve. Similarly, in the chapters written by Eigen, Rogers, and Ferguson the unwillingness of medical practitioners to comply with categories of medical testimony or attempts to fit medical diagnoses and concepts within legal categories of illness, debility, or rights are clearly drawn out.

In each case the struggles of medical practitioners not to be thus curtailed also resulted in concerted efforts by those practitioners to change the legal structures and concepts to which they had become subject. As stated by Eigen, in their refusal to accept the court's definitions of madness, 'medical witnesses were reframing the law's criterion of cognitive impairment'. However, in other cases the refusal of practitioners to bend to the requirements of the law resulted in the marginalisation of their evidence, as shown by Davidson.

The first of the papers in this collection, 'Parliamentary Inquiries and the Construction of Medical Argument in the Early 19th Century', by Catherine Kelly, traces the significant increase in parliamentary interest in medical matters, particularly military medical matters, over the course of the Napoleonic Wars and in the years following. In particular, through several case studies, it examines parliamentary review of military medical practice during the Wars in the form of the parliamentary select committee of inquiry. Such committees were used by parliament to investigate controversial matters or issues on which the 'facts' needed to be established before parliament would consider a motion, and their reports and published evidence reveal much about the interaction between parliament and military medicine during this period, the status of military practitioners compared with civilian practitioners, the problems of finding an agreed evidentiary model for medical debates, and the ways in which parliament attempted to influence medical practice.

What emerges clearly from this paper is that as Parliament's interest in military medicine increased, it in turn drew more on the professional opinion of medical practitioners to inform, but not determine, the legislative approach to be taken to medical issues which it sought to regulate. Involving military medical officers in the process of legislating also brought controversies in medical theory and over medical practices to the attention of Parliament. Kelly's paper demonstrates that while it was medical practitioners who raised these issues, it was Parliament that resolved them. Not only did Parliament regard itself as legally authorised to do so, many parliamentarians considered themselves eminently qualified to make such determinations, and they were supported in that conclusion by some medical practitioners who espoused the availability of medical knowledge to all. Although many practitioners continued to claim the exclusivity of knowledge and authority, that authority was ceded, in part, to parliamentarians the moment the question was taken up by them. As a result, medical authority took a secondary role in determining how medical matters were to be regulated, despite the greater knowledge and understanding of medical matters possessed by its practitioners, military and civilian.

Kelly's paper also shows how the ways in which medical practitioners chose to interact with Parliament, and to present medical 'facts' to non-experts, affected the importance Parliament placed on the various evidence presented to it. Medical evidence grounded in personal observation and experience held greater sway with parliamentarians, and those medical practitioners who recognised this had greater success in promoting one type of medical practice or opinion over another. As a result, Kelly argues, the educational model promoted by military medical officers was tacitly endorsed.

Kelly's paper, like the next in the collection by James Hanley, demonstrates that the way in which medical practitioners interact with legal institutions has had a significant impact on the regulatory approach of Parliament to some medical issues. Through their use of Parliament as a forum in which to promote their medical opinions, some military practitioners in the period considered by Kelly had a noteworthy effect on government policy in relation to medicine. Their efforts were all the more effective for being informed by an appreciation of the conventions of the parliamentary process and the kinds of evidence which would appeal in that context.

In Bye Laws, the Environment, and Health before Chadwick, 1835–40, James Hanley examines the numerous bye-laws dealing with the control of health nuisances submitted for approval by the newly-reformed municipal corporations in England and Wales following the passage of the Municipal Reform Act 1835. Hanley argues that the bye-laws reveal a persistent refusal on the part of corporations and the Home Office to involve medical personnel in the suppression of nuisances; the permissive character of the statute meant, for the medical profession, that lay understandings continued to dominate the practice of nuisance control. However, as he points out, the bye-laws nonetheless demonstrate an ambitious extension of traditional nuisance law, especially in terms of developing health as a rationale for action. As Kelly's chapter also reveals, government in this period was willing to draw on the opinions of the medical profession, but retained the final authority to apply its own understandings to the evidence presented to it, and on this basis retain authority over determining health care goals and the measures by which to achieve them.

However, while Kelly's chapter demonstrates the influence of medical practitioners on developing laws, Hanley's illustrates the way in which legal regulation shaped the development of medical practice and/or theory. His analysis reveals that one of the more striking features of the bye-laws is a growing emphasis on Chadwickian-style sanitary reform before Chadwick appeared on the scene, an example of the legal system leading the medical profession on issues of public health reform. Taken together, these chapters illuminate not only the nature of interactions between the medical profession and legislative bodies, but demonstrate further that this interaction had influence in both directions—both the medical profession and the legal system were shaped by their interactions with the other.

The third paper in this collection, 'Is a Burn a Wound? Vitriol-Throwing in Medico-Legal Context' takes up the second theme, exploring the tensions between the medical and legal understandings of the concept of a 'wound' and medico-legal responses to the crime of vitriol throwing. Katherine Watson's paper delves into the conflict between different professional conceptualisations and the problems this presented when the justice system attempted to determine how the criminal law should address the then increasing incidence of vitriol-throwing. She traces this conflict from the passing of the 1803 Malicious Shooting and Stabbing Act (better known as Lord Ellenborough's Act), which had created ten new capital felonies, most of them offences against the person. Watson argues that despite the use of the word 'wound' in the act's long title, the precise use of the terms stab, cut, and poison in the actual text of the statute implied that other forms of injury were excluded from the provisions of the law. Lawyers clearly saw 'wounding' in this sense as purely a form of stabbing,[18] and judicial decisions upheld this interpretation: 'whenever a wound could not be considered a cut or a stab, the prisoner was entitled to an acquittal if tried under this statute'.[19] The word 'wound' itself did not appear in the text of the new law, which required proof of an incised cut for a felonious assault charge to succeed.[20]

This legal understanding of 'wound' directly conflicted with some contemporaneous medical understandings, particularly in the case of burns such as those that might be caused by vitriol throwing. While some doctors considered burns wounds, others maintained the more traditional view of a wound as deriving from mechanical means. Watson's paper demonstrates how this conflict over what

---

[18] JF Archbold, *A Summary of the Law relative to Pleading and Evidence in Criminal Cases* (1st American edn) (New York, Stephen Gould and Son, 1824) 246. The index (p 429) under 'wounding' says 'see stabbing', implying equivalence. See also P Handler, 'The Law of Felonious Assault in England, 1803–61' (2007) 28 *The Journal of Legal History* 183, 189–91.

[19] AS Taylor, *Elements of Medical Jurisprudence* (London, Deacon, 1836) 480; EW Cox (ed), *Reports of Cases in Criminal Law, argued and determined in all the Courts in England and Ireland*, vol 3, 1848–1850 (London, 1850) 145, 148–50.

[20] For the full text of the statute, see WD Evans, A Hammond and TC Granger (eds), *A Collection of Statutes Connected with the General Administration of the Law*, 3rd edn, vol 5 (London, Blenkarn, Lumley and Bond, 1836) 206–09.

constituted a wound created a loophole for those who had caused a serious injury in medical terms to escape punishment in proportion to the wrong.

The law's approach to vitriol throwing in the early 19th century developed in part due to the complex interaction between the medical profession and the justice system. Watson argues that one explanation of the court's refusal to adopt the medical definition of a 'wound' was that such a definition remained a matter of dispute within the medical profession. Her analysis shows, however, that over time the opinions of doctors, as well as concerns about disproportionality in punishment, led lawyers and the courts to broad their understanding of what constituted a 'wound' to encompass a more medically-sophisticated interpretation. In doing so, this paper shows both the complexity of this interaction, and the practical implications disputed understandings between law and medicine had on the operation of the legal system.

As with Watson's chapter, Joel Eigen's 'Not Their Fathers' Sons: The Changing Trajectory in Psychiatric Testimony, 1760–1900' brings to the fore the difficulties inherent in communication between the medical and legal professions. Roger Smith has argued that 'the early Victorian debate over criminal responsibility can be characterised as one between two incommensurable discourses. For law, to be "responsible" meant to be able to understand the law's threats ... for medicine it meant that one's actions were controlled by the higher centre of the brain'.[21] This understanding of the interaction between the medical profession and the law is reflected in Eigen's paper, in which he details the emergence of a new form of expert witness at London's central criminal court, the Old Bailey, from 1760. This new type of witness began to assert that insanity was a medical condition. Drawing on the Old Bailey Sessions Papers to examine a series of trials heard in London from 1760–1913, Eigen explores the range of imagery used by specialist witnesses to address legal concerns of intention and culpability, highlighting the tension between medical and legal conceptions of madness. In doing so, it becomes clear that these conceptions were shaped by the roles they were intended to play, and the discourse within which they developed. Each conception bore the hallmarks of its origins, and the conflict between them illuminates the difficulty that dogs communication between such distinct discourses, for reasons of language and of more fundamental perspectives on the reason for defining madness. For the law, madness determined culpability or otherwise, for the doctor it determined a disease condition that was then to be treated. As Eigen shows, these differing goals, as well as the shifting institutional settings in which mental examination occurred, had a profound influence on the conceptions of madness within each profession, with each influencing the other.

---

[21] R Smith, *Trial by Medicine: Insanity and Responsibility in Victorian Trials* (Edinburgh, Edinburgh University Press, 1981), as cited in T Ward, 'Law, Common Sense and the Authority of Science: Expert Witnesses and Criminal Insanity in England, Ca 1840–1940' (1997) 6 *Social and Legal Studies* 343, 348–9.

Eigen's chapter also draws out another aspect of the interaction between the medical profession and the legal system—that doctors were not always willing to comply with categories of medical testimony, or prepared to fit medical diagnoses and concepts within legal categories of illness, debility, or rights, a theme also picked up in Angus Ferguson's paper 'Speaking Out about Staying Silent: A Historical Examination of Medico-legal Debates over the Boundaries of Medical Confidentiality'. Where Eigen's doctors resisted legal categorisations of madness, Ferguson's objected to the legal system's refusal to recognise medical confidentiality as binding the medical practitioner to maintain that confidence in the court. Ferguson's paper examines the development of ethical guidelines and medical law in relation to confidentiality, and the conflict that arose between the legal system and the medical profession in negotiating what information doctors could rightfully refuse to provide to the courts.

In Britain it is generally accepted that medical confidentiality cannot be absolute, that at times it must be limited by other considerations, and Ferguson demonstrates that historical examination reveals an ongoing negotiation of where and when medical confidentiality should be kept or breached. While a range of groups have expressed views on medical confidentiality at different times, the medical and legal professions have been the most common and prominent protagonists in the ongoing debate. In large part, Ferguson argues, this is because the courtroom has provided a key arena in which traditional medical ideas about doctor–patient confidentiality have been directly and publicly challenged by the law's desire for medical testimony. He explores two main areas in which doctors' assertion of their ethical duty to maintain confidence came into direct conflict with the demands of government and the legal system—the treatment of socially and physically stigmatic diseases such as VD and doctors' need to breach confidentiality in their defence during cases involving accusations of malpractice—to draw out the nature and resulting outcomes of this conflict.

One vital conclusion to emerge from this analysis in the context of the themes of this collection is the tension between professional claims to authority over behaviour. Ferguson contends that on one level the courtroom clashes between judges and medical witnesses can be viewed as a clash of duties: the doctor emphasising his professional duty to the patient while the law stresses the doctor's civic duty to the law. On another level, there is an element of inter-professional rivalry between the medical and legal professions. Lawyers have long enjoyed a privilege exempting them from disclosure of discussions held with their client in preparation for legal proceedings. While this has been justified on the grounds that a fair adversarial system of law requires that each party in a case is free to consult legal expertise, some doctors have argued that the interests of public health require a similar exemption for patients' consultations with their doctors. Not only has this argument generally been dismissed by judges, but at times it has appeared, to certain of the medical lobby at least, that judges have used medical testimony as an unnecessary short-cut to processing cases.

Ferguson's paper also makes the point that while the courtroom has been a flashpoint between the two professions, historians must look beyond it to obtain a fuller picture of medical and legal discussion of medical confidentiality by examining a broad range of formal and informal medico-legal interactions. Many of the papers in this collection analyse a wide variety of ways and forums in which doctors and the legal system interacted, from Kelly's exploration of the doctor's role in select committees and Goold's examination of the Warnock Committee's work, to Eigen's work on asylum doctors to the next paper in this collection, Roger Davidson's, which draws on the testimony of medical witnesses to the Wolfenden Committee on Prostitution and Homosexual Offences (1954–7) and doctors' reports to parole hearings, amongst other sources.

In his paper 'Law, Medicine and the Treatment of Homosexual Offenders in Scotland, 1950–80', Davidson draws on a range of archival material to examine the medical perception and treatment of male homosexuality that prevailed in the courts and prisons after 1945, an area he argues has received little attention from historians and social scientists, despite the growing body of work on the social politics and legal and medical discourses surrounding homosexuality in the 20th century. Focusing on the Scottish experience, which has been the subject of a notably small body of research, Davidson explores the Scottish evidence submitted to the Wolfenden Committee by medical officials and experts, and by practising psychotherapists on the adequacy and suitability of existing provisions for the medical treatment of homosexual offenders.

One striking conclusion Davidson's paper makes is that medical evidence, though readily brought by both the defence and the Crown Office, was often marginalised in legal proceedings. This stemmed in part, he argues, from the lack of consensus within the medical profession over the aetiology of medical treatment in homosexual cases, picking up on an issue that has been noted in a number of the chapters in this collection—that where the medical profession could not or would not present the legal system with an agreed view on a medical matter, courts or the legislature were often likely to set the medical view to one side in favour of their own judgment.

Davidson argues further that although the courts and parole boards invited medical evidence on homosexuality and its treatment to inform sentencing and parole decisions, the impact of this evidence on sentencing was often limited to, and mediated by, legal discourses that reflected broader moral assumptions and concerns within Scottish civil society. Such moral assumptions operated in the context of the enduring tensions between medical conceptions of homosexual behaviour as a pathology or intrinsic condition and judicial conceptions of it as embodying criminal sexual acts. Davidson's paper, like those of Watson and Eigen, demonstrates that, where there is unresolved disagreement between the legal system and the medical profession over understandings of a medical condition, the implications of this are often the marginalisation of medical views in favour of legal ones.

Three chapters in this collection present work on Scotland. In an area of study that has often focused on the English experience, Davidson's and Gayle Davis' chapters in particular demonstrate how its national culture and history of medical practice, as well as it distinct legal system, have often shaped medico-legal interactions in a way that sets them apart.

Davis' chapter explores an area that, like many of those considered in this collection, has received only scant attention from historians. In focusing upon the role of the medical profession within the process of abortion law reform, Davis' chapter addresses similar issues to those of Ferguson, Goold and Wilson by teasing out how the medical profession has attempted to influence the development of law.

Academic attention has tended to focus on the social history of abortion law reform, or examined abortion as a political issue. As a result, most work has considered either the interplay between pressure groups and professional bodies in shaping abortion policy, or its implications for a broader interpretation of sexuality, morality and citizenship. A final group has explored abortion within the gendered context of the politics of reproductive control and women's rights. All of this research has tended to focus—either explicitly or implicitly—upon the English experience.

Taking a partially comparative approach, Davis surveys abortion law and practice as it existed in Britain prior to 1967 by addressing the differing legal status of abortion in England and Scotland, and the inconsistencies in practice between different parts of the country. By switching the focus to Scotland, she argues that the distinctive traditions of law and medical practice found north of the Border had crucial input into the 1967 Abortion Act. Her chapter examines the personalities involved in the successful passing of the Act, and in doing so Davis demonstrates how the medical profession played a significant role in shaping the operation of the law in this area, both through pressing directly for change, and through its application of the law as written.

Like other chapters in this collection, Davis also demonstrates that the interaction between the medical profession and the legal system had influence in both directions, as she explores the degree to which that law has influenced, and been interpreted within, medical practice. Her chapter draws out a crucially important point for the explorations of medico-legal interaction—that doctors' attitudes to laws and their application of them significantly affects their operation. She charts the impact of the legislation and the medical problems which were perceived to have been created by the Abortion Act and teases out medical attitudes to abortion in the early years of its legalisation. Davis shows how the medical community responded to the challenge of this new responsibility, showing that some employed a range of strategies to minimise or devolve their role in the decision-making process. Whereas the conventional historiography largely stereotypes and simplifies the response of the medical community towards abortion, Davis argues that there is a need for a more nuanced approach which captures the diversity and ambiguities that characterised the medical community's response to the enforced medicalisation of abortion in these decades.

The final two chapters in this collection cover more recent events in the historical interaction of law and medicine. Unlike the periods considered in the early papers, a new discourse emerged in the late 20th century that has importance influences on how the medical profession, government and the legal system determine how medicine should be practiced and regulated. Bioethics, as an academic discipline, traces its origins to the 1970s, and the work produced by those who would eventually describe themselves as 'bioethicists' informed debate over medico-legal issues in the 40 subsequent years, adding a further dimension to the complex ways in which medicine and law were shaped.

Imogen Goold's chapter examines how the medical profession and legal system determined how to regulate the new assisted reproductive technologies that emerged in the late 1970s. Increasing public concern, and indeed unease, about these techniques following the birth of Louise Brown had made this need all the more pressing and as the chair of the committee that would fundamentally shape the debate on this issues, Mary Warnock noted, legislation was needed to 'reassure the public that we were not entering an era of totally uncontrolled manipulation of the future of the human race'. The Warnock Committee was established in 1982 to make recommendations for regulation. Its report met with both support and condemnation, and was vigorously debated in both Houses of Parliament during 1985.

Examining the moral and ethical concerns that informed the debate over how to manage these new technologies, Goold's chapter 'Regulating Reproduction in the United Kingdom: Doctors' Voices, 1978–1985', shows how the medical profession was an influential voice. Doctors gave evidence to the Warnock Committee, in a manner not unlike that of the military doctors discussed in Kelly's paper. They also, like Kelly's doctors, took an active role in shaping policy by making presentations to Members of Parliament and actively participating in lobby groups, but in addition began themselves to write on and debate ethical issues, as the new bioethicists moved into hospitals to provide guidance on the challenges facing doctors. Like Davis's paper, Goold's also demonstrates how the influence worked both ways. While the medical profession lobbied, as well as producing its own ethics guidelines to control practices, its practices were later shaped by the constraints (and lack thereof) placed on it by the law.

The final chapter in the collection takes this history up to the present day. In 'Nobody's Thing? Human Tissue in Science, Ethics and the Law during the late 20th Century, Duncan Wilson analyses how judicial decisions both shaped medical research practice, but more importantly in the context of this collection, how the efforts of researchers and clinicians to shape the law was spurred on by their concerns about how the law might constrain their practices due, to some degree, to a lack of appreciation of research practices. Wilson explores the lead up to, and reception of, the Human Tissue Act 2004 by doctors and medical researchers, many of whom regarded the stringent regulations covering tissue acquisition and use as unnecessary. To them, their practices to that time had been adequate, given cultural and psychological understandings of human tissue prevalent in the community. Wilson draws on this view to explore the role public opinion, or more particularly, public opinion as it was presented in the debate by both sides, shaped both the law and medical practice.

Wilson focuses on the impact of the John Moore case, in which a patient brought legal claims after his bodily tissue was removed and used to produce a commercially valuable cell-line without his consent.[22] While the *Moore* case has often been cited as sparking off debate about the use of human tissue in medicine, Wilson argues that lawyers, scientists and ethicists had all turned their attention to this subject well before the case. In doing so, he rejects the simple view that this legal decision was the major influence on changes in medical research practices, arguing instead that these debates arose due to historical trends that reshaped these 'worthless' tissues, namely, the rising emphasis on patient autonomy in healthcare and, later, questions about commerce and exploitation in biotechnology. As Wilson points out, much of the drive for changes to practices came from the medical profession and the science community, who, through the expression of their views were a vital force in shaping the current law.

---

[22] *John Moore v the Regents of the University of California* (1990) 51 Cal 3d 120.

2

Parliamentary Inquiries and the Construction of Medical Argument in the Early 19th Century, 1793–1825

CATHERINE KELLY[*]

The vast expansion of the British Army's medical department during the French Revolutionary and Napoleonic Wars (1793–1815) was a significant contributing factor to many developments in British medicine, not the least of which was the creation of a distinct cohort of medical professionals, 'military medical officers', who emerged with their own professional identity, based on distinct educational experiences and theoretical perspectives.[1] During the Wars, and in the years following, these military medical men came into conflict with civilian practitioners both in the medical marketplace and in theoretic disputes. It was also during this period that medical men, particularly those of the military, began to involve politicians and Parliament in medical debates.

This chapter will examine the rise in parliamentary involvement in military medical matters over the first quarter of the 19th century. It will demonstrate how, through that involvement, parliamentarians became more educated about medicine, the 'military medical' perspective came to the fore and was preferred by parliamentarians, and how Parliament's role in deciding medical debates contributed to questions over what forms of medical argument were persuasive in the context of competing medical paradigms.

In order to understand the importance of Parliament's involvement in disputes between medical practitioners at this time it is first necessary to outline briefly the features of what this chapter terms 'military medicine'. In the early 19th century,

---

[*] Acknowledgements: The research for this chapter was undertaken with the generous financial support of the Wellcome Trust. Limited excerpts of this chapter appeared previously in C Kelly, '"Not from the College, but through the public and the legislature": Charles Maclean and the Relocation of Medical debate in the Early Nineteenth Century' (2008) 82 *Bulletin of the History of Medicine* 545, © The Johns Hopkins University Press. Reprinted with permission of the Johns Hopkins Press.

[1] For more on medicine during the Wars see N Cantlie, *A History of the Army Medical Department* (Edinburgh, Churchill Livingstone, 1974); RL Blanco, *Wellington's Surgeon General: Sir James Macgrigor* (Durham, Duke University Press, 1974); M Ackroyd, L Brockliss et al, *Advancing with the Army* (Oxford, OUP, 2007).

disputes within medicine arose about what type of medical education was best, what value could be placed on classical medical texts, and what type of observations contributed to the improvement of medical knowledge. The theories behind these debates are too complex to be gone into in detail here, and it should not be concluded that practitioners fell neatly into defined categories. However, large numbers of practitioners who served in the armed forces believed in the superiority of 'on-the-field training' over academic study, expressed a preference for empirical approaches to medicine over theoretical, and challenged the traditional division between surgery and physic. They also believed that military medicine was distinct from civilian medicine and advocated a 'military medical specialty'.[2] They began to derive statistics from observation of populations of sick, rather than basing their theories on individual cases.[3] They made arguments to support their practices based on those statistics and on principles of 'manpower economy', and from their experiences began to question the received learning they had been given about certain therapeutics and diseases, particularly fevers and dysentery.[4] Much of this new thinking brought them into conflict with more traditional practitioners and, in the early stages of the Wars, with the Army Medical Department which was headed by eminent 'establishment' practitioners who had never seen military service.

Select Committees of Inquiry and Military Medicine

Historians of the British Parliament have identified a marked increase in petitions, royal commissions and parliamentary inquiries in the years after 1780.[5] The degree of parliamentary involvement in medical matters can be seen most clearly in an examination of parliamentary inquiries conducted by select committees during this period. Select committee inquiries were a tool used by Parliament to investigate controversial matters or issues on which the 'facts' needed to be established before Parliament would consider a motion. While they do not

---

[2] See generally C Kelly, *Not Surgeons Alone but Medical Officers: The Effects of the French Revolutionary and Napoleonic Wars on British Military Medicine*, (University of Oxford, unpublished thesis, 2008).

[3] Similar techniques were also being developed in the larger civilian hospitals.

[4] 'Manpower economy' was a form of argument which sought to use the concept of a man's economic value to the service as a justification for certain medical practices. At this time it became employed more frequently by military practitioners in their writings, see for example the works of Robert Robertson and Thomas Trotter.

[5] P Jupp, *British Politics on the Eve of Reform—The Duke of Wellington's Administration 1828–1830* (London, Macmillan, 1998); P Jupp, 'The Landed Elite and Political Authority in Britain c1760–1850' (1990) 29 *Journal of British Studies* 70; J Innes, 'Legislation and Public Participation: Aspects of a Changing Relationship 1760–1830' in D Lemmings (ed), *The British and their Laws in the Eighteenth Century* (Woodbridge, Boydell Press, 2005) 102–32; JC Sainty, *The Origin of the Office of Chairman of Committees in the House of Lords*, (House of Lords Record Office, 1974) <http://www.parliament.uk/documents/upload/chairmn.pdf> accessed 7 July 2007.

Parliamentary Inquiries and the Construction of Medical Argument 19

represent the entirety of Parliament's dealings with medicine (or any subject which came to the attention of Parliament) they were the method usually employed if Parliament wanted to form an opinion about any medical practice. Committees could have various powers, including the calling of papers, reports, and even the examination of witnesses *viva voce*. They would produce a report which would then be tabled in Parliament with a view to the passing of a motion, or drafting of legislation. The reports and published evidence of select committees reveal to the historian the issues parliamentarians considered to be important, the types of witness thought to be worth questioning, and the styles of evidence used by witnesses to make their arguments. Towards the end of this period, historians have identified an increase in the interest of the press in select committees and their findings.[6] Consequently, in addition to the select committee's function in educating Parliament, it became a potential tool in the education of the public and in the formation of 'public opinion'.[7]

From the beginning of the Wars, and throughout the first part of the 19th century, Parliament engaged in a significant number of inquiries into aspects of medicine, particularly into army medicine and medical issues related to army experience.[8] In the preceding century, a similar parliamentary interest is not apparent.[9] This growth may have resulted from increased concern for the health and welfare of soldiers, or from a heightened appreciation of the economic advantage in maintaining the health of soldiers,[10] or may have been linked to the rise in the use of the parliamentary inquiry generally. However, while these factors may partially account for the phenomenon, an examination of the

---

[6] Innes, above n 5, at, 111.

[7] SE Finer, 'The Transmission of Benthamite Ideas 1820–50' in G Sutherland (ed), *Studies in the Growth of Nineteenth-Century Government* (London, Routledge, 1972).

[8] The details of those inquiries can be found in 51 *Commons Journals*, 450, 512–17: 'Petition of Matthew Baillie physician and Everard Home, Esq, surgeon', 29 February 1796 and 16 March 1796; and in the following committee reports presented to Parliament: *Commons Committee Reports* [*CCR*] 1801–1802, ii, (75), 267–318: 'Report from the committee on Dr Jenner's petition, respecting his discovery of vaccine Inoculation', 6 May 1802; *CCR* 1801–1802, ii, (114), 381–499: 'Report from the committee on Dr C Smyth's petition, respecting his discovery of nitrous fumigation', 10 June 1802; *CCR* 1818, vii, (285), 59–71: 'Report from the select committee on the contagious fever in Ireland', 8 May 1818; *CCR* 1818, vii, (332), 1–52: 'Report from the select committee on contagious fever in London', 20 May 1818; *CCR* 1819, ii, (449), 537–638: 'Report from the select committee appointed to consider the validity of the doctrine of contagion in the plague'; *CCR* 1821, iv, (732), 335–40: 'Report from the select committee on the ophthalmic hospital', 3 July 1821; *CCR* 1824, vi, (417), 165–287: 'Second report from the select committee appointed to consider the means of improving and maintaining the foreign trade of the country', 14 June 1824. These are not the only select committees to have investigated matters related to medical questions, however they are the only ones which have any military focus or which consider a medical controversy.

[9] A review of the General Indexes to the *Commons Journals* for the years 1697–1800 reveals only 11 inquiries related to medicine, most of those being related to the administration and financial management of medical institutions. Only three inquiries could be said to have considered issues related to medical practice or treatment and only one could be said to have any military aspect.

[10] H Cook, 'Practical Medicine and the British Armed Forces After the "Glorious Revolution"' (1990) 34 *Medical History* 1–26; M Harrison, 'Medicine and the Management of Modern Warfare' (1996) 34 *History of Science* 379–410.

inquiries demonstrates that at least part of the explanation must be the decision of medical men themselves to seek out this forum.

The first 'military medical' issues to be considered by select committees of inquiry in the early 1800s were raised in the Commons when medical practitioners petitioned Parliament for public funds as a reward for their inventions. The petitions required Parliament to determine the value of the discovery to the nation, and in both instances select committees were established to investigate that question. These committees considered respectively Dr Edward Jenner's discovery of vaccine inoculation, and Dr Carmichael Smyth's discovery of nitrous fumigation, both in 1802. They were extensive inquiries that called on a large number of medical witnesses. Examples of similar petitions (and related petitions for patents), in all areas of scientific endeavour, can be found in parliamentary records dating back several decades before the Wars.[11]

The history of Dr Edward Jenner's discovery of vaccine inoculation (vaccination) is well documented.[12] However, the parliamentary inquiry which considered the significance of his discovery has received comparatively little attention. It is not feasible here to examine all aspects of that inquiry, instead only the contribution of a military medical voice in its determinations will be considered. The inquiry was proposed on 17 March 1802, by the Chancellor of the Exchequer, Henry Addington. A committee was chosen from the members comprising 'Admiral Berkeley, Mr Foster, &c.' with a quorum of five.[13] Berkeley was Jenner's neighbour, and Berkeley and his wife had organised the political support Jenner needed for the petition.[14] Although Berkeley did not move the petition he was appointed chairman of the committee.

Of the oral evidence given to the committee, 36 medical witnesses were examined, and six of those were practitioners strongly connected with the military— Sir Gilbert Blane, Mr Francis Knight, Dr Joseph Marshall, Dr Lind, Mr Thomas Keate, and Mr Robert Keate. However only Blane, Marshall and Thomas Keate, gave evidence related to the effectiveness of vaccination within the forces. Their evidence was significantly different to that adduced from the overwhelming majority of medical witnesses to the committee, who had usually testified to their personal experience of vaccination, their opinion of Jenner's originality, and that they had caused their own children to be vaccinated. These three witnesses did address those issues, but also discussed their own attempts to introduce vaccination into the service(s) for which they had responsibility, and the efficacy of that

---

[11] See, eg 'Report from the Committee considering the Petition of Sir Henry Phillip's composition for destroying insects' 38 *Commons Journals*, 16 May 1781, 467–472; 'Report from the Committee considering the Petition of Thomas Foden respecting his chrystalline size,' 55 *Commons Journals*, 23 May 1800, 564–566.

[12] The best account is probably RB Fisher, *Edward Jenner, 1749–1823* (London, A Deutsch, 1991), which in chapter 6 contains a good review of the lead up to, and proceedings for, the presentation of the petition to Parliament, and the workings of the select committee.

[13] 57 *Commons Journals*, 240.

[14] Fisher, above n 12, 120.

measure. In particular, they gave evidence on the ability of soldiers and sailors to perform their duties after vaccination (in contrast to smallpox inoculation), whereas no 'civilian' witness gave evidence on the ability of men, women or children to be productive after vaccination. These witnesses also introduced into evidence the positive opinion of vaccination held by senior military leaders under whom they had served. Marshall referred to Admiral Lord Keith and General Sir Ralph Abercromby.[15] Blane presented testimonials from Lord Keith and General Hutchinson in its favour.[16]

The contribution of military medical officers to this select committee was, admittedly, not overwhelming. However, the quality and content of the military medical submissions does reveal a focus on populations as opposed to individuals, in contrast to the evidence of their civilian colleagues. The only comparable civilian evidence, in this respect, was given by practitioners in charge of large hospitals.[17] It is not possible to determine, from the summary form in which the evidence was reported by the committee, how extensively the military practitioners were questioned about the productivity of servicemen following inoculation, but the inclusion of the evidence at all suggests that the committee members considered it important. When viewed with evidence given to the Committee on Nitrous Fumigation, a good case can be made that parliamentarians had received significant exposure to the distinctive concerns of military medicine, and of 'manpower economy' reasoning, following these two inquiries.

The petitioner in the case of Nitrous Fumigation was Dr James Carmichael Smyth. Smyth obtained his MD at Edinburgh University in 1764. In 1788 he was elected a fellow of the Royal College of Physicians, and was elected to the Royal Society in 1799.[18] He had previously been commended by Parliament for his efforts in managing an outbreak of fever among Spanish prisoners in Winchester in 1780, where he had used nitrous fumigation to destroy and prevent contagion.[19] His method was to mix 'pure nitre in powder and concentrated vitriolic acid' in a pipkin which was then carried through an infected area.[20] Fumigation had long been used in the fight against contagion, however Smyth's claim to innovation lay in the ability of patients to remain in the room and breathe during

---

[15] 'Jenner's Petition', above n 8, 18.
[16] ibid 14.
[17] Dr Woodville, Physician to the Small Pox Hospital, Mr John Griffiths, Surgeon to St Georges Hospital, and Dr Nelson, Physician to the Vaccine pock Institution, all gave evidence of large numbers of inoculations within their establishments: 7,500; 1,500; and 700 respectively.
[18] G Stronach, 'Smyth, James Carmichael (1742–1821)', rev J Loudon, *DNB* <http://www.oxforddnb.com/view/article/25950> accessed 8 April 2008.
[19] 'Smyth's Petition', above n 8, app 1.
[20] ibid 24–25; see also JC Smyth, *The Effect of the Nitrous Vapour, in Preventing and Destroying contagion; ascertained from a variety of trials, made chiefly by surgeons of His Majesty's Navy, in Prisons, Hospitals, and on Board of Ships: with an introduction Respecting the Nature of Contagion, which gives rise to the Jail or Hospital fever; and the various Methods Formerly Employed to Prevent or Destroy This.* (London, J Johnson, 1799) 59.

the administration of his fumigation, a circumstance not possible in the common fumigations at the time which used muriatic or sulphuric acids.

In 1795, under the orders of the Lords Commissioners of the Admiralty, he had organised a trial of the nitrous fumigation method on His Majesty's Ship *The Union* at Sheerness, where there had been an outbreak of fever.[21] According to Smyth, his experiments were a success and his methods were then used widely in the navy, by military surgeons, and in prisons.

The select committee investigation into Dr Smyth's discovery of 'Nitrous Fumigation' was initiated by Mr Bragge in the Commons on 25 February 1802. Smyth's petition specifically referred to the usefulness of his discovery to the armed forces.[22] In its report the committee commended not only the practicality of his method 'in situations, such as Ships of War and Transports, where the Removal and Separation of the Sick may be impractical',[23] but also highlighted a consideration it believed to be 'forcibly affecting':

> [C]ontagious Fevers have been apt particularly to prevail and make the most dreadful Ravages in Ships of War, or among soldiers, when confined in transports or crowded into Hospitals. It cannot but enhance the Value of the Petitioner's Discovery ... that it provides the Means of arresting the Progress of a most fatal Disease, to which the brave Defenders of their Country must ... be particularly exposed.[24]

The committee concluded that the public had benefited from Smyth's discovery, 'especially in the Persons of our brave Soldiers and Sailors.'[25]

Nearly all the witnesses to the committee, both those who appeared in person and those who gave written testimonials, were connected with either naval or military practice. Their evidence focused strongly not only on the efficacy of Smyth's discovery but also on the practicality of administering it in the less than ideal circumstances of crowded transports and hospitals.

However, the evidence presented was not entirely supportive of Dr Smyth's petition. In particular Dr John Lind, surgeon to The Royal Hospital at Haslar, and Dr Thomas Trotter, late Physician to the Fleet, both objected vehemently to his claims, instead arguing that the widely accepted practices of discipline, separation of the sick, and rigorous hygiene were the only sure preventatives against contagion, and that Dr Smyth's fumigation only appeared to be effective because of the time at which it was employed (ie at the natural decline of the fever after the aforementioned methods had taken effect).

Lind's arguments against Smyth were apparently motivated by a desire to defend his father Dr James Lind's measures to prevent contagion, and were

---

[21] For his account of these trials see: *JC Smyth, An Account of the Experiment made at the desire of the Lords Commissioners of the Admiralty on Board the Union Hospital Ship to determine the Effect of the Nitrous Acid in Destroying Contagion and the Safety with which it may be Employed, In a letter addressed to the Rt Honorable Lord Spencer, &c, &c, &c,* (London, J Johnson, 1796).
[22] 57 *Commons Journals,* 173.
[23] 'Smyth's Petition', above n 9, 4.
[24] ibid 4–5.
[25] ibid 8.

ultimately dismissed by the committee because of some inaccuracies.[26] However, Lind's criticism of Smyth's use of statistical tables to prove his success demonstrates the difficulties facing both medical and non-medical experts in inquiries such as this when the efficacy of a particular measure was called into question. Lind's argument was that, despite the apparent success of Smyth's measures as shown in the tables presented in his book, the decrease in morbidity and mortality demonstrated by the tables was actually attributable to the measures that had been put in place before Smyth's methods were implemented and that the tables on their own (or in the context that Smyth had placed them) were misleading. The thrust of Lind's argument was that

> while the Nitrous Acid is used only in Combination with Means, which if employed alone, would have been sufficient to have destroyed the Contagion, its Efficacy cannot receive Support from any Result of the combined Means, unless it could have been proved to accelerate them, which is not attempted.[27]

Conversely, Smyth's response to Lind reiterates his support for the evidentiary power of statistics. He stated:

> [T]hose Regulations of the late Doctor Lind, were either entirely neglected, or executed in so careless and imperfect a Way, as to be totally useless; and that they were so the Returns of the Prison and Hospital for the Six Weeks after he left Winchester, prove in the clearest Manner.[28]

Exchanges such as this, and those which were aired in the Ophthalmia Inquiry discussed later in this chapter call into question any perception that the rise of statistics, in the form of naval or military returns, presented an unproblematic way in which to make judgements about medicine and medical efficacy, and certainly did not resolve a failure within the profession to 'achieve a shared framework for interpreting reliable evidence'.[29] The usefulness or ways of using those records in actual debate had not been established and many, like Lind, instinctively grasped the meaninglessness of statistics divorced from the circumstances in which they were produced.

Trotter's antagonism to Smyth's method appears to have been based in a strong philosophical objection to the use of fumigation per se. In his evidence he stridently objected to the practice of fumigation which he insinuated was supported only by superstition.[30] Trotter is well known for his commitment to achieving health through discipline, the enlistment of officers in hygienic measures, and the

---

[26] These inaccuracies should not have been fatal to his evidence and the committee's dismissal of Lind would appear to have more to do with his character and reliability as a disinterested man of his word, see S Shapin, *A Social History of Truth: Civility and Science in Seventeenth-Century England* (Chicago, University of Chicago Press, 1994) for the importance of such qualities in the preceding century.

[27] 'Smyth's Petition', above n 8, 69.

[28] ibid 73.

[29] For a discussion of the rise of statistical record keeping and its use in medicine during this period see U Tröhler, *To Improve the Evidence of Medicine': The 18th Century British Origins of a Critical Approach* (Edinburgh, Royal College of Physicians of Edinburgh, 2000).

[30] 'Smyth's Petition', above n 8, 81.

occupation of the mind.[31] His evidence against fumigation was entirely consistent with his philosophy. Fumigation only appeared to work, he argued, because it was inevitably used at the same time as those other methods of combating disease. Moreover, he warned that fumigation gave a false sense of security which could undermine the practice of the necessary discipline and hygiene that in reality prevented contagion.

The more interesting argument offered by Trotter was his analysis of Smyth's case for fumigation which Trotter labeled 'assertion instead of proof'.[32] What Trotter required for proof he said, was reasoning based in theory and accepted principles, not speculation and conjecture. Trotter's evidence demonstrates the complexities of the divisions within the medical profession regarding the probative value of certain types of proof: his thoroughly modern, military medical officer–like support for preventative measures and the importance of support from officers in their implementation was expressed at the same time as his much more 'establishment' view that deduction from 'mere observation', even in large volume, should not be enough to change accepted medical views, and only innovations which could be explained by new discoveries in the history of the disease or the specific nature of the medicine were acceptable.[33]

The committee gave extensive consideration to Trotter's allegations but in the end tacitly endorsed Smyth's rebuttal that, in fact, it was Trotter who was making the 'assertions'.[34] It does appear that the committee members were not prepared, or possibly able, to engage with the theoretical position presented by Trotter, and it is possible that evidence they were able to understand—'experiential' evidence—carried more weight with them.

The committee's report was presented to the Commons on 10 June 1802[35] and on 24 June 1802 the House resolved that Smyth's discovery had:

> already been attended with the most beneficial effects, especially in His Majesty's Naval and Military Hospitals ... it may justly be expected to be hereafter productive of the most extensive advantages, particularly to his Majesty's fleets and armies,

and recommended an award of £5,000.[36]

These two committees demonstrate that medical issues were being considered by Parliament early in the Wars, and that the military medical voice at those investigations was given significant weight. They also demonstrate that modes of persuasion beginning to be used by military practitioners, such as 'manpower economy' arguments and statistical evidence were aired in Parliament, albeit with varying levels of success. Importantly, it was parliamentarians who decided

---

[31] M Harrison, *British Medicine in an Age of Commerce and Empire, 1660–1830* (forthcoming, OUP, 2010).
[32] 'Smyth's Petition', above n 8, 80.
[33] ibid 80–82.
[34] ibid 7.
[35] 57 *Commons Journals* 565.
[36] 57 *Commons Journals* 650.

the importance of these discoveries, their originality, and what monetary reward they merited. This was particularly important in cases, such as the latter, when questions of 'medical expertise' were raised, and the value of various types of evidence brought to the attention of the committee.

Military medical issues were soon brought to the attention of Parliament again, in the form of the Commissioners of Military Inquiry's investigation of the Army Medical Department, as part of a series of inquiries into the running of the army initiated by Spencer Perceval and the Treasury.[37] Ostensibly, the Commissioners of Military Enquiry were only to examine 'the Public Expenditure, and Conduct of Public Business' in various military departments.[38] However, their investigation of the Army Medical Department was significantly wider ranging. The issues which they canvassed went to the heart of debates within the service over the reward of experience rather than theoretical education and the derivative question of whether military medicine required specialised knowledge.

The Commissioners took evidence from large numbers of medical men, both traditionalists and those who advocated the specialist status of military medicine. They were heavily influenced by one of the most prominent military medical officers of the time, Dr Robert Jackson, referring to his publications constantly in their report and even going so far as to say, 'Our remaining suggestions will apply to the whole Army Medical System … and we rely much on the opinions of Dr. Jackson.'[39] Their investigation of medical practice was supportive of Jackson and their report supported the philosophy of military medicine as a specialty distinct from civilian physic and surgery.[40]

Parliamentarians were exposed to more claims for the superiority of military medical experience in one of the most important developments in the regulation of medical education in Britain immediately following the Wars, the Apothecaries Act of 1815. The genesis and operation of this Act has been extensively researched by Irvine Loudon in his seminal work on the general practitioner.[41] However, one particular aspect of that Act that is regularly mentioned, but which remains under-researched, is the attempt to have army and navy surgeons exempted from its operation in relation to the education and examination required for certification.

The initial bill included a clause excluding persons acting or having acted as full surgeon or apothecary in the army or navy from examination under the Act; however, it was removed after the bill was sent to the 'Act of Parliament Committee of the Society of Apothecaries' and no such exclusion was legislated until 1825.[42]

---

[37] 'Fifth Report of the Commissioners of Military Enquiry' *House of Commons Sessional Papers* 1808, v.
[38] ibid 3.
[39] ibid 81.
[40] ibid 16.
[41] I Loudon, *Medical Care and the General Practitioner 1750–1850* (Oxford, Clarendon Press, 1986) esp ch 7.
[42] ibid 66. Cantlie, above n 1, 435–6, makes brief reference to the proposed exclusion and the feelings of military practitioners; Ackroyd, above n 1, 57 states 'Army and naval surgeons were not affected by the legislation.'

That committee, which was not a parliamentary committee, had received a letter from the College of Physicians in January 1814 commenting on the then proposed bill and requiring 'that all persons who have acted in any Department of the Army or Navy as Medical Practitioners should not thence derive any authority to practice unless examined by the constituted bodies'.[43] The non-inclusion of the exemption caused problems for the examiners under the Act almost as soon as it was passed, because many army and navy surgeons had not served a five-year apprenticeship as required by the legislation. The examiners requested advice from counsel on the matter, asking what to do regarding army and navy surgeons 'whose qualifications are in many instances superior to those of others'.[44] The position of the military surgeons remained unclear and further opinions from counsel were sought and applications to Parliament to resolve the matter considered.[45] Many of the arguments put to counsel for consideration were based on the notion that the education of army and navy surgeons was equal, and probably superior to, that of a 'regular' candidate for examination who had served the requisite time in an apprenticeship. In April 1816 the Army Medical Board requested a conference with the Principal Officers of the Company of Apothecaries, or the Court of Examiners.[46] At that meeting the Chairman of the Committee told the Army Medical Board 'that the Society had no intention whatever of taking any measures to prevent such surgeons of the Army whose warrants bear date previously from practicing as Apothecaries.'[47] The Committee also passed a resolution to that effect.[48] In May that year it was proposed to make an application to Parliament to amend the Apothecaries Act to enable surgeons of the army and navy of certain years' standing to practice without certificate, and to that end members of the Committee sought a meeting with Lord Palmerston who apparently gave his wholehearted support to the measure.[49] It does not appear that any such amendment was actually legislated; however, the position of the army and navy surgeons may have been considered settled by the resolution of the Committee.

Lord Palmerston was only one of several parliamentarians involved in the creation and administration of the Apothecaries Act; however, it is not clear whether any of the wrangling over the position of military surgeons came directly to the attention of a wider parliamentary audience. What is clear is that parliamentarians such as Lord Palmerston were approached to help resolve the matter, further

---

[43] Letter of Doctor Latham, President of the Royal College of Physicians to the Rt Hon George Rose, 27 January 1814', *Society of Apothecaries, Act of Parliament Committee Minutes 1814–1834*, Apothecaries Hall Archive, MS 8211/1, 7 (*Committee Minutes*).
[44] *Committee Minutes*, 23 August 1815, 87.
[45] 'Extract from the Minutes of the Court of Examiners, 19 January 1816' *Committee Minutes*, 90–91; 'Opinion of C Warren, 19 January 1816', *Committee Minutes*, 98; 'Letter to Mr Buckler, 28 March 1816', *Committee Minutes*, 99–100; *Committee Minutes*, 104.
[46] 'Letter from the Army Medical Board Office, 19 April 1816', *Committee Minutes*, 105.
[47] ibid 106.
[48] ibid.
[49] ibid.

establishing the impression that Parliament was seen by many practitioners as a forum for deciding medical debates. It is also clear from the failure of military surgeons to keep the exclusion in the bill, that by the end of the Wars, army and navy surgeons did not feel that they had the necessary authority and backing to convince Parliament that the education they had received and their experience on the field of battle were examination enough to place them ahead of their civilian counterparts who had to be examined under the Act.

The Opthalmia Inquiry

Competition between civilian and military practitioners was played out in two further select committee inquiries following the Wars. In these inquiries the questions of what type of medical experience, and what medical paradigm, would be considered 'best' was brought squarely to the attention of Parliament, as military medical officers made calculated attempts to gain the ascendancy. These two inquiries related to diseases which had been encountered during the Egyptian Campaign of 1801: ophthalmia and plague.

Not long after the Commissioners of Military Enquiry issued the Fifth Report, a disease called Egyptian ophthalmia (now thought to be a form of trachoma) reached epidemic proportions in the British Army. The disease had first been encountered on the Egyptian campaign of 1801, and raged in British Regiments long after its conclusion. In the decade following 1809 it produced a vast number of invalids and pensioners over which military and civilian practitioners, backed by their political patrons, engaged in a bitter dispute for the right to treat.

The civilian protagonist at the centre of this dispute was Sir William Adams.[50] Adams had trained under John Cunningham Saunders at The London Infirmary for Curing Diseases of the Eye in Charterhouse Square. In 1807, he had established his own practice in Exeter, where he helped to establish the West of England Infirmary for Curing Eye Disease. He claimed marvellous success in the treatment of gutta serena and cataracts and also to have developed a procedure to treat the third stage of the Egyptian ophthalmia, which involved the repeated removal of granulations on the palpabrae with a scalpel. Adams became very successful and was made surgeon and oculist-extraordinary to the Prince Regent and to the dukes of Kent and Sussex, and he was knighted in 1814. He had other powerful patrons, The Commander in Chief, Sir David Dundas, and the Secretary at War, Lord Palmerston. In 1817, he was given the charge of an ophthalmic hospital in Regents Park, and set up by his patrons in opposition to army medical officers who claimed superior skills in the treatment of the Egyptian ophthalmia. Eventually,

---

[50] For an overview of his career see WP Courtney, 'Adams, Sir William (1783–1827)', rev JM Tiffany, *DNB* <http://www.oxforddnb.com/view/article/23200> accessed 18 April 2006.

the post of ophthalmic surgeon to the army was also created for Adams, at a salary of £1,500, which Courtney understates 'greatly offended the military surgeons'.[51]

Adams' elevation incurred the particular ire of the Army Medical Board and its Director General, Sir James McGrigor. Their dispute over the territory of ophthalmia was made known to the public through the publication of various pamphlets and reports by each side, through the medical press, a select committee inquiry, and was finally debated in Parliament.

Adams' side of the story is set out in detail in several documents; his letter to the Directors of the Greenwich Hospital,[52] a report of the Directors of Greenwich Hospital,[53] and another published anonymously in 1821.[54] The thrust of those documents was that despite Sir David Dundas' attempts to procure a trials of Adams' practice on soldiers afflicted with the ophthalmia, the Army Medical Department created obstacles which prevented the trials from going ahead, was 'decidedly hostile' and tried to 'frustrate his views and counteract his efforts'. It appears that following a letter issued by the Adjutant General to the Director General of the Army Medical Board on 2 December 1812, Adams made several experiments on pensioners but the results of those experiments were contested by army practitioners.

Unfortunately for Adams, the hostility of the Army Medical Board continued. His anonymous supporter recorded that in 1813, the Commander in Chief gave directions that an inquiry into Adams' practice 'should be taken entirely out of the hands of Army Practitioners (who at that time, most pertinaciously denied its efficacy), and that it should be placed in those of ... eminent Civilian Practitioners.'[55]

Despite the resulting favourable reports Adam's plans were thwarted by James McGrigor, the Director-General of the Army Medical Board. The report alleges that on 4 July 1815, McGrigor wrote to the Adjutant General regarding the Egyptian ophthalmia, stating that there were at that time very few cases remaining in the Army.

Despite McGrigor's claims, the Secretary at War called for the returns of ophthalmic diseases treated in the Army Hospitals since 1810. They showed, contrary to McGrigor's figures, that the malady was extensively prevailing. Adams' supporter

---

[51] ibid.

[52] W Adams, *A Letter to the Right Honourable and Honourable the Directors of Greenwich Hospital, containing an exposure of the measures resorted to, by the Medical Officers of the London Eye Infirmary, for the purpose of retarding the adoption, and execution of plans for the extermination of the Egyptian Ophthalmia from the Army, and from the Kingdom, submitted for the approval of Government* (London, Baldwin, Craddock and Joy, 1817).

[53] *Official Papers relating to Operations Performed By Order of the Directors of The Royal Hospital for Seamen, at Greenwich, on Several of the Pensioners Belonging thereto, For the Purpose of Ascertaining the general Efficacy of the New Modes of Treatment Practised By Sir William Adams, for the Cure of The Various Species of Cataract, and the Egyptian Ophthalmia, published by Order of the Directors,* (London, Manufactory for Employment of Deaf and Dumb, 1814).

[54] Anon, *Facts and Documents Relating to the Establishment of the Ophthalmic Hospital,* (London, L Harrison, 1821).

[55] ibid 4.

then asserted that in 1816, McGrigor used all his influence to form an Eye Infirmary placing, 'an Army Surgeon, a personal friend of the Director General … at the head of this institution'.[56]

The army surgeon and personal friend of McGrigor referred to was Dr John Vetch. Vetch and Adams turned to the press to assert their respective claims to superiority. In 1817, Adams published his *Letter*, and in the following year Vetch published a pamphlet of observations on Adams' treatment.[57] Adams believed he was the victim of a conspiracy of army medical officers and purported to be defending himself against attacks made on his 'honor and integrity'. Vetch repeatedly made claims that his experience in Egypt and with the military gave him superior skills in the treatment of the disease, not possessed by Adams.

The existence of two institutions for the treatment of the ophthalmic pensioners soon came to the attention of a budget-conscious Parliament, and on 11 May 1819, Mr JP Grant rose to ask why

> the ophthalmia having prevailed to a considerable extent in our army, an hospital had, during the war, been established at Bognor for the cure of that disorder; great cures of it had been effected; and the disease was found of late years to have happily abated in the army. Notwithstanding this, in a time of peace, and at a moment when public economy was so much talked of, not only a new establishment was formed, but a gentleman (Sir W Adams) was placed at the head of it, who had never been in the army; and who had therefore no claim to military patronage … and who, though he was not even now in the army was placed over the heads of many eminent men who had devoted their lives to the service of their country.[58]

Grant set out an argument very similar to that advanced in Vetch's works, stressing the priority of army medical officers in the treatment of this disease. He called for an inquiry into the establishment of the second institution and for all the papers relating to its establishment.

Lord Palmerston responded to Grant's motion and used the opportunity to give his version of the history of the establishment of Adams' Ophthalmic Hospital.[59] Palmerston stated that the army medical practitioners had been so opposed to Adams and his mode of treatment, that 'it was useless to think of associating Sir W Adams with them; and the only way of rendering his system generally available was to place himself at the head of the establishment'.[60] Palmerston

---

[56] ibid 8; Adams' claims regarding the hostility of army medical practitioners are repeated in private letters to Lord Palmerston, see British Library (hereafter BL), Add 48432, (Palmerston Papers), ff 129–132: Adams to Palmerson, 5 December 1816; BL, Add 48436, (Palmerston Papers), f. 162: Memoranda (unattributed); and the 2nd Earl of Liverpool, see BL, Add 38267, (Liverpool Papers), f. 157: Adams to Liverpool, 21 June 1817; and BL, Add 38267, (Liverpool Papers), ff 188–195: Adams to Liverpool, 24 June 1817.
[57] J Vetch, *Observations relative to the Treatment by Sir William Adams, of the Ophthalmic Cases of the Army*, (London, J Callow, 1818).
[58] Hansard, 10 May 1819, 316.
[59] ibid 317.
[60] ibid 318.

also introduced to the House his personal observations of the patients in Adams' hospital, and invited the members to go there and judge for themselves. Finally, to prove the hostility of the medical men of the army, Palmerston read to the House an intercepted letter which appeared to prove a conspiracy in which an army practitioner connived to get Adams' patients drunk and thus induce a relapse of the disease before an inspection. Palmerston did not consent to the production of the papers because they would 'not contribute to real information, or lead to useful discussion'.[61] The motion was debated but finally it was negatived without any call for a division.[62]

In response, Vetch wrote Palmerston a public letter.[63] In that letter he stressed the importance of army medical experience for treating soldiers. This superiority of army practitioners was not a negative reflection on Adams, but arose instead 'from the superior experience of the Medical Officers of the Army in these diseases.' Vetch supported this claim by stating that army practitioners could devote all their time to the ophthalmia spreading through the forces whereas the civil oculist was more diversely occupied. Vetch also drew attention to the high number of desertions which he claimed Adams caused because he didn't understand soldiers.

Vetch also made reference to the initial trial undertaken by Adams, and to the conflicting evaluations of that trial. Vetch expressed particular outrage at Palmerston's reasons for suppressing a Report critical of Adams' practice, challenging Palmerston's view that it was 'dictated by a spirit of professional jealousy and hostile combination against Sir William Adams'. Furthermore Vetch did not agree 'that your Lordship's own testimony, and the statement given by Sir William Adams himself, render further evidence not only unnecessary, but inadmissible'. To this end Vetch included the text of a report made by Dr Moseley, Physician to Chelsea Hospital, Thomas Keate, Esq Chairman to the College of Surgeons and the late Surgeon-General to the Army, and William North, Esq dated 17 March 1818. That report found that of 64 Scottish pensioners selected by Adams for treatment 30 were still unfit and the 34 'supposed' to have been cured, had not been and were very liable to relapses.[64]

Finally, on 6 March 1821, it was moved in Parliament that a committee of inquiry be established to give Adams 'an opportunity of vindicating his reputation, and proving the merits of the institution over which he presided'. The motion was supported by supporters of Adams and others who knew medical gentlemen 'at variance' with Adams and wanted to get to the bottom of the matter.[65] The motion was carried, and in 1821 the committee issued its report. Its findings were generally supportive of Adams' practice, although it questioned his discovery of the palpabrael

---

[61] ibid 323.
[62] ibid 330.
[63] J Vetch, *A Letter to the Rt Hon Lord Viscount Palmerston, Secretary at War, &c &c on the Subject of the Ophthalmic Institution for the Cure of Chelsea Pensioners*, 2nd edn (London, 1819).
[64] ibid 25.
[65] *The Times Digital Archive*, 7 March 1821, 2.

cure, suggesting instead that he had merely revived something that had been known since antiquity. The commissioners also stated that they were 'induced to think very highly' of the 'knowledge and skill of Dr Vetch'. They found that, 'the objects of the Establishment, having now been attained', there did not appear to be 'any public inconvenience [that] would now arise from its discontinuance'. They recommended that Adams be awarded four thousand pounds for his services to the public. That award was contested by Mr HG Bennet who 'was one of those who thought that not a penny of the public money should be given to that gentleman'.[66] Lord Palmerston defended the claim and the full sum was paid to Adams.

In the course of this debate, Adams had made overt claims of McGrigor's untruthfulness, and those claims had been (less overtly) repeated by Lord Palmerston. Unusually, McGrigor, who was given to strident rebuttals of any such allegation of made against him, did not issue any statement denying that he had lied to his superiors about the extent of the ophthalmia. In 1819, however, McGrigor had published a document which set out his opinion of Adams and strongly asserted the superiority of army practitioners for the treatment of this disorder. McGrigor argued that Adams was no better than many civil and army oculists, and in the treatment of Egyptian ophthalmia he was worse than army medical officers because he did not have their experience. McGrigor further explained that Adams' lack of understanding was not only medical but also cultural in that he did not understand soldiers' dislike of submitting to operations at the judgement of only one person, and that in army practice (under the orders of the Commander-in-Chief) there was always, in such cases, a consultation (or second opinion). McGrigor further claimed that as result of Adams' practice there had been many desertions. In support he attached medical reports not favourable to Adams.[67]

It appears that the case conducted by the Medical Board against Adams before the Select Committee had been vitriolic. Mr J Dawson commented on the proceedings defending the non-production of the papers to Parliament, stating:

> The quarrels between nations and empires were never carried on with half the ferocity which distinguished the quarrels of bigots and authors. But of all the quarrels that had ever occurred between men of science, there was not one that displayed more ill feeling than that which distinguished the dispute between the Medical Board and Sir William Adams.[68]

Concerns were also raised that parliamentarians were not qualified to be the arbiters of medical debates.[69] The fact remained however, that Parliament was,

---

[66] *The Times Digital Archive*, 11 July 1821, 2; *The Times Digital Archive*, 25 July 1822, 2.
[67] Chelsea Hospital, *Report to HRH The Commander-in-Chief upon the subject of the out pensioners of Chelsea hospital, that have been under treatment for diseases of the eyes: Also, the reports made by the medical officers of Chelsea hospital upon the cases of those patients* (London, 1819).
[68] *The Times Digital Archive*, 11 July 1821, 2. Unfortunately, I have been unable to discover any official record of the proceedings before this select committee.
[69] 'Pamphlets on the Ophthalmic Question' (1821) 17 *Edinburgh Medical and Surgical Journal* 608–19.

by this time, deeply involved in medical debates, and had been embroiled in those relating to the military medical profession for over ten years. The pamphlets published by the central players in the ophthalmia debate show that Parliament was faced with a civilian versus military practitioner dispute that was very marked, very open, and very bitter. It was also presented with varying types of medical evidence, not the least of which were statistical tables and refutations of those tables. It was even confronted with different assertions of who was cured and who wasn't. It is perhaps not surprising in these circumstances that members of the House chose instead to assert their own ability to assess medical practices and decide between two practices in competition with one another.

The make-up of the select committee in this instance is worth noting as it was comprised of many very senior and influential men, several of whom requested to join the committee after it had initially been formed.[70] Most importantly, in the debates in Parliament it is apparent that the medical protagonists had procured powerful political patrons who felt very passionately about the issue themselves. It seems clear that the participants on both sides of the debate were keen for the issue to be taken to Parliament, and also that they supplemented their efforts in that direction with appeals to the public through written works.

The Inquiries into the Plague

The greatest example of a medical practitioner employing these techniques can be found in the final inquiry considered in this paper: the parliamentary inquiry into the contagiousness of the Plague, held in 1819. This inquiry was precipitated by the manoeuvring of a very politically active medical practitioner, Charles Maclean.[71] Maclean had served extensively overseas with the East India Company, and had made strenuous efforts to be promoted while serving with the army in the years 1804–05. He thought he would make an outstanding military medical practitioner, but believed he had been denied that opportunity by recruitment practices early in the Wars that favoured practitioners trained at Oxford and Cambridge. Maclean championed the value of medical experience gained overseas, and of experience over theory in general.

---

[70] The Committee ordered on 10 May 1821 was: Lord Viscount Palmerston, Mr Chancellor of the Exchequer Nicholas Vannisttart, Sir Thomas Acland, Mr George Banks, Mr Joseph Foster Barham, Mr Grey Bennett, Mr George Dawson, Lord Viscount Ebrington, Sir Ronald Ferguson, Mr Grant, Mr Holmes, Mr Hutchinson, Sir Charles Long, Sir James Mackintosh, Mr Tremayne, and Mr Wilmot, 76 *Commons Journals*, 325; Sir Thomas Pechell joined on 10 May 1821, 76 *Commons Journals*, 330; Sir Lowry Cole, Sir Henry Hardinge and Mr Wood joined on 14 May 1821, 76 *Commons Journals*, 341; Mr O'Grady and Mr Macqueen joined on 15 May 1821, 76 *Commons Journals*, 345.

[71] M Harrison, 'Maclean, Charles (fl 1788–1824)', *DNB*. <http://www.oxforddnb.com/view/article/17649> accessed 24 May 2006.

Maclean believed that almost no diseases were contagious. He was particularly adamant in this respect about the Plague.[72] He had been trying to persuade the medical profession of his 'theory of epidemic disease' and non-contagion since the turn of the century, but had been spectacularly unsuccessful. Eventually he gave up trying to persuade the medical profession, and turned his attention to the public and Parliament, perhaps thinking that if he could persuade them, his theory would become the dominant one.[73]

He did this in several different ways. First through articles in newspapers and journals and also by making his 'theory of epidemic disease' more exciting, adding some elements sure to catch the attention of politicians, businessmen and the public, such as an attack on the Catholic Church or the economic cost of quarantine. Importantly for the purposes of this discussion, he also cultivated politically powerful patrons and agitated to have the issue debated in Parliament.

Since 1813 Maclean had been cultivating the patronage of the Duke of Kent, the Levant Company, Lord Grenville and the East India Company.[74] They supported him in an expedition to the Levant to research the plague in late 1815. *Results of an Investigation regarding Epidemic and Pestilential Diseases*, the two-volume account of his research there, is usually seen as the catalyst for the 1819 inquiry.[75] Lord Grenville presented *Results* to the Levant Company Court who, in turn, asked Grenville to present it on their behalf to the Prince Regent and request an inquiry.[76]

In February 1819, Sir John Jackson, a director of the East India Company, rose in the Commons to call for a select committee to consider the 'Validity of the Doctrine of Contagion in the Plague'. He was supported by Mr Robinson, treasurer of the navy and member of the Board of Trade.[77] The inquiry that followed is particularly interesting in the context of this chapter, not because of the complex opinions that were aired about the nature of contagion, but because the way in which Maclean directed the debate required practitioners to address the question of what type of evidence should be probative: theoretical or experiential. However, despite the 'expert' status accorded medical practitioners by the inquiry,

---

[72] For a detailed description of Maclean's medical philosophy see C Kelly, '"Not from the College, but through the public and the legislature": Charles Maclean and the relocation of medical debate in the early 19th century', (2008) 82 *Bulletin of the History of Medicine* 545–69.

[73] On Maclean's strategy, see ibid.

[74] See Maclean's account of his correspondence with these persons and companies detailed throughout C Maclean, *Specimens of Systematic Misrule* (London, H Hay,1820); also BL, Add 59265, (*Dropmore Papers*), ff 92–188.

[75] C Maclean, *Results of an Investigation regarding Epidemic and Pestilential Diseases including Researches in the Levant, Concerning The Plague*, vols 1 and 2 (London, Thomas and George Underwood, 1817–18).

[76] Dropmore Papers, above n 74, f 175.

[77] 74 *Commons Journals*, 122: The committee ordered comprised: Sir John Jackson, Mr Bennet, Mr Boswell, Mr Fowell Buxton, Mr Henry Clive, Mr Cust, Mr Dawson, Mr Fazakerley, Mr Fleming, Mr Davies Gilbert, Mr Sandford Graham, Mr Hudson Gurney, Mr Heygate, Mr Legh, Mr Macqueen, Sir Charles Monck, Mr Morritt, Dr. Phillimore, Mr Frederick Robinson, Mr Wallace, and Mr Wilberforce.

the ultimate decision on a point of medical philosophy, the question of contagion, was to be made by politicians, not practitioners. Despite the weight given to expert witnesses, the questions posed by the inquirers were those of non-medical men. The committee concluded that there was no evidence to support a change to the 'received doctrine of contagion' but specifically stated that the question of quarantine was outside its remit.

The committee thoroughly investigated the opinion of nearly every witness on the quarantine laws and found that the great majority supported their amendment. Sir John Jackson chaired the inquiry and was clearly persuaded by the argument of the anti-contagionists.[78] He refused to sign the contagionist report of the committee and spoke against it in Parliament.[79] Maclean appeared as both the first witness, and the last. He was the only witness to be called twice and his *Results* informed much of the questioning. He claimed in his critique of the inquiry to have actually drafted questions for Jackson, but was disappointed that Jackson did not use them verbatim.[80] Of the 19 medical practitioners examined by the committee, nine had served with the army or navy. Practitioners were specifically questioned as to whether their knowledge of the plague came from personal experience, or the accounts of others.

The exclusive ability of medical practitioners to determine the question of contagion was raised by Jackson, and the opinions of Maclean and other practitioners were specifically sought on the issue. Maclean was given the floor in his second address to the committee and definitively stated, 'In conclusion, I may observe, that the question of contagion in epidemic diseases, as acknowledged even by its advocates, is entirely one of fact, not of physic, of which all persons of a liberal education are as competent to judge as physicians'.[81]

A further committee in 1824 considered the effect of quarantine on the foreign trade of Britain but not the question of contagion, which was considered settled by the 1819 Report.[82] Medical witnesses were consulted by this committee, but only contagionists, as the opinion of anti-contagionists on quarantine regulations was considered a foregone conclusion. The committee concluded that the quarantine system was too onerous and recommended that the length of quarantine be reduced and penalties for contravention made less harsh. Debates on the successful Quarantine Laws Bill in Parliament in the following year were accompanied by a petition from Maclean introduced into Parliament by John Smith.[83] Smith gave strong support to Maclean and advocated the view that 'the question, as to its

---

[78] Jackson was born in Jamaica in 1763, the son of a surgeon. He entered Parliament in 1806 as Member for Dover. In April 1807 he became a director of the East India Company. For further details see his biographical entry in RG Thorne (ed), *The History of Parliament: House of Commons 1790–1820* (London, Secker and Warburg, 1986).
[79] Hansard, 1st ser, vol 40, (1819), 1133–4.
[80] Maclean, above n 74, 166.
[81] 'Contagion Report', above n 8, 97.
[82] 'Foreign Trade Report', above n 8.
[83] Hansard, 2nd ser vol 12, (1825), 993–6.

contagious or non-contagious quality, was not so much a question of science as a question of fact, on which any man who was in the habit of weighing testimony, was qualified to decide'.[84]

However, the parliamentary forum for medical debate was not approved of by many practitioners, who felt that non-medics would only be able to appreciate experience-based evidence and not the finer points of medical learning and theory that they believed were essential. It was feared that division within the profession would cause authorities to turn to 'members of the bench or the bar accustomed to weigh evidence, and investigate facts, or even of such plain men as compose juries'.[85] Repeated complaints were made regarding Maclean's decision to take the debate to the public, 'to whom it should be observed he always addresses himself',[86] and were usually accompanied by an observation that the public and the legislature were not qualified to decide 'questions of which they must be necessarily ignorant'.[87]

Professional privilege was reasserted through statements explicitly alleging the inadequate standard of proof required by non-medical men to decide the question: '[Maclean's arguments are] the kinds of arguments that might do very well for a wrong-headed reformer in the House of Commons, but which must greatly injure a medical writer in the eyes of his brethren'.[88]

The participants in this debate were conscious of the evidentiary problems with which they struggled, referring to 'the unsettled nature of the laws of evidence in regard to medical inquiries',[89] and the need to establish meaningful ground on which to engage in a conflict of ideas. The debates over the type of evidence presented to the committee mirror those encountered in the select committee inquiries considered earlier in this chapter. The essential point being that according a higher value to 'experience' based evidence placed the educational model of men like the military medical officer above those who had been traditionally educated. The statements of witnesses to the inquiries and the writings of eminent physicians demonstrated a struggle on both sides of the debate to establish what type of evidence would be probative in not only this, but all medical debates, and what type of witness would be considered competent to give it.

Predictably, the Royal College of Physicians maintained most strongly the value of ancient texts, asserting in their report to Parliament that considerable evidence would be required to counterbalance the 'weight of ages'.[90] However this position was undermined by some 'establishment' practitioners who, while not rejecting

---

[84] Hansard, 2nd ser vol 12, (1825), 1315.
[85] G Blane, *Elements of Medical Logick* (London, T&G Underwood, 1819) 182.
[86] 'Fever in Ireland' (1826) 10 *The Lancet*, 721.
[87] ibid.
[88] 'Fever-Contagion-Quarantine' (1 January 1825) 2 *Medico-Chirurgical Review* 18.
[89] 'Critical Analysis' (1825) 24 *Edinburgh Medical and Surgical Journal* 100.
[90] 'Contagion Report', above n 8, 100.

the importance of theory, argued for the importance of experience, even the eminent naval physician Sir Gilbert Blane, when considering the question, concluded that the two modes of reasoning should be given equal weight.[91]

This conflict between two probative systems was evident to the layperson, and in the 1819 inquiry, Jackson directly asked Dr William Gladstone, surgeon to the Naval Asylum at Greenwich, whether he would 'rather be governed by modern facts' or 'historical reports?'[92]

The debates aired during the contagion inquiry threw into sharp relief the evidentiary struggle between two paradigms, the importance of which to military medical officers lay in the experiential model valuing more highly the observations of practitioners who had personally observed and treated a disease. The gradual acceptance of that form of evidence by men such as Mr Hume, who stated in parliamentary debate that he 'would certainly prefer the opinions of those who had visited the countries in which the plague occasionally showed itself',[93] plausibly then affected the ways in which medical practitioners directed their efforts at medical investigation going forward.

Conclusion

This chapter has demonstrated a significant increase in parliamentary interest in medical matters, particularly military medical matters, over the course of the French Revolutionary and Napoleonic Wars and in the years immediately following. More particularly, it has shown that parliamentarians directed their attention not only to questions of medical administration as they had principally done before 1793, but also to controversies in medical theory and over medical practices. Much of this interest was created by military medical officers themselves, who took their issues to Parliament and to their political patrons. This was especially the case in issues relating to divisions between the military and civilian arms of the medical profession, and in cases where an intra-professional resolution was not possible because of a lack of an agreed probative basis for engaging in medical debate. Medical practitioners supplemented their appeals to Parliament with pamphlets addressed to the public, and at the same time assiduously cultivated political patrons. These patrons appear to have become significantly interested in the medical perspectives they championed and the involvement of men such as Viscount Palmerston and Lord Grenville in medicine during this period warrants further research.

The effect of this increased parliamentary attention to medical matters was inevitably that the medical debates raised in Parliament were resolved in

---

[91] Blane, above n 85, 92, 96.
[92] 'Contagion Report', above n 8, 29.
[93] Hansard, 2nd ser, vol 12 (1825), 1326.

Parliament, not by medical practitioners themselves. It also appears that many parliamentarians considered themselves eminently qualified to make such determinations, and that they were supported in that conclusion by some medical practitioners who espoused the availability of medical knowledge to all. Although many practitioners continued to claim the exclusivity of knowledge and authority, that authority was ceded, in part, to parliamentarians the moment the question was taken up by them. The availability of knowledge was closely linked to the constitution of that knowledge, and accordingly medical practitioners attempted different ways of proving medical facts to Parliament. The types of evidence that appear to have been favoured in the parliamentary forum were those grounded in personal observation and experience. Thus the educational model promoted by military medical officers was tacitly endorsed, as was the concept of a 'military medical specialty'. The ability of Parliament to promote one type of medical practice or opinion over another was perceived by medical practitioners who exploited the potential thus presented.

3

Bye Laws, the Environment, and Health before Chadwick, 1835–1840

JAMES HANLEY

In 1835, the British Parliament gave newly-reformed municipal corporations in England and Wales the power to formulate bye laws for the suppression of nuisances subject only to the condition that they be submitted to the central government for review.[1] From 1835 through 1840, more than 100 corporations submitted one kind of bye law or another to the Home Secretary, and many submitted more than one version.[2] Historians of medicine have not generally paid much attention to these bye laws.[3] Some of the neglect may be due to the fact that the bye laws have not been seen to be important in the history of the urban environment.[4] It is undoubtedly true that many of these early bye laws were weakly enforced. However, it is not the purpose of this chapter to consider the enforcement of these laws, but rather to analyse them less as indicators of action than as registers of opinion. In so doing, the historian can take the making of these bye laws as seriously as did the people who made them. Indeed, councils spent many hours and days studying and drafting bye laws, many of which dealt with

---

[1] The Municipal Reform Act 1835 s 90 permitted corporations to make bye laws for the good governance of the town and for the prevention and suppression of such nuisances as were already not punishable in a summary manner by virtue of any Act then in force in the borough. It required corporations to submit their bye laws, if they made them, to one of His Majesty's principal secretaries of state, and required the Privy Council to disallow them within 40 days, unless more time had been requested. The affairs of the municipal corporation were directed by a Council, composed of directly elected councillors and indirectly elected aldermen.

[2] Based on the bye laws records found at The National Archives, Kew (TNA) /HO/70/1-6. There may well be bye laws, copies of which were not retained in these records. Terminology was not consistent at the time: I use 'bye laws' except where quoting.

[3] Housing bye laws have received some attention; R Harper, *Victorian Building Regulations: Summary Tables of the Principal English Building Acts and Model By-Laws, 1840–1914* (London, Mansell, 1985); SM Gaskell, *Building Control: National Legislation and the Introduction of Local Byelaws in Victorian England* (London, Bedford Square Press, 1983).

[4] On the limitations of municipal councils at this time, see S Szreter 'Economic Growth, Disruption, Deprivation, Disease, and Death: On the Importance of the Politics of Public Health for Development' (1997) 23 *Population Development Review* 705–8; M Daunton, 'Taxation and Representation in the Victorian City' in R Colls and R Rodger (eds), *Cities of Ideas: Civil Society and Urban Governance in Britain, 1800–2000* (Burlington, VT, Ashgate, Ashgate, 2004) 21–45. For a more sympathetic review of council activity, see P Harling, 'The Powers of the Victorian State' in P Mandler (ed), *Liberty and Authority in Victorian Britain* (New York, OUP, 2006) 43–7.

subjects of interest to medical historians. Furthermore, councils produced the first sets of bye laws between the 1831 cholera epidemic and the emergence of Edwin Chadwick's sanitary movement in 1838, and they thus provide a glimpse into a wide cross-section of provincial opinion at a transitional moment in the history of English public health.[5]

An examination of the bye laws submitted for review and the responses to these bye laws by the central government illustrates the ways in which these bye laws, themselves shaped by statute and common law, in turn influenced the development of central theories and practices of health. Specifically, I want to argue in this paper that the history of bye laws provides us with further evidence of the independent provincial roots of the early public health movement,[6] thereby further questioning the traditional formulation in which the early public health movement is associated with Edwin Chadwick, Secretary to the Poor Law Commission. His 1838 and 1839 reports to the Poor Law Commission and 1842 *Report on the Sanitary Condition of the Labouring Population of Great Britain* are usually heralded as the germinal documents of the movement.[7] Although the content of Chadwick's sanitary program evolved over time, at its core was a belief in the pathological effects of exposure to miasma or effluvia from decomposing animal and vegetable matter. Chadwick's insistence on importance of miasma has been interpreted in a variety of ways by historians, but most accounts agree that he forged a stronger (and much more dogmatic and ideological) link between filth and disease than most of his medical contemporaries.[8]

Chadwick undoubtedly differed from doctors in the overriding importance he attached to sanitary measures, but the bye laws reveal that municipal politicians (and their legal staff), often inspired by provincial examples, had already prioritised, at least in theory, the development of summary procedures to deal with just such decomposing organic matter, and they often did so in the face of central government resistance. In keeping with the bye law powers granted them, they expressed their concern in terms of certain kinds of common nuisance on private land, yet the different form of expression should not blind us to the conceptual similarity. Chadwick was writing a report for a non-specialist audience; municipal councils were drafting bye laws meant stand up in a court of law, and they were obliged to express themselves in the language of nuisance law. This basic conceptual similarity between municipal thinking and Chadwick's must go some way to

---

[5] The bye laws dealt, on occasion, with a very wide range of topics. In this chapter, my focus is mainly on the bye laws dealing with health.

[6] Historians have long recognised that the provinces led the central government in health matters. Liverpool, for example, appointed the first Medical Officer of Health; WM Frazer, *Duncan of Liverpool* (Preston, Carnegie, 1997).

[7] Chadwick's role is strongly emphasised in MW Flinn, 'Introduction', in E Chadwick, *Report on the Sanitary Condition of the Labouring Population of Great Britain*, reprint (Edinburgh, Edinburgh University Press, 1965) 35.

[8] M Pelling *Cholera, Fever and English Medicine 1825–1865* (Oxford, OUP, 1978); C Hamlin, *Public Health and Social Justice in the Age of Chadwick: Britain 1800–1854* (New York, CUP, 1998).

explaining the speed with which Chadwick's analysis gained provincial support; Chadwick told them what they already believed.

This chapter has four sections. In the first section I describe the background to bye laws, including mechanisms that existed to regulate the urban environment prior to 1835. This section will show that well before 1835, local authorities of one sort or another had developed summary mechanisms for regulating what might be called sanitary public nuisances such as privies, slaughter houses and various kinds of hazardous materials on public land, yet they had made only tentative progress in identifying, or developing procedures for dealing with, common nuisances on private land. The second section, based on a detailed study of sanitary nuisance provisions in bye laws produced in three different regions, argues that corporations very deliberately and very carefully used the bye law making process to provide summary remedies for common nuisances on private land, particularly nuisances that were perceived to be a danger to health. The third section demonstrates that although corporations emphasised new kinds of nuisance, they did so from a lay perspective; medicalised procedures, so recently in operation during the 1831–32 cholera epidemic, were ignored. The final section illustrates that the process of constructing a new urban sanitary order was highly contested. Councillors disagreed among themselves about what should be done, but even more importantly they differed with the central government which, in the name of the Home Secretary, routinely challenged local practice. Yet even as the Home Office rejected some bye laws, it promoted others, forcefully illustrating the role of the bye laws in shaping central understandings of health.

The Statutory Background to Bye Laws

The ability of urban authorities to regulate their environments was well recognised prior to 1835. Municipal corporations and other urban authorities had three principal mechanisms for regulating the environment: bye laws, the common law, and local Acts. According to long established tradition, municipal corporations made bye laws for the good government of their cities on the basis of powers granted to them in their charters. These bye laws did not require central government sanction, though they were of course subject to legal challenge by local citizens.[9] The common law was another important mechanism

---

[9] HA Merewether and AJ Stephens, *The History of the Boroughs and Municipal Corporations of the United Kingdom*, reprint, vol 2 (Brighton, Harvester Press, 1972) 1443–52. For a listing of these bye laws, see Royal Commission of Inquiry into Municipal Corporations of England and Wales, 'Analytical Index to the Reports of the Commissioners Appointed to Inquire into the Municipal Corporations' HC (1839) 402, 83–5.

for regulating the urban environment, and in theory a wide range of nuisances could be prosecuted under common law procedures.[10]

Because only some urban settlements had corporate charters, and because the common law was often seen as an imperfect mechanism, urban elites often resorted to a third means of regulating the urban environment: local Acts of Parliament that created local commissions of one kind or another.[11] These acts, promoted by local notables but passed by Parliament, both established the constitution of local governing bodies and stipulated their powers, including powers to regulate aspects of the urban environment.[12] From the perspective of historians of medicine, these acts are of interest as they contained a wide range of provisions governing what would soon be called sanitary nuisances; indeed, there were already semi-standard sanitary nuisance provisions.[13] There were, for example, usually regulations about the time at which privies and slaughter houses could be emptied of their contents and about penalties for spilling the contents as they were moved in the streets.[14] There were, in addition, almost always regulations, usually found within the general street code, governing nuisances from slaughter houses and swine styes running into the streets and from other offensive matter left in the streets.[15] The desire by local authorities to control what we may call

---

[10] J Hanley, 'Parliament, Physicians and Nuisances: The Demedicalization of Nuisance Law, 1831–1855' (2006) 80 *Bulletin of the History of Medicine* 702–32; C Hamlin, 'Public Sphere to Public Health: The Transformation of "Nuisance"' in S Sturdy (ed), *Medicine, Health and the Public Sphere in Britain, 1600–2000* (London, Routledge, 2002) 189–204.

[11] F Clifford, *A History of Private Bill Legislation*, reprint, vol 2 (New York, Kelley, 1968); F Spencer, *Municipal Origins: An Account of English Private Bill Legislation Relating to Local Government, 1740–1835* (London, Constable, 1911). These bodies were called by a variety of names in law but are usually called Improvement Commissions by historians. They often co-existed with Municipal Corporations in the same location, the latter having a much narrower range of powers. The existence of two sources of authority in the same town could be productive of much controversy. See D Fraser, *Urban Politics in Victorian England: The Structure of Politics in Victorian Cities* (London, Macmillan, 1979) 91–102, 154–75.

[12] Parliament responded to this avalanche of private regulation with a series of acts in 1847 designed to simplify the local Act process, including the Towns Police Clauses Act and the Towns Improvement Clauses Act. See J Prest, *Liberty and Locality: Parliament, Permissive Legislation and Ratepayers' Democracies in the Nineteenth Century* (New York, OUP, 1990).

[13] My conclusions in what follows are provisional, based on a preliminary review of nuisance provisions in a select number of local Acts. Spencer described the characteristics of the 'normal' local Act in *Municipal Origins*, above n 11, 178–263.

[14] Short titles for statutes were not used consistently until the 1840s. I use short titles as given retrospectively in R Devine (ed), *Index to the Local and Personal Acts, 1797–1849* (London, HMSO, 1999). As per convention, local Act chapter numbers are given in Roman type. Dorchester Improvement 1834 (4 Wm 4 c xvi) s 55; Gravesend and Milton Improvement 1833 (3&4 Wm 4 c li) s 12; Tetbury Improvement 1817 (57 Geo 3 c ii) s 23; Metropolitan Paving 1817 (57 Geo 3 c xxix) s 73.

[15] Great Bolton Improvement 1817 (57 Geo 3 c lix) s 6; Hastings Town and Port Improvement 1820 (1 Geo 4 c xii) s 39; Bury St Edmunds Improvement 1820 (1 Geo 4 c lxi) s 17; Stockton Improvement 1820 (1 Geo 4 c lxii) s 21; Dorchester Improvement 1834 s 53. Taunton Town and Market Regulation 1833 (3&4 Wm 4 c xlvii) s 12 and Gravesend and Milton Improvement 1833 s 79 had more elaborate street codes. On occasion, sanitary nuisances in public streets were found with other nuisances in clauses apart from the general street nuisance clause; Hastings Town and Port Improvement 1820 s 32.

sanitary nuisances was, as many historians have noted, already of long standing before 1835.[16]

In addition to these standard nuisance provisions, many local Acts of the pre-Municipal Reform Act period also contained provisions against what were variously called 'other nuisances' or 'particular nuisances', including, to take one example, a prohibition on any 'Slaughter House, Hog Stye, or other noisome Building' that was a nuisance.[17] Given that the general street codes usually permitted local improvement commissioners to control nuisances from slaughter houses and other comparable premises, one might wonder why these supplementary statutory provisions were necessary. They were necessary in part because the supplementary provisions did not deal with street nuisances but rather with the premises themselves; they concerned not blood running into the street from a slaughter house but the slaughter house itself. Additional statutory provisions were thus necessary because the provisions dealt with a different set of facts.

Yet the supplementary statutory provisions also categorised and policed these nuisances differently. The street code, an unwieldy list of offensive situations and/or things sometimes several pages long, usually did not have special procedures attached to it, nor did it always claim that the offense in question had to be a 'nuisance'. The acts usually permitted any constable or commissioner to apprehend any violator of the street code 'without any Warrant whatsoever' and bring them to the magistrates.[18] The local notables who sponsored the acts and the parliamentarians who approved them appeared to believe that little judgment was required beyond the register of a conviction by the magistrates. The mere fact of the occurrence such as blood from the slaughter house running in the street was all that was required for conviction.

For the supplementary nuisances, in contrast, the local Acts frequently developed additional procedural safeguards. Hastings' 1820 local Act required that to be removed a hogpound or stye or other public or common or private nuisance had to be investigated by the commissioners for the act and identified as such. At least seven commissioners were required to order a direct abatement. No comparable procedure existed for street nuisances. Stockton's 1820 act empowered its improvement commissioners to remove any hogstye or other noisome building provided that it was a nuisance 'in the legal Acceptation of that Term', again

---

[16] B Keith-Lucas, 'Some Influences Affecting the Development of Sanitary Legislation in England' (1954) 6 *Economic History Review*, 2d ser, 290–96; R Porter, 'Cleaning up the Great Wen: Public Health in Eighteenth-Century London,' in (1991) Suppl 11 *Medical History* 67; S Webb and B Webb, *Statutory Authorities for Special Purposes* (London, Longmans, Green, 1922) 235–349; Hamlin, above n 8, 257–64; P Carroll, 'Medical Police and the History of Public Health' (2002) 46 *Medical History* 461–94.

[17] Quote from Stockton Improvement 1820 s 24. See also Tetbury Improvement 1817 s 26; Metropolitan Paving 1817 s 67; Hastings Town and Port Improvement 1820 s 37; Taunton Town and Market Regulation 1833 s 13; York Improvement and Markets 1833 (3&4 Wm 4 c lxii) s 97; Gravesend and Milton Improvement 1833 s 82; Bermondsey (St Mary Magdalen) Improvement 1834 (4 and 5 Wm 4 c xcv) s 70;

[18] Quote from Bury St Edmunds Improvement 1820 s 17; see also Taunton Town and Market Regulation 1833 s 12; Gravesend and Milton Improvement 1833 s 79.

in contrast to violations of the act's street code. Taunton's 1833 act allowed its improvement commissioners to remove any slaughter house, hogsty, necessary house, manure heap, or other noisome or offensive building, matter or thing whatsoever if, after due investigation which the commissioners were required to conduct, they found it to be a 'Nuisance'. Taunton and York had in their 1833 acts specific appeal procedures for these particular nuisances, again in contrast to the general street codes.[19]

The fact that local Acts usually stipulated different and more rigorous procedures for the supplementary nuisances indicates that the framers saw them differently. It wasn't just that the slaughter house itself was a circumstantially different nuisance from its blood running in the street; it was categorically different, and required different standards of proof before it could be abated. The nature of the difference between these two kinds of nuisance was not made explicit in the acts. The most obvious distinction between the two kinds of nuisance would have been the common law distinction between private (affecting an individual) and common or public (affecting the community) nuisances, each of which was defined and dealt with differently.[20] Yet the distinction between general street nuisances and particular nuisances did not correspond to the common law distinction between common and private nuisances.

The feature that united most of the 'particular nuisances' was that they were nuisances on private land. A nuisance on private land could be, under the common law, a common or a private nuisance, depending on the circumstances. It is difficult to determine from the Acts if the particular nuisances were seen as common or private nuisances. The language of the Acts generally, but not exclusively, permitted action against them if they were a nuisance to any inhabitant. However, it was highly unlikely that local Acts would have been drafted to permit public monies to be spent on a purely private nuisance, that is, a nuisance affecting one individual only. Rather, the acts appeared to contemplate nuisances on private land that were potentially common, although complaints against them could be initiated by a single individual. The procedural distinction these acts drew was effectively one between common nuisances on public land (the street code) and common nuisances on private land (the particular nuisances).[21]

---

[19] Hastings Town and Port Improvement 1820 s 37; Stockton Improvement 1820 s 24; Taunton Town and Market Regulation 1833 s 13; York Improvement and Markets 1833 s 97.

[20] JT Smith, *The Laws of England Relating to Public Health, Including an Epitome of the Law of Nuisances* (London, S Sweet, 1848); JA Paris and JSM Fonblanque, *Medical Jurisprudence*, vol 1 (London, W Phillips, 1823), 330–54. Briefly, private nuisances affected an individual, and the remedy for them was to sue for damages (through an action on the case). Public, or common, nuisances affected the public, and the remedy for them was through indictment at the Quarter Sessions.

[21] It is clear that not all common nuisances on private land were captured by these local Acts. Apparently they could only be dealt with if they were next to a public street, and nuisances in private courts escaped. On this see Royal Commission for Inquiring into the State of Large Towns and Populous Districts, 'Second Report of the Commissioners for inquiring into the State of Large Towns and Populous Districts,' 1845 (C (1st series) 602) 40–44.

By 1835, then, many urban authorities had already begun to regulate nuisances that would one day figure as public health hazards, and in so doing they had begun to develop procedures not commonly presented in expositions of the common law of nuisances.[22] Common nuisances, according the common law, were all dealt with in one way, by indictment before a Quarter Sessions grand jury. Local authorities, with parliamentary sanction, had long introduced summary procedures for dealing with common nuisances in public streets into the general street codes of local Acts. Local authorities also clearly recognised that the common law did not adequately protect the public against common nuisances on private land, and they developed new procedures to deal with them. Yet common nuisances on private land, according to local authorities and Parliament, required a higher degree of procedural scrutiny than common nuisances on public land. In the next section, we will see that when corporations made bye laws, they pushed these procedural novelties even further.

The Bye Laws of Health

While it is thus clear that several mechanisms, especially the local Act mechanism, permitted 19th-century urban authorities to regulate the urban environment, the 1835 Municipal Reform Act provided a simple and low cost mechanism. Under the Act, 178 named corporations were given a new structure and franchise. The only additional compulsory new power given to the newly-reformed corporations was the establishment of a borough police force.[23] The 1835 Act also permitted newly elected town councils to make bye laws for the good governance of the town and for the prevention and suppression of such nuisances as were already not punishable in a summary manner by virtue of any act then in force in the borough. Newly-reformed municipal corporations seized the Municipal Reform Act's bye law-making power with alacrity. The new councils first met in January 1836, and by December 1837 more than 75 corporations submitted bye laws to the Home Secretary. Most revisited these bye laws several times in the future, and quite a number did so in the short term.[24]

---

[22] Smith, above n 20 and Paris and Fonblanque, above n 20 did not discuss summary mechanisms for dealing with common nuisances, but one would not expect discussion of the common law to refer to mechanisms contained in local Acts, local Acts not being common.

[23] Derek Fraser argued that Parliament's reluctance to give these corporations power was the single strongest argument that can be advanced against the claim that 1835 was a revolution in municipal government; D Fraser, *Power and Authority in the Victorian City* (Oxford, Basil Blackwell, 1979) 12, 164. But these bye laws were real power, as contemporary commentators anxiously noted. See H Chapman, *The Act for the Regulation of Municipal Corporations in England and Wales* (London, Charles Ely, 1835) 72.

[24] My discussion in this section and the next relies on bye laws as they were submitted. As section IV makes clear, the Home Office caused many bye laws to be altered, and the bye laws as submitted often did not take effect, but I am interested in the original formulation.

This suggests that the usual means for regulating the urban environment were not wholly satisfactory, although one of the features of the bye laws passed from 1835–40 was their continuity with what came before, particularly in terms of what might be called health or sanitary nuisances. The regulation of night soil, the control of sanitary nuisances in the streets, and the regulation of particular nuisances were found in the earliest bye laws, and their presence only increased over time.[25] Yet in addition to these elements of continuity, the bye laws displayed important discontinuities, especially an increased emphasis on nuisances on private property. The attention paid to nuisances on private land was, furthermore, focused on sanitary nuisances. The nature and timing of this interest was, I suggest, too closely linked to the 1831–32 cholera epidemic to be a coincidence and highlights a second, related feature of this discontinuity: an increased emphasis on health.[26] In the remainder of this section I will focus in detail on sanitary nuisance bye laws produced in three parts of the country: Liverpool, the north-east, and the county of Worcestershire, although other places will be occasionally drawn upon.

Liverpool was chosen because it was one of the most active local Act promoters, including one passed in 1835, as well as one of the most active bye law promoters. The existence of these local Acts, some of which allowed magistrates to make bye laws and some of which contained provisions of a bye law-like character, did not deter the council from making its own bye laws. The council chose to make bye laws in part because the passage of the Municipal Reform Act gave it the chance to harmonise to some extent the variety of regulations then in force within the various boundaries of the town.[27] Yet the council's bye laws were more than just an exercise in standardisation. The opportunity to make corporate bye laws forced councilors systematically to scrutinise their existing provisions. The bye law committee of the council spent weeks preparing bye laws for the full council's consideration, and the full council debated the committee's recommendations over five consecutive council meetings.[28] The council's 1836 bye law code was probably the single most extensive code in the country for the time.

The surprising feature of Liverpool's 1836 bye law code, at least in terms of sanitary nuisances, was its rejection of the model provided by Liverpool's 1835 local Act. The relevant section of the 1835 act, restricted to the old city boundaries, prohibited throwing or leaving any offensive matter in any public street, as was commonly seen in local Acts of the time, but it also prohibited throwing or leaving the same matter on any open or uncovered place, whether surrounded by

---

[25] See, for examples of different types of early nuisance bye law, TNA/HO/70/1, Buckingham (9 November 1836); TNA/HO/70/3, Kingston-upon-Thames (10 August 1836); TNA/HO/70/5, Rye (20 October 1836); TNA/HO/70/2, Denbigh (4 July 1836); TNA/HO/70/3. Liverpool (29 October 1836).

[26] The argument here complements that developed in detail in Hanley, above n 10.

[27] Some of the local Acts regulated the Docks, some the old city limits. The corporate boundary under the 1835 Municipal Reform Act was the parliamentary borough; 5 and 6 Wm 4 c 76, sch A.

[28] Liverpool Record Office (LRO), Report of Bye Law Committee, 352 MIN/COU/II/1/1, 21 September 1836. Council meetings dealing with bye laws took place on 30 September and 17, 18, 19, 24 and 26 October.

a wall or not, if it was within 10 feet of any public street.[29] That second provision was a step beyond most local Acts and was clearly intended to regulate offensive matter on private land. This provision had passed parliamentary scrutiny, and the bye law committee, not surprisingly, brought it forward unaltered for inclusion in the 1836 bye laws. Remarkably, the council did not adopt the proposed bye law. Councillors were particularly concerned with the possibility that the 10 foot rule was too broad. 'Ultimately', the *Liverpool Mercury* reported, suggesting a rather protracted conversation, council referred the matter back to the committee.[30] In the end, the council turned the local Act provision into two bye laws. The prohibition on offensive matter in the public streets remained. A new bye law governed offensive matter on open private land, which could be acted on only if it was a common nuisance.[31]

The transition from one provision in the local Act to two bye laws may seem trivial, but drafting fresh language that was not consistent with their local Act was not something the council undertook lightly; the bye law committee obviously believed the statutory provision should be incorporated into the bye law code, the mayor and the clerk drew the council's attention to the fact that it was a statutory provision, and at least one member urged councillors not to vary the language used in the local Act.[32] The two bye laws expressed an understanding of the issue, furthermore, that was non-trivially different from the statutory provision they supplanted. The council believed, based on the first of these two bye laws, that nuisances on public streets could be dealt with in a summary fashion without having to be identified as a common nuisance. They also clearly believed that offensive matter on private property was a problem that required urgent procedural attention, but the prohibition sanctioned by Parliament in 1835 was too indiscriminate. As they struggled to reconcile their belief that something had to be done about nuisances on private property with their anxiety over the rights of private property, councillors reached back to one of the elements of the common law; nuisances on private property had to be common nuisances, even if they were within 10 feet of a public passage. Even as they streamlined common law process, they still wanted common law definitions.

Their decision illustrates the continuing hold the common law had on councillors. Common nuisances on private property had to be dealt with differently than those on public land. The 1835 local Act effectively equated common nuisances on public land with nuisances on private land, at least if the latter were within 10 feet of a public passage; both could be dealt with in a summary fashion with little

---

[29] Liverpool Buildings Regulation, Improvement &c 1835 (5 and 6 Wm 4 c liv) s 37.
[30] 'Council Proceedings' *Liverpool Mercury* (21 October 1836) 374.
[31] 'Council Proceedings' *Liverpool Mercury* (28 October 1836) 382. The bye laws may be found at LRO/MIN/COU/II/1/1 (29 October 1836) 299–334. The bye laws are numbered 4 and 5.
[32] 'Council Proceedings' *Liverpool Mercury* (21 October 1836) 374. To be clear, the 1835 Act applied to the old, smaller corporate boundaries. The new 1836 bye laws applied to the new, larger corporate boundaries. The council could not amend an act of Parliament, but they could alter the language they drew from the act as they drafted new bye laws for a new jurisdiction.

procedural requirement. Yet councillors resisted the equation. This bye law shows the difficulties councillors had in extending summary procedures to nuisances on private land even when Parliament essentially invited them to do so.

This chapter has dwelt at some length on Liverpool, as a similar bye law governing nuisances on private land, including virtually the same list of nuisances in the same order, appeared in the bye laws of three different north-eastern councils: Newcastle (1837), Sunderland (1837), and Stockton (1838).[33] Stockton's case is noteworthy as its local Act had only passed in 1820, but when Stockton council created bye laws it relied not on its own local Act but instead on the Newcastle's and Sunderland's already-formed bye laws.[34] Stockton council may have chosen to work from bye laws rather than Stockton's existing 1820 local Act as the latter was limited even by the standards of the time. Indeed, sanitary nuisances hardly figured at all in the local Act. In the bye law code, however, they were found in four different bye laws.[35]

The shift in emphasis in Stockton's case from an 1820 local Act scarcely touching sanitary hazards to an 1838 bye law code in which they figured prominently, particularly as common nuisances on private land, was rapid and resembled changes in Worcestershire.[36] Worcester was the first council to prepare bye laws in the county. The City of Worcester was already governed under a local Act passed in 1823,[37] and like so many local Acts it contained a number of statutory provisions that had the character of bye laws, but the Worcester bye law committee thought the local Act was deficient in two ways. First, the corporate boundary was more extensive, the local Act being confined to the smaller limits of the old City of Worcester. For that reason alone, the bye law committee recommended adopting as bye laws 11 provisions from the local Act that extended what were effectively the old city bye laws to the new, larger corporate boundaries.[38]

Although the bye law committee claimed that all they did was extend the relevant sections of the local Act to the corporate borough, they actually slightly modified some of the clauses. In one small wording change, the committee prohibited privies or necessary houses if they annoyed the neighborhood by reason of effluvia they generated, whereas the local Act prohibited them if they

---

[33] TNA/HO/70/4 (Newcastle, 2 August 1837); TNA/HO/70/5, Stockton (sent 10 March 1838), and Sunderland (5 October 1837). It is not clear if Newcastle and Sunderland worked from Liverpool's bye laws or from some other local Act or set of bye laws. Hull council specifically worked from Liverpool's bye laws and it would not surprising if Newcastle and Sunderland did as well; 'Town Council Meeting' *Hull, Rockingham and Yorkshire and Lincolnshire Gazette* (17 June 1837) 3.

[34] TNA/HO/70/5, Stockton to Home Office (7 September 1838).

[35] The three north-eastern councils included a bye law not found in Liverpool's code, regulating, in Newcastle's bye law, 'private Drains, Gutters or Sewers' in tenements communicating with the common sewers. Sunderland and Stockton amended this to regulate 'private dung-hills, midden-steads, drains, gutters, or sewers' within tenements. All three were, however, clearly attempting to reach private property.

[36] Bewdley Corporation's records have not been examined.

[37] Worcester Water and Improvement 1823 (4 Geo 4 c lxix).

[38] 'Meeting of the Town Council' *Berrow's Worcester Journal* (13 April 1837) 3.

annoyed passersby.[39] These apparently trivial modifications were, I would again argue, highly significant. The new bye law conceptualised the problem differently, redefining the spatial dimension and specifying the source of the problem. Decomposing matter did not just annoy passersby because it smelled, it polluted the neighborhood because it produced effluvia. And effluvia did not just annoy people; it made them sick. Though the wording change was small, the change in thought behind it was not. This was not a bye law about comfort; it was a bye law about health.

However, the deficiency of Worcester's local Act extended beyond the geographic limitations inherent in the old city local Act, and the bye law committee drafted an additional set of bye laws not drawn from or based on the local Act. Of particular interest to this chapter were the provisions relating to health. Although Worcester's local Act already contained provisions around night soil and general street nuisances, the committee recommended and the council enacted a further bye law regulating nuisances on private land.[40] If a 'pig sty, or any other matter' were presented to two or more justices of the peace, the justices were obliged to strike a five-member 'inspection inquest'. The inquest members had to be drawn from different wards and had to view and report on the alleged nuisance within three days, failure to serve being a met with a fine. The complainant had to pay to initiate the process, but recovered from the respondent if the nuisance was proved.

The model for this procedure is not clear, although a coroner's inquest is an obvious candidate.[41] What is striking, though, is the fact that the committee developed this process at all. This procedure raised a number of issues. How many members should the inquest have? How should they be chosen? How quickly should they act? Should they be fined, and how much, for not acting? What sort of appeal should there be for respondents? How much should the complainant pay? It is extremely unlikely that the answers to these questions were uncontroversial, and probably every element entailed debate and discussion. All of the men on the council were volunteers, and though service undoubtedly had its own rewards, they would not unnecessarily multiply their committee work unless they thought it mattered. That the committee worked through the details of this inspection inquest is an indication of the seriousness with which they viewed the problem.

Some insight into the committee's rationale for the procedure emerged the following year, after the Home Office challenged the bye law. The phrase 'any other

---

[39] Compare Worcester local Act s 44 with bye law no 1. The bye laws may be found at WRO/b261.5/BA7123/parcel 10.

[40] 'Meeting of the Town Council' *Berrow's Worcester Journal* (13 April 1837) 3. This bye law was, according to the *Journal*'s report, meant to catch private and public nuisances. The corporation would not have involved itself in the prosecution of private nuisances, and the reporter or speaker must have meant public nuisances on private land; no other construction makes sense. The other 'health' bye law concerned the sale of unwholesome food.

[41] For coroner's inquests, see I Burney, *Bodies of Evidence: Medicine and the Politics of the English Inquest, 1830–1926* (Baltimore, Johns Hopkins University Press, 2000) 4–6.

matter' was deemed too general, and in response the council stipulated a more defined list of nuisances and required that they be prejudicial to the public health as a nuisance before they could be acted on.[42] It is interesting that they had to be a danger to the public health. Nuisances under the common law did not have to be a danger to health. That Worcester council, like the Stockton council, decided to extend its bye laws after only 14 years is significant; it is not as though nuisances on private land first appeared after 1823. Since the council intended the new bye law to permit the control of nuisances to health on private land, one must assume that some event since 1823 convinced the council that they needed to worry about that and that they needed to worry about effluvia. The cholera epidemic is the most obvious candidate; the inability to control nuisances on private land was one of the most common complaints during the epidemic.[43]

Worcester's bye laws' influence extended beyond Worcester, as they served as a model for other corporations in the county. Droitwich's bye law-making members were probably the most careful students of Worcester's bye laws. When Droitwich began to prepare bye laws, it first prepared a draft of all potentially desirable bye laws. The bye law committee, as was the case for Sunderland and Stockton, appeared not to work from any local Act but rather from other bye laws; the order and content of Droitwich's draft bye laws were virtually identical to Worcester's 1837 bye laws. Yet this draft was extensively revised; 12 of the bye laws were marked for deletion and did not appear in the next draft.[44] However, Droitwich retained the two bye laws related to health added by the Worcester bye law committee, including the 'inspection inquest'. But even here the Droitwich council tightened the Worcester bye law, deliberately modifying Worcester's clause to make explicit the wider range of nuisances to which it applied.[45]

Kidderminster's bye law history tells a similar story with a slight variation. The short bye law code the council passed in February 1838 contained few provisions. Unlike Worcester and Droitwich, Kidderminster council decided not to institute proceedings to abate common nuisances on private land. Yet Kidderminster's council revisited their bye laws in 1840 and extended the bye law regulating the movement of offensive matter to new types of situation.[46] Of the four sets of

[42] Worcester to HO, 23 October 1838, TNA/HO/70/6.

[43] Worcestershire certainly had exposure to the epidemic; see British Library Add MS 39,167, ff 158–71 for records of correspondence over the epidemic. On nuisance control during the epidemic, see Hanley, above n 10; M Durey, *The Return of the Plague: British Society and the Cholera, 1831–32* (New York, Humanities Press, 1979) 83.

[44] Drafts are at WRO/261.4/BA1006/parcel 29.

[45] Worcester's bye law no 20 regulated 'a pigsty, or any other matter' that was a nuisance. Droitwich's first (23 bye law) draft kept this, as did its second (11 bye law) draft, but the latter was annotated with 'cess hole privy'. This minutely altered but carefully prepared article appeared in the version of the bye laws sent to the Home Office 22 May 1838; TNA/HO/70/2.

[46] The 1838 bye laws regulated the movement of soil and dung around the city, but exempted from regulation any soil or dung kept in any 'Stable or Yard'; TNA/HO/70/3 (13 February 1838). The amended bye laws (19 May 1840) removed the exemption. Kidderminster council may have had short bye laws as the Kidderminster Improvement Commission was thought to be the responsible body for these matters in the town; Royal Commission for Inquiring into the State of Large Towns and

bye laws examined from Worcestershire, only Evesham produced a code with no reference to sanitary nuisances.[47]

This review of early bye law production in Liverpool, the north east, and Worcestershire shows us the care and deliberation with which councils fashioned bye laws relating to sanitary nuisances: Liverpool council bothered to debate the propriety of its 10-foot rule, Sunderland and Stockton minutely scrutinised and amended Newcastle's list of nuisances, Worcester amended its own act's list of nuisances and drafted provisions to catch new ones, and Droitwich minutely clarified Worcester's list. Even the non-making of bye laws was time consuming; Evesham's bye law committee deliberated for five nights before they produced their very short code, and no doubt most of the time was spent reviewing, and rejecting, other towns' bye laws. The review also shows us that councils had different ideas about what needed to be done in terms of bye laws pertaining to health; some drafted elaborate new precautions, others did less. Several factors undoubtedly influenced the decision whether to produce these sorts of bye laws and the final form the bye laws assumed, although the existence and perceived adequacy of a local Act and the presence of regional models seem to have been particularly important determinants.[48] It is unlikely that these different bye laws can be explained solely or even mainly as a result of the objective sanitary conditions of the respective towns.

The fact that eight out of nine councils from Liverpool to Worcestershire to Tyneside and Teesside displayed an increased commitment to the management of common nuisances on private land is noteworthy. Anything, be it on public land or private, was subject to indictment (if a common nuisance) or action (if a private nuisance) under the common law. In that sense, these bye laws regulated that which was already potentially actionable or indictable. Yet councils clearly thought that was necessary, and the kind of nuisance on private land to which they directed their attention was, furthermore, a subset of potential legal nuisances. They paid little attention in bye laws dealing with nuisances on private land to, for example, the stopping of light. The fact that councils emphasised sanitary hazards on private land alerts us to a second discontinuity in the bye laws: a focus on health as the rationale for action.

The focus on health as the spring to action, while often implicit, occasionally appeared explicitly. The clearest example was outside the range of corporations hitherto described. Pwllheli council explicitly drew attention in several of its bye laws to situations or things 'detrimental to Public Health', which it distinguished

---

Populous Districts, 'Appendix to the Second Report of the Commissioners of Inquiry into the State of Large Towns and Populous District, 1845 (C (1st series) 602) app pt 1, 42, query 19.

[47] WRO/b261.5/BA7123/parcel 22, Bye-Law Committee Minute Book (20 November 1838). Evesham's committee requested bye laws from six different places and the Clerk obtained another set on his own. The committee deliberated for five evenings. The bye laws are at 4 February 1839.

[48] Gerry Kearns draws attention to the neglected aspect of inter-urban cooperation. See G Kearns, 'Town Hall and Whitehall: Sanitary Intelligence in Liverpool, 1840–63' in S Sheard and H Power (eds), *Body and City: Histories of Urban Public Health* (Burlington, VT, Ashgate, 2000) 108.

from things that were annoying, offensive and injurious to individuals. They specifically prohibited any 'Night Soil or other decomposed substances emitting noxious or unhealthy effluvia' and permitted justices to fine individuals who refused to remove decomposing substances or stagnant waters deemed to be capable of causing any dangerous or malignant disease.[49] It is hard not to detect in Pwllheli's concern about decomposing things causing malignant disease an echo of the cholera epidemic that had occurred, after all, only five years earlier. Even in the case of some of councils considered in this section, the emphasis on health emerged explicitly. Worcester's bye laws empowered the justices to act upon nuisances on private land if they were 'calculated to be prejudicial to the public health as a nuisance'.[50] In two additional bye laws passed by the Liverpool council in 1836 and 1838 to regulate chemical nuisances and slaughter houses respectively, the council explicitly proscribed nuisances that prejudiced the 'health or comfort' of the citizens.[51]

It is possible that these references to health were simply more non-specific bye law boilerplate, as Peter Hennock suggested many years ago with respect to references to health in local Act preambles.[52] Certainly the common law of nuisances did not require nuisances to be prejudicial to health. When the first cases under Liverpool's 1836 noxious vapour bye law came to trial, the corporation's counsel, after reading the bye law for the record, observed that 'It was hardly of any consequence whether the gas, or vapour, was prejudicial to the health of the inhabitants or not, if it were prejudicial to their comforts.' The presiding magistrate too noted, in ruling against the defendant, that nuisances did not have to affect the health of inhabitants if the inhabitants were rendered uncomfortable.[53] The Liverpool council, its clerk, and the legal counsel on whom they relied in drafting the bye law of course knew this, yet they inserted health into the bye law regardless. Even if they did not succeed in convincing the magistrates, or their own counsel, that health mattered by itself, they at least got them talking about it. And changing the terms of a debate is sometimes, in the long term, more important than winning it.[54] Parliament did not medicalise noxious trades such as slaughter houses in 1847 out of the blue.[55]

---

[49] TNA/HO/70/4, Pwllheli (26 November 1836) 5, 7, 8.

[50] Worcester (29 November 1838); WRO/261.5/BA7123/parcel 10. This is an amended set of bye laws produced in response to Home Office questioning.

[51] The two bye laws in question were passed separately from the major 1836 code; TNA/HO/70/3, Liverpool, bye laws dated 8 August 1836 and 1 August 1838.

[52] EP Hennock, 'Urban Sanitary Reform a Generation before Chadwick?' (1958) 10 *Economic History Review*, 2d ser, 113–20. The language of local Acts, furthermore, did not often refer to health when it discussed nuisances; health was not usually part of the specific rationale for a specific provision.

[53] 'Chemical Nuisances' *Liverpool Mercury* (30 December 1836) 454.

[54] AE Dingle, '"The Monster Nuisance of All": Landowners, Alkali Manufacturers, and Air Pollution, 1828–64' (1982) 35 *Economic History Review*, 2d ser, 529–48, argued that alkali regulation had little if anything to do with public health. I do not mean to disagree; I do want to suggest that concerns over health partly informed the debates over noxious trades, and those debates should not be seen in isolation from other debates over health hazards occurring at the same time.

[55] Towns Improvement Clauses Act 1847 (10 and 11 Vict c 34) s 104. In the absence of an inspector of nuisances, nuisances had to be certified by a medical person.

The Lay Perspective

The increasing attention paid to sanitary nuisances on private land was, I have argued, an important discontinuity. But where did it come from? The similarity of these new nuisances to nuisances the public health movement, often seen to be led by Edwin Chadwick, would soon be strongly associated with is striking. Indeed, they were not only conceptually similar but chronologically nearly coincidental. The first public report linked with Chadwick to draw attention to sanitary nuisances was the 4th report of the Poor Law Commissioners published in mid 1838.[56] Yet the chronology makes clear that, at least for the councils in this study, the linkage between decomposing animal and vegetable matter and hazards to health had already been made. Pwllheli may be an extreme example, with its bye laws submitted in late 1836, but even if we restrict ourselves to Liverpool, Worcestershire and the north-east, the picture is clear. Liverpool had already displayed concern with sanitary nuisances on private land in its 1835 local Act. Worcester council, the county leader, drafted its bye laws on nuisances on private land in 1837, as did Newcastle, the temporal leader of the three north-eastern towns. It may be the case that councils in 1838 and 1839 were influenced by centrally-disseminated propaganda, but they were possibly even more influenced by the knowledge and practice they gleaned from regional counterparts. At all events, the central government was by no means the temporal leader in this movement.

The context in which councils created bye laws was likewise different from Chadwick's. Chadwick partly developed his strong sanitary program in the context of struggles to vindicate the New Poor Law, but councillors knew little of Chadwick's machinations. The sources of provincial sanitarianism perhaps lay elsewhere. Of course there was a long-standing belief in the deleterious effects of filth, yet the roots of the Liverpool council's sanitary program, for example, may be productively sought in the law which shaped and guided understanding and action. They were not a medical body, and they understood nuisances entirely in the context of the common law which framed the conceptualisation of the problem and provided the remedies for it.

It is possible that councils drew on the writings of physicians, long conscious of the potentially dangerous consequences of filth.[57] One of the most well known of these, James Phillips Kay's *Moral and Physical Condition of the Working Classes ... in Manchester*, first appeared in the aftermath of the 1831 cholera epidemic, a crucial event, as I have argued. While Key's pamphlet may have played such a role, there is no indication that it did, even in the northern towns of this study. Nor would

---

[56] For discussions of Chadwick's entry into this field, see Hamlin, *Public Health*, above n 8, 85; C Hamlin, 'Edwin Chadwick, "Mutton Medicine" and the Fever Question' (1996) 70 *Bulletin of the History of Medicine* 233–65; SE Finer, *The Life and Times of Sir Edwin Chadwick* (London, Methuen, 1952) 155–6; MW Flinn, above n 7, 43.

[57] Flinn, above n 7, 10, 44; Hamlin, 'Edwin Chadwick', above n 56, 236; Keith-Lucas, 'Some Influences', above n 16; Porter, 'Cleaning up the Great Wen', above n 16, 71–4.

we necessarily expect it to have played a role. Lay people did not need physicians to tell them that foul smelling waste was potentially hazardous. It is far more likely that the cholera epidemic reinforced this popular notion notwithstanding the Privy Council's attempt to medicalise sanitary nuisances during the epidemic.

The bye laws councils drafted after 1835 did not suggest any retreat of lay judgment in the aftermath of cholera. Liverpool and the northeastern councils prescribed no specific procedures to assess whether a common nuisance existed or not, relying entirely on private citizens to complain. The only corporations in this sample where specific procedures existed were Worcester and Droitwich. The Worcester and Droitwich bye laws were interesting in that they did not reflect any awareness that these nuisances, designated during the cholera epidemic as hazards to health requiring medical certification, required any sort of medicalised procedures to deal with them. They were unusual bye laws in the sense that they had explicit procedures attached to them, but these procedures reflected the non-specialist orientation of local nuisance practice in the 1831–32 cholera epidemic and what would be its continuing non-specialist interpretation through 1855. The reliance on the common law thus re-asserted lay control over what had been, in the cholera epidemic, newly medicalised health hazards.

A similar reliance on lay judgment was found in bye laws surrounding unwholesome meat and fish. In the mid 1850s, parliamentary hearings on adulterated food took testimony from medical men on the identification and ill effects of consuming bad food, tacitly endorsing medical expertise, and John Simon issued a major report on food in the 1860s.[58] Yet some local authorities had already taken this under lay control in local Acts.[59] In Liverpool's 1820 local Act, the Mayor and Inspector of Markets were empowered to enter any slaughter house and if they found meat which appeared to them diseased they were empowered to seize it. It was then to be examined by 'competent Persons, according to the usual Course and Practice heretofore adopted'. If the competent persons found it bad, it was to be destroyed.[60] In no place was it stipulated what constituted competency. In early bye laws, corporations continued this reliance on lay judgment.[61]

---

[58] Select Committee to Inquire into the Adulteration of Food, Drinks, and Drugs, 'Report from the Select Committee on Adulteration of Food, Drinks, and Drugs' HC (1856) 379 qq. 1446–66; Report of the Medical Officer of the Privy Council, 'Fifth Report,' HC (1863) 161 app 206. For this issue later in the century see K Waddington, '"Unfit for Human Consumption": Tuberculosis and the Problem of Infected Meat in Late Victorian Britain' (2003) 77 *Bulletin of the History of Medicine* 636–61.

[59] This was not so common that it formed a part of Spencer's typical local Act, and no entry regarding unwholesome food is found in the index to Clifford's study of local legislation.

[60] Liverpool Improvement 1820 s 21. Bermondsey (St Mary Magdalen) Improvement 1834 s 69 had a provision similar to Liverpool's. Taunton Town and Market Regulation 1833 s 22 empowered destruction of meat.

[61] Coventry (22 November 1836), found at TNA/HO/70/4 with Northampton; Northampton (9 April 1838) TNA/HO/70/4; Grantham (11 May 1837) TNA/HO/70/2. Even Liverpool (29 October 1836) abandoned its old competent persons process; TNA/HO/70/3. In some cases, the process of deciding that food was unfit for sale was not stipulated, but the seizure and destruction of meat required approval of the justices; Southwold (23 April 1839) TNA/HO/70/5. In a possible echo of Liverpool's old procedure, Derby (7 July 1838) had specialist officers—the Searchers of Flesh—who were responsible for drawing magisterial attention to unwholesome food, but there was no indication that they required specialist training, and they could in any event delegate their duties to police or

The final area in which we can see lay control was the regulation of noxious trades such as slaughter houses and other noisome premises, regulations which were, as we have already seen, often found in pre-1835 local Acts. One of the notable features of some of the bye laws was the increasing attention that began to be devoted to such potential nuisances.[62] Liverpool's 1836 bye laws, for example, contained a relatively elaborate slaughter house code, regulating the frequency of cleaning, the movement of offal, the placement of privies, and the presence of animals. Notwithstanding this detailed code, the council passed, in August 1838, a fresh bye law regulating the vapours and gases from slaughter houses that affected the health and comfort of the citizenry. Although Parliament would require medical certification of nuisances such as this in certain circumstances in 1847, the 1838 Liverpool bye law required no medical participation. Other corporations' 'noxious trades' bye laws were similarly devoid of professional medical involvement.[63]

Over the middle decades of the 19th century, Parliament repeatedly re-visited the procedures necessary to process both sanitary nuisances and nuisances from noxious trades, alternately requiring and deleting medical participation. Sanitary nuisances had required medical involvement during the 1831–32 cholera epidemic and would again in 1846, and in 1847 Parliament could require medical certification of noxious trades such as slaughter houses in the Towns Improvement Clauses Act.[64] At the local level, in contrast, even as councils categorised and identified new nuisances, they continued to rely on non-medical procedures which invariably relied on the common judgment of the propertied citizenry.

The Role of the Home Office

The maintenance of domestic order was the Home Office's most important responsibility, so it was only natural that the Office was responsible for perusing bye laws in the first instance. The character of bye laws as a whole, furthermore, made this even more sensible; although this paper has focused on hazards to health of one sort or another, many of the bye laws contained numerous provisions policing a

---

constables; TNA/HO/70/2. According to Joseph Fletcher's survey of municipal institutions, it appears that fewer than ten corporations had specialist officers dealing with meat and fish, though many more minor officers probably had this task; J Fletcher, 'Statistics of the Municipal Institutions of the English Towns' (1842) 5 *Journal of the Statistical Society* 163–66. 'Searchers of Flesh' did not appear on the list.

[62] The smoke nuisance did not figure prominently in these bye laws, although Derby's bye laws (7 July 1838) were a notable exception; TNA/HO/70/2. On responses to the smoke nuisance, see S Mosley, *The Chimney of the World: A History of Smoke Pollution In Victorian and Edwardian Manchester* (Cambridge, White Horse Press, 2001) 133–43; Harold Platt, *Shock Cities: The Environmental Transformation and Reform of Manchester and Chicago* (Chicago, University of Chicago Press, 2005) 442–67. Hanley, 'Parliament', above n 10, 706, 711 mistakenly claimed that the 1821 Smoke Nuisance Bill did not pass.

[63] Coventry (22 November 1836) found at TNA/HO/70/4 with Northampton; Northampton (9 April 1838) TNA/HO/70/4; Warwick (15 March 1836) TNA/HO/70/6; Liverpool (1 August 1838) TNA/HO/70/3.

[64] Towns Improvement Clauses Act 1847 (10 and 11 Vict c 34) s 104.

wide range of behaviours and situations in public streets. Indeed, the history of police and policing has been an important context for the analysis of bye laws.[65] More recently, historians have begun to study bye laws from a disciplinary perspective, reflecting a historiographic shift in emphasis from overt to implicit methods of social control in the making of the liberal city.[66] The insights of these scholars have greatly increased our view of the meaning and function of municipal bye laws, relatively neglected next to the criminal law. This section turns to a consideration of the bye laws as a whole in order to argue that an examination of the process by which these bye laws made it into the municipal code reveals some of the tensions, contradictions, and ironies at work in the creation of the liberal city.[67]

One of the most striking features of the bye law-making process was the level of central-local disagreement involved, and this tension developed very quickly. Although for most of 1836 and 1837 the Home Office challenged bye laws infrequently, by the end of 1837 the Office rarely accepted without amendment any bye laws sent to it.[68] The root of this conflict lay in the different meaning councils and the Home Office attached to the statute. In some cases, councils and the central government disagreed about the kind of nuisance against which the statute permitted councils to make bye laws, as is apparent from the comments made on the bye laws. The Home Office normally retained its copy of the bye laws even when it rejected them, and the bye laws were often annotated. The annotations, furthermore, were not just proof-readers' marks, with particular sections marked for deletion, but evaluations, explanations, and exclamations. 'Too general', 'minute', 'trifling', and 'vexatious' appear not infrequently, and sometimes in combination.[69]

---

[65] R Storch, 'The Policeman as Domestic Missionary: Urban Discipline and Popular Culture in Northern England, 1850–80' in RJ Morris and R Rodger (eds), *The Victorian City: A Reader in British Urban History, 1820–1914* (New York, Longman, 1993) 281–306; VAC Gatrell 'Crime, Authority and the Policeman-State' in FML Thompson (ed), The *Cambridge Social History of Britain, 1750–1950*, vol 3 (New York, CUP, 1993) 244–5; D Reid, 'Playing and Praying', in M Daunton (ed), *The Cambridge Urban History of Britain*, vol 3 (New York, CUP, 2000) 758–78.

[66] P Joyce, *The Rule of Freedom: Liberalism and the Modern City* (London, Verso, 2003) 87–8; S Gunn, 'From Hegemony to Governmentality: Changing Conceptions of Power in Social History' (2006) 39 *Journal of Social History* 705–20. See also C Otter, 'Making Liberalism Durable: Vision and Civility in the Late Victorian City' (2002) 27 *Social History* 1–15.

[67] This process can be studied by the annotations made on the draft bye laws and through the letters sent by the Home Office to the relevant corporation. The documents do not, unfortunately, unambiguously identify the person responsible for the annotation. According to one historian of the Home Office, the Home Secretary in 1835 would have been expected to be involved in the response to every single letter that was sent to the office; J Pellew, *The Home Office, 1848–1914: From Clerks to Bureaucrats* (East Brunswick, NJ, Associated University Presses, , 1982) 5–7. The Home Office history states that only the most senior officials would have been allowed to minute documents; TNA/HO/415/1 (accessed 8 August 2007).

[68] There was some earlier attention; see Home Office Correspondence TNA/HO/43/52, HO to Flint (23 February 1837); HO to Hythe (20 April 1837). For late 1837 and early 1838, TNA/HO/43/53-55, letters to Swansea, Hull, Bridgnorth, Weymouth, Richmond, Arundel, Stockton, Calne, Northampton, Oswestry, Congleton, Droitwich, Maidenhead, Bewdley, Carnarvon, Stafford, and Tewkesbury.

[69] TNA/HO/70/1, Carnarvon (10 July 1838) 5; TNA/HO/70/2 Calne Wells (3 May 1838) bye law no 10; TNA/HO/70/2, Droitwich (2 July 1838) bye laws nos 3 and 10; TNA/HO/70/2, Devonport (4 October 1838) 13.

Indeed, readers occasionally lost patience with the bye laws. One exasperated reader noted on Bewdley's bye laws that 'There are so many of these bye laws objectionable ... I think the best course will be to disallow them altogether.' Another reader responded: 'Cannot we give some of these boroughs a good model for bye laws?'[70] The annotations suggest that the central government did not share local enthusiasm for a micro-regulatory state.

In other cases, councils and the central government agreed that particular situations were at least potentially nuisances, but they disagreed about the statute's summary remedy. On some bye laws, for example, a Home Office reader has noted that the remedy for the nuisance in question was by indictment at common law.[71] In these cases, the Home Office's continued preference for common law remedies thus conflicted not only with the obvious preference of councils but even with the Municipal Reform Act itself. The Act permitted councils to make bye laws for nuisances not dealt with in a summary manner in any existing legislation; it was intended to provide an alternative to the common law. The Home Office's revision of bye laws from 1835–40 thus continued, even if inconsistently, the pattern that had been established in the 1831–32 cholera epidemic where local authorities wanted summary power and central authorities did not want to give it.

The frustration central officials felt with municipal councils was, of course, matched by the frustration councils felt for the central government, notwithstanding the fact that the statute clearly allowed the Privy Council to disallow bye laws. To be sure, some corporations meekly submitted to the Office's demands. But other corporations simply refused to pass any bye laws at all after the Office rejected their first set.[72] Still others actively resisted. Hull council, for example, wrote a 12-page, closely-spaced letter explaining their rejected bye laws, certain that once the Home Secretary had a '<u>full knowledge of the circumstances</u>', he would accept them. Surprisingly, the Home Secretary did not regard this as presumptuous; rather, he approved most of the previously rejected bye laws.[73] Other councils challenged central interference by pointing out, even if diplomatically, examples of differential treatment. Thus Droitwich council, noting that Worcester council already had a similar bye law, wished to preserve the right to destroy unfit food, yet 'have not any wish to press it' if the Home Secretary thought it unnecessary.[74] Some councils rather more tartly pointed out differential treatment.[75] Others recruited their MP into the battle,

---

[70] TNA/HO/70/1, annotation on letter from Bewdley to Home Office (2 June 1838).
[71] TNA/HO/70/1, Bridgnorth (sent 27 November 1837); TNA/HO/70/2, Devonport (4 October 1838) 14.
[72] An example is Tewkesbury; see WRO/b261.5/BA7123/parce110, Tewkesbury to Evesham, 22 November 1838.
[73] TNA/HO/70/3, Hull to HO (8 November 1837) 1 (Emphasis in original).
[74] TNA/HO/70/2, Droitwich to HO (9 July 1838).
[75] TNA/HO/70/1, Congleton to HO (2 May 1838) Congleton to G Wilbraham (26 July 1838).

though on the whole it appears that the Home Office got its way far more often than not.[76]

To say that there was central-local conflict is not to suggest that there was a unity of purpose either in the provinces or at the Home Office. In the case of councils, we have very little surviving material that reveals much about the debates around bye laws. Bye-laws committees did not meet in open session, and when bye laws came before the full council reporters often left the room even if, or perhaps because, the debate lasted for days. In terms of central government, the records do not suggest complete unanimity. Devonport, for example, had a variety of bye laws for the prevention of indecency. The section included separate bye laws for the suppression of indecent exposure, public bathing, indecent prints, and indecent language. The Home Office had a variety of questions about them; indeed, this was the most heavily annotated section of the bye laws. The provision regulating indecent language was marked 'too general and objectionable'. The provision surrounding indecent prints was marked 'very questionable as at present'. Someone at the office appeared to believe that the section as a whole was unnecessary. Scrawled along the side of the page is a faded query which appears to read: 'are not these all punishable at common law'[?] In spite of the fact that the Home Office had reservations, some of the bye laws were marked 'I w^d allow this'[.][77] Clearly there were differences of opinion within and between the Home Office and corporations.

A second feature of the bye law making process was its inconsistency. On occasion, the Home Office disallowed as a bye law a provision the corporation simply wished to import from its local Act into its new bye laws.[78] In addition, the Home Office's somewhat belated attention to bye laws occasionally meant that bye laws disallowed in one town were already in force in another. The provisions governing the seizure and destruction of unwholesome food, not disallowed in so many places, were one of the bye laws increasingly challenged by the Office. Liverpool, Kidderminster, Worcester, and Droitwich kept their bye laws on the subject, though the latter two were forced to amend them, yet others were told to strike them out in whole or in part.[79] The same inconsistency can be seen in bye laws governing noxious trades. The Home Office did not challenge Coventry's and Warwick's fairly drastic 1836–37 prohibitions on some noxious trades. In contrast, it rejected Devonport's 1838 prohibition against any 'noisome or injurious Smells or Vapours' as it 'might interfere with some trades now carried on'.[80] The

---

[76] For MPs, see Evesham, WRO/b261.5/BA7123/Parcel 10, Clerk to Lord Marcus Hill (25 February 1839); TNA/HO/70/1, G Wilbraham to HO (29 July 1838).

[77] TNA/HO/70/2, Devonport (4 October 1838) 20.

[78] See, for example, TNA/HO/70/3, Hull to HO (8 November 1837) 4.

[79] Compare Worcester bye laws of 11 April 1837 and 29 November 1838 at TNA/HO/70/6 and Droitwich bye laws sent 22 May 1838 and 3 August 1838 at TNA/HO/70/2. Welshpool (4 December 1838 at TNA/HO/70/6) and Southwold (23 April 1839 at TNA/HO/70/5) bye laws have part of the unwholesome meat provision struck.

[80] TNA/HO/70/2, Devonport (4 October 1838) 17; Oswestry's bye laws were also thought to impose a restraint on trade; TNA/HO/70/4, Oswestry to Home Office (16 May 1839).

bye laws on sanitary nuisances received similarly inconsistent treatment. Once again, the earlier a corporation got their bye law in, the better off they were; there is no record, for example, of Liverpool's, Newcastle's, or Sunderland's bye laws being challenged. Yet Stockton's, Droitwich's and Worcester's were. A number of other corporations' nuisance bye laws were modified, sometimes severely.[81] The bye laws remind us of the extent of local variation, even under the operation of the same statute.

Finally, although the Home Office policed bye laws as best it could, its efforts at controlling the content of bye laws were not uniformly successful and may have contributed to the success of the very measures they sought to ban. As a result of council pressure, the Home Office found itself forced both to defend its inconsistencies and to respond constructively to the avalanche of bye laws; they couldn't just be negative. In 1858, the Local Government Act Office would prepare sets of model bye laws for the local authorities in need of them.[82] In mid-1838, in the absence of any official model bye laws, the Home Office began to suggest models of various sorts, often relying on bye laws already sent by other corporations such as Derby and Carnarvon.[83] Not only was the Home Office playing catch up, it was relying on other councils to tell them how to do so, thereby forcefully illustrating the role of the bye laws in shaping central understandings of health.[84]

The extent of municipal council influence on central thinking extended beyond specific examples such as Derby and Carnarvon. In each of the three areas under consideration in this paper, unwholesome meat, noxious trades, and sanitary nuisances, bye laws rejected by the central government ended up on the statute book in one form or another after 1845.[85] It seems reasonable to suggest that at least part of the inspiration for this had to have come from bye laws as the Home Office reviewed literally hundreds of them from 1835–45. Bye laws may not have been very effective in promoting the cleaning up of towns in the 1830s, but they were important models in influencing the development of statutory nuisance law in the 1840s and beyond.

---

[81] TNA/HO/70/5, Southwold (23 April 1839); TNA/HO/70/2, Devonport (4 October 1838); TNA/HO/70/3, Hull, 'Copy of a bye law made … 9th October 1837 and 3rd January 1838'; TNA/HO/70/6, Great Yarmouth (23 March 1840 and 14 May 1840).

[82] The Secretary of State for the Home Department, 'First Annual Report on the Execution of the Local Government Act, 1858,' 1859 sess 2 (C (1st series) 2585) app C 30.

[83] For Derby see Droitwich bye laws sent 9 July 1838 (bye law no 9) at TNA/HO/70/2. For Carnarvon, see TNA/HO/43/55, HO to G Wilbraham (31 July 1838). Carnarvon's model bye laws imposed only modest restraints on trade.

[84] Kearns, 'Town Hall and Whitehall', above n 48 drew attention to the absence of any simple model of central local relations in sanitary intelligence.

[85] Parliament made the destruction of unwholesome food part of the 1855 Nuisances Removal Act. Parliament's decision to permit the regulation of some noxious trades in the 1847 Towns Improvement Clauses Act again seems to be an echo of corporate bye laws. And the medicalisation of sanitary nuisances in 1846, barely a year after the Health of Large Towns Commission recommended no change in the law of nuisances, is noteworthy.

4

Is a Burn a Wound? Vitriol-Throwing in Medico-Legal Context, 1800–1900

KATHERINE D WATSON

This chapter traces the evolution of medico-legal responses to a crime that was largely (but not exclusively) confined to the 19th century: vitriol throwing. Accounts of this offence indicate that English law was for many years unequal to its seriousness: although it could be prosecuted under statutes against damage to property or wounding, the penalties were light because the strict legal definition of a 'wound' long excluded the injuries caused by vitriol (generally defined in medical terms as 'burns') and courts consequently downgraded charges to the misdemeanour offence of common assault. But the use of vitriol in industrial disputes in Glasgow during the 1820s led Parliament to extend an English Act against maiming and wounding to Scotland, and vitriol throwing was added to a list of capital offences against the person which included stabbing, shooting and poisoning.[1] Two key issues emerge at this point. The first is the definition of the word 'wound', and the competing medical and legal understandings of its meaning; these will be discussed below. The second is the legal definition of an offence as either a misdemeanour or a felony. The former were indictable offences which did not amount to felony and generally merited lesser penalties such as fines, corporal punishment or imprisonment. Felonies were such serious crimes that, at common law, conviction led to a forfeiture of life or property or both.[2]

In Scotland then, during the mid-1820s vitriol throwing was specifically defined in law as a felony, clearly distinct from other forms of wounding. In England, by contrast, in 1835 an assailant escaped a charge of felonious assault because it could not be considered in law that sulphuric acid was capable of producing a wound (the woman having been indicted for wounding); two surgeons argued opposing views.[3] However, by the provisions of an Act passed in July 1837, throwing

---

[1] R Christison, *A Treatise on Poisons, in relation to Medical Jurisprudence, Physiology, and the Practice of Physic* (Edinburgh, A Black, 1829) 115.

[2] AH Manchester, *A Modern Legal History of England and Wales 1750–1950* (London, Butterworths, 1980) 194. See also JH Baker, *An Introduction to English Legal History*, 4th edn (London, Butterworths, 2002) 502.

[3] AS Taylor, *Elements of Medical Jurisprudence* (London, Deacon, 1836) 487. The trial of Ann Murrow at Liverpool on 19 August 1835 is discussed in detail below.

destructive matter with intent to do grievous bodily harm became a form of felonious assault, carrying a maximum penalty of transportation for life, but loopholes relating to the definition of a wound remained because, in order to sustain an indictment, bodily injury had to be achieved.[4] It was not until the Offences Against the Person Act of 1861 that vitriol throwing was effectively dealt with in English law, when it became a felony to burn, maim, disfigure or disable anyone with a corrosive fluid or destructive substance, or to attempt to do so—whether or not an actual injury resulted.[5] With the removal of the word 'wound' from the relevant section of the statute, the medico-legal focus shifted to the nature of the substance involved. Although the criminal justice system tended to deal harshly with offenders after that date, particularly when a case went to the assizes, the intent to injure the person that the law required continued to offer vitriol throwers the possibility of acquittal.

In order to trace the evolution of vitriol throwing in its medico-legal context, this chapter will approach the subject both chronologically and thematically, using case studies of specific trials to highlight key incidents in relation to contemporary laws. The focus will be mainly on England from the late-18th century to the mid-19th century, but two important Scottish cases will serve to emphasise the differences in the medico-legal situation north and south of the Border. These differences were related not to medical issues, but to the way in which the law was framed: in 1825 the new Scottish statute referred specifically to vitriol throwing,[6] but this did not happen in England until 1861. Until then, the wording of the various English laws against malicious injuries tended to be so precise that the relatively unique crime of vitriol throwing became subject to a key difference of interpretation between medical and legal definitions of certain terms, particularly the words 'wound' and 'burn', and this could lead to difficulties in prosecuting criminal charges. This was actually a greater problem in crimes involving other forms of violence against the person, particularly violence that did not draw blood,[7] but the offence of vitriol throwing offers a neat example of how medical and legal issues were argued and resolved over the course of several decades.

The chapter will begin with an overview of the place of sulphuric acid in relation to crime, to lay a foundation for the subsequent sections, which will consider

---

[4] AS Taylor, *The Principles and Practice of Medical Jurisprudence* (London, J Churchill and Sons, 1865) 593.

[5] An Act to consolidate and amend the Statute Law of England and Ireland relating to Offences against the Person (6 August 1861); specifically s 29.

[6] 6 Geo IV c 126, discussed in detail below.

[7] For an example of some of these arguments in relation to the Offences Against the Person Act 1837, see the case of *Thomas Shea and William Dwyer v The Queen*, 5 and 6 May 1848, in EW Cox (ed), *Reports of Cases in Criminal Law, argued and determined in all the Courts in England and Ireland, vol 3, 1848–1850* (London, J Crockford, 1850) 141–58. For a more specifically medico-legal discussion of such problems, see AS Taylor, *Medical Jurisprudence*, 4th American edn (Philadelphia, Blanchard and Lea, 1856) 175–80. For a detailed analysis of the problems encountered in prosecuting interpersonal violence, see P Handler, 'The Law of Felonious Assault in England, 1803–61' (2007) 28 *The Journal of Legal History* 183.

the medical context, and then the legal context of the crime, especially in relation to wounding. The third section will look specifically at vitriol throwing in its medico-legal context. Methodologically, the work relies primarily on three types of sources: newspaper and archival accounts of criminal cases (which are more detailed than most case reports); medico-legal textbooks; and legal publications such as law reports and compendia. The text of relevant statutes will feature prominently, as will trials in which the laws were tested. Although the story of vitriol-throwing is one that continued, in Britain, up to the Second World War, and remained of medico-legal interest until the 1960s, this chapter will look mainly at the period up to and immediately following the introduction of the 1861 Offences Against the Person Act, many of the provisions of which remain in effect to this day.[8]

Sulphuric Acid and Crime

Oil of vitriol was the common name for strong sulphuric acid, an oily liquid heavier than water which was colourless when entirely pure, but was usually brownish and generally odourless. In the 18th century it became an increasingly important chemical due to its use in dyeing, calico printing, bleaching and alkali manufacture—soda was an essential raw material in making soap, glass and paper.[9] In the rapidly industrialising society of the 19th century, sulphuric acid became a relatively ubiquitous substance because it had a wide variety of legitimate uses in agriculture and manufacturing. Furthermore, it was often diluted and used domestically for cleaning, especially copper pots. It could be purchased at any chemist's shop or oil shop, and it was cheap: in 1850 two teaspoonfuls of the concentrated acid cost about half a penny. These facts, combined with its strongly corrosive properties, meant that of the irritant mineral poisons recognised in chemistry and medicine, sulphuric acid far exceeded in medico-legal importance its two mineral acid cousins, nitric acid and hydrochloric acid.

There were two main circumstances when a medical professional might be called to test for the presence of vitriol: in the vomit or stomach contents of deceased persons; and in the form of alleged stains on clothing. By the late 1820s, when the professor of medical jurisprudence at the University of Edinburgh, Robert Christison, published his groundbreaking textbook on toxicology,[10]

---

[8] Ss 28, 29, 30, 64 and 65 created a range of criminal offences which supplement the Explosive Substances Act 1883 and the Explosives Act 1875. These remain in force except that the Criminal Damage Act 1971 covers all aspects of the resulting damage to property and the Terrorism Act 2000 links possession to terrorist purposes. See 'Offences Against the Person Act' <http://www.wikicrimline.co.uk/index.php?title=Offences_Against_The_Person_Act_1861> accessed 15 November 2008.
[9] WH Brock, *The Fontana History of Chemistry* (London, Fontana, 1992) 276–93.
[10] Christison, above n 1.

sulphuric acid had a well deserved reputation for its role in suicidal and accidental deaths. Statistics on fatal cases of poisoning in England in 1837–38 showed that of 36 deaths attributed to the mineral acids, 32 were caused by sulphuric acid, of which 21 were accidents, seven were suicides, and four were undetermined. Together these amounted to one-fifteenth of the total number of deaths caused by poison in that two-year period, and by the early 1860s sulphuric acid had become the fifth most common substance found in poisoning fatalities.[11] It was extremely rare for the acid to be used in homicides, because of its strong taste and immediately painful effects, but textbooks of forensic medicine were quick to notice a worrying trend that dated from the early years of the 19th century: the use of sulphuric acid to kill babies, usually by their parents.[12] But it had one other criminal function that medico-legal writers clearly recognised as a problem that doctors might encounter: its use to disfigure the person, or to destroy clothing, usually by being thrown from a cup or bottle.

By the 1830s all the principal writers of British medico-legal texts, including Christison, Michael Ryan, Alfred Swaine Taylor, and William Guy, agreed that this was a new type of crime. Christison dated its origins quite precisely:

> It originated in one of our great manufacturing towns, Glasgow, during the quarrels a few years ago between masters and workmen regarding the rate of wages, and became at last so frequent, that the present Lord Advocate, in applying for an act of Parliament to extend the English Stabbing and Maiming act to Scotland, added a clause which renders the offence now alluded to capital. In 1828 a woman Macmillan was tried here and condemned under that act. The crime has also become lately common in England. I observed three cases noticed in the London papers as having occurred in London last November, and two others near Manchester last spring.[13]

Vitriol throwing, which seems to have been a largely urban phenomenon which originated in industrial disputes in both Scotland and England, continued to be mentioned in textbooks of forensic medicine for well over a century. In 1845 Christison asserted that it was 'now much less frequent',[14] and in the 1920s it was alleged by another writer to be 'a practice more frequent on the Continent than in England',[15] but during the intervening years the crime actually experienced a period of increased frequency in both Scotland and England. More cases were tried in the High Court of Justiciary[16] in the decades between 1860 and 1880

---

[11] WA Guy, *Principles of Forensic Medicine* (London, 2nd edn, H Renshaw, 1861) 328.

[12] JG Smith, *The Principles of Forensic Medicine, systematically arranged, and applied to British Practice* (London, 2nd edn, T and G Underwood, 1824) 140; Christison, above n 1, 114.

[13] Christison, above n 1, 115. Smith, above n 12 makes no mention of vitriol throwing in his section (pp 138–41) on sulphuric acid, another indication that it was largely unknown before the latter part of the 1820s.

[14] R Christison, *A Treatise on Poisons, in relation to Medical Jurisprudence, Physiology, and the Practice of Physic*, 4th edn (A and C Black, Edinburgh, 1845) 151.

[15] WA Brend, *A Handbook of Medical Jurisprudence and Toxicology, for the use of Students and Practitioners*, 6th edn (London, Charles Griffin, 1928) 234.

[16] The High Court of Scotland.

than in the preceding 20 years,[17] while English legal officials also noted a rise in incidence. In 1854 a London magistrate claimed that it 'was very much practised in the north',[18] and the Recorder of London in May 1881 thought that it was 'becoming very common'.[19] In 1860 American medico-legal experts thought that numerous cases had occurred recently in England,[20] and in 1910 an authoritative British text stated that 'scarcely a month goes by without an example of greater or lesser magnitude'.[21] My own research on cases noted in *The Times* between 1785 and 1940, and on references to vitriol throwing in literature and popular culture,[22] shows that although its prevalence declined after the 1890s, it continued to happen fairly regularly right up until the beginning of the Second World War.

The Medical Context: Wounds and Burns

This section will consider the actual effects caused by sulphuric acid, and their relation to medical thinking about how to classify the damage that it did to the human body. There were two options: to call the damage a burn or a wound. In the opinion of some, a burn was a type of wound, but to others, it was not. The following section will discuss the legal position on this issue.

The effects caused by oil of vitriol on flesh were dramatic: in 1930 a horrified witness described how a victim's skin sizzled and moved as the acid acted.[23] Vitriol mutilated and maimed victims by destroying skin and supporting tissues; its corrosive action could liquefy muscle and dissolve bone. It combined with water in organic matter, generating a considerable amount of heat, to which the resulting damage was in part due—a charring effect that caused noticeable blackening. If the acid got into the eyes it caused blindness. If the injuries were extensive victims could be permanently disabled; those who recovered were likely to be badly disfigured, with no hope of regaining a semblance of their former appearance prior to the advent of plastic surgery.

In trying to determine how medical men classified the damage caused by vitriol, I have relied on textbooks of forensic medicine and toxicology, rather than on general works of medicine, because medico-legal writers consistently recognised

---

[17] National Archives of Scotland (hereafter NAS), 'Solemn Database' of 19th-century High Court cases: 18 cases of vitriol throwing were tried 1860–80, but only six during the period 1836–59.
[18] *The Times*, 15 September 1854, 9e.
[19] *The Times*, 24 May 1881, 7f.
[20] F Wharton and M Stillé, *A Treatise on Medical Jurisprudence*, 2nd edn (Philadelphia, Kay and Brother, 1860) 485, para 519.
[21] AS Taylor, *The Principles and Practice of Medical Jurisprudence*, 6th edn, vol 1 (London, JA Churchill 1910) 605.
[22] KD Watson, 'Crimes of Passion? Vitriol Throwing in Victorian England', *Victorian Criminalities*, University of Exeter, 18–19 April 2005.
[23] *The Times*, 23 June 1930, 11c.

the acid as an important topic given its possible application in accidents, suicides and homicides. It was always classed as a poison and considered largely in relation to its internal effects on the person, which were excruciatingly painful and typically fatal. Although vitriol throwing was certainly painful, it was rarely fatal. So we find an increasing distinction made between the two main modes of application: treatments for and the medico-legal features of cases of ingestion (or poisoning) were discussed in the toxicology section of texts, while the external effects caused by sulphuric acid were usually dealt with in chapters devoted to burns and scalds.

This, for example, is what England's leading medico-legal expert did in the numerous editions of his *Manual of Medical Jurisprudence*, which first appeared in 1844.[24] During his lifetime Alfred Swaine Taylor, of Guy's Hospital, revised this volume several times, changing its title in 1865, when it became *The Principles and Practice of Medical Jurisprudence*.[25] He died in 1880 but the book lived on, the 13th edition appearing in 1984. In each and every edition except the last, vitriol throwing was included in the chapter on burns, with its own subheading. Until the 20th century it tended to be labelled 'burns by corrosive liquids', thereafter 'vitriol throwing', until in 1965 the section was renamed 'chemical burns'. This was reflective of changing medical opinion on the characteristics of the damage caused by vitriol.

In both Taylor's textbooks and those of a later Manchester-based expert, John Dixon Mann (whose textbook on forensic medicine and toxicology appeared in six editions between 1893 and 1922), discussion of burns by corrosive fluids tended to come immediately after a rather longer section on spontaneous human combustion. Even books that did not devote a separate subheading to vitriol throwing acknowledged that the surface excoriations it caused to the body must be treated like burns,[26] and there seems to have been a general acceptance amongst practitioners of forensic medicine that lesions caused by corrosive fluids, as by dry heat, were burns, in distinction from scalds, which were caused by steam or hot fluids.[27] By making this differentiation, they clearly hoped to influence the generations of medical practitioners who might one day be called upon to offer an opinion on the subject in a legal setting.

But where did burns lie in relation to the much broader category of 'wounds'? It seems that standard medical thinking did not allow for burns to be included within the definition of a wound. Rather, wounds were defined by the nature of the instrument with which they were inflicted, and by the effect produced. They were consequently divided into four categories: gunshot wounds, simple

---

[24] AS Taylor, *A Manual of Medical Jurisprudence* (London, J Churchill, 1844).
[25] Taylor, above n 4.
[26] See, eg WA Guy and D Ferrier, *Principles of Forensic Medicine*, 6th edn (London, H Rensaw, 1888) 362, 366.
[27] See, eg Brend, above n 15, 58; DJA Kerr, *Forensic Medicine: A Textbook for Students and a Guide for the Practitioner*, 2nd edn (London, Black, 1936) 110.

incised wounds, lacerated or contused wounds, and punctured wounds.[28] Thus, during the 19th century doctors typically assumed that a wound involved breaking of the skin by the use of some instrument—a surgical designation. Burns were not defined as a type of wound, but stood as a category in their own right.

In a purely surgical sense, in the early 19th century a wound was defined as 'a recent solution of continuity in the soft parts, suddenly occasioned by external causes'.[29] According to Taylor, those who adopted this view did not regard as wounds, burns by heated bodies or corrosive liquids, ruptures of the internal organs, or simple fractures and dislocations—although such injuries were, in his estimation, fully encompassed by such a definition.[30] In 1844 he asked three eminent London surgeons for their definition of a wound, and was supplied with three slightly different accounts: 'A solution of continuity from violence of any naturally continuous parts; An external breach of continuity directly occasioned by violence; An injury to an organic texture by mechanical or other violence'.[31] In Taylor's opinion, 'we shall look in vain for any consistent definition of a wound, in works on medicine and surgery',[32] and he advocated that the English adopt the Continental definition, which included every description of personal injury arising from whatever cause, applied externally.[33] It was to take well over a century before this goal was achieved, but it is clear that medical opinion on the definition of a wound began to expand, and this chapter contends that, in the forensic sphere (and probably more generally also) this happened as a result of the wording of various 19th-century legal statutes. Although the surgical definition of a wound remained largely unchanged throughout our period of interest, the medical interpretation of the types of injuries encompassed by the term clearly reacted to the legal definition of a wound, and expanded in relation to the meaning of the word as it was used in the 1861 Offences Against the Person Act.

For example, in 1888 the sixth edition of Guy's *Principles of Forensic Medicine* referred to 'the old surgical definition of a wound', which he understood to mean the damage done by mechanical injury. Crucially, his definition had expanded to encompass dislocations, sprains and fractures, though not burns.[34] Similarly, Dixon Mann acknowledged that the surgical definition of a wound had grown: 'Almost all injuries to the body produced by mechanical violence are comprehended, in the legal sense, under the title of "wounds"'. However, he continued to

---

[28] A Macaulay, *Dictionary of Medicine, Designed for Popular Use*, 8th edn (Edinburgh, Adam and Charles Black, 1846) 587; S Thomson, *A Dictionary of Domestic Medicine and Household Surgery* (London, Groombridge and Sons, 1852) 568.
[29] Taylor, above n 3, 486.
[30] ibid 485–6.
[31] Taylor, above n 24, 280; Taylor, above n 7, 175.
[32] Taylor, above n 7, 175.
[33] ibid.
[34] Guy and Ferrier, above n 26, 268.

classify burns as a separate category.[35] The 1922 edition of his text was even more explicit about the link between the law and the definitions that had to be applied in a courtroom setting:[36]

> The definition is enlarged beyond that given by the surgeon by the words which follow in the statute: 'Whosoever shall, by any means whatsoever, wound or cause any grievous bodily harm to a person.' The last clause of this sentence obviates the necessity for defining whether a given injury is or is not a wound, which was a question that formerly led to much discussion at almost every trial relating to matters of personal violence, and which not unfrequently facilitated the escape of a guilty person.

In effect, then, the medical, legal and medico-legal understanding of a wound developed away from the idea of a division of the skin that was understood in the 1840s, to include a growing number of types of injury. Interestingly, however, the wording of the definition of a wound did not change noticeably. So although by the early decades of the 20th century we find much the same formal definition of a wound put forward as was commonplace in the 1840s—a wound was defined as a solution of the natural continuity of any tissue of the living body—its now very broad reach was usually stressed, as for example in the 1928 edition of Taylor's classic text, edited by the famous medical detective Sydney Smith.

Smith claimed that because this definition omitted any mention of flowing blood, the severing of skin, the nature of the tissue damaged, or the cause of the solution of continuity, it had a distinct advantage. This was because it included bruises, the effects of burns by any means,[37] all lacerations, dislocations, and fractures; in effect, it included all possible injuries and 'grievous harm' that can be done to a body.[38] It is surely no coincidence that Smith preceded his definition of a wound by stating the terms of the 1861 Offences Against the Person Act as it related to wounding and causing grievous bodily harm. In 1936 Douglas Kerr explicitly linked the two when he stated that:

> Such a definition has a very wide application and in England is still further increased by the words "any grievous bodily harm" (the Offences Against the Person Act 1861). This term "grievous bodily harm" is not used in Scotland. It applies to injuries causing some pain or inconvenience and so prejudicing for a time the bodily health.[39]

In lauding the usefulness of this definition, 20th-century forensic experts seem to have forgotten that the selfsame designation was once highly exclusive in both medical and legal understanding. The next section of this chapter examines

---

[35] J Dixon Mann, *Forensic Medicine and Toxicology*, 6th edn (London, C Griffin and Co, 1922) 256.
[36] ibid 219.
[37] By heat, chemicals or electricity.
[38] S Smith (ed), *Taylor's Principles and Practice of Medical Jurisprudence*, 8th edn, vol 1 (London, Churchill, 1928) 317.
[39] Kerr, above n 27, 60.

the legal interpretation of a wound, in order to show how that too evolved over time.

The Legal Context: Wounding

The penalties for physical assaults which did not result in death evolved in a piecemeal fashion over the course of several centuries. This is because, according to the historian of English legal history, JH Baker, such offences 'fell only partially within the range of common-law felonies',[40] and were thus punishable only under statute law, which tended to be created to address problems that were specific to the time. Baker continues:

> A maiming—a serious incapacitation or loss of limb—could be made the subject of an appeal of mayhem; but this form of redress gave way in practice to the action of trespass, and mayhem did not become an indictable felony.[41]

Mayhem, a medieval concept, could be considered both a civil injury (a trespass) or a criminal offence, but only if the injury was such as to weaken the ability of the individual (in practice, a man), to fight and defend himself; injuries that only disfigured, according to the 18th-century jurist Sir William Blackstone, were not held to be mayhems at common law.[42] Thus, even violent assaults were mere trespasses or misdemeanours until a number of offences akin to mayhem were made felonies by statute.

The first of these dated from the reign of Henry IV and concerned the cutting out of tongues and eyes, in the context of a robbery, so as to prevent the victim giving evidence against the perpetrators.[43] A better known statute of 1670 made it a capital felony to cut off parts of the body, put out an eye or slit noses with intent to maim or disfigure. This was known as Coventry's Act, because it resulted from the angry reaction of Parliament to a street assault made on Sir John Coventry MP, who had his nose slit in revenge for some obnoxious comments he had made in the House of Commons.[44] Under both these statutes no offence was committed unless a wound was inflicted. But the Black Act of 1723 made it a capital offence to make an attempt on someone's life by shooting, even if no wounding occurred.[45] These then were

---

[40] Baker, above n 2, 531.
[41] ibid.
[42] W Blackstone, *Commentaries on the Laws of England*, reprint, vol 4 (Chicago, University of Chicago Press, 1979) 205–06. So, the loss of a hand, limb, eye or front tooth constituted mayhem, but not the loss of an ear or a molar.
[43] 5 Hen IV c 5; see Blackstone, above n 42, 206.
[44] See Blackstone, above n 42, 207. For more on this incident, see S Porter, 'Coventry, Sir John (c.1636–1685)' *DNB*, <http://www.oxforddnb.com/view/article/6479> accessed 29 May 2007.
[45] See Blackstone, above n 42, 208 and 'Trial of James Thomas Earl of Cardigan, in the House of Lords, on the 16th day of February 1841, for Felony', in *The Annual Register, or a view of the History and Politics, of the Year 1841* (London, JGF and J Rivington, 1842) 244.

the only situations where, in England, assaults that did not lead to death could be punished severely, as felonies; all other instances were common misdemeanours.

By the early years of the 19th century the rising incidence of attempted murder had become so alarming that the chief justice, Lord Ellenborough, who was a keen supporter of capital punishment, decided that something had to be done.[46] His solution to this problem came in the form of a new Act of Parliament, and it was this Act which led to the creation of a new set of problems; these revolved largely around the very precise way in which certain injuries were described.

Problems with 'Wounds' and Lord Ellenborough's Act

Ellenborough referred to his Bill as the Maiming and Wounding Bill, but its full title was

> An Act for the further Prevention of malicious shooting, and attempting to discharge loaded Fire-Arms, stabbing, cutting, wounding, and poisoning, and the malicious using of Means to procure the Miscarriage of Women; and also the malicious setting Fire to Buildings; and also for repealing a certain Act, made in England in the twenty-first Year of the late King James the First, intituled, An Act to prevent the destroying and murthering of Bastard Children; and also an Act made in Ireland in the sixth Year of the Reign of the late Queen Anne, also intituled, An Act to prevent the destroying and murthering of Bastard Children; and for making other provisions in lieu thereof.[47]

This act, the Malicious Shooting and Stabbing Act 1803, which came into effect on 1 July 1803 and applied to England, Wales and Ireland, is best known to historians as the Act that repealed the 1624 law, which had forced unmarried women accused of newborn child murder to prove that the child had been born dead, a law that had in effect made a single woman guilty of murder until proven innocent whenever she concealed her pregnancy and the baby died.[48]

But Lord Ellenborough's Act, as it has always been known, accomplished a great deal more. The first section created ten new capital felonies, most of them offences against the person, as spelled out in the bill's lengthy title. Shooting at or stabbing with intent to murder, rob, disfigure, disable, do some grievous bodily harm, or to prevent the lawful apprehension of the defendant or his accomplices became forms of felonious assault, as did administering drugs to procure abortion in a pregnant woman, attempted poisoning, and arson with intent to injure or defraud. These were all now hanging offences, so it is little wonder that individuals

---

[46] *The Times*, 29 March 1803, 2a.

[47] WD Evans et al (eds), *A Collection of Statutes connected with the General Administration of the Law*, 3rd edn, vol 5 (London, Thomas Blenkarn, Edward Lumley and WH Bond, 1836) 206.

[48] There are numerous works that look at this law. The best monograph study is M Jackson, *Newborn Child Murder: Women, Illegitimacy and the Courts in Eighteenth-Century England* (Manchester, Manchester University Press, 1996).

indicted under the terms of this statute, where they could afford counsel, challenged its specificity. For it soon became clear that, despite the use of the word 'wound' in the act's title, the precise use of the terms stab, cut, and poison in the actual text of the statute implied that other forms of injury were excluded from the provisions of the law. Lawyers clearly saw 'wounding' in this sense as purely a form of stabbing,[49] and judicial decisions upheld this interpretation: 'whenever a wound could not be considered a cut or a stab, the prisoner was entitled to an acquittal if tried under this statute'.[50] The word 'wound' itself did not appear in the text of the new law.[51]

This, of course, led to problems, not least when individuals found guilty of causing serious physical harm to another person had to be acquitted on a technicality; if an indictment was carefully framed, they could be convicted of an aggravated assault, or committed for retrial on a lesser charge, but this was scarcely satisfactory. The main area of contention involved the definition of a wound, as the statute required proof that an incised wound had been inflicted; contused or lacerated wounds did not come within the meaning of the Act.[52] Assaults committed by blunt instruments were most obviously problematic, therefore, but it seems likely that the injuries caused by vitriol would also have caused consternation. However, the law was not put to the test: English cases of vitriol throwing seem to have been indicted as malicious damage to property (clothing), with no mention made of personal injury.[53] In the one case identified thus far in which physical harm was done, the accused man, who was a deaf mute, was acquitted because there was no interpreter in court.[54] Vitriol throwing was apparently not yet common enough in England to pose the sorts of problems that blunt instruments did, but it was only a matter of time before it did.

The Scottish Response

The lack of legal recourse against the crime of vitriol throwing in Britain was clearly demonstrated in Scotland during the 1820s, when, as Robert Christison tells us, vitriol throwing began to become so frequent, in the context of industrial disputes in Glasgow, that the chief Scottish judge asked Parliament to extend the provisions of Lord Ellenborough's Act to Scotland. Entitled 'An Act to make

---

[49] JF Archbold, *A Summary of the Law relative to Pleading and Evidence in Criminal Cases* (New York, Stephen Gould and Son, 1824) 246. The index (p 429) under 'wounding' says 'see stabbing', so implying equivalence. See also Handler, above n 7, 189–91.
[50] Taylor, above n 3, 480; Cox, above n 7, 145, 148–50.
[51] For the full text of the statute, see Evans, above n 47, 206–09.
[52] Archbold, above n 50, 246.
[53] See, eg the following cases reported in *The Times* 7 January 1815, 3e; *The Times* 28 April 1817, 3e; *The Times* 22 October 1821, 3c; *The Times* 1 August 1823, 3e; *The Times* 1 April 1824, 3e.
[54] *The Times*, 8 November 1825, 3f.

provision in Scotland for the further Prevention of malicious shooting, and attempting to discharge loaded Fire Arms, stabbing, cutting, wounding, poisoning, maiming, disfiguring, and disabling His Majesty's subjects' (6 Geo IV c126), the new bill received royal assent on 5 July 1825.[55] It criminalised most of the same offences that Lord Ellenborough's Act had, but added a unique clause about vitriol throwing. Christison gives us its exact wording:

> The clause of the Scottish act against this crime is as follows: 'If any person shall wilfully, maliciously, and unlawfully throw at or otherwise apply to any of his Majesty's subject or subjects any sulphuric acid or other corrosive substance, calculated by external application to burn or injure the human frame, with intent in so doing or by means thereof to murder, or maim, or disfigure, or disable such his Majesty's subject or subjects, or with intent to do some other grievous bodily harm to such his Majesty's subject or subjects; and where in consequence of such acid or other substance being so wilfully, maliciously, and unlawfully thrown, or applied with intent as aforesaid, any of his Majesty's subjects shall be maimed, disfigured or disabled, or receive other grievous bodily harm—such person being thereof lawfully convicted, shall be held to be guilty of a capital crime, and shall receive sentence of death accordingly.[56]

The first person to be so convicted was a woman named Euphemia McMillan. She was tried at Edinburgh in December 1827, along with her husband, Hugh, for throwing sulphuric acid over Archibald Campbell, a painter and dancing instructor, with the intent to murder, maim or disfigure him. The incident occurred on 17 October 1827 and he died in hospital on 30 October, but although the indictment included a separate charge of murder, the prosecution did not proceed with it for two reasons: the charge of vitriol throwing was a capital offence on which the evidence was strong; and Campbell's death had resulted not from the direct effects of the acid but from an infection contracted in hospital.[57] This raised a separate medico-legal question that will not be discussed further here, because generally the victims of vitriol throwing did not die.[58]

The facts of the McMillan case were these. Euphemia and Hugh lived on the same staircase as Archibald Campbell and his wife, with whom they were on bad terms. Just a few days earlier, Campbell had had Euphemia McMillan arrested for forcing open the door to his flat, and she had had to pay bail to get out of gaol. Witnesses heard her threaten to damage his cloak with sulphuric acid (at which time she also apparently said that she intended to do it while her husband was

---

[55] Evans, above n 47, 209 gives the full title of the Act, but not its text.
[56] Christison, above n 1, 115.
[57] In order to relieve high pressure in his damaged left eye, his doctors bled him from the right arm. A few days later, inflammation and fever set in, and a post-mortem examination proved that he died from blood poisoning that got into his lungs. The prosecution could not have proceeded with the charge of murder without raising the legal question of the responsibility of the prisoners in the case of death from a secondary cause that arose as a consequence of a surgical operation that was necessary and skilfully performed. See Taylor, above n 3, 336–41.
[58] My own research bears this out (of 216 British cases studied thus far, only three resulted in death), and medico-legal writers also noted that the crime was rarely fatal.

asleep), saw her with a jug that was later found broken under the window of her flat with traces of acid still in it, and followed a trail of acid from her door to the spot on the landing where Campbell was attacked. Although he had not seen who threw the acid at him, the evidence was enough to convict McMillan, who was 26 years old, but her husband was acquitted.[59] The judge sentenced her to death, but because this was the first conviction under the new statute, her sentence was commuted to perpetual banishment.[60]

The 1825 Scottish Act was repealed in 1829 and replaced by a new law which brought suffocation, strangulation and drowning within its remit. It maintained a clause against vitriol throwing, which remained a capital crime.[61] In 1832 a woman was sentenced to 14 years transportation for throwing vitriol,[62] but the first (and, it transpired, only)[63] person to actually be executed under the provisions of the Scottish version of Lord Ellenborough's Act was hanged in Glasgow in January 1834. Hugh Kennedy, aged 27, was convicted of attempting to murder James Goodwin, a fellow servant, by throwing sulphuric acid mixed with sand over him while he slept.[64]

The English Response: Lord Lansdowne's Act and the Murrow Case

The 1820s and 1830s were in Britain a time of criminal law reform, when numerous obscure and repetitive statutes were consolidated, if not actually modernised to any great extent. In 1828, a total of 56 statutes concerning malicious injuries, from medieval laws through Coventry's Act and including Lord Ellenborough's Act, were repealed and consolidated in the Offences Against the Person Act (9 Geo IV c 31), known as Lord Lansdowne's Act after the then Home Secretary. This Act retained many of the provisions of its predecessors, such as those of the infamous

---

[59] *The Times*, 21 December 1827, 4a; National Library of Scotland, Ry.III.a.2(81), broadside detailing the trial and sentence of Hugh and Euphemia McMillan; NAS, AD14/27/14, precognition against Hugh and Euphemia McMillan for the crime of murder at High Street, Edinburgh, 1827. Scottish legal records regularly recorded married women under their maiden names, so the accused was also known as Euphemia Lawson.

[60] R Christison, 'Disfiguring of the Countenance with Sulphuric Acid' (1829) 31 *Edinburgh Medical and Surgical Journal* 230–36.

[61] *An Act for the more effectual Punishment of Attempts to murder in certain Cases in Scotland* (10 Geo IV c 38); this became law on 4 June 1829. Section 3 dealt with vitriol throwing, and remained in effect throughout the century. For the full text, see Evans, above n 47, 209k–209l.

[62] *Return of Number of Persons committed for Trial in Scotland, 1832* (London, House of Commons, 1833) 26 (no 62, throwing vitriol with intent to injure). This was the case of Mary MacKay, NAS, AD14/32/3, precognition for assault at Perth, 1832.

[63] NAS, 'Solemn Database' of 19th-century High Court cases.

[64] *The Times* 11 January 1834, 3f; 24 January 1834, 3d.

Murder Act of 1752,[65] and sections 11 and 12 of Lord Ellenborough's Act. In addition, however, to maintaining the 1803 provisions, there was a key innovation: as well as adding a specific phrase about drowning, suffocating and strangling, the law now stated that anyone who shall 'unlawfully and maliciously stab, cut or wound any person, with intent, in any of the cases aforesaid to murder such person' (section 11) or with intent to 'maim, disfigure or disable ... or to do some other grievous bodily harm' (section 12) was subject to capital punishment.[66] The addition of the word 'wound' was done specifically to avoid the sorts of problems that had arisen due to the lack of generality in the 1803 Act.[67]

But these changes did not prove sufficient to clear up inconsistencies in the sorts of assaults that could be tried as capital offences in England. The word 'wound' was added to the new Act to expand the coverage of the law away from incised injuries by providing for the infliction of wounds by blunt instruments: in order to bring a case within the statute, the continuity of the skin had to be broken, though not necessarily by an incised wound (a hammer blow was now included within its scope, for example.)[68] This left open the question whether a wound could be produced without a weapon, and of course continued the problems associated with actually defining a wound.[69] Recall that at the time, although some doctors might have accepted that fractures, dislocations and burns were wounds, these would not typically be considered as such in the surgical sense, and therefore individual doctors might differ in their opinions. Although Michael Ryan wrote confidently in 1836 that vitriol throwing was now a felony,[70] he was rather too hasty in his judgement, as just the year before a woman named Ann Murrow was tried and acquitted on a technicality. This case was seized upon by Alfred S Taylor, who noted disapprovingly that it showed that an offence which amounted to a capital felony in Scotland constituted only a misdemeanour in England.[71]

Ann Murrow was tried before the Lord Chief Justice at Liverpool on 19 August 1835, charged with having 'thrown a quantity of vitriol upon the face of John Wade, with intent to disfigure him, or do him some grievous bodily harm'; the indictment was framed under section 12 of Lord Lansdowne's Act.[72] Murrow, aged 48, had been a servant in Wade's family, but had been discharged following a house fire he suspected her of starting. She asked for her job back, was refused

---

[65] *An Act for better preventing the horrid Crime of Murder*; this stipulated that murderers were to be executed two days after sentence was passed and their bodies hung in chains or anatomised. For the full text, see Evans, above n 47, 204–06.

[66] For the full text, see Evans, above n 47, 209–209k.

[67] Cox, above n 7, 145; Handler, 'Law of Felonious Assault', above n 7, 195–9.

[68] J Chitty, *A Practical Treatise of Medical Jurisprudence, Part 1*, 2nd American edn (Philadelphia, Carey, Lea and Blanchard, 1836) 430.

[69] Taylor, above n 3, 481–6.

[70] M Ryan, *A Manual of Medical Jurisprudence and State Medicine*, 2nd edn (London, Sherwood, Gilbert, and Piper, 1836) 386.

[71] Taylor, above n 3, 487, fn 1.

[72] ibid 486–87; *The Times* 21 August 1835, 4d.

and started using abusive language, at which he had her committed to the House of Correction for a month. When she got out, she again went to Wade's house, and asked him for money. He was about to give her a shilling when she threw the contents of a cup at him. His sight was destroyed, and the skin on his face came off in blisters, leaving ulcerated patches. Two surgeons attended him and testified at the trial. The first said that 'the injury caused by the action of the vitriol was not what he would call a wound'.[73] The second considered that the acid had produced a wound. Murrow had confessed to the constable who arrested her, Wade's clothes were burnt by the vitriol, and the jury found her guilty of the capital offence. But the judge reserved it for the opinion of his common law colleagues as to whether the injury sustained by Wade could come within the meaning of the word 'wound' in the Act. The judges decided that it did not, so Murrow was acquitted of felony, though she was later tried for a misdemeanour (assault by throwing vitriol with intent to maim) and sentenced to two years imprisonment.[74]

Over the six years following the passing of Lord Lansdowne's Act, the average annual number of committals made under sections 11 and 12 was 136,[75] but a number of cases resulted in acquittal for individuals who were clearly guilty of causing physical damage but whose acts could not be brought within the meaning of the statute. These acquittals hinged on the interpretation of the word wound, judges tending to the view that a wound must be inflicted by some instrument. This meant that offenders were either capitally convicted or subject only to punishment for an assault—a fine and imprisonment without hard labour. The Commissioners appointed in 1836 to enquire into the state of the criminal law highlighted this disproportion, and proposed that the law be amended to add a form of words that would embrace all acts of violence.[76]

The 1836 Commission and the 1837 Act

The Royal Commission on the Criminal Law was appointed by Lord John Russell when he became Home Secretary during the second premiership of Lord Melbourne. Its main task was to investigate the infliction of capital punishments, but the resulting legislation was also relevant to serious assaults. The Offences Against the Person Act received royal assent on 17 July 1837, and was intended to embrace the sorts of violent acts that had formerly been excluded by statute. It maintained the main provisions of its predecessors, reduced the severity of the

---

[73] *The Times* 21 August 1835, 4d.
[74] The National Archives, Kew, PL 28/6, Palatinate of Lancaster, Minute Book: August 1835 Liverpool assizes; March and April 1836 Liverpool assizes.
[75] Taylor, above n 3, 498.
[76] *Correspondence between His Majesty's Principal Secretary of State for the Home Department and the Commissioners appointed to Inquire into the State of the Criminal Law* (London, 1837) 11–12.

possible sentence in most cases, added words meant to include all forms of violence and, crucially, referred specifically to throwing of any corrosive fluid or other destructive matter with intent to maim, disfigure, disable or do other grievous bodily harm (section 5). However, for the charge to stick, harm actually had to be done. The penalty in such cases was transportation for life, or for any term not less than 15 years, or to be imprisoned for any term not exceeding three years.[77] The Commissioners, who did not specify vitriol throwing in their report, had recommended that the minimum prison term should be five years,[78] but at least vitriol throwing was now placed largely on a par with stabbing, shooting and poisoning.

Largely, but not entirely: other clauses stipulated the same penalty even when no harm was actually done in cases of stabbing, shooting and poisoning. Overall, the new law penalised vitriol throwers in the form of those who caused a bodily injury dangerous to life with intent to commit murder (a capital offence but a charge which could rarely be sustained in cases of vitriol throwing), and those who caused grievous bodily harm, but tended to exclude them from the understanding of wounding, which was usually held to be instrumental in nature.[79] As in previous statutes, the word wound was not specifically defined, and in 1851 the Act for the better Prevention of Offences (14 & 15 Vict c 19 s 4) provided a legal remedy for this, by stipulating that grievous bodily harm inflicted with or without any weapon or instrument (without the intent to murder) was a misdemeanour subject to a prison term of up to three years.[80]

Although this was by no means the end of the medico-legal uncertainty surrounding malicious injuries to the person, it did mark a turning point in the prosecution of vitriol throwers. In England, it is clear from trial reports that appeared in *The Times* that there was an increase in the reporting of and/or incidence of vitriol throwing after 1837, and by the early 1840s judges were making use of the full range of penalties laid out in section 5, from a year in prison to transportation for life for a repeat offender.[81] This apparent rise in the profile of the crime was almost certainly related to an increased use of the new law, in circumstances that might previously have led to cases being tried as assaults at quarter sessions. *The Times* tended to report cases from the assizes in preference to those from the lesser courts, with the exception of the London police courts. There, a great many cases of vitriol throwing were heard in the middle part of the century, and either dealt with as misdemeanours or committed for trial at the Old Bailey as felonies.[82]

---

[77] WA Guy, *Principles of Forensic Medicine* (London, H Renshaw, 1844) 343; *The Standard Library Cyclopaedia of Political, Constitutional, Statistical and Forensic Knowledge*, vol 3 (London, Bohn, 1849) 189–90.
[78] *Correspondence*, above n 76, 13.
[79] Cox, above n 7, 155–6.
[80] *The Statutes of the United Kingdom of Great Britain and Ireland, 14 and 15 Victoria 1851* (London, 1851) 73–76.
[81] See, eg four cases reported in *The Times* in 1840: 4 March 1840, 6e; 21 March 1840, 7b; 20 April 1840, 5c; 24 August 1840, 6d.
[82] Watson, above n 22.

In Scotland, by comparison, under the revised law of 1829 (10 Geo IV c 38 s 3, which remained in effect throughout the period with which this chapter is concerned), throwing vitriol and causing bodily harm in circumstances that amounted to attempted murder remained a capital offence, but it was usually possible for defendants to claim that they had acted out of passion, reducing the circumstances to those that attended manslaughter. The word 'wound' did not appear in the Scottish law, although it did use the word 'burn'.

The 1861 Act

The final stage in the medico-legal evolution of the crime of vitriol throwing came in 1861, when English and Irish laws relating to offences against the person were amended and consolidated in the Offences Against the Person Act, which came into effect on 1 November 1861 and remained the principal source of statute law on this subject in England and Wales until well after the Second World War; the law did not pertain to Scotland. The word 'wound' remained in some sections, again undefined, but vitriol throwing was considered in its own clause, where the word 'wound' was removed and the word 'burn' inserted. In its entirety, section 29 stated that:

> Whosoever shall unlawfully and maliciously cause any Gunpowder or other explosive Substance to explode, or send or deliver to or cause to be taken or received by any Person any explosive Substance or any other dangerous or noxious Thing, or put or lay at any Place, or cast or throw at or upon or otherwise apply to any Person, any corrosive Fluid or any destructive or explosive Substance, with Intent in any of the Cases aforesaid to burn, maim, disfigure, or disable any Person, or to do some grievous bodily Harm to any Person, shall, whether any bodily Injury be effected or not, be guilty of Felony, and being convicted thereof shall be liable, at the Discretion of the Court, to be kept in Penal Servitude for Life or for any Term not less than Three Years—or to be imprisoned for any Term not exceeding Two Years, with or without Hard Labour, and with or without Solitary Confinement, and, if a Male under the Age of Sixteen Years, with or without Whipping.[83]

So we see that vitriol throwing was included with terrorist bombings. While the latter is now subject to the Terrorism Act 2000, the 1861 statute against vitriol throwing is still in force. The wording of the statute made it possible for a conviction for felony to be achieved even when no injury to the person was done, but in cases where clothing only was damaged magistrates had the option of treating the case as one of malicious damage to property, incurring a fine and payment of damages. This was another angle to the story of vitriol throwing, which in the 18th and early 19th centuries could also be prosecuted as a felonious crime against property, but the subject is beyond the scope of this chapter.

---

[83] *A Collection of the Public General Statutes passed in the 24th and 25th Years of the Reign of Her Majesty Queen Victoria* (London, 1861) 386–99.

In trials for vitriol throwing, following the passage of the 1861 Act, the main issues to be determined involved the element of intent, the nature of the injury done to the person, the identity of the substance thrown, and whether it should or should not be considered a corrosive fluid or a destructive substance. The latter were questions for doctors and chemists, but the first was usually established by non-medical evidence. Unfortunately, whenever a clear intent to injure could not be proved, the defendant had to be acquitted of the felonious assault, so vitriol throwers could still cause severe injury yet escape any form of punishment, or suffer a mild penalty only. This happened in a Liverpool case in 1867,[84] but generally the act of throwing vitriol was suggestive of intent to injure. Since an assault could be perpetrated even when no bodily injury was done, we occasionally find individuals charged with making threats to throw vitriol—an indication of how the law had broadened its view of what precisely constituted a malicious injury. Finally, in the absence of an injury the identity of the fluid thrown was of importance, and where this could not be established by scientific evidence, an acquittal might follow.

Conclusion

Under the terms of the 1861 Act, the injury caused by sulphuric acid was called a burn, but not a wound. Medico-legal writers thereafter tended to base their definition of burns and wounds around the wording used in the statute, but not all seem to have accepted that a burn was also a wound in the medical sense. Alfred Swaine Taylor and his many editors clearly thought that the medical definition of a wound should and did include burns, but others, like William Guy and John Dixon Mann, retained the more traditional view of a wound as deriving from mechanical means. Under the terms of the law as it now related to vitriol throwing, however, this was unproblematic: the statute was clear enough to encompass nearly all the forms of malicious assault that one person could inflict on another.

It is perhaps more interesting to reflect on the changing legal definition of these words, which was clearly linked to cases that came before the courts but which had to be dismissed on points of legal interpretation. Although lawyers and lawmakers would not adopt the medical definition of a wound, possibly because it remained in dispute among medical men, they do at least appear to have stretched their construal of its meaning to encompass a more medically-sophisticated interpretation, so that crimes of the type perpetrated by Ann Murrow in 1835 became increasingly and uniformly subject to the punishments they deserved.

---

[84] *The Times* 14 December 1867, 9e.

5

Not Their Fathers' Sons: The Changing Trajectory in Psychiatric Testimony, 1760–1900

JOEL PETER EIGEN

Testifying at the case of a London surgeon on trial for assaulting two police officers, Richard Parramore—member of the Royal College of Surgeons—described the defendant in the following words:

> I believed he was labouring under a delusion—he said a mesmerist was downstairs below him who was trying to throw him out of the window by force, trying experiments ... there were wires from the room below to his room, that he was cutting these wires, and while he was cutting them he was interrupted, and that he was sorry he had shot the policemen.

Parramore was followed in the witness box by John Rowland Gibson, medical officer of Newgate Gaol, who regularly visited with prisoners suspected of contemplating an insanity plea:

> In the course of my duty I have had my attention called to a great many cases involving insanity—I have heard the evidence of the last witness as to the appearances he observed and the statements the prisoner made at the time—these appearances and statements are no doubt consistent with his suffering from delirium at the time he committed this act.

The trial ended with the prisoner's statement that he could not sleep, having become convinced that somebody below his rooms was 'making me an experiment for mesmerism or electro biology.' Sensing the preliminary symptoms of an epileptic fit coming on, he had shouted: 'Stop that devilry, I will have no more of it,' and it was at that moment the police had burst into his rooms. Apparently persuasive to the jury, the defendant's words prompted an acquittal on the grounds of insanity and he was detained 'awaiting her Majesty's pleasure.'[1]

There are any number of forensic terms in this 1876 case to capture the attention of an historian of law and medicine; indeed, the prosecution of surgeon Charles Grimes fairly brims with medical terms that defined 19th-century insanity trials. Delusion and epilepsy had long enjoyed a historical pedigree in

---

[1] *Old Bailey Sessions Papers* (hereafter, *OBSP*) 1875–76, 8th sess, case 400, 151–55.

medical testimony. Mesmerism itself was a topic of intense public interest in an era awash in hypnotism, somnambulism, and 'doubled consciousness'.[2] One also finds in trial testimony allusions to vacancy and states of absence, increasingly present in descriptions of states of suspended consciousness in the second half of the 19th century.

Almost obscured by these vividly theatrical mental states was the unexpected appearance of delirium, a term decidedly out of place in late-Victorian medicolegal discourse. Odd that such a totemic term of the late 1700s should find its way back into the Old Bailey almost a hundred years after it had passed from courtroom use. Insanity in the 18th century had been a matter of a global derangement: insensibility, incoherence, or 'being out of one's wits.' Delirium's place in the history of madness had been ensured by its resemblance to the last stages of febrile delirium: insanity was described as 'delirium without fever' as far back as antiquity. What business did it have in the courtroom of Henry Maudsley and Forbes Winslow? Forensic psychiatry had come a long way since the early days of forensic medical witnesses in the 1760s … or had it?

The 1876 trial of Charles Grimes sits at the beginning of a third phase of a survey of insanity trials undertaken to examine the rise of forensic-psychiatric testimony in common law courts.[3] The initial period—1760–1843—began with the first appearance by a medical witness at the Old Bailey, London's central criminal court, to testify about insanity as a medical condition and ended with the trial of Daniel McNaughtan, which led to the articulation of a formalised insanity plea in response to the testimony of the nine medical witnesses. The second period began with the introduction of the McNaughtan Rules in 1843, ending in 1876 with a trial in which a medical witness adamantly denied that the defendant's mental condition could be described in any way as insanity, yet nonetheless merited an acquittal because her actions had been those of an automaton.[4] In sum, medical testimony in

---

[2] Mesmerism and its cultural resonance have been most recently examined in A Winter, *Mesmerised: Powers of Mind in Victorian Britain* (Chicago, University of Chicago Press, 1998).

[3] Spanning the years 1760 to 1900, this survey includes all criminal trials heard at London's central criminal court, the Old Bailey, in which mental derangement was raised as a possible exculpatory defence. Today's historian of law and medicine is fortunate to be able to consult verbatim testimony narratives of these trials, taken down in shorthand during the proceedings, printed each night, and sold the following day on the London street. Known as the *Old Bailey Sessions Papers*, these accounts of courtroom testimony served as the basis for my earlier work on the evolution of forensic psychiatry, *Witnessing Insanity, Madness and Mad-Doctors in the English Court* (New Haven, Yale University Press, 1995) covering the years 1760–1843, and *Unconscious Crime, Mental Absence and Criminal Responsibility in Victorian London* (Baltimore, Johns Hopkins University Press, 2003), surveying the years 1843–1876.

[4] Following the acquittal of Daniel McNaughtan for killing the personal secretary of Robert Peel—whom the defendant had mistaken for the prime minister—the House of Lords asked the trial judges to formulate standard language that could be given to future juries to determine culpability when faced with a defence based upon insanity. The judges' responses, known today as the McNaughtan Rules, articulated the criterion, 'knowing right from wrong'; subsequent juries were henceforth to be instructed that they could acquit an allegedly insane prisoner if, in their opinion, the accused's defect or disease of the mind precluded the capacity to recognise the legal wrong he or she was committing. The questions asked by the House of Lords and the judges' answers are given in *McNaughtan's*

this second installment introduced various states of unconsciousness: automatism, somnambulism, and a curious import from France, *vertige épileptique*.

To be sure, forensic–psychiatric witnesses in this second period continued to employ medical terms heard earlier in the century—delusion and moral insanity, for example—but conspicuously missing from their testimony were the states of 'global delirium' and 'insensibility', which had been so prominent in the later 1700s. Before the acquittal of James Hadfield in 1800, only a total want of understanding and memory satisfied the law's criterion of a level of derangement sufficiently debilitating to merit an acquittal. It was therefore totally unanticipated to find in the third sequence of trials—from 1876–1900—the reappearance of delirium and an even more outdated diagnosis, melancholia, proffered by medical witnesses from the witness box. Although the historian of science has learned not to be surprised by the discontinuous arc of specialist ways of seeing and explaining, one wonders how to account for medical witnesses dusting off long-discarded terms associated with an era when little distinguished medical testimony from the common cultural consciousness invoked by neighbours, lovers, and other decidedly non-specialists in the field of mental medicine.

Tracking forensic testimony over time engages one of the most intriguing issues at the heart of the history of medicine: the fine art of naming an affliction. Whether one is diagnosing heart disease or hernia, diabetes or dysentery, medical texts and medical practitioners alert the clinician to the ambiguous nature of a suspected malady's symptoms and signs, the unpredictable 'life-course' of a disease, and the consequent need for sober and detached interpretation. Although all medical specialties face unique challenges in making medical sense out of mysterious matter, any student of medical history would acknowledge that the attempt to isolate and characterise discrete states of mental derangement presents a minefield all its own. Owing to the absence of reliable materialist cues, analysis of symptoms and the subsequent naming of mental diseases were thought to be dependent upon the patient interview. It was the significance of conversation—of listening attentively to the flow of ideas—that led to the medical conviction that psychiatric diagnosis was imparted 'though the ear.'

For the neighbour or the family member, however, the putative madman's behaving 'more like a mad bullock than anything else' constituted sufficient grounds to justify the inference of madness.[5] Medical men who treated the deranged were much more likely to base their diagnoses on the lurching, rambling flow of conversation, specifically the inability of the mad to respond to a question with an appropriate answer. The major reason that delusion surfaced as the first medico-legal term to distinguish lay from medical testimony was that,

---

Case (1843) 8 Eng Rep 718; 10 Clark and Fin 200, 302–14. The most comprehensive analysis of the McNaughtan trial and its historical context is given in R Moran, *Knowing Right from Wrong: The Insanity Defence of Daniel McNaughtan* (New York, Free Press, 1981) 168–75.

[5] JP Eigen, *Witnessing Insanity: Madness and Mad-doctors in the English Court* (New Haven, Yale University Press, 1995) 82–107.

unlike the neighbour or family member, the experienced physician 'persisted in the interview', realising that 'the smallest rivulet flows into the great stream of … derangement. Ordinary persons [were] much deceived by the temporary display of rational discourse.'[6] Attention to the way in which ideas were expressed did not of course rule associated behavioural cues; facial expression, random gestures, and a catalogue of bodily movements could easily frame how the verbal outpourings of the putative patient were interpreted. Still, it was the content of their conversations—not the external signs of distraction—that informed medical assertions to have discerned madness, asserted forcefully both in medical texts and courtroom testimony in the formative years of forensic-psychiatric practice.

This chapter examines an unexpected turn in the historical content of medical diagnosis by exploring the setting and professional experience that structured the medical interviews of the putatively mad criminal. That medical ideas changed significantly over the years 1760–1900 is hardly exceptionable: this was the era that witnessed an emerging specialty in mental medicine, expressed both in a host of medical texts on insanity and an emerging professional voice of forensic-psychiatric witnesses in court. What is singular is the sudden lurching back in clinical imagery to an era that recognised no particular specialty in mental medicine, revealing anything but a progressive 'march of the Enlightenment' into the witness box.

Testimony Overview: 1760–1843

Capturing the voice of the first self-proclaimed medical specialists in madness presents few difficulties for today's historian. There is no shortage of 19th-century medical tracts written by asylum doctors and general practitioners who turned their attention increasingly to mental derangement. One also finds contemporary medical journals devoting increasing space to professional debate surrounding the diagnosis and treatment of the mad. But it was the courtroom that provided the setting that matters most to historians of forensic psychiatry: the very public forum in which the emerging specialists in mental medicine asserted their professional opinion not only to peers, but to a lay—and legal—audience. To assert professional expertise in the pages of an esoteric medical tome or to fellow practitioners in the folds of an in-house medical journal was one thing; to stake one's claim to a unique field of knowledge in the face of a courtroom dominated by legal rules and community common sense was quite another. One wonders what was said in court, by whom, and to what effect. Who constituted the most suspicious audience to medical testimony: the jury, the prosecutor, the judge, or the general medical community?

[6] J Haslam, *Medical Jurisprudence as It Relates to Insanity According to the Laws of England* (London, C Hunter, 1817) 15–19.

The trial of Charles Grimes, for example, provides clear evidence that privately-retained physicians and surgeons were followed to the witness box by medical men employed by the gaol whose sustained familiarity with mental derangement exceeded that of even the most celebrated private practitioners and medical authors of the day. Trial testimony is therefore central to charting the odyssey of this new medical specialty, and in this regard, today's historian of medicine and law is fortunate indeed. In the 1970s, John Langbein published two seminal articles that alerted the academic world to the historical utility of the *Old Bailey Sessions Papers (OBSP)*, verbatim narratives of courtroom testimony taken down in shorthand during trial sessions, transcribed at night, and sold on the London street the next day.[7] After verifying their accuracy against a contemporary judge's own notes from the 1760s, Langbein invited legal scholars to mine the *Papers*, a source that had already been employed to great effect by Nigel Walker in his magisterial history of the insanity defence from the Middle Ages into the early modern England, focusing particularly on the legal response to the increasing presence of medical men in the courtroom.[8]

Walker's interests, however, did not extend to the content of medical testimony and the examination of forensic-psychiatric witnesses. How did medical witnesses enter a setting whose rules and procedures had been set by a powerful judiciary and attempt to convince the court that they could see and hear things that had eluded even the most attentive neighbour? Although their credentials rivalled those of their medical brethren, their role in the witness box was a bit trickier. When the general medical practitioner was called to decode ambiguous signs surrounding an enigmatic death, the practical significance of the specialist's testimony was evident. Only a man trained in anatomy and physiology could account for seemingly inexplicable phenomena: a wound that yielded no blood, a drowned person with no water in her lungs, a fatal head wound that could have been resulted from either a fall or from the blow of a blunt object. No neighbour or relative was really qualified to aver on such a matter; expert testimony was unambiguously called for.

Madness, however, was anything but mysterious. As the late historian Roy Porter long maintained, 18th-century madness was spectacularly on view; few observers doubted nature's legibility. It was therefore the utter conspicuousness of the prisoner's distraction that neighbours and relatives of the accused transported into the Old Bailey in the late-18th and early 19th centuries: delirious raving, wild histrionics, baying at the moon while naked. Consequently, conventional images found their way into both lay and medical testimony. Indeed, little distinguished the specialist from the neighbour until 1800, when the trial of James Hadfield introduced the concept of delusion into courtroom testimony. As the first term

---

[7] J Langbein, 'The Criminal Trial Before the Lawyers' (1978) 45 *University of Chicago Law Review* 263; J Langbein, 'Shaping the Eighteenth-Century Criminal Trial: A View from the Ryder Sources' (1983) 50 *University of Chicago Law Review* 1.

[8] N Walker, *Crime and Insanity in England: Vol 1, The Historical Perspective* (Edinburgh, Edinburgh University Press, 1968).

of preference for 19th-century medical witnesses, delusion came to demarcate the expert's gaze precisely because of the deft questioning needed to uncover a hidden and, in some cases, tenaciously circumscribed universe of deranged beliefs lurking just below pacific composure. Only the trained listener and practiced clinician knew to probe; the neighbour's inference was dismissed, so readily was he duped by surface impressions of equanimity.

The preference for delusion, however, did not preclude specialists in mental medicine from introducing affective states of being, long familiar to Western folklore and likely to be on the minds of jury. Perhaps the oldest of these was melancholia which, along with mania, can be found not only in early 19th-century courtroom testimony but also in medical writings dating to Hippocrates, eventually developed into a discrete states of temperament by Galen. Evidenced by brooding dejection, consumed with fears—some of which rose to the level of delusion—melancholia was a derangement of temperament and emotion, although its legal significance for matters criminal had been circumscribed by Matthew Hale, who famously rejected 'melancholy distempers' as not significantly debilitating to preclude culpability.[9] Up until 1800, only a total—not a partial—want of memory and understanding could rise to the level of a legally significant madness.

Delusion was the first of the partial states of insanity to make its way into the Old Bailey, but others were waiting in the wings. The early decades of 19th century witnessed the introduction of an expansive array of states of derangement that stopped conspicuously short of a total want of memory and understanding; indeed, they did not even implicate cognitive faculties. For all its association with an *idée fixe*, melancholia was predominantly a disturbance in mood, and helped to clear the way for other states of deranged affect that offered a 'clear-thinking' madness which swept one 'quite away' by a force independent of will. Initially termed *manie sans délire* by Philippe Pinel, these afflictions revealed no global state of confusion or incoherence.[10] The Parisian clinician and medical superintendent of Bicêtre gave birth to a circle of acolytes who parcelled out the derangement of volition into an array of innovative categories of madness. Most prominent of Pinel's students was Jean-Etienne-Dominique Esquirol who, in 1817, proposed his own neologism, monomania, to describe the overwhelming force let loose by a malevolent impulse: *monomanie homicide*, or a more generic, unreflective urge, *monomanie instinctive*.[11] Most often, monomania conveyed one's total absorption by an all-consuming fear or false belief, and thus appeared to borrow a good part of its conceptual resonance from the centuries-old, familiar affliction, melancholia. Esquirol retained the content of melancholy—self-absorption by an overwhelming fear—but discarded melancholia's historical—and unscientific—association with black bile.[12] By coupling

---

[9] M Hale, *The History of the Pleas of the Crown* (London, E and R Nutt, 1736) 30–37.
[10] P Pinel, *A Treatise on Insanity* (Sheffield, Cadell and Davies, 1806).
[11] JED Esquirol, *Mental Maladies: A Treatise on Insanity* (Philadelphia, Lea and Blanchard, 1845).
[12] J Goldstein, *Console and Classify: The French Psychiatric Progression the Nineteenth Century* (Cambridge, CUP, 1987).

insistent fear with an expansive, lively temperament, Esquirol thus fashioned monomania, consigning melancholy, supposedly, to the clinical ash heap.

It is consequently monomania, not melancholia that one finds featured more frequently in Old Bailey testimony in the 1830s and 1840s. As employed by medical witnesses, a lucid madness could explain how 'insane persons have pursued an object with a degree of cunning which belongs to very few except the most exalted talents',[13] and yet be perfectly unmindful of the moral transgression they were about to commit. Moral imbecility and clear thinking could thus exist side by side. This was, of course, conscious deliberation of a very particular sort, revealing a capacity to reason divorced from moral context or consequence. The vivid separation of legal from moral wrong made it much easier for the introduction of other conceptions of mental functioning that placed the offender practically in the role of a moral bystander to his own crime. Some defendants were said to suffer from an impairment of volition—described as a 'lesion of the will' or the more generic term, 'moral insanity'; others were captive to a monomaniacal obsession that commanded them to kill their children, or as in the case of the person cited above with 'most exalted talents', to forge a cheque.[14]

In an effort to staunch the feared torrent of such non-intellectual forms of insanity into the courtroom, the McNaughtan verdict was seized upon as the opportunity to establish criteria for a legally sufficient madness. A derangement of morals, of will, of any kind of insanity that left the afflicted perfectly coherent while supposedly in the throes of monomaniacal excitement was left conspicuously out of the McNaughtan Rules. Only a cognitive impairment—an inability to know the nature and quality of the act—would rise to the level of a derangement that could justify an acquittal. The second phase of the survey of insanity trails was therefore undertaken to gauge how effectively the law was able to circumscribe medical witnesses' testimony to the prisoner's capacity to 'know' what he was about. Having given them a berth in the witness box, would it be possible to preclude asylum physicians and general practitioners from extending the jury's consideration to the defendant's failure to exert self-control?

Testimony Overview: 1843–1876

Surveying the years following the McNaughtan verdict, one soon realises that whatever the Rules might have been designed to exclude from courtroom testimony, medical witnesses were not so easily muzzled. Moral insanity showed no signs of retreat; indeed, medical witnesses displayed voluble professional

---

[13] *OBSP* 1833, 7th sess, case 104, 733.
[14] JC Prichard, *A Treatise on Insanity and Other Disorders Affecting the Mind* (London, Sherwood, Gilbert, and Piper, 1835); and JC Prichard, *On the Difference Forms of Insanity in Relation to Jurisprudence, Designed for the Use of Persons Concerned in Legal Questions Regarding Unsoundness of Mind* (London, Hippolyte Baillière, 1842).

confidence in their adamantine refusal to answer questions phrased in ways that restricted the grounds for inferring insanity. Responding to a judge's admonition that he answer only the question asked, madhouse superintendent John Conolly responded in 1853, 'I am perfectly aware that is the question ... [but] ... I think it can only be answered in the manner in which I have answered it.'[15]

While legal and medical practitioners actively struggled to confine insanity to their own professional preserves, their lively debate was apparently lost on a newly emerging cadre of prisoner who had quite literally wandered, unannounced, into the Old Bailey. Although many 19th-century defendants continued to articulate insanity defenses that featured conventional elements of mental impairment—delusion, hallucination, and homicidal mania—a noticeable population of prisoners presented the court with a type of alienation that called into question their 'authorship' of the crime. Sleepwalkers, automatons, and persons afflicted with a curious variant of epilepsy referred to in medical testimony as 'epileptic vertigo' challenged the court to assign responsibility to the defendant on trial when it was arguably another person who committed the physical act. This second phase of the trial survey ended accordingly with a verdict that reveals the jury's acceptance of the possibility of goal-directed behaviour bereft of conscious thought.[16]

Jurors in this trial had been faced with a conundrum: the defendant had sliced off her infant daughter's hand while in a state of epileptic vertigo. Upon entering the kitchen to cut a piece of bread, the defendant seemed to disappear into a state of unconsciousness said by French clinicians to intervene between two separate episodes of convulsive epilepsy. In such a period of absence, epileptic patients had been known to carry on conversations and perform feats of considerable physical dexterity, all while 'asleep'.

Medical testimony in this 1876 trial explicitly disavowed the presence of insanity—'epilepsy has nothing to do with insanity. ... I do not consider the patient is in the slightest degree insane', and yet no other verdict owing to mental impairment was at the jury's disposal.[17] Offered the findings of guilty, not guilty, or not guilty on the grounds of insanity, the jury returned a verdict of 'not guilty on the grounds of unconsciousness'. The judge was evidently appalled with the verdict, refused to release the prisoner, and announced his intention to write to the Home Office to explain the singularity of the verdict. Despite his professional pique, a compelling precedent had been set: just six months later, another judge

---

[15] *OBSP* 1850–51, 9th sess, case 1502, 368–69.

[16] Analyses of these trials can be found in JP Eigen, *Unconscious Crime: Mental Absence and Criminal Responsibility in Victorian London* (Baltimore, Johns Hopkins University Press, 2003). One's choice of end points regarding how to separate historical periods is obviously at the discretion of the historian. As mentioned earlier, there appeared to be compelling reasons for breaking the data at 1843, with the formalisation of the insanity plea at the McNaughtan trial, and again in 1876, with medical testimony that denied the presence of insanity and yet alleged the exculpatory significance of the prisoner's mental state. In retrospect, these three resulting periods reveal not only significant stages in the emerging role of the medical witness, but defining shifts in the content of medical testimony as well.

[17] *OBSP* 1875–76, 11th sess, case 413, 495–97.

advised jurors to consider the possibility that epileptic vertigo lay behind the prisoner's actions.[18]

In the years 1843–76 therefore, states of suspended consciousness took their place among those terms most frequently cited by medical witnesses: delusion, 'women's problems', fits (including epilepsy), and brain fever or concussion. The second category represents a significant departure in forensic-psychiatric testimony: the presence of a gender-specific derangement. Among the issues mentioned in regard to 'women's problems' were pregnancy, delivery, 'suppression of menses', and menopause. The diagnosis used most often in court to subsume all of these was puerperal mania (or puerperal insanity), a term heard only twice in the 80 years that preceded McNaughtan. Although other forms of insanity could also be unambiguously physically grounded—brain fever, concussion, a fall on the head—an impairment linked directly to reproductive functions was obviously unique to women. A defence strategy that employed this variant of insanity usually ended in acquittal for reasons that are not difficult to imagine: the victims were predominantly the defendant's children and neighbours invariably described the accused as a loving and devoted parent. Even in cases where the killing was clearly premeditated—one mother methodically mixed Battle's Vermin Powder into her children's rice pudding—the jury was prepared to regard the tragic women as driven by physiological impulse owing to the upheaval of birth or lactation.[19] In all cases, the tragic mother was depicted as having been compelled to destroy those creatures 'nearest and dearest' to her.

In sum, forensic-psychiatric testimony from 1843 to 1876 continued to invoke terms familiar to medical and lay audiences but also introduced an innovative variation in mental derangement that conspicuously sidestepped the 'knowing' element of insanity. To be sure, delusion remained a staple in the expert witness's vocabulary while monomania faded precipitously. Moral insanity continued to frame medical testimony, with gender-specific puerperal mania also becoming a frequent topic for the jury's deliberation. Both conditions were (usually) free from intellectual derangement, endowing the passions with a will of their own, a force that the afflicted was powerless to restrain. For all the clinical sense that a derangement of 'how one ought to feel' toward one's children or intimates made to medical authors and medical witnesses, moral insanity met vocal opposition in court as judges fulminated at the idea of framing a wicked will as a disease category. Still, the noted jurist James Fitzjames Stephen averred in 1883 that he had ultimately accepted the notion of an insanity of morals, although it is difficult to know if his gradual acceptance of non-intellectualist insanity was shared among his brothers on the bench.[20] Clearly, judges at the Old Bailey could let their displeasure be known, as witnessed in the trial that yielded the anomalous verdict, 'not guilty on the grounds of unconsciousness'. In retrospect, it is hard to imagine

---

[18] *OBSP* 1876–77, 4th sess, case 246, 434–60.
[19] Eigen, above n 16, esp 69–85.
[20] JF Stephen, *A History of the Criminal Law of England*, vol 2 (London, Macmillan, 1883).

who was more shocked by the verdict: the judge, the defendant, or the historian of forensic psychiatry reading the case in the 21st century.

Testimony Overview, 1876–1900

The third and final survey of the *Papers* was therefore undertaken to examine how issues of 'unconscious crime' were put before the jury after the unexpected verdict in 1876. Did epileptic vertigo disappear from medical testimony as suddenly as it had surfaced? Were subsequent juries likely to follow the lead of these singularly disposed community members and acquit because the actual physical act appeared not to 'belong' to the accused? And most importantly, did the possibility of disembodied criminality inaugurate a new set of questions about instinctual drives 25 years before Freud?

Heretofore conceptualised as only the repository of forgotten associations linking one idea to another, one is tempted to conceive of the unconscious as a silent co-defendant in offenses that signified a certain social death for the offender.[21] The victims of 'unconscious crime'—like the victims of women in the throes of puerperal mania—were no strangers to the assailants: they were their beloved children, spouses, and close friends. Although no mention is made at trial of anything suggesting 'buried resentment' or 'repressed hostility', it cannot have been lost on the jury that the defendants and their victims shared precisely the sort of affectionate and intimate bond that should have rendered them the least likely of targets of mortal violence. Might courtroom inquiry into the nature of the bond that united victim and assailant illuminated how the unconscious was reconceived as something more than a vast file of forgotten memory links, a reservoir perhaps of inexpressible, explosive hostility? Just as the sleepwalking defendant had unexpectedly wandered into the Old Bailey while legal and medical practitioners were consumed with negotiating the fate of moral insanity, a similarly unanticipated courtroom player would emerge in third sequence of trials.

In 1898, Edgar Smith was prosecuted for the murder of his fiancée. At the beginning of the trial, prison surgeon James Scott employed the medical term 'melancholia' to account for the degree of seeming equanimity the defendant retained in the face of an impelling delusion. The historian of medicine would be forgiven for smiling at the prison surgeon's mention of melancholia.[22] Similar to delirium—a term that was also believed to have fallen into clinical desuetude—melancholia with its 25-century pedigree had also all but vanished from medical

---

[21] For a comprehensive look at medical psychology's views of the unconscious before Freud, see W Hamilton, *Lectures on Metaphysics and Logic* (Edinburgh, W Blackwood and Sons, 1859).
[22] *OBSP* 1898–99, 12th sess, case 704, 929–41.

testimony by the early 19th century and was rarely invoked after McNaughtan.[23] Perhaps it was just an odd reference made by a prison surgeon who had casually gathered his observations while the defendant was awaiting trial.

But the trial of Edgar Smith was anything but anomalous: in trial after trial in the late 1870s and into 1900, melancholia had reappeared as a disease, not just as a synonym for depressed affect. And, as in the 1898 trial, it was invoked to describe the impairment of male as well as female defendants. A term that one might have been convinced had gone the way of the dodo had returned with a vengeance, and not just for female depressives. In fact, the last third of this research—the years that cover 1876 to 1900—featured the (re)introduction of terms that had defined the testimony of the first generation of medical witnesses—those who appeared in the late 18th century up to the McNaughtan trial—employing terms such as delirium, insensibility, and most frequently, melancholia.

When examined comprehensively, the trajectory of forensic testimony from 1760–1900 suggests the presence of three separate generations of medical men: 1760–1843, 1843–1876, 1876–1900. The first two periods are distinguished for the reasons given earlier: the moment when the first medical witness appears in the Old Bailey to speak of insanity as a medical condition (1760), the verdict and Rules accompanying the trial of Daniel McNaughtan (1843), and the explicit introduction of states of unconsciousness into medical testimony and expert testimony addressing consequent issues of volition (1876). From employing states of 18th-century global delirium and eventually delusion, the first generation of medical witnesses eventually gave way to a subsequent cohort that expanded the scope of expert testimony to engage not only cognitive but volitional chaos as well. Sleepwalkers, after all, are not mad; automatons are not deranged; prisoners afflicted with epileptic vertigo are not insensible. They were instead not really 'there' at the crime. The jury's verdict of 'not guilty on the grounds of unconsciousness' was therefore a useful place to demarcate the second generation of medical witnesses, active in the courtroom and especially active in expanding medical testimony and challenging directly the law's ability to ascribe responsibility to behaviour.

The final section—canvassing the years from 1876 to the end of the of the century—constitutes a third generation of medical witnesses, precisely because

---

[23] Along with mania and phrenitis, melancholia was one of the earliest terms used to denote severe mental affliction, dating to antiquity. Long associated with a brooding, sorrowful temperament, melancholia's association with humoral origins was thought by French clinicians early in the 19th century to betoken a pre-scientific conception of mental derangement, and was summarily dropped in favour of the neologism, *monomanie*. For a discussion of the changing fortunes of melancholia at the hands of the Pinel's circle, see Esquirol, above n 11 and Eigen, above n 5, 72–6. Melancholia's status as a *legally* significant ailment was circumscribed by Hale in his *History of the Pleas of the Crown* (first printed in 1736), which referred to 'melancholy distempers' as a degree of distraction that still allowed for 'as great [an] understanding as ordinarily a child of 14 years hath … [and] such a person may be guilty of treason or felony'. For Hale, as for jurists until the trial of James Hadfield in 1800, only a *total* want of memory and understanding rose to the level of a legally significant madness. See M Hale, above n 5, esp 30–7.

the medical terms that surface mark such a departure from the middle years of the Victorian Era. One might have fully expected this third generation to continue along the avenue of their 'fathers'—focusing on unconscious states of being, and eventually anticipating Freudian concepts of unconscious motivation by the turn of the century. What one notices instead is a curious skipping of a generation, with the grandsons of the forensic psychiatric profession reverting to their grandfathers' diagnoses, not their fathers'.

The Dynamics of Diagnosis

Social scientists have long been intrigued by psychiatric diagnosis because of the interactional components of the interview between patient and physician. The diagnosis of aberrant mental and behavioural states is not a question of blood work, diseased intestines, or atrophied reflexes; it is instead a matter of an impression made on the observer's organs of sense. Classic studies in American sociology have highlighted the role of the social setting that brings classifier and the classified together—whether in a state hospital, jail cell, or private clinic. The influence of the interview's setting on eventual diagnosis has forever alerted behavioural and social scientists as well as practitioners; to the role that social surrounding can play in diagnosis.[24]

With these classic findings as a guide, the role of social setting was examined in all trials in which a medical witness appeared at the Old Bailey to aver on the defendant's mental condition. Table 1 offers these findings, separated into six different time periods that are explained below.

Table 1: How the Prisoner Met the Doctor

Affiliation	1760–1800	1801–30	1831–43	1844–76	1877–99
Social/Private	33%	14%	7%	4%	1%
Professional acquaintance (Pre-existing)	61%	37%	22%	17%	15%
Prison/Jail/Asylum Interview		40%	58%	51%	63%
On-scene witness			7%	25%	19%
No previous contact			3%	2%	1%
Insufficient data	6%	9%	3%	1%	1%
	100%	100%	100%	100%	100%
Total No	18	35	74	241	341

---

[24] AB Hollingshead and FC Redlich, *Social Class and Mental Illness: A Community Study* (New York, Wiley, 1958).

The first period—the years comprising the latter half of the 18th century—is unique in that one finds no appearance by a gaol or prison surgeon; the most frequent associations were those that grew out of professional acquaintance. These consultations were most often prompted by a physical injury or disease, which had over time revealed a psychological dimension. While treating a family member, the physician happened to notice the sullen, lachrymose relative in the corner, and it was this impression that the medical witness later delivered to the court. Fully a third of the medical witnesses in this earlier period were testifying about a purely private association: neighbours, co-workers, and in one case, an apothecary testifying about his business partner who happened to kill a lover.[25]

What changes immediately at the turn of the century is the entry, of asylum, prison, and gaol surgeons to the witness box, and in significant numbers. This should not be surprising on an institutional level because the asylum movement did not really take hold in Britain until the early 19th-century. When it did, these institutions served as an ideal spot to converse with the accused awaiting trial. This category was dominated by one particular medical man, Gilbert McMurdo, surgeon to Newgate Gaol. An ophthalmologist in the employ of the Corporation for the City of London, McMurdo was often directed by the court to visit with prisoners whom the state believed were contemplating an insanity plea. Up to the McNaughtan trial, he was the most frequent medical witness at the Old Bailey, testifying about the alleged derangement of the prisoner, and most often denying any evidence of insanity.[26] There is a telling observation to be made here: for all the popular association one reads of medical testimony laid at the door of an increasingly activist defence, the Old Bailey trial narratives make it abundantly clear that it was the prosecution that regularly enlisted medical testimony.[27] One could well argue that the growth of medical participation in insanity trials was spearheaded by the state, with defence counsel calling medical witnesses of its own to counter the all too predictable finding of sanity reported by the gaol surgeon.

---

[25] Eigen above n 5, esp 108–32.
[26] In 1833, McMurdo described his assignment in Newgate as follows: '[T]he clerk of arraigns told me it was very likely I should be wanted; and I had better be in attendance, on one occasion the Lord Mayor met me and said, Mind you see that prisoner, for it is very likely we shall want your evidence. … I go to the Compter daily to see the prisoners.': *OBSP* 1833, 5th sess, case 814, 402.
[27] Defence attorneys made a late entry into common law courts, having been formally excluded until the Treason Act 1696. Believing that '[N]o one could speak more effectively for those accused of crimes than [they] themselves', judges traditionally relegated counsel for defence to the role of questioner of witnesses; a defence 'case,' as such, was not laid before the jury, nor indeed were opening statements offered. Initially permitted legal representation for only treasonous offences, criminal defendants were gradually given the opportunity for legal representation—and a continuing 'activist' one at that—by the 1730s. Analyses of the historical emergence of defence counsel in common-law courts can be found in DJA Cairns, *Advocacy and the Making of the Adversarial Criminal Trial, 1800–1865* (Oxford, Clarendon, 1998), JM Beattie, 'Scales of Justice: Defence Counsel and the English Criminal Trial in the Eighteenth and Nineteenth Centuries' (1991) 9 *Law and History Review* 221, esp 236–44, and JH Langbein, 'Historical Foundations of the Law of Evidence: A View from the Ryder Sources' (1996) 96 *Columbia Law Review* 1168.

Also in this second period—from 1801–1830—one sees a precipitous fall in the number of cases where there was a private association between the medical witness and the prisoner, dropping by more than a half, and continuing to slide down to barely one per cent in the very last period. It is not immediately obvious what this suggests about the apparent attenuation in casual acquaintance between medical men and their neighbours. One thing is clear, however; the early years of the 19th century mark the introduction of an associational base that will predominate throughout the 1800s. The prison, the gaol, and the workhouse will serve as the most frequent meeting point for medical professional and the accused. By the end of the years surveyed, fully three in every five meetings took place in an institutional setting.

Over time, professional acquaintance also dropped noticeably, trading per centages almost exactly with prison and gaol meetings. Although it does not appear to have shared the fate of 'private' associations, existing professional association clearly slipped to no more than one or two in 10. The other basis for association that matched it in proportion was 'on scene or after' meetings between medical personnel and the accused. These were occasioned by physicians or other medical men being called to attend a victim or who visited an injured accused and later reported their impressions to the court. Together, the professional acquaintance and the on-scene meetings constituted about a third of the meetings by the end of the period of study.

Clearly, there was no apparent shift in associational patterns that could account for the third generation of medical witnesses ignoring the forensic terms introduced by their fathers, and opting instead for their grandfathers' diagnoses. Even if one could chronicle some anomalous new forum—or the return of an old one, for example, 'professional' acquaintance—it would be important not to succumb to some essentialist notion of diagnosis: that medical interpretation is ineluctably framed by the physician and prisoner meeting in one setting rather than another. Aside from the rigidly reductive implication this would carry for the mechanics of crafting a diagnosis, one would also be drawing a shade over the subject sitting at the centre of the interview. Persons are not plants after all; they talk back, they migrate from initial diagnostic boxes to others, they may even challenge the observer to justify a diagnosis. Such confrontations could occasionally take place in the midst of a trial. In 1848, a defendant cross-examined prison surgeon McMurdo after his testimony, eliciting an admission that if his—the defendant's—account of the alleged assault was indeed accurate, 'delusion' could not possibly describe his mental state, leaving the medical witness without of a diagnosis.[28]

Taken together—interview setting, voluble 'subjects', changing professional association—the elements that produce a diagnosis become every bit as important

---

[28] *OBSP* 1853–54, 12th sess, case 1122, 1365–6. For another instance of a putatively insane defendant deriding the inference of the mad-doctor testifying at his trial—'you judge from ideas? You have a good opinion of yourself.' See *OBSP* 1813, 1st sess, case 11, 14.

to the historian of forensic medicine as the official name given to any particular ailment. That the evolution of these terms reveals not a linear, smooth progression in acceptance but rather a discontinuous lurching from later to earlier usage invites further speculation about what the medical witness was up to. With the exception of delusion—the medical term of preference throughout the century—no term was invoked more frequently than melancholia in late-19th-century efforts to house insanity in diagnosable medicine. Further, melancholia was something more than depression, a term one is likely to find in many trials, but one that was not a diagnosis or a discrete disease category. One did not suffer from depression in and of itself; it was rather a by-product of melancholia itself or described simply as a profoundly dejected temperament.

Analysis of courtroom testimony late in the 19th century reveals melancholia to have been a disease eminently conformable to lay notions of derangement. Melancholia could be folded directly into the most familiar of gender ailments, for example:

> the prisoner was suffering from puerperal melancholia, a form of mental disease not infrequently following childbirth ... persons suffering from that disease are fully aware of what they are doing ... very often the woman is seen to be affectionate a short time before the act—the suppression of milk is a frequent cause.[29]

Everything in this description was familiar to the Victorian jury except the conjoining of melancholia with puerperal insanity. The capacity to retain an awareness of what one was doing and the addition of 'homicidal impulses' served to give melancholia the substance of moral insanity without naming it as such, sidestepping the derision such 'clear-thinking' madness had elicited from the bench.[30] When one examines testimony in trials in which melancholia had no puerperal involvement (about half of the women defendants and obviously all of the men) one begins to suspect that medical witnesses were employing melancholia to continue courtroom inquiry into states of impaired mental functioning that did not directly implicate the intellectual faculties.

Even so, medical witnesses were adroitly reframing the law's criterion of cognitive impairment to conform to emotional and volitional derangement. They were therefore able to question explicitly the defendant's ability to distinguish right from wrong, describing prisoners as 'suffering from melancholia, so as not to know the quality of his acts'[31] or 'incapable of understanding the position in which he now is.'[32] Other physicians invoked the existence of suspended unconsciousness introduced earlier in the century but now conjoined with melancholia: 'it is quite possible for a woman in such circumstances to be unconscious of

---

[29] *OBSP* 1902–03, 11th sess, case 766, 1142.
[30] Cases that feature melancholia paired with homicidal 'tendencies' can be found in *OBSP* 1886–87, 8th sess, case 659; 1893–94, 6th sess, case 380; 1895–95, 12th sess, case 831.
[31] *OBSP* 1900–01, 11th sess, case 628, 788.
[32] *OBSP* 1901–02, 12th sess, case 702, 994.

her doings at times.'[33] Most often, medical witnesses in this third period left the legal consequences of melancholia implicit, but nonetheless vivid, coupling the newly recovered mental state with homicidal monomania—long familiar with the Old Bailey jury—or with acute mania.[34] In an age of instincts, uncontrollable impulses, and homicidal tendencies, the law's concern with knowing right from wrong was eclipsed not by moral insanity but by 'maniacal attacks of mania' coupled with melancholia.

The Utility of Melancholia

The greatest similarity between men and women said to suffer from melancholia was to be found in their victims: almost all targeted their own children. This was true for women, whether or not their melancholia was linked to reproduction. Men with the same diagnosis also targeted their children. The similarity with moral insanity was even closer in these cases: just as medical witnesses had cited a derangement of volition—a 'lesion of the will'—to account for senseless crime in the 1840s, so the following generation of forensic-psychiatrists invoked melancholia to frame the tragic event as an unintentional, involuntary response to a diseased impulse. That a loving and devoted parent could destroy those nearest and dearest had been central to mid-19th-century puerperal mania; it had not been standard feature of the few Victorian women who were described in court as melancholic, whatever the cause. And it was certainly not a feature of men's functioning; only by the end of the century does one find the treacherous, propelling forces of melancholia capable of animating such a motiveless attack.

The association of melancholia with homicidal as well as suicidal impulses would continue into the 20th century. In 1905, Henry Walter Poppel stood trial for the wilful murder of his two daughters, Violet and Ada. After slitting the throat of each, the prisoner had attempted to do away with himself by similar means, but the razor had apparently been dulled by the earlier attacks. Having survived the suicide attempt, he was taken to the police station and examined by a physician who informed the court that 'he did not seem conscious of his position—he was dull and rather apathetic—someone was cutting a bandage and the scissors were blunt—they remarked on it, and the prisoner said, "it is only fit for the scrapheap, like my razor."'[35]

The prisoner's general state of depressed mood was also mentioned by his wife at the trial, as well as the fact that he made no distinction between their own children and his stepchildren who also lived with them. This would become a matter

---

[33] *OBSP* 1900–01, 4th sess, case 172, 232.
[34] For the explicit pairing of melancholia with homicidal monomania, see *OBSP* 1890–91, 11th sess, case 727; 1892–93, 7th sess, case 482, and with homicidal mania, 1879–80. 7th sess, 428.
[35] *OBSP* 1904–05, 11th sess, case 708, 1543.

of importance in the lengthy medical evidence offered at his trial. Appearing in court to testify about the defendant's manifest melancholia was William Stoddart, assistant medical officer at Bethlem Hospital. His participation in the trial is noteworthy precisely because the testimony of asylum physicians had become increasingly rare in the early 20th century. Only 50 years before, physicians, surgeons, and apothecaries affiliated with asylums would brandish the professional experience gained from 'hundreds of patients' to confer authority to their diagnoses and to distance their insight not only from that of the lay person, but from the general practitioner.[36] By the late 1800s, however, the asylum doctor faded appreciably from the courtroom, replaced by the private practitioner who claims no particular expertise in the diagnosis and treatment of insanity. Perhaps this is a sign that professional training in mental medicine was so well accepted in the curriculum that no particular institutional apprenticeship was deemed necessary.

In the event, Dr Stoddart did not have to be coaxed to refer to his 'large experience in these matters, [having] been at Bethlem in my present position of for seven years.' He continued:

> I came to the conclusion that he was suffering from melancholia. ... [H]e had lost the natural instinct of self-preservation. ... [H]e told me he had intended to commit suicide for three days and that he did not intend to kill his children until the last minute when he was about to commit suicide, when he thought he could not leave his wife with the responsibility of raising these starving children—I did not think of the fact that he had killed his own children rather than his step children but it strikes me now that it is a natural instinct to preserve one's own offspring and that instinct had obviously gone—my opinion is that at the time he committed these acts he was prevented by mental disease from controlling his conduct.

On cross-examination, the medical witness reasserted that 'the natural instinct of self-preservation is inborn. ... I consider that a man who takes away the life of those he loves must do it from an insane point of view.'[37]

The association of melancholia with instincts was a novel combination, even for a court that was finding melancholia to be the most hospitable of diseases. Indeed, there were few forensic concepts—delusion, homicidal impulse, inability to know right from wrong—that could not be brought into melancholia's orbit. The innovative element in Dr Stoddart's testimony, however, was his pronouncement that natural instincts were overridden by 'mental disease'. Instincts were never mentioned in the trials of Victorian women who killed their children in the throes of puerperal mania; implicated instead was some as yet unnamed physiological reflex thought to be responsible for throwing children into the Thames or mixing poison in with their children's pudding. Melancholia had grown to be not only the second most frequently invoked disease category in late 19th century insanity trials after delusion, but a state of being that seemed in consequence to

---

[36] For an examination of the institutional affiliations of the first generation of forensic-psychiatric witnesses, see Eigen, above n 5, esp 122–32.
[37] *OBSP* 1904–05, 11th sess, case 708, 1547–8.

encompass a type of derangement, circumscribed to be sure since victimisation was likely to be confined to one target, but sufficiently robust to include men as well as women, and women with no reproductive involvement either.

That melancholia is given such a prominent place in Dr Stoddard's testimony underscores the emerging forum that brought medical man and the accused together: Bethlehem Hospital. As a medical officer of the most well known of mental institutions, Stoddard had the opportunity to examine and monitor the conversation and behaviour of a range of patients, a frequently invoked professional vantage point articulated by medical witnesses in insanity trials throughout the Victorian era. But it was not only a hospital physician who drew upon his experience to articulate melancholia and its features in relation to crime. In the years that witnessed the re-emergence, indeed, the near-dominance of melancholia in the witness box, it was the prison surgeon and physician who conveyed the term to the Old Bailey. By far the most frequently appearing medical witness was John Scott, medical officer at Holloway and later Brixton Prison. The noteworthy aspect of his participation in the trials, and that of his fellow prison physicians, is that they would appear for either the prosecution or the defence. In contrast to their forebear—Newgate surgeon Gilbert McMurdo—who almost always supported the State's case that the defendant was sane, Scott and his peers appeared for the defence in almost half of the trials in which they testified.

In terms of professional dynamic, this was remarkable. These men were paid by the Corporation for the City of London, and there could be little doubt regarding how their employers wished them to testify. But their employment did not preclude their appearing for the defence, with or without a subpoena. Even when they appeared for the state, they were fully capable of finding a sufficient level of insanity owing to the ravages of melancholia. Of course, they could also refute the evidence of the defence's medical witness. Still, the observation that they might just as easily deduce a level of derangement that in their opinion precluded the defendant's capacity to know what she was about or if she did, to understand why it was wrong, suggests that the social setting that witnessed the doctor/prisoner interaction also contributed to an increasingly self assured attitude toward the medical witness's professionalism. This is the reason why careful scrutiny of courtroom testimony is so critical to the effort to recreate the emergence of this new professional role. A simple frequency distribution of 'how the prisoner met the doctor' could easily obscure the emerging professional independence of the prison doctor, for all his numerical dominance.

That they were employed by the prison—or in receipt of a particular order by the Secretary of the Treasury to visit a prisoner suspected of being likely to raise an insanity plea—only ensured their participation at the trial. A review of the courtroom testimony suggests not only a level of professional independence, but that the sustained familiarity with the prisoner, the capacity to gauge the level of derangement against the population in the prison, the ability to witness behaviour over time, appears to have insulated the physician from institutionally-generated expectations, providing a setting for the proffering of opinion informed by work experiences and an evolving conception of the ravages of an emotionally-based insanity. This is not to argue that all the medical observer did was to 'read' madness in the behaviour of the mad; it is to suggest that sustained contact and a capacity to position particular manifestations of derangement against a spectrum of distracted people might well have framed the diagnostic categories that emerged in the late 19th century.[38]

Sustained attention to an emerging independence on the part of forensic-psychiatric witnesses does not of course account for melancholia's return specifically, although one begins to suspect that contemporary notions of derangement may well have helped shape the medical gaze. For the greater part of the Victorian era, medical writers—and not a few medical witnesses—endeavoured to account for crime that had no meaning in the context of purposeful behaviour. Motiveless criminality that left the offender vulnerable to criminal punishment for an outrage he or she had no particular interest in committing had progressed from moral insanity to forms of unconscious crime. Each served its time upon the stage—the witness box—and then was heard, practically, no more. For all the worry that attended the supposed introduction of 'partial insanity' after the acquittal of James Hadfield in 1800, the Old Bailey judiciary had remained almost unanimously opposed to a defence based on impaired will, greeting a defence of the prisoner's action in such a frame with adamantine rejection.

The *OBSP* reveal, however, that this visceral rejection was not always shared by the jury. Though particular terms fall from favour, the widely shared sentiments regarding uncontrollable impulses found resonance with long standing cultural beliefs about disturbance in mood and the failure of self-control. Medical witnesses were able to enlist these beliefs by initially fashioning the diagnoses of moral insanity—with lesion of the will being perhaps the most graphic—all in an effort to challenge the law's insistence that delusion laid at the heart of insanity.

A review of medical testimony over time therefore reveals that the possibility that involuntary action lay at the root of some forms of criminal behaviour, revealed most clearly in the choice of victim more than anything else, found its way into the courtroom under a series of diagnoses. The law has a way of working itself into a conceptual corner when jurists insist that intentional resolve should sit at the heart of assigning culpability. The first sign of the court's inability to accommodate purposeless crime was moral insanity, followed in turn by automatic states of functioning that seemed to separate the defendant from the perpetrator. Further into the 19th and early into the 20th centuries, instincts appear to frame the same purposeless, self-destructive actions, symbolised by the murder of beloved children, surely a more searing sort of suicide than anything a felon could do to herself. In many ways, it was the very inexplicability of the crime that gave melancholia its newfound berth in this latest incarnation of medical testimony.

---

[38] This point has also been made in reference to the origin and defence of monomania among French clinicians. JP Eigen, 'A mania for diagnosis: unravelling the aims of nineteenth-century French psychiatrists' (1989) 2 *Journal of the History of the Human Sciences* 241.

This last phase of research had been envisioned as a way to examine whether the imagery of unconscious crime—so apparent in the years running up to the 1876 'not guilty on the grounds of unconsciousness'—could anticipate Freud's reworking of the unconscious as something more than a storehouse of forgotten memory links. Certainly one does not expect to find 'repressed hostility' articulated at the Old Bailey; even today's medical witness would venture very gingerly into a defence based on unconscious motivation. But one had to be surprised to find an association of instincts with melancholia in Old Bailey testimony, years before Freud published his seminal essay, *Mourning and Melancholia*. Although natural, it is perhaps ultimately not terribly important to try to decide which influenced which: do insights flow from the courtroom to the clinic, or do ideas take the opposite route? Rather than try to track the odyssey of pathological categories, it might be more fruitful to use both as indicators of larger cultural questions.

Just as the mid-19th-century's anxiety about a 'will out of control' could be found in popular literature, tracts on population theory and publications of 'social statistics', so the same disquiet could be discerned in species of derangement that attacked the will separately, infecting it with a lesion capable of carrying the afflicted 'quite away'.[39] By the end of the Victorian era, instincts appear prominently in the critical forums of the clinic and the courtroom. Although 'lesion of the will' had managed to mix metaphysical and physical imagery together, few really believed that the will had a suppurating character all its own. Instincts, however, carried the suggestion of materialism. It would appear that the threat they posed to free will and voluntary choice would engage fundamental issues of responsibility on an entirely more significant plane.

---

[39] MJ Weiner, *Reconstructing the Criminal: Culture, Law, and Policy in England, 1830–1914* (Cambridge, CUP, 1990) esp 14–45.

6

Speaking Out about Staying Silent: An Historical Examination of Medico-legal Debates over the Boundaries of Medical Confidentiality

ANGUS H FERGUSON

Medical confidentiality has always been stressed, in theory at least, as a central part of ethical medicine—a cornerstone of the doctor–patient relationship, playing an important role in efficient and effective medical practice.[1] The understanding that the doctor will respect the patient's confidentiality is intended to encourage patients to divulge all information which may be relevant to the diagnosis and treatment of their ailment without fear that the information will be misused. Professional codes of medical practice have always stressed the importance of respecting the confidentiality of the doctor–patient encounter. From the time of the Hippocratic Oath this ideal has been incorporated in the words:

> Whatsoever I shall see or hear in the course of my profession, as well as outside my profession in my intercourse with man, if it be what should not be published abroad, I will never divulge, holding such things to be holy secrets.[2]

In practice, the respect given to this principle has varied according to both the context of the medical consultation, and the relative importance of public interest in the information learned by the doctor during it.[3]

---

[1] The current law on medical confidentiality can be summarised as recognising, in both common law and statute, an obligation of confidence within the doctor–patient relationship. However, this does not extend to recognition of a privilege to non-disclosure of such confidences during court proceedings. For further information see chapter 8 of I Kennedy and A Grubb, *Medical Law*, 3rd edn (London, Butterworths, 2000); and chapter 8 of JK Mason and GT Laurie, *Mason and McCall Smith's Law and Medical Ethics*, 7th edn (Oxford, OUP, 2006).

[2] There are many variants on the wording of the Hippocratic Oath, this version is taken from CJ McFadden, *Medical Ethics* (London, Burns and Oates, 1962) 366. It should also be noted that no professional body existed to enforce the ideals incorporated in the oath.

[3] While the level of privacy which a patient received during his or her consultation was dependent on the context of that consultation—a wealthy patient, able to pay for a consultation in their own home, enjoying greater privacy than a patient obtaining treatment in the more public surroundings of a barber shop—the obligation of confidentiality related to the doctor's use of the information once obtained, regardless of the context.

Their professional position entails that doctors learn information of interest to other parties, be it patients' relatives, employers, the government or the law. While the ideal of medical confidentiality emphasised the importance of respecting the confidentiality of the individual patient, during the course of the 19th and 20th centuries this emphasis was challenged by the rise of interest in, and focus on, the collective.[4] With growing concern about public health, and national concerns about issues such as abortion, doctors found themselves at the centre of an increasingly complex set of competing agendas on the use of medical information. Over this period, a history of debate, disagreement, even open confrontation, between medicine and the law on the issue can be discerned. From legislation compelling the notification of contagious or infectious diseases, through to judicial demands for medical testimony in court, the law challenged, and doctors defended, the boundaries of medical confidentiality. Added edge was given to these discussions by the fact that the confidentiality of the doctor–patient relationship has never gained the protected status enjoyed by lawyers and their clients. This chapter demonstrates some of the ways in which the medical profession attempted to gain judicial recognition of medical privilege during the early 20th century.

The multifarious and changing contexts of medical practice—from private practitioners to public medical officers of health, ship surgeons to consultants at venereal disease clinics—as well as the various demands which can be placed on medical information—by patients, their relatives, employers, public health bodies and the law—made establishing comprehensive rules on medical confidentiality an exceptionally difficult task. Arguments about doctors' civic duty versus their professional duty were juxtaposed with debates over the importance of medical confidentiality to public health measures or the utility of medical evidence in the law courts. Examination of the history of debates over medical confidentiality illustrates that such issues and agendas do not form a neat dialectic, with doctors defending the importance of confidentiality against legal encroachment in a series of debates over specific issues. Rather, issues overlap and professional agendas are muddled by sub-groupings and interests. As the examples discussed later in this chapter demonstrate, public health doctors normally interested in the breach of confidentiality for the notification of infectious disease could emphasise the importance of maintaining confidentiality to the treatment of sexually transmitted diseases. Lawyers could at times be found supporting the case for a stronger recognition of medical confidentiality.[5] The historical debates have been further clouded by additional considerations: from issues of professional status and inter-professional rivalry; through the self-interest and needs of individual medical practitioners to breach confidentiality to mount a defence in malpractice

---

[4] The shift away from laissez faire, towards legislation based upon collectivist ideology had implications in a number of fields including medicine. See, eg the introduction to AV Dicey, *Lectures on the Relation Between Law and Public Opinion in England During the Nineteenth Century*, 2nd edn (London, Macmillan, 1962).

[5] See for instance the views of the *Law Journal* after a case in the early 1920s; see n 82.

cases; to the pecuniary interests of doctors in maintaining a public perception of professional integrity in a competitive medical marketplace. As a result, the history of medical confidentiality is a complex array of overlapping issues, interest groups and individuals, fluid in time and location—from courtroom showdowns between judges and medical witnesses, to private meetings and correspondence between key representatives of the medical and legal points of view. Only a taste of these formal and informal interactions can be given in the space of a chapter. Two examples will be discussed, the first relating to the notification of abortion around the turn of the 20th century, the second focussing on the debate over medical privilege in the early interwar years.

These examples are selected from the period around the turn of the 20th century into the 1920s—a period of intense debate on the subject of medical confidentiality, reflecting broader changes in the medical and legal worlds at the time. As Catherine Crawford has noted, modern scholarship has focussed on the changing power relationship between medicine and law. She notes: 'In Foucault's influential analysis, "juridical power" (that of a sovereign) has, during the past few centuries, been overtaken in significance by "biopower" (the power of the norm), a process that has tended to enhance the power and importance of medicine'.[6] This rise in medical power inspired confidence amongst the medical profession to challenge legal authority on its demands for medical information. The examples discussed in this chapter highlight the implications of the changing structure of medical practice and growing political interest in, and influence on, medical matters. During this period, medicine was moving from an individually-minded, competitive, and private market place, towards an environment which increasingly emphasised collectively-funded and oriented healthcare in the form of national insurance and public health doctors. Measures such as Acts compelling the notification of infectious disease, required doctors to override the confidentiality of the individual patient in favour of the collective interest of the community.[7] While statute law was placing greater demands on medical information, the opening up of the civil law system to larger sections of society was also posing a challenge to medical confidentiality. Doctors were frequently subpoenaed to give evidence in the flood of civil divorce cases in the aftermath of World War I. Although circumstances had changed considerably in the intervening years, doctors who wished to assert medical privilege in such cases were bound by a common law precedent set in the latter half of the 18th century, which forbade it.[8] That case was The Duchess of Kingston's Trial for Bigamy.

---

[6] C Crawford, 'Medicine and the Law' in WF Bynum and R Porter (eds), *Companion Encyclopedia of the History of Medicine* (London, Routledge, 1993) 1619.

[7] G Mooney, 'Public Health versus Private Practice: The Contested Development of Compulsory Infectious Disease Notification in Late Nineteenth Century Britain' (1999) 73 *Bulletin of the History of Medicine* 238.

[8] 'Medical privilege' refers in this context to the ability of doctors to refuse to give evidence in court on grounds that it would constitute a breach of patient confidentiality.

The Duchess of Kingston's Trial for Bigamy

The modern law on medical confidentiality in Britain is built upon the precedent set by Lord Mansfield in the trial of the Duchess of Kingston for bigamy in 1776. Heard in the House of Lords, the case revolved around whether Elizabeth Chudleigh, Duchess Dowager of Kingston, had committed bigamy by marrying the Duke of Kingston whilst she was already secretly married to Augustus John Harvey, the Earl of Bristol.[9] Amongst the list of witnesses called to testify during the case was Caesar Hawkins, surgeon to King George III and a friend to both Elizabeth Chudleigh and Augustus John Harvey. When called on to answer questions regarding the nature of his friends' relationship, Hawkins protested that he was bound to non-disclosure by medical confidentiality, stating: 'I do not know how far any thing, that has come before me in a confidential trust in my profession, should be disclosed, consistent with my professional honour.'[10] Elsewhere I have argued that this protest was both inaccurate and motivated by Hawkins's personal desire to further his interests by portraying himself as a gentleman of honour.[11] The information he was asked to disclose had not been learned in his capacity as a medical man but rather in his position as a friend and confidant of the couple. Nonetheless, his claim to medical privilege provoked the Lord Chief Justice, Lord Mansfield, into stating that doctors had no authority to claim medical privilege:

> [T]o save your Lordships the trouble of an adjournment, if no Lord differs in opinion, but thinks that a surgeon has no privilege to avoid giving evidence in a court of justice, but is bound by the law of the land to do it; (if any of your Lordships think he has such a privilege, it will be a matter to be debated elsewhere, but) if all your Lordships acquiesce, Mr Hawkins will understand that it is your judgement and opinion, that a surgeon has no privilege, where it is a material question, in a civil or criminal cause, to know whether parties were married, or whether a child was born, to say, that his introduction to the parties was in the course of his profession, and that in that way he came to knowledge of it. ... If a surgeon was voluntarily to reveal these secrets, to be sure he would be guilty of a breach of honour, and of a great indiscretion; but, to give that information in a court of justice, which by the law of the land he is bound to do, will never be imputed to him as any indiscretion whatever.[12]

Although this point was not the central question on which the case was argued, or decided, the wide reporting of the case led to a common perception amongst medics and lawyers that there was no privilege of medical confidentiality. As

---

[9] A highly controversial figure in her lifetime, Elizabeth Chudleigh has received much attention from biographers, most recently in C Gervat, *Elizabeth. The Scandalous Life of the Duchess of Kingston* (London, Century, 2003).

[10] *The Trial of Elizabeth Duchess Dowager of Kingston for Bigamy* (London, Bathurst, 1776) 119.

[11] AH Ferguson, 'The Lasting Legacy of a Bigamous Duchess: The Benchmark Precedent for Medical Confidentiality' (2006) 19 *Social History of Medicine* 37.

[12] Above n 10, 120.

such, it became the foundation for the common law approach to medical confidentiality in Britain in the course of the 19th century.[13]

However, the 18th century medical profession which Hawkins represented, and which the court's ruling bound, underwent significant changes during the course of the 19th and early 20th centuries. From the individualistic world of competitive private practice, developments in medical education, organisation, and practice produced a more coherent body of practitioners operating both within private practice and the growing number of collective, and, with the introduction of National Insurance in 1911, partially publicly-funded, healthcare schemes.

Changes in medical education in the century after the Duchess of Kingston's trial reflected the growing understanding of medicine and disease based on pathological anatomy, and latterly incorporating germ theory.[14] The old three-tiered hierarchy of physicians, surgeons and apothecaries, gave way to a binary distinction between general practitioners and increasingly specialised consultants attached to hospitals.[15] The Medical Act 1858 established a register of qualified practitioners as well as the General Medical Council with disciplinary powers over registered members of the profession.[16] Professional organisations, such

---

[13] A number of printed accounts of the trial were produced in addition to the 1776 account cited above, n 10. See F Hargrave, *A Complete Collection of State Trials vol 11* (London, 1781); TB Howell, *A Complete Collection of State Trials* (London, 1816); L Melville, *Notable British Trials* (Edinburgh, W Hodge, 1927 and 1996 reprint). It is still cited as the earliest case in textbooks on the subject. For modern citations of the importance of the precedent see F Gurry, *Breach of Confidence* (Oxford, Clarendon Press, 1984) 352; JV McHale *Medical Confidentiality and Legal Privilege* (London, Routledge, 1993) 13. McHale's work is in turn cited on the issue of medical privilege by M Brazier, *Medicine, Patients and the Law*, 3rd edn (London, Penguin, 2003) 72; I Kennedy and A Grubb, *Medical Law: Text with Materials* (London, Butterworths, 2000) 1061. For recognition of the precedent by historians of medicine see AAG Morrice, '"Should the Doctor Tell?": Medical Secrecy in Early Twentieth-Century Britain' in S Sturdy (ed), *Medicine, Health and the Public Sphere in Britain 1600–2000* (London, Routledge, 2002) 64; AH Maehle, 'Protecting Patient Privacy or Serving Public Interests? Challenges to Confidentiality in Imperial Germany' (2003) 16 *Social History of Medicine* 400. It should be noted that as the ruling was part of a criminal trial it was not binding under Scots' law. However, in the absence of any specific Scottish case on the point, the court's ruling was generally acknowledged to hold in Scotland too. See Ferguson, above n 11, 47–8.

[14] See, eg C Brooks and P Cranefield, *The Historical Development of Physiological Thought* (New York, Hafner, 1959); T Gelfand, *Professionalizing Modern Medicine: Paris Surgeons and Medical Science and Institutions in the Eighteenth Century* (Westport, Greenwood Press, 1980); R French and A Wear, *British Medicine in an Age of Reform* (London, Routledge, 1991); WF Bynum, *Science and the Practice of Medicine in the Nineteenth Century* (Cambridge, CUP, 1994); K Codell Carter, *The Rise of Causal Concepts of Disease* (Aldershot, Ashgate, 2003); though it should be stressed that more traditional ideas of medicine, tied in with questions of social status and honour, persisted into the twentieth century, see C Lawrence, 'Incommunicable Knowledge: Science, Technology and the Clinical Art in Britain 1850–1914' (1985) 20 *Journal of Contemporary History* 503.

[15] See, eg I Waddington, *The Medical Profession in the Industrial Revolution* (Dublin, Gill and Macmillan, 1984); WF Bynum and R Porter, *Medical Fringe and Medical Orthodoxy 1750–1850* (London, Croom Helm, 1987).

[16] Medical Act 1858. For details regarding the GMC see, eg RG Smith, 'Legal Precedent and Medical Ethics: Some Problems Encountered by the General Medical Council in Relying Upon Precedent When Declaring Acceptable Standards of Professional Conduct' in R Baker (ed) *The Codification of Medical Morality (vol 2)* (Dordrecht, Kluwer Academic Publishers, 1995) 205–218; RG Smith, 'The Development of Ethical Guidance for Medical Practitioners by the General Medical Council' (1993) 37 *Medical History* 56.

as the British Medical Association (BMA), aimed to represent the interests of a larger section of the profession than the Royal Colleges had done in the past.[17] Periodicals such as *The Lancet* and the *British Medical Journal* provided a forum in which doctors could air their views, and, in the case of the latter, a mouthpiece with which the BMA could shape the opinions of the profession on topical issues—including medical confidentiality.[18] In Roy Porter's words, Thomas Wakley, the founder of *The Lancet*, 'battled to raise medicine into a respected profession, with structured, regulated entry and lofty ethical ideals'.[19] One consequence of these ongoing medical developments was increased patient faith in the doctor, based on the ability of the latter to diagnose more accurately and give a prognosis for disease. As Edward Shorter notes, even before the new understanding of disease had been translated into effective therapeutics: 'doctors in the modern period often involved themselves in counseling patients in intimate problems, indeed presuming to advise society as a whole in a wholly unfamiliar extension of this new medical authority'.[20]

However, if the 19th-century changes produced progress towards a more coherent and more authoritative medical profession, demands for medical information also increased with the state's growing agenda in public health. Large cities, such as Liverpool and Glasgow, employed a medical officer of health, whose task it was to improve the health of the local population, prioritising the collective welfare over private doctors' interest in individual patients. The growing interest in producing statistics on the health of local and national populations, and the ensuing attempts to tackle diseases of particular concern, posed challenges for doctors.[21] Increasingly, statute laws stressed the doctor's duty to the collective interests of society, reflecting concerns about public health and national efficiency at a time of international economic and military competition. Yet, while doctors were increasingly being used as tools for information gathering and surveillance by the state, most still relied on private paying patients as their main source of income. It is notable that in the lead up to the introduction of National Insurance and the National Health Service, large numbers of doctors expressed concern about becoming, in effect, civil servants.[22] General practitioners were particularly concerned about the potential loss of their autonomy, and while their concerns were in large part focussed on financial considerations, the change in status also carried implications for their relative obligations to the patient and the state. The

---

[17] P Bartrip, *Themselves Writ Large: the British Medical Association 1832–1966* (London, BMJ, 1996).
[18] P Bartrip, *Mirror of Medicine: a History of the British Medical Association* (Oxford, Clarendon Press, 1990).
[19] R Porter, *The Greatest Benefit to Mankind* (London, HarperCollins, 1997) 351.
[20] E Shorter, 'The History of the doctor–patient relationship' in Bynum and Porter, above n 6, 791.
[21] For background information see E Higgs, *Life, Death and Statistics: Civil Registration, Censuses and the Work of the General Register Office, 1836–1952* (Hatfield, Local Population Studies, 2004).
[22] C Webster, *The National Health Service: A Political History* (Oxford, OUP, 1998) 9–11, 27–8.

confidentiality of the doctor–patient encounter was one way of exploring, testing and negotiating these relationships and defining the evolving medical profession's role in a rapidly changing society.

Starting with Graham Mooney's work on infectious disease notification legislation in the later 19th-century, Andrew Morrice has traced the evolution of legal demands on doctors to breach confidentiality in the key areas of abortion and venereal disease (VD).[23] Both issues provide an interesting juxtaposition of medical and legal authority. Statute law classified abortion as an illegal operation, though there was an exception for cases of therapeutic abortion.[24] What constituted therapeutic abortion was largely determined by medical opinion, giving doctors a deal of authority in determining how the law on the matter was applied in individual cases. Similarly the renewal of state interest in the question of VD was stimulated, in part, by advances in medical understanding, diagnosis and treatment of syphilis in the first decade of the 20th century. Yet, while medicine's growing authority on both these matters seemed to enhance the profession's power and standing, the law showed a determination to subjugate medical interest to legal interest, by imposing demands for medical information against the will of doctors. It is the tension produced by these competing medical and legal agendas, which provides the subject matter for the following two case studies.

Notification of Abortion

While judges of the 18th century held considerable power to make the law through their rulings in individual cases, by the late 19th century, Parliament had become a much more active law-making body, making greater use of its legislative power. Consequently, the task of the judge increasingly became the interpretation of growing amounts of statute law. As the government took a keener interest in the health of the population, more and more legislation was enacted which affected medical practitioners. However, as the example of notification of abortion demonstrates, legal interpretation of the doctor's duty was not always clear and consistent—causing confusion for doctors as to their position under the law.

In Britain, the Offences Against the Person Act 1861 established severe penalties for women, and any accomplice, who procured an illegal abortion. Section 67 of the Act set out punishments for anyone considered as an accessory before or after any felony contained in the Act, and included the words: 'whosoever shall

---

[23] See Mooney, above n 7, 241; Morrice, above n 13.
[24] What constituted an illegal as opposed to a therapeutic abortion was a penumbral area of law. See B Brookes, *Abortion in England 1900–1967* (London, Croom Helm, 1988) 22–78; B Brookes and P Roth, '*Rex v Bourne* and the Medicalisation of Abortion' in M Clark and C Crawford (eds), *Legal Medicine in History* (Cambridge, CUP, 1994) 314–43; J Keown, *Abortion, Doctors and the Law* (Cambridge, CUP, 1988) 49–83.

counsel, aid or abet the commission of any indictable misdemeanour punishable under this Act shall be liable to be proceeded against, indicted and punished as a principal offender'.[25] Doctors were most likely to come into contact with women suffering ill-effects from the operations carried out by backstreet abortionists and there was some debate as to whether their involvement could be regarded as making them accessories after the fact if they did not report the crime to the police. While doctors were quick to condemn unqualified abortionists, they were often reluctant to inform on women who had survived the risks associated with illegal termination—believing it would deter such women from seeking necessary medical assistance from qualified practitioners.[26] Furthermore, judges were inconsistent in their views on the importance of notification. Professor John Glaister, an expert in medico-legal issues and author of *Medical Jurisprudence and Toxicology*, indicated that while the law was generally understood by medical practitioners to impose on them a duty to notify the authorities of cases in which illegal abortion was suspected, the view expressed by the judge during *Kitson v Playfair* (1896) had 'traversed that understanding'.[27] In this highly-publicised case, the royal accoucheur, William Smoult Playfair, was found guilty of slander and fined £12,000 after he disclosed to his brother-in-law, Sir James Kitson, his suspicion that Sir James' sister-in-law, Linda Kitson, had recently had an abortion or miscarriage.[28] Given that Linda Kitson's husband had been in Australia for the previous 15 months, Playfair's allegation carried an implicit accusation of adultery. As Angus McLaren has shown, the trial resulted from an accusation of slander against Playfair and notification of abortion was not directly at issue. Nonetheless, the judge, Henry Hawkins, did comment on a distinction he perceived between the letter and the spirit of the law. In court he effectively suggested that the law should be ignored if a doctor believed that a woman had acted with good intention when procuring an illegal abortion and was making a good recovery.[29] However, this was an expression of opinion on a matter not at issue in the trial, obiter dicta rather than a ruling, and held no formal authority.[30] Nonetheless, as Glaister noted, such

---

[25] Offences Against the Person Act 1861 s 67.

[26] The exceptions to this reluctance to notify were cases where the effects of the illegal termination were so severe that the patient seemed likely to die. In such circumstances doctors were inclined to regard the threat to future women using the same abortionist as of utmost importance, and notification was more likely. As the case of Annie Hodgkiss, discussed below, demonstrates, the difficulty of predicting the survival of each patient made this far from an exact science.

[27] J Glaister, *Glaister's Medical Jurisprudence and Toxicology*, 6th edn (Edinburgh, E and S Livingstone, 1938) 358. There is no official transcript of the case, only a report in *The Times* (see n 28).

[28] While there is no official transcript of this case, the coverage in *The Times* indicates that, at his wife's request, Playfair made the disclosure to his brother-in-law. *The Times* 26 March 1896, 13.

[29] A McLaren, 'Privileged Communications: Medical Confidentiality in Late Victorian Britain' (1993) 37 *Medical History* 145.

[30] Obiter dicta refers to judicial opinion expressed during a case which does not form part of the official ruling on the issue in question. As such, it is not binding, however it can have persuasive authority on issues on which no prior ruling has been made.

statements served to confuse doctors in relation to their duty to notify cases of illegal abortion.

In an attempt to clarify the position, the Royal College of Physicians held a consultation on the issue in 1896. As part of this process, opinions were sought from two lawyers: Sir Edward Clarke[31] and Horace Avory[32]. Avory and Clarke indicated that doctors were permitted to carry out abortions, before or during birth, where the mother's life was at risk; that they should treat medically, but in no other way assist, women who came to them after a criminal abortion; and that there was no absolute obligation to notify the law in such cases. One of the attendees at this consultation was Professor Robert Saundby, a fellow of the Royal College of Physicians and chairman of the British Medical Association council. In 1902 he published a textbook entitled *Medical Ethics: A Guide to Professional Conduct*, which became a key text in the development of BMA policy on many ethical issues.[33] In his section on confidentiality, Saundby followed the line of thought which Clarke and Avory had given to the Royal College of Physicians, stating that the requirement to disclose had been:

> to the effect that a medical man should not reveal facts which had come to his knowledge in the course of his professional duties, even in so extreme a case as where there are grounds to suspect that a criminal offence had been committed.[34]

In 1914, Avory sat as judge in the prosecution of Annie Hodgkiss for the manslaughter of Ellen Armstrong.[35] Hodgkiss was alleged to have performed an illegal abortion on Armstrong, who, having taken ill as a result, was admitted to the Birmingham Women's Hospital. She was visited there by her family's physician, referred to in the trial as Dr A.[36] During the visit, Armstrong told Dr A that she had undergone an abortion and gave the name of the woman who had performed it. She explicitly asked Dr A not to tell anyone, a promise Dr A considered binding. Armstrong subsequently, and very abruptly, died of a haemorrhage. Having examined the details of the case, Avory was forced to conclude that in the absence of evidence, such as a dying deposition from Armstrong naming Hodgkiss as the abortionist, the case could not proceed. Avory was clearly frustrated by these circumstances, because they prevented him from using this case as an opportunity to clarify the law on medical confidentiality. When instructing the jury, therefore,

---

[31] Clarke (1841–1931) was a pre-eminent Queen's Counsel and Member of Parliament for Plymouth. He was appointed Solicitor General in 1886 and held the post until the fall of Lord Salisbury's government in 1892. When Salisbury returned to power in 1895, Clarke turned down the position of Solicitor-General to concentrate on private practice and in 1897 he declined an offer to become Master of the Rolls.

[32] Having 'devilled' for Clarke as a junior counsel, Avory (1851–1935) became a King's Counsel in 1901 and by 1910 was a judge on the King's Bench Division of the High Court.

[33] R Saundby, *Medical Ethics: A Guide to Professional Conduct* (Bristol, Wright, 1902).

[34] R Saundby, *Medical Ethics: A Guide to Professional Conduct*, 2nd edn (London, Charles Griffin, 1907) 114.

[35] Birmingham Assizes, 1 December 1914, [78 JP 604].

[36] 'Medicine and the Law. A Judge on Professional Secrecy' (1914) 184 *The Lancet* 1430.

he emphasised that Saundby's textbook misrepresented the opinion he and Clarke had given to the Royal College of Physicians in 1896. The implication was that, in Avory's opinion, doctors did have a clear obligation to notify and that, in the case before him, Dr A had failed to perform the duty required of him.[37]

This opinion was picked up by Sir Charles Mathews, Director of Public Prosecutions, who wrote to William Hempson, solicitor to the BMA, requesting that Avory's views be given wide circulation amongst the medical profession in order that they might correct the 'inaccuracy' of Saundby's book.[38] Hempson was reluctant to comply, citing the contradictory positions taken by judges in previous cases, notably *Kitson v Playfair*, as a reason not to be dictated to by Avory's views.[39] When they met at Whitehall later that month, Mathews emphasised to Hempson that doctors 'were citizens of the state, [and] that as such they owed a higher duty to the state in aid of the suppression of crime than to their patient.'[40] Furthermore he indicated that the Lord Chief Justice[41] had considered and expressed approval of Avory's views and, as chief coroner, had proposed that a copy should be sent to every coroner in England and Wales 'as a guiding light as to the attitude which it was their duty to adopt should similar cases arise at any inquest before them.'[42] Hempson could only have been left with the impression that, while contradictory views had been expressed in the past, there was a growing uniformity of opinion amongst key legal figures that doctors should be made aware of their ultimate duty to the state and their necessary contribution to the ends of justice.

However, if Mathews believed that the weight of his argument and the support of the Lord Chief Justice would be sufficient to cause the BMA to capitulate under pressure, he was mistaken. In January 1915, the BMA council, having drawn on the discussions and proposals of its central ethical committee, adopted resolutions demonstrating its opposition to the legal viewpoint.[43] The first indicated that doctors should not give out information without patient consent. The second declared that the state had no authority to claim that doctors were obliged to disclose patient information. The third proposed sending a copy of these resolutions

---

[37] While this appears to contradict the views attributed to him during his earlier consultation with the Royal College of Physicians, it is possible that his view on the notification of abortion was dependent on the likely fate of the woman involved: see above n 24 and n 26. His criticism of Dr A would therefore stem from the latter's failure to notify in a case where the woman was at high risk of dying as a result of an illegal abortion. This interpretation is similar to that given by Mason and Laurie, above n 1, 260.

[38] This, and all following BMA references, comes from the archive of the British Medical Association, BMA House, Tavistock Square, London. British Medical Association Central Ethical Committee (BMA CEC) minutes, Mathews to Hempson 14 December 1914.

[39] BMA CEC minutes, Hempson to Mathews 15 December 1914.

[40] BMA CEC minutes, Hempson's report of meeting with Mathews at Whitehall 22 December 1914.

[41] Rufus Isaacs, Lord Reading.

[42] BMA CEC minutes, Hempson's report of meeting with Mathews at Whitehall 22 December 1914.

[43] For a fuller discussion in the lead up to the adoption of the council's resolutions see AH Ferguson, *Should a Doctor Tell? Medical Confidentiality in Interwar England and Scotland* (unpublished PhD thesis, University of Glasgow) 53–9.

to the relevant department of state and further ventilating the issue in the medical press. While the first two resolutions made clear that the BMA had no intention of responding in a conciliatory manner to the judiciary's attempt to impose its will on doctors, the last was a deliberate affront to the Director of Public Prosecutions. Throughout his correspondence and meetings with Hempson, Mathews had stipulated that the matter should be kept private and away from the press. Thus, the BMA resolutions were not only denying state authority over doctors to compel notification of abortion, they were advocating a ventilation of the whole question in the medical press against the expressed wishes of the Director of Public Prosecutions. The gauntlet laid down by Avory and Mathews had been taken up by the BMA which showed no intention of pulling its punches.

With both sides holding firm to their position, and poised on the verge of confrontation, the question was in hiatus by summer 1915 when the disruption caused by the First World War engaged the resources of the BMA, which undertook the organisation of medical provision for the war effort.[44] While medical confidentiality in cases of abortion was more or less sidelined as an issue as the war enveloped attention, the differences between legal and medical opinion, on the relative merits of the doctor's duty to the patient and the state, pointed towards a reigniting of controversy in the near future. The episode reveals a number of important factors in the debate over medical confidentiality. Initially at least, the position on notification of abortion was not clear. The obligation on doctors to notify the crime was blurred both by the opinions expressed by legal figures such as Hawkins or Avory and Clarke, and by doctors' own sense of what should be done. When, in 1915, the judiciary sought to impose on doctors an obligation to notify cases of abortion, they stressed the doctor's duty to the state and the ends of justice, which, from a legal perspective, overrode any duty to the patient. Yet, far from capitulating to legal pressure, the medical profession strove to reassert the importance of medical confidentiality and, in its third resolution, the BMA demonstrated a willingness to rally its members and fight against legal encroachment. When the debate resumed in the early interwar years, notification of VD cases had surpassed abortion as the key issue under dispute and the establishment of the Ministry of Health added a new voice to the discussions.

Confidentiality of VD Treatment

The English divorce courts were a key arena in which the law, public health policy and medical tradition came into confrontation over the boundaries of medical confidentiality in the early 1920s. A sharp rise in the number of divorce petitions following the First World War, coupled with the importance of medical evidence

---

[44] Bartrip, above n 17, 181.

of VD in many of these cases, placed medical confidentiality as an obstacle to the rapid processing of the growing backlog of divorce hearings.[45] As a result, individual divorce cases became battlegrounds for competing medical and legal ideas about confidentiality and public interest. Andrew Morrice's examination of the key issues tackled by the Central Ethical Committee of the British Medical Association in the first half of the 20th century provides a taste of this confrontation.[46] However, while Morrice charts the increasing polarisation of medical and legal views on VD testimony in divorce cases, the apparent absence of a courtroom showdown on the issue leaves an unsatisfactory 'anti-climax' to Morrice's account.[47] What follows demonstrates that such a showdown was closer to being realised than has hitherto been acknowledged. While, at first, the case of *Needham v Needham* (1921)[48] does not appear to be significant, closer examination reveals how near the medical witness came to an outright refusal of the court's demand to give evidence—risking contempt of court and going to prison as a medical martyr.

Developments in Government policy on VD in the second decade of the 20th century represented the first concerted political effort to tackle the problem since the Contagious Disease Acts of the 1860s.[49] David Evans notes that, as well as moral concerns and pressures from social hygienists, the renewal of medical interest in VD was stimulated by developments in medical knowledge in the first decade of the 20th century—from the identification of the causative organism in syphilis, through Wasserman's development of a diagnostic blood test, to Erlich's discovery of Salvarsan as a treatment for the disease.[50] A Royal Commission on VD, established in 1913 to investigate and provide recommendations on tackling the problem, published its final report in 1916.[51] The Government agreed to implement the main proposals of the report and in July that year the Local Government Board issued The Public Health (Venereal Disease) Regulations 1916, providing publicly-funded VD clinics where individuals could be diagnosed and treated. Following the reasoning of the Royal Commission that, for such a

---

[45] R Phillips *Putting Assunder. A History of Divorce in Western Society* (Cambridge, CUP, 1988) 516–17.

[46] AAG Morrice, *Honour and Interests: Medical Ethics in Britain and the Work of the British Medical Association's Central Ethical Committee, 1902–1939* (unpublished MD Thesis, University of London, 1999) 265–6.

[47] Morrice, above n 13, 75.

[48] While there is no official report of this case, it was reported in *The Times* 10 June 1921; *The Daily Chronicle* (10 and 11 June 1921); and the *Law Journal* (18 June 1921).

[49] Contagious Diseases Prevention Act 1864; Contagious Diseases Act 1866; Contagious Diseases Act 1869; earlier Acts repealed by the Contagious Diseases Acts Repeal Act 1886. The earlier Acts had designated policing duties to the medical profession, giving them authority for the 'forcible examination of prostitutes' in dockyards and garrison towns and the power to confine those with VD for up to three months. See G Savage, '"The Wilful Communication of a Loathsome Disease": Marital Conflict and Venereal Disease in Victorian England' (1990) 34 *Victorian Studies* 35.

[50] D Evans, 'Tackling the "Hideous Scourge": The Creation of Venereal Disease Treatment Centres in Early Twentieth-Century Britain' (1992) 5 *Social History of Medicine* 415.

[51] *Royal Commission on Venereal Diseases. Reports and Minutes of Evidence* PP 1914 (Cd 7475) XLIX; PP 1916 (Cd 8189) XVI; PP 1916 (Cd 8190) XVI.

scheme to be successful, consultations and treatment should carry a guarantee of confidentiality, under article II(2) of the Regulations all proceedings at these clinics were to be regarded as confidential. Advertising material emphasising this pledge was a key component of efforts to persuade those who believed they might have VD to seek early treatment.[52]

The greatest challenge to the confidentiality of treatment at these centres came from the divorce courts. As Roderick Phillips has shown, the years after World War I saw a sharp rise in the number of divorce cases, caused in part by the disruptive circumstances of the war, but also reflecting the fact that the divorce courts were increasingly open to those who would previously have been excluded on financial grounds.[53] With a growing backlog of hearings, the courts were keen to process cases as efficiently as possible. A disparity in English divorce law at the time meant that while a man only had to prove that his wife had committed adultery in order to divorce her, a woman had to prove both her husband's adultery and that he had committed an act of cruelty towards her.[54] Evidence of VD could assist plaintiffs of either sex in certain circumstances—for a disease-free man to prove that his wife must have contracted the disease from an adulterous relationship, and for a woman to prove that her husband had caught VD in an adulterous relationship and subsequently committed an act of cruelty by infecting her.[55] In such circumstances, doctors from the VD treatment centres began to be subpoenaed to appear as witnesses in divorce hearings.

The precedent on medical confidentiality that is most frequently cited from the early interwar years comes from the case of *Garner v Garner* (1920).[56] Clara Garner was seeking a divorce on grounds that her husband contracted VD from another relationship and then infected her. In order to support her case, she subpoenaed Dr Salomon Kadinsky from the Westminster Hospital to give evidence on her behalf. Appearing in court, Kadinsky was reluctant to breach medical confidentiality. Before being sworn in as a witness, he produced a note from the chairman of the house committee of the Westminster Hospital, which cited the emphasis placed on confidentiality by the 1916 Regulations on VD. The judge, Alfred McCardie, refused the protest stating that 'in a court of justice there were "even higher considerations than those which prevailed with regard to the position

---

[52] For an example of such propaganda see R Davidson, *Dangerous Liaisons: A Social History of Venereal Disease in Twentieth-Century Scotland* (Rodopi, Amsterdam, 2000) 137.

[53] Phillips, above n 45, 516–17.

[54] Separate divorce legislation, with greater parity of proof for men and women, applied in Scotland.

[55] Though as Worboys notes, the medical understanding of the etiology, transmission and treatment of venereal disease at the time was far from exact. See M Worboys, 'Unsexing Gonorrhoea: Bacteriologists, Gynaecologists and Suffragists in Britain 1860–1920' (2004) 17 *Social History of Medicine* 41.

[56] *Garner v Garner* [1920] TLR 36, See, eg S Michalowski, *Medical Confidentiality and Crime* (Ashgate, Aldershot, 2003) 168; McHale, above n 13, 13–14; Morrice, above n 13, 69; B Reid, *Confidentiality and the Law* (London, Waterlow, 1986) 149.

of medical men'".[57] Kadinsky took the oath and testified that Clara Garner suffered from syphilis.

While Garner is generally cited as the decisive case from the period, the details were not particularly controversial. As the Ministry of Health noted at the time, Kadinsky's objection was based on a rather extreme interpretation of the 1916 VD regulations as preventing any disclosure, even when (as with Clara Garner) the patient in question had given her consent.[58] Although the Ministry saw no difficulty in a doctor breaking confidentiality at the patient's request, the press coverage of Garner caused them great concern.[59] A leading article in *The Times* suggested that 'the whole Government scheme for exterminating venereal diseases must be reduced to a nullity if secrecy of treatment cannot be guaranteed with the assistance of the courts', for, otherwise, 'the endeavours which have long been made to root out a hidden plague in the community must be allowed to rank among the pious futilities of the government.'[60] Naturally, the Ministry was concerned that in the rush to condemn the aims of the public VD treatment scheme as nullified by McCardie's ruling, *The Times* had failed to publicise the fact that disclosure was made with the full consent, indeed, at the request, of the patient. Nonetheless, it was clear that a similar case could arise in which a doctor would be faced with disclosure against the patient's wishes.

Over subsequent months the Minister for Health, Christopher Addison,[61] attempted to gauge the opinion of the Lord Chancellor, the Earl of Birkenhead,[62] on the advisability of inserting a clause in the statute providing that information about patients acquired by doctors in the course of their work at the public VD treatment clinics was privileged from being given in evidence.[63] Clearly

---

[57] *Garner v Garner* [1920] TLR 36, 196.

[58] While Kadinsky's refusal might be interpreted as an attempt to use medical confidentiality to protect the husband, *Needham v Needham* [1921], discussed later in this paper, provides a counter example where a doctor protested giving medical evidence against the wife. In neither case was there an explicit indication that the doctor's claim to medical privilege was affected by the gender of the patient.

[59] The Ministry of Health had taken over the running of the VD treatment scheme, from the Local Government Board, when it came into being in 1919.

[60] 'Medical Evidence in Divorce' *The Times* 14 January 1920, 13.

[61] Christopher Addison, first Viscount Addison, was a qualified medical doctor. He served as Minister for Health 1919–1921. See K Morgan and J Morgan, *Portrait of a Progressive. The Political Career of Christopher, Viscount Addison* (Oxford, OUP, 1980).

[62] FE Smith, First Earl of Birkenhead, served as Lord Chancellor from 1919–1922, during which time he himself heard divorce cases in order to assist in processing the backlog. See J Campbell, *FE Smith, First Earl of Birkenhead* (London, Cape, 1983).

[63] In order to avoid delays in implementing the treatment scheme, the Local Government Board had not sought to get parliamentary support for the incorporation of the Royal Commissions' recommendations as a statute law. Rather, using powers provided by the Public Health Act 1913, the Local Government Board declared venereal disease a national emergency, allowing it to insist that local authorities adopt the measures for treatment contained in the 1916 VD Regulations. See Evans, above n 50, 421–2. The Venereal Disease Act 1917 outlawed the sale of remedies for VD and the treatment of VD by anyone other than a duly qualified medical practitioner—thereby giving the medical profession a monopoly on VD treatment.

not enthused by the idea, Birkenhead made no pretence of proceeding with the urgency that the Ministry felt the matter required, citing the need to consult broader judicial opinion as a reason to delay his response.[64] By February 1921, after protracted correspondence with the Lord Chancellor's Office, Addison showed signs of losing his patience. He wrote to Birkenhead on St. Valentine's Day 1921 expressing keen disappointment that Birkenhead had yet to furnish him with an adequate response and emphasising the pressing nature of the question. His attempt to pressure Birkenhead into supporting the Ministry's position was dealt a blow by Birkenhead's reply:

Dear Minister for Health,

You must allow me to point out that it is perfectly futile of you to write me such letter on grave legal matters as that which I received from you this morning. The changes which you desire are far-reaching and highly disputable. I am myself at present opposed to them. The President of the Probate, Divorce and Admiralty Division is strongly opposed to them. The delay, therefore, to which you make such querulous reference, until the Lord Chief Justice is appointed and possibly the new Attorney-General, is entirely in your favour, as it may conceivably, however improbably, supply you with two judges who agree with your views. Nothing in the meantime is to be gained by concealing from you my own views

1. That it is highly doubtful whether you will ever obtain the modification of the existing law you desire, and
2. That it is even more doubtful whether such a modification, if admitted, would not be extremely pernicious.[65]

Unperturbed by what Sir Maurice Linford Gwyer,[66] the Ministry's lawyer, termed the 'very strange' reply from the Lord Chancellor, Addison subsequently met with Birkenhead who undertook to raise the matter within two weeks of the appointment of a new Lord Chief Justice, discuss it with other judges and report back.[67] Displaying considerable optimism, Gwyer suggested that Addison should not read too much into Birkenhead's unfavourable stance since 'the letter scarcely represented his considered judgement, and indeed bore the appearance of having been written in a moment of pique.'[68] A month later the Lord Chancellor's private

---

[64] For more detail on this see Ferguson, above n 43, 79–84.
[65] Files of the Lord Chancellor's Office held at Public Record Office, Kew, London (PRO LCO). PRO LCO 2/624, Birkenhead to Addison 14 February 1921.
[66] Sir Maurice Linford Gwyer served as legal advisor and solicitor to the Ministry of Health from 1919 until his appointment as Treasury solicitor in 1926.
[67] The vacancy in the post of Lord Chief Justice had been created when Lloyd George had moved Rufus Isaacs (Lord Reading) to become Viceroy of India. Sir Gordon Hewart, the Attorney-General was the obvious replacement but, at a time of mounting pressure for his coalition government, Lloyd George wished to keep Hewart as an ally in the cabinet. Much to the annoyance of Birkenhead, a deal was struck between Lloyd George and Hewart whereby an elderly judge would be appointed as Lord Chief Justice to be replaced by Hewart in due course.
[68] Files of the Ministry of Health held at Public Record Office, Kew, London (hereafter PRO MH). PRO MH 78/253, Gwyer to Machlachlan 5 April 1921.

secretary indicated that, having met with the new Lord Chief Justice,[69] Birkenhead had found him to be in full agreement with his own view and that of the President of the Probate, Divorce and Admiralty Division.[70] Clearly, this did represent the considered judgement of the relevant judiciary and its foundation could not be so easily questioned. To Birkenhead, the unanimity of legal opinion meant that Addison's idea of statutory recognition for a limited privilege for doctors could be taken no further. It was just as the Ministry of Health reached this apparent dead-end that it received a letter from Dr John Elliot, an employee of the VD clinic in Chester, who had been subpoenaed to give evidence in a forthcoming divorce hearing.[71]

Dr Elliot: The Ministry's Medical Martyr

Elliot was in urgent need of advice. A patient had attended his clinic with her child who suffered from the gonorrhoeal eye infection opthalmia neonatorum. Her husband, claiming to be disease-free himself, took the presence of disease in the child as evidence that his wife had contracted gonorrhoea in an adulterous relationship. Elliot had been subpoenaed to provide medical evidence backing this claim. Writing to the Ministry, he was keen to know if he had no choice but to breach confidentiality in the impending trial. Replying the following day, Dr Francis Coutts, the senior medical officer in charge of the Ministry's work on VD, explained the position as the Ministry currently understood it. Having been subpoenaed, Elliot must attend the court but could protest against being required to disclose confidential information acquired during his work at the VD treatment centre, making clear that it was in the public interest that such matters should remain confidential. If exemption was not granted, Elliot was left with two options: to have the protest recorded and then answer the questions; or, to refuse to give evidence. If he took the latter course, he ran the risk of imprisonment for contempt of court, which, while being of personal discomfort, would 'no doubt very effectively draw attention to the hardship of the position'.[72] Perhaps, Coutts continued, Elliot could furnish the Ministry with details of when the trial was to take place in order that it could send a shorthand writer to take notes on the court's actions, and Elliot himself could call at the Ministry to discuss the best way to put any protest he wished to make. Coutts also suggested that Elliot might wish

---

[69] Alfred Tristram Lawrence, first Baron Trevethin, had, at the age of 77, been given the dubious honour of keeping the seat warm for Hewart who duly took up the post in 1922.

[70] Sir Henry Duke, first Baron Merrivale, was President of the Probate, Divorce and Admiralty Division of the High Court from 1919 until 1933. During this time the Matrimonial Causes Act 1923 was passed which put the sexes on an equal footing for divorce on grounds of adultery under English law. See Phillips, above n 45, 526.

[71] PRO MH78/253 Elliot to Coutts 3 June 1921.

[72] PRO MH78/253 Coutts to Elliot 4 June 1921.

to get in touch with legal counsel, though it was unlikely he would be permitted to use them in court.

Elliot's next letter stated that the importance of the case was such that he felt he might not have the confidence to put his protest effectively and so he had corresponded with Honaratus Lloyd KC.[73] Clearly passionate about the issue, Elliot claimed to be of a mind to decline to answer questions and face the consequences, though he reserved final judgement until he had talked the matter over with Lloyd. The case was *Needham v Needham* and while Elliot felt sure he would have the support of the whole medical profession, he hoped he would also have the support of the Ministry, as far as this was possible. The latter, it turned out, was an important qualification.

On receiving this letter, Coutts sent a note to Gwyer indicating that, although Elliot had engaged the services of a lawyer, it appeared he might be a willing, and timely, martyr in the cause of medical privilege.[74] Coutts suggested:

> I think it is very probable that if we gave him direct encouragement he would decide to decline to give evidence and thus make it a test case. I recognise however, that we could not well do this officially, and it is a great responsibility to advise him unofficially in this direction.[75]

A great responsibility, indeed, but also a great opportunity. Having received a negative response from Birkenhead on their proposal to extend a statutory form of legal privilege to doctors, the senior members of the Ministry were keen to continue their promotion of what they believed was a justified and necessary cause. The coincidental arrival of Elliot's plea for help knocked ajar the door the consulted legal opinion had seemingly closed. The circumstances seemed ideal. In the course of researching the matter over the previous months, the Ministry had frequently come across references to an informally recognised privilege granted to clergymen when appearing as witnesses in court. It appeared to them that judges were reluctant to imprison clergymen for refusing to disclose information confided in them, recognising that no form of punishment the court could impose would be sufficient to counter the witness's sense of a higher duty. The Ministry now seemed keen to test whether the same leniency would be shown to a doctor, who, in face of dire consequences, resolutely stood by his belief in the ancient and venerable principle of medical confidentiality. Thus, the public health wing of government was engineering a face-off between the medical profession's traditional ethic of confidentiality and the law's right to demand disclosure based on a 150-year-old precedent. Elliot could provide them with their test case, but first he had to be persuaded of the contribution his potential sacrifice would make to the cause. Yet, the matter was more delicate. The guiding hand of the Ministry must leave no obvious fingerprints on the wary Dr Elliot's back as it eased him into the

---

[73] PRO MH78/253 Elliot to Coutts 5 June 1921.
[74] PRO MH78/253 Coutts to Gwyer 6 June 1921.
[75] ibid.

spotlight of public attention, or, viewed another way, into prison for contempt of court.

However, the Ministry was not alone in advising Elliot. Lloyd counselled him that after initially refusing to give evidence, if the court continued in its demand, Elliot should comply.[76] In addition to appearing as a witness, Elliot was required to bring the hospital records with him and the secretary to the infirmary was also likely to be subpoenaed. Writing on a Tuesday, Elliot was to meet with the Infirmary's chairman, secretary and solicitor on the following day before travelling to London on Thursday to meet with the London & Counties Medical Protection Society, from whom he had requested counsel. He understood the trial could be called on the Friday. With so many demands upon him it is little wonder Elliot concluded by stating 'I don't quite know what to do.'[77]

The Daily Chronicle ran two stories relating to the *Needham v Needham* trial on 10 June 1921.[78] A follow-up article gauging the medical profession's reaction the next day eagerly recounted Elliot's performance in court.[79] The reports noted his prolonged attempt to have medical privilege recognised, arguing that the 1916 VD regulations were statutory authority for him not to disclose, and that it was on this understanding that he and others had taken up posts as medical officers at VD clinics.[80] The judge, Justice Horridge, held that sufficient statutory authority to support a claim for privilege had not been demonstrated. Despite further protests that confidentiality between doctor and patient was one of the principles held dearest by the medical profession and that protection of it was essential to public health measures to combat VD, Horridge ordered Elliot to assist in the administration of justice and answer all questions. Elliot acquiesced.

In sweeping style, the *Daily Chronicle* announced to its readers:

> It is clear that if there is no guarantee of professional secrecy in certain kinds of clinic the whole object of the Ministry of Health acting in the interests of the public is likely to be defeated. The matter requires legislation.[81]

The *Law Journal* concluded an article criticising Horridge's decision with the words: 'A strong judge is required to create a precedent that would be beneficial to the public as well as fair to medical men'.[82] This point was not lost on the Ministry. A memo from Coutts to Sir George Newman, the chief medical officer at the Ministry, indicated that, along with Gwyer, he had met with Elliot prior

---

[76] PRO MH78/253 Elliot to Ministry 7 June 1921.
[77] ibid.
[78] PRO MH78/253 Articles: 'Doctors and Patients', *The Daily Chronicle* (London, 10 June 1921) and 'Doctors must tell' *The Daily Chronicle* (London, 10 June 1921).
[79] PRO MH78/253 'Should a doctor tell? BMA takes serious view of Judge's decision' *The Daily Chronicle* (London, 11 June 1921).
[80] The 1916 regulations were not statutory authority but had been implemented as required measures under the national emergency clause of the Public Health Act 1913. See, above n 63.
[81] PRO MH78/253 'Doctors and Patients' *The Daily Chronicle* (London, 10 June 1921).
[82] PRO MH78/253 'Doctors as Witnesses' *Law Journal* (London, 18 June 1921).

to his court appearance to discuss the line of argument he should take. They decided that counsel from the London & Counties Medical Protection Society should be used, if possible, to put forward the case. Horridge had not granted this request, though Coutts clearly believed that Elliot presented their argument well. Though eventually agreeing to give evidence after entering his protest, Elliot later acknowledged that he would have been willing to go to jail if it had only been for a few days, but imprisonment lasting six months was too much to bear.

The Ministry's problems were mounting. Elliot, their spokesman in the case, had failed to convince the judge of the need for medical privilege. Moreover, he had flinched in court at the prospect of a prolonged imprisonment. But losing its martyr was only the beginning of the Ministry's predicament. The detrimental impact that the ruling, and particularly the press reports of it, could have in deterring people from seeking treatment at the Government's clinics was exacerbated by the possibility that doctors at the clinics were themselves becoming disillusioned with the system. Coutts noted that Elliot was seriously contemplating giving up his position at the VD clinic, and another letter received from Dr Gibson, a VD medical officer in Oxford, made clear the strong feeling that 'this ruling of Mr Justice Horridge puts us in an altogether false position with our patients'.[83]

The prospect of losing medical officers from VD clinics was potentially very damaging for the Ministry. Coutts proposed that the issue should be pressed, that strong leading articles on the subject should appear in the medical journals, and that the Ministry should meet for discussions with the Royal College of Physicians, the Royal College of Surgeons and the BMA.[84] He suggested that some of the daily newspapers might also be willing to take the matter up. Concurring with Coutts' assessment of the seriousness of the situation, Newman forwarded the memo on to Gwyer with a note stating: 'You will wish to see this in view of your memo for the minister. I think we ought to try and act at once. It is important we should not lose our VD officers'.[85]

A week later, Hugh Woods, secretary to the London & Counties Medical Protection Society wrote to the Ministry, inviting it to meet the costs which the Society had incurred in their support for Elliot.[86] He insisted that the Ministry act to ensure that medical officers who took up their posts believing that confidentiality would be observed would see the regulation protected and enforced. It could not be expected that busy practitioners would risk prolonged imprisonment for carrying out what they believed was their ethical duty. If the legislature failed to deliver such protection then 'it may be necessary for some members of our profession to incur martyrdom of the kind with a view to awakening the consciousness

---

[83] PRO MH78/253 Gibson to Coutts 10 June 1921.
[84] PRO MH78/253 Coutts to Newman 13 June 1921.
[85] PRO MH78/253 Newman to Gwyer 13 June 1921.
[86] These amounted to £32 15s.

of the public'.[87] The onus was on the Ministry to provide the circumstances in which the medical officers could maintain their duty of secrecy, which the Ministry's regulations had enshrined. A further letter from Woods, seeking advice in relation to an impending divorce case in which, again, VD doctors had been subpoenaed as witnesses, ended on an ominous note, stating that the very existence of public VD clinics was dependent on the question.[88] The Ministry sent a negative reply with regard to the request for expenses. It claimed there were no funds for this purpose, and that it had been made clear to Elliot, in the meeting before the case, that while the Ministry sympathised with his position it could offer him no financial assistance.[89]

Having failed in its attempt to convince Birkenhead of the need for a level of statutory protection for medical privilege, and then seen its medical martyr capitulate in his challenge to the common law, the Ministry decided to change tactics. Rather than attempting to alter the law, Sir Alfred Mond, who had replaced Addison as Minister for Health, sought to encourage the judiciary to show greater understanding of the predicament in which doctors were placed when subpoenaed to give medical evidence in court.[90] If it was clear that they were called to testify only when absolutely necessary and not, as had been suggested for the growing number of civil divorce hearings, as a means to rapidly process cases and make things more convenient for the courts, then doctors would be more willing to comply with the courts' demands. In this way, the negative publicity which the confidentiality of the VD treatment scheme had received in the press might be averted.

Though Elliot's capitulation marked the end point of the Ministry of Health's interest in medical martyrdom, his courtroom experience rekindled the fighting spirit amongst members of the BMA. At the annual meeting of representatives, which took place shortly after the Needham trial, the membership passed a resolution in favour of the BMA supporting a direct challenge to the law on medical privilege. Over the course of the following year, a specially constituted Medical Secrecy Committee was established to consider the format which such support would take. Their initial recommendations read somewhat like a manifesto for medical martyrdom—offering a bona fide martyr assurances that his family would receive financial support during the period of his imprisonment and that the local division of the BMA would cover the needs of his practice. It even suggested that martyrdom could be good for business—attracting patients to a doctor who demonstrated such a high regard for their confidentiality. However,

---

[87] PRO MH78/253 Woods to Ministry 20 June 1921.
[88] The case referred to was *Atwood v Atwood*.
[89] PRO MH78/253 Slator to Woods July 1921.
[90] Mond replaced Addison as Minister for Health after Lloyd George moved the latter amidst controversy over post-war government expenditure on Addison's ambitious housing program. From 31 March 1921, Addison became Minister without portfolio. See KO Morgan, *Consensus and Disunity. The Lloyd George Coalition Government 1918–1922* (Oxford, Clarendon Press, 1979); K Morgan and J Morgan, above n 61, 131–4.

underneath their desire to fight the law, there remained an acute awareness of the difficulty of accurately defining the boundaries of the privilege they sought. Having drafted the professional secrecy committee's report to council in preparation for the BMA's annual representatives meeting in Glasgow 1922, Alfred Cox expressed grave doubts as to the validity of the position they were advocating:

> I have never felt less comfortable over anything than I do over this. … I have tried to make it, within the limits of a short report, as convincing to myself and others as I could. But frankly I am not convinced that the line we are suggesting will stand criticism. … The attitude rests on sentiment and tradition and it is no good trying to invest it with logical consistency.[91]

Sentiment and tradition were not likely to persuade the judiciary to exempt such a valuable source of information from the court. Moreover, while the BMA had been considering its position on a policy of martyrdom, Birkenhead had consolidated the legal opposition. The publication of his essay 'Should a Doctor Tell?' was designed to provide a conclusive argument against medical privilege, and he distributed it to all members of the judiciary.[92] Coupled with insecurities about their own argument, Birkenhead's rallying of the judiciary dampened the confrontational spirit of most at the BMA. Though not formally abandoned, the policy of supporting martyrs in the cause of confidentiality was shelved indefinitely.

The Medical and Legal Perspectives

It is evident that there were competing ideas about the duty of a doctor and the consequences of a breach of medical confidentiality. As the Director of Public Prosecutions stressed in 1915, doctors had a duty as citizens to assist the law, which, in his opinion, overrode their professional duty to the patient. Similar sentiments were expressed by McCardie in *Garner v Garner* (1920), and Horridge in *Needham v Needham* (1921). Without doubt, the medical profession's obligations to the communal interest were increasing with legislation requiring notification of infectious disease cases; participation in the national insurance scheme; growing numbers of municipally-funded medical officers of health; and the instigation of schemes such as the publicly-run VD treatment centres. However, the vast majority of doctors were not employed by the state. Most still had to compete for business in a marketplace where reputations counted. Just as Caesar Hawkins had been aware of the threat posed by any public perception that he was breaking medical confidentiality during the Duchess of Kingston's trial, so too the doctors

---

[91] BMA CEC correspondence, Cox to Hempson 6 April 1922.
[92] FE Smith, 'Should a doctor tell?' in *Points of View* (London, 1922).

involved in the interwar divorce cases were sensitive to the need to make a show of their respect for the confidentiality of their patients' medical information in the public setting of the court. Yet, there was more to the medical protests over abortion and VD than a façade of honour designed to protect professional reputation. In both 1915 and 1921, the medical profession showed a willingness to stand up and fight for the principle. The resolutions passed by the BMA council in 1915, coupled with Elliot's courtroom appearance and its immediate effect on the BMA membership in 1921, demonstrated a passion to resist further legal encroachment into doctor–patient confidentiality that went beyond personal self-interest. The fact that, in the end, no medical martyr provoked a test case can be seen as a matter of timing. When the Ministry, in the aftermath of Birkenhead's dismissal of the idea of medical privilege, had the will and, in John Elliot, the potential martyr, to challenge the law, they could not provide the practical support and financial security for Elliot to proceed. By the time the BMA, provoked by Elliot's experience, had decided to offer practical support to a bona fide martyr, the will for challenging the law had waned: in part as a result of the difficulty of defining the privilege they sought; in part because Birkenhead's published essay had rallied the judiciary against the idea of medical privilege.

While duty was stressed by both sides of the debate, consequences seemed of most importance to the law. For judges, the efficient and effective administration of justice was paramount to the confidentiality of the individual patient, and so the doctor's duty to inform the law trumped any duty of medical confidentiality to the patient. Yet, doctors also gave consequentialist arguments for protecting confidentiality. Notification to the authorities of all women who sought assistance after an illegal abortion would deter women in these circumstances from turning to medical help. Similarly, encouraging individuals, who suspected they may have contracted a form of VD (a physically and socially stigmatic set of diseases) to seek early medical assistance, was seen to depend on the provision of assurances that all diagnosis and treatment would be confidential. This was the belief of the Royal Commission on VD, whose recommendations provided the basis of the VD Treatment Regulations of 1916, and of both the Local Government Board and the Ministry of Health who implemented and ran the scheme.[93] Fears that a lack of confidentiality would deter people from seeking treatment, and lead to further spread of the disease, can be seen in the reactions of the newspaper reports, the

---

[93] Evidence of this can be found in some of the Parliamentary debates on the question. In one, the President of the Local Government Board, Walter Long, stated: 'there is a feature attached to these diseases which does not belong to the ordinary troubles of health. The patient does not like it to be known that he or she is suffering from this disease; they like to conceal the fact; they do not want it notified. Therefore if we are really going to deal with our suffering population, we must take care not only that there is proper provision for their treatment, but that everything is done that can be done to get it without notification. ... What I am imploring them [hospitals running the VD treatment schemes] to do is to take the patients in and welcome them from wherever they come, to ask them no questions, and seeking in no way to identify them with this horrible misfortune that has overtaken them'. *Parliamentary Debates (HC) Fifth Series* vol 84, 239.

Ministry of Health, and the VD officers themselves when doctors from the clinics were forced to breach the guarantee of confidentiality in order to facilitate the processing of a backlog of civil divorce suits. These cases gave the impression that the law was giving precedence to its own convenience over the public health claims of the medical profession, sparking Lord Dawson of Penn, at a meeting of the Medico-Legal Society, to suggest that the law was the 'spoilt child of the professions'.[94]

There is no doubt that there was an element of professional rivalry involved in the question. In part this stemmed from the similarities in the basic unit of both the medical and legal encounter. While both the doctor–patient and lawyer–client relationship depend on a level of professional confidentiality, only the latter has this formally recognised by a privilege of non-disclosure in a court of law. Legal privilege had been justified on the grounds that the complexity of the law entailed that, under a fair justice system, individuals need access to legal expertise and advice. The guarantee that the lawyer was bound by confidentiality, even in the courtroom, allowed the client to be open and honest and thereby facilitated the legal process. The development of medical knowledge founded on pathological anatomy, germ theory and other modern science-based sources of information in the 19th and 20th centuries, increasingly gave medicine an opportunity to make a similar claim for privilege. This change in medical knowledge, combined with a growing sense of a communal professional identity and the rise of mass representation in organisations such as the BMA, endowed the medical profession with greater authority to stand up against legal dictate.[95] The inter-professional rivalry over confidentiality in the early 20th century can be seen as reflecting this growing status of the medical profession. Where, in the late 18th century, Caesar Hawkins had sought from the court some recognition that he was an honourable gentleman, the doctors appearing as witnesses in the divorce courts in the 1920s were already aware of their growing value to the state. Operating under regulations on confidentiality of VD treatment that were sanctioned by government, these doctors were in a stronger position to challenge the law on the principle of the matter.[96] However, as the cases discussed above show, circumstances contrived against them. Garner, the early case which triggered the debate and set the precedent for the rejection of protests from VD doctors in the divorce courts, was based on an extreme interpretation of the rules of confidentiality.[97] Salomon Kadinsky's

---

[94] Lord Dawson of Penn, 'An Address on Professional Secrecy Delivered at a Meeting of the Medico-Legal Society, held on 21 March 1922' (1922) 202 *Lancet* 619, 620.

[95] The medical profession's position would become stronger yet with the rise of greater numbers of effective therapeutics in the course of the twentieth century; a fact tempered by the establishing of the NHS in 1948 by which the duty for mass healthcare provision was undertaken by the state.

[96] It should be noted that the government, in the form of the Ministry of Health, was normally interested in the breach of individual patient medical confidentiality in situations where there was a communal public health interest. VD represented a specific instance in which the protection of public health relied on the pledge that individual patient confidentiality would be protected, thereby encouraging people to seek early diagnosis and treatment.

[97] See above n 57.

position in Garner mirrors Caesar Hawkins' in the Duchess of Kingston's trial, in so far as neither case involved a controversial breach of medical confidentiality. In Hawkins' case the information he disclosed was not obtained in his professional capacity; while Kadinsky was asked to give evidence with the full consent, indeed at the request, of his patient. Yet the cases in which Hawkins and Kadinsky were involved have had a lasting impact on the legal position.

Aside from the well-known precedents, the debate over the principles involved in the question, of whether the testimony of VD doctors should be exempt from use in civil divorce courts, took place in private meetings and discussions. Only after the failure of their attempts to convince Birkenhead and his colleagues of the need for a limited medical privilege, did the Ministry look to promote a test case. As already noted, Elliot's appearance in *Needham v Needham* had the potential to put the law to the test, but it foundered in the absence of practical support. Though it provoked the BMA to consider actively supporting a policy of martyrdom, the issue's momentum had been lost: a result of Birkenhead's shoring-up of legal opposition, combined with the difficulty of comprehensively defining the boundaries of the privilege that was sought. Would it apply only to VD doctors? Only in divorce cases? Only under civil law? While it was claimed that medical privilege was sought in the interests of the patient, it was clear that there was an underlying measure of self-interest involved. In an era when the majority of doctors still had to rely on private paying patients as a key source of income, serious damage could be caused to professional reputation if the newspapers reported, in their sensationalist manner, that a doctor had broken the pledge of confidentiality. Perhaps more fundamental than this, doctors at times needed to breach medical confidentiality in self interest. In the event of an accusation of malpractice from a patient, a doctor needed to be able to defend himself with evidence taken from his encounter with the patient.[98]

These considerations tempered both the BMA and the Ministry of Health's drive for a medical martyr, and were still fresh in the mind of both bodies when attempts were made to promote a private member's bill on medical privilege in the House of Commons in 1927.[99] Just as the confrontation over the notification of abortion in 1915 failed to reach a climax when war intervened, so the disagreement over judicial demands for testimony from VD doctors in divorce hearings in the early interwar years, also seemed to peter out. Examination of the correspondence between John Elliot and the Ministry of Health prior to Needham, and the effect this case had on the BMA, indicates that a showdown between medical and legal interests was closer to reality than has hitherto been acknowledged. Nonetheless, the obituary of medical martyrdom over confidentiality in the early interwar years simply reads: Elliot acquiesced.

---

[98] For an example see the case of the 'Kissing Doctor' in Ferguson, above n 43, 207.
[99] A similar attempt was made in 1936. For details of both see Ferguson, above n 43, 154–89.

Looking Beyond Laws, Precedents and Professional Guidelines

As an issue of long-standing, and ongoing, controversy, medical confidentiality provides a wealth of information on the history of medico-legal interaction. Both the common law and statutes have challenged and curtailed traditional ideas about medical confidentiality held by the medical profession. While debates over these challenges have often revolved around central principles: competing duties or projected consequences, they have also been influenced by a myriad of other more pragmatic matters. From the pecuniary interests of doctors in maintaining their professional reputations, to the rapid processing of a lengthy backlog of civil divorce cases, both medical and legal self-interest have influenced the direction and outcome of debate. Perhaps more striking still is the important role that chance played in the delineation of the boundaries of medical privilege. Caesar Hawkins's dubious claim to medical privilege during the Duchess of Kingston's trial in 1776 led to the setting of a precedent which has bound the medical profession ever since. The timely arrival of a letter from Dr John Elliot, allowed the Ministry of Health the chance to contemplate a direct challenge to judicial demands on medical witnesses in the early 1920s. The attempt failed because the nascent Ministry of Health could not give Elliot the professional and financial support he needed if sent to jail. Yet his appearance in court provoked the BMA, temporarily at least, seriously to consider providing practical assistance for bona fide martyrs. While this demonstrates the strength of medical feeling on the need to challenge legal encroachment into the confidentiality of the doctor–patient relationship, it also illustrates the importance of timing. Had the BMA's offer of support been available to Elliot at the time of his courtroom appearance the story of the medical martyr may have ended with the legal system being forced to reconsider the applicability of the Duchess of Kingston's precedent in the changed circumstances of contemporary VD treatment.

In conjunction with the earlier confrontation over abortion, the debates over the confidentiality of VD treatment highlight the changes which were occurring in medicine. In the 18th century, all but the elite of the profession occupied a relatively low status in society; competing against each other, and a range of informal healers, for their livelihood. By the turn of the 20th century, new foundations for medical knowledge and practice meant patients increasingly attributed status and authority to doctors. This growth in authority was further strengthened by growing state demands on the medical profession—recognition that they had a role in improving the common welfare of the population. However, this proved to be a double-edged sword. As doctors found growing demands placed upon information they possessed, traditional ideals of medical confidentiality were challenged by statute and common law, both of which recognised the value of modern medical information to their ends. Yet, the popular and state recognition of their new status gave doctors greater confidence to stand up against such legal demands. Whereas Caesar Hawkins had been asked to reveal details from personal conversations relating to his friends' marriage, the modern medical profession was involved in debates over notification of illegal abortion or the disclosure of details of patients treated for VD, the latter carrying a government-backed pledge of confidentiality. Although it was still individual doctors who took to the witness stand, it is evident that the defence of medical confidentiality in the early 20th century was made by representatives of a more coherent medical profession. Nonetheless, while greater professional coherence, coupled with a growing sense of medicine's authority and status in society, gave it confidence to stand up to the law, it is clear that the law was unwilling to treat the question of medical confidentiality any differently. Indeed it might be argued that the rising status of medicine was concurrent with a diminishing of the boundaries of medical confidentiality: the utility of modern medicine's knowledge and information increasing the demand for it. Far from 'juridical power' being overtaken by 'biopower', in the debates over medical confidentiality, judges continued to assert their right to demand medical information, even when it meant overriding public health regulations.[100] In part, this reflected changes in the law; for instance the opening-up of the civil divorce courts to larger sections of society, which made medical testimony invaluable to the efficient processing of the backlog of cases in the interwar years. The courts' rejection of doctors' attempts to maintain the confidentiality of VD treatment seems evidence of the prioritisation of legal over medical interests. Yet, it is just as dependent on the fact that defining the boundaries of medical privilege is an exceptionally difficult task. While neither the law nor medicine could maintain that the presence or absence of medical privilege was a perfect position, the fact that it had been denied in law for over 150 years made the defence of the status quo considerably easier for the law than any medical attempt to argue for an imperfect alternative.

---

[100] For the distinction between 'juridical power' and 'biopower' see Crawford, above n 6.

7

Law, Medicine and the Treatment of Homosexual Offenders in Scotland, 1950–1980

ROGER DAVIDSON

Introduction[*]

In recent years, the social politics and the legal and medical discourses surrounding homosexuality in 20th-century Britain have attracted increasing attention from historians and social scientists. Within the growing literature, the medical perception and treatment of homosexuality and homosexual offences have been treated from a variety of standpoints. Many studies address the subject as a central aspect of the politics surrounding either the regulation of dangerous sexualities or the process of homosexual law reform.[1] Others, often from a social constructionist viewpoint, have focused on the competing sexological and psychoanalytical discourses surrounding homosexuality and their impact upon public policy.[2]

---

[*] Acknowledgements: I am greatly indebted to the Wellcome Trust whose financial support made possible the original research upon which this chapter is based, I also wish to thank the Lord Justice General for permission to consult and cite selected Scottish High Court trial processes and appeal papers held at the National Archives of Scotland.

[1] See, eg J Weeks, *Sex Politics and Society: The Regulation of Sexuality since 1800*, 2nd edn (London, Longman, 1989) chs 6, 8; P Higgins, *Heterosexual Dictatorship: Male Homosexuality in Post-War Britain* (London, Fourth Estate, 1996) 51–8; R Davenport-Hines, *Sex, Death and Punishment: Attitudes to Sex and Sexuality in Britain since the Renaissance* (London, Collins, 1990) ch 8. For an overview of the social politics of homosexual law reform in Scotland, see R Davidson and G Davis, '"A Field for Private Members": The Wolfenden Committee and Scottish Homosexual Law Reform, 1950–67' (2004) 15 *Twentieth Century British History* 174; R Davidson and G Davis, 'Sexuality and the State: The Campaign for Scottish Homosexual Law Reform, 1967–80' (2006) 20 *Contemporary British History* 533.

[2] See, eg C Waters, 'Havelock Ellis, Sigmund Freud and the State: Discourses of Homosexual Identity in Interwar Britain' in L Bland and L Doan (eds), *Sexology in Culture: Labelling Bodies and Desires* (Cambridge, Polity Press, 1998) ch 10; C Waters, 'Disorders of the Mind, Disorders of the Body Social: Peter Wildeblood and the Making of the Modern Homosexual' in B Conekin, F Mort, and C Waters (eds), *Moments of Modernity: Reconstructing Britain 1945–1964* (London, Rivers Oram, 1999) 135–51. ID Crozier, 'Taking Prisoners: Havelock Ellis, Sigmund Freud, and the Construction of Homosexuality 1897–1951'(2000) 13 *Social History of Medicine* 447; M Houlbrook, *Queer London: Perils and Pleasures in the Sexual Metropolis, 1918–1957* (Chicago, University of Chicago Press, 2005) 195–8, 257–62.

126   Roger Davidson

Anecdotal evidence of medical attitudes and therapies is also scattered in the written and recorded testimonies of homosexuals.[3] However, with the notable exception of the oral history recently undertaken by King, Smith and Bartlett,[4] there has been little systematic primary research into the medical perception and treatment of male homosexuality that prevailed in the surgeries, clinics, courts and prisons of the land since the Second World War. This is especially true in relation to the Scottish experience, despite the distinctive traditions of law and medical practice north of the Border, as well as, arguably, Scotland's distinctive civic and sexual culture.

This paper seeks to begin to make good this omission by documenting the medical perception and treatment of homosexual offenders in Scotland in the period 1950–80, and the role that medical evidence played in the prosecution and sentencing of such offenders. Two main sources of evidence are explored. First, the verbal and written evidence of Scottish witnesses before the Wolfenden Committee is examined in order to identify how homosexual offenders were treated—or allegedly treated—in the 1950s. The Wolfenden Committee was appointed in 1954 in response to a moral panic surrounding an apparent escalation in urban vice, and with a remit to consider the law and practice relating to homosexual offences and prostitution. Secondly, a systematic analysis is undertaken of the medical reports on homosexual offenders submitted by psychiatrists and other doctors to Scottish High Court trials and appeals during the period 1950–80, and of their role in court proceedings. This will serve to throw important light on the degree to which medical views and practices pertaining to homosexual offenders in Scotland changed over the quarter century following Wolfenden and how far and in what ways they influenced the legal process.

The View from Wolfenden

Scottish evidence to the Wolfenden Committee varied as to the extent to which medical considerations played a part in the sentencing of homosexual offenders in the 1950s. James Adair, former Procurator-fiscal for Edinburgh and Glasgow, was of the opinion that: 'Some judges were very responsive to suggestions by medical men about treatment, while others agreed that these were not the

---

[3] See, eg A Jivani, *It's Not Unusual: A History of Lesbian and Gay Britain in the Twentieth Century* (London, Michael O'Mara, 1997) 122–8; B Cant (ed), *Footsteps and Witnesses: Lesbian and Gay Lifestories from Scotland* (Edinburgh, Polygon, 1993) 49; T Davidson (ed), *And Thus Will I Freely Sing: An Anthology of Gay and Lesbian Writing from Scotland* (Edinburgh, Polygon, 1989) 154–9.

[4] M King, G Smith and A Bartlett, 'Treatments of Homosexuality in Britain since the 1950s—An Oral History: The Experience of Patients' (2004) 328 *British Medical Journal* 427; M King, G Smith and A Bartlett, 'Treatments of Homosexuality in Britain since the 1950s—An Oral History: The Experience of Professionals' (2004) 328 *British Medical Journal* 429.

concern of the judge.'[5] Certainly, under the Criminal Justice (Scotland) Act of 1949, courts had explicit powers both to call for medical reports on offenders and to prescribe medical treatment (although not its specific nature) as part of a probationary sentence. Thus, an offender could, with his consent, be required under a probation order to undertake remedial treatment, either as a resident or non-resident of an institution or as a patient of a named doctor.[6] Some legal witnesses before the Wolfenden Committee considered that, compared with legal practice in inter-war Scotland,[7] there was an increasing trend in Scottish Courts for medical reports to be used in cases involving homosexual offences, and that the practice was 'much more the custom in Scotland than in England'.[8] Dr W Boyd, Consultant Psychiatrist to the Scottish Prison and Borstal Service, testified that he was:

> in charge of a Mental Health Service where both the Procurators-fiscal and the Sheriffs were willing to recognise that we could have cooperation, and many offenders were placed on probation on the condition that they attended hospital.[9]

Indeed, in Glasgow, whereas formerly the magistrates had tended to process homosexual offenders without any consideration of medical issues simply 'as men who were doing a dirty thing', and to routinely 'fine them a fiver each', in the 1950s, such cases were increasingly remitted to the Sheriff Court to ensure some level of medical examination.[10]

---

[5] The National Archives, Public Record Office, Kew (PRO), HO345/9, Proceedings of the Wolfenden Committee on Homosexual Offences and Prostitution (PWC), Summary Record of 21st Meeting, March 1956. On the issue of variance in judicial practice, see also *Report of the Wolfenden Committee* (*RWC*), PP 1956–7, Cmnd 247, XIV, p 63, para 182; DK Henderson, *Society and Criminal Conduct* (Edinburgh, Royal College of Physicians of Edinburgh, 1955) 25.

[6] PRO, HO345/9, CHP/108, PWC, evidence of Faculty of Advocates, March 1956; NAS, HH60/268, evidence of Scottish Home Department, October 1954.

[7] Evidence suggests that, prior to the Second World War, the police and judiciary in Scotland were often extremely hostile to the efforts of psychiatrists to secure medical treatment rather than imprisonment for their clients. See, eg W Merrilees, *The Short Arm of the Law: The Memoirs of William Merrilees OBE: Chief Constable The Lothians and Peebles Constabulary* (London, John Long, 1966) 121–2. This attitude was strongly reinforced by the judgement of the Lord Justice Clerk in the case of *HM Advocate v Morison* (1944) JC 132 in March 1944. M had been charged on indictment in the Sheriff Court of the Lothians and Peebles at Edinburgh with a number of homosexual offences under the 1885 Criminal Law Amendment Act. The Sheriff had been sympathetic to sentence being deferred until the likely response of the panel to psychotherapeutic treatment under a probationary order had been assessed. However, the Lord Justice Clerk determined that it was not the Courts prerogative merely to approach such cases 'from the purely medical standpoint', and with a 'single eye to the possible rehabilitation of the offender'. Instead, he ruled that 'the duty of the Court was to give effect to the law which punished such offences as crimes' without delay, and he imposed a sentence of eighteen months' imprisonment [NAS, ED15/109, Note by Scottish Home Department, 18 March 1946].

[8] PRO, HO345/15, CHP/TRANS/42, PWC, evidence of KM Hancock, Director of the Scottish Prison and Borstal Services, 1 November 1955; PRO, HO345/16. CHP/TRANS/60, evidence of Association of Sheriffs Substitute, 9 April 1956. See also LJ Moran, *The Homosexual(ity) of Law* (Routledge, London and New York, 1996) 116. It was obligatory to have a medical report on any person under the age of 21 involved in such cases.

[9] PRO, HO345/15, CHP/TRANS/41, PWC, evidence of W Boyd, 1 November 1955.

[10] PRO, HO345/16, PWC, evidence of Magistrates of Corporation of Glasgow, 9 April 1956.

In line with the recommendation of the Scottish Advisory Council on the Treatment and Rehabilitation of Offenders that psycho-therapeutic and other medical treatment should be more widely available for convicted sexual offenders,[11] the Scottish Home Department had, it claimed, by the mid-1950s, begun to press for the provision of more psychiatric services within the Scottish prison system. The Department recommended that all first offenders should have a full medico-psychological assessment prior to sentencing.[12] Further, it advocated that all male prisoners convicted of homosexual offences should be interviewed at some point by a psychiatrist and that, if the offender was suitable for treatment and was willing to undergo it during his sentence, he should be admitted to a psychiatric hospital as an in-patient or given treatment at a psychiatric clinic as an out-patient. Similar psychiatric examination and treatment was viewed as desirable for all male Borstal inmates.[13]

However, despite such aspirations, Dr Inch, the Medical Adviser to the Scottish Prison and Borstal Services, maintained that the resources for treatment within Scottish prisons remained 'pitifully inadequate' and 'barely scratching the surface of the problem'.[14] With first offenders, who often served short sentences, at best only a 'few psychotherapeutic talks' were possible. Apart from Barlinnie, where a new medical psychiatric unit was being built, there were no special psycho-therapeutic units in Scotland such as existed at Wormwood Scrubs and Wakefield and many of the prisons were too small to justify in-house psychiatric provisions.[15] For any 'deep treatment', such as it existed, the Scottish Prison Service relied entirely on external psychiatric provisions within the NHS. Within the Borstal system, treatment was, in practice, largely confined to casual, ad hoc

---

[11] Scottish Advisory Council on the Treatment and Rehabilitation of Offenders, *Psycho-Therapeutic Treatment of Certain Offenders with Special Reference to the Case of Persons Convicted of Sexual and Unnatural Offences* (Edinburgh, 1948) 6–9.

[12] NAS, HH60/268, PWC, memo by Scottish Home Department, October 1954. In the opinion of Dr TD Inch, Medical Adviser to the Scottish Prison and Borstal Services, offenders who were mentally defective, neurotic or psychotic should be hospitalised and the 'homosexual psychopath' subjected to an indeterminate sentence within a 'special institution or colony'. The routine provision of medical reports was also advocated by some magistrates, but not by the Crown Agent [PRO, HO345/16, evidence of Magistrates of the Corporation of Glasgow, 9 April 1956; evidence of LI Gordon, Crown Agent, 9 April 1956].

[13] NAS, HH60/268, PWC, memo. by Scottish Home Department, October 1954.

[14] NAS, HH57/1287, PWC, note by TD Inch, 13 October 1955. On the scarcity of psychiatric resources in Britain, see also RWC, p 62, para 180; G Westwood, *Society and the Homosexual* (London, Gollancz, 1952) 89.

[15] PRO, HO345/15, CHP/TRANS/41, PWC, evidence of W Boyd, 1 November 1955. In view of this, the policy of the Scottish Home Department, in direct contrast to that of the Home Office, was to integrate the prison medical service with mainstream and psychiatric medicine within the NHS. The lack of adequate resources for the implementation of probationary treatment for sexual offenders in Scotland was an enduring problem. In 1959, a Glasgow psychiatrist reported that, due mainly to a shortage of qualified staff, provisions were still 'ludicrously inadequate. … The usual treatment is to administer some drugs and to perform a little elementary psycho-analysis' (*The Scotsman*, Edinburgh, 6 June 1959). See also DK Henderson and IRC Batchelor, *A Textbook of Psychiatry for Students and Practitioners*, 9th edn (London, OUP, 1962) 206; K Wardrop, *Psychiatry and Probation* (London, Institute for the Study and Treatment of Delinquency, 1971) 8.

advice conveyed by the Governor, chaplain and psychiatrist to inmates, and to the enforcement of 'hard work and varied recreation, especially of an athletic nature' to counteract 'homosexual tendencies'.[16]

Scotland did vary from England and Wales in the type of medical treatment administered in prison to convicted homosexual offenders. According to the evidence of Scottish Prison Medical Officers, no use was made of electro-convulsive therapy (ECT) in Scottish prisons. Narco-analysis (psycho-analysis undertaken during a light phase of anaesthesia) had been used to a limited extent during the war but had been deemed unsuited to 'civil life'.[17] However, in contrast to England and Wales, where the practice had been discontinued as too dangerous, oestrogen treatment had been used in Scottish prisons on sexual offenders for some time (especially at Perth), largely inspired by the work of FL Golla at the Burden Neurological Institute in Bristol.[18] It was only given to prisoners who signed an agreement to the procedure and then only under strict medical supervision. According to Inch, oestrogen treatment had never been pushed 'to its limits'—'to the extent of producing atrophy of the testicles or even gynaecomastia [excessive enlargement of the male breasts]—but only to the point of eliminating or at least greatly reducing libido'.[19] The prime objective was to make the prisoners less anxious, more 'adaptable' and 'easier to handle', and to provide the 'small maintenance dosage that reliev[ed] tension' without producing any physical change in the patient. Significantly, such treatment regimes were not public knowledge. According to Inch, the Scottish Prison Service had 'never said anything'. 'We have', he noted, 'just kept very quiet about it'.[20]

The fullest and most compelling Scottish evidence to the Wolfenden Committee in favour of homosexual law reform did come from medical witnesses. Perhaps the most influential evidence was that submitted by Drs Inch and Boyd from the Scottish Prisons and Borstal Services.[21] Echoing the previous recommendations of the Scottish Advisory Council on the Treatment and Rehabilitation of Offenders, they aired serious doubts as to the value of imprisonment in reforming sexual offenders and favoured the decriminalisation of homosexual behaviour

---

[16] NAS, HH57/1287, PWC, Note by Scottish Home Department on Scottish Prisons and Borstal Institutions, October 1955.

[17] ibid.

[18] For Golla's use of hormone treatment, see FL Golla and RS Hodge, 'Hormone Treatment of the Sexual Offender' (1949) 256 *The Lancet* 1006.

[19] NAS, HH57/1288, memo by TD Inch, 'Sexual Offenders: Treatment in Prisons'; PWC, PRO, HO345/15, CHP/TRANS/42, PWC, evidence of TD Inch, 1 November 1955. More routinely, homosexual offenders suffering from anxiety states were treated with Langactic and Sodium Amytal (NAS, HH57/1288, HS Walter, Psychiatric Clinic, Aberdeen Royal Infirmary to GI Manson, Medical Officer HM Prison, Peterhead, 3 December 1957).

[20] PRO, HO345/15, CHP/TRANS/42, PWC, evidence of TD Inch, 1 November 1955. The subsequent disclosure by the Wolfenden Committee of the use of hormone therapy produced some colourful headlines. See *Sunday Pictorial*, 16 February 1958: 'Sex Pills for Scots in Jail'.

[21] See NAS, HH57/1287, note by TD Inch for PWC, October 1955; PRO, HO345/15, CHP/TRANS/42, PWC, evidence of TD Inch and W Boyd, 1 November 1955.

for consenting adults over 21.[22] In their view, a range of alternative provisions was necessary. In accordance with Freudian interpretations, there needed to be more child guidance and child psychiatric clinics to 'treat deviation as early as possible before fixation occurred'. Courts should have routine psychiatric reports on all homosexual offenders prior to sentencing, supplied by a properly-staffed University or Regional Hospital Board clinic, and more extensive use needed to be made of probationary orders for treatment of first offenders under the 1949 Criminal Justice (Scotland) Act. For the homosexual recidivist or 'homosexual psychopath', there should be a separate psychopathic institute, as in Denmark. Finally, treatment regimes had to be more effectively monitored and sustained by means of improved staff resources for after-care and social work. Underlying their evidence was a belief that a less punitive policy would in fact produce a more liberal and sympathetic attitude to homosexuality in British society.

Evidence submitted by Drs Winifred Rushforth and WP Kreamer, respectively founder and Medical Director of the pioneering Davidson Clinic in Edinburgh, established in 1940 to provide family therapy and psychoanalytical treatment to the general public, also favoured the decriminalisation of homosexual behaviour between consenting adults as integral to changing social attitudes and to a refocusing of public debate onto issues of aetiology rather than punishment.[23] In their view, in many cases, homosexuality was 'neither a disease nor a matter of choice' but compulsive behaviour contingent on emotional immaturity.[24] They stressed the value of psychotherapy in bringing some homosexuals 'into a more mature state' in which they could relate to women. They considered that imprisonment merely reinforced the mental and social problems of homosexuals and should only be used for 'hardened offenders' who were 'a potential danger to young people'. They did not feel that prison predisposed homosexual offenders to effective treatment, and viewed the existing prison medical staff as unsuited to addressing sexual problems. At the very least, they advocated the general introduction of group psychotherapy for offenders. However, significantly, their evidence still identified homosexuals as fundamentally dysfunctional and anti-social and, in part, their opposition to legal coercion was that it served merely to magnify

---

[22] Significantly, this was not a view shared by many Scottish Prison Medical Officers (PRO, HO345/15, CHP/TRANS/42, PWC, evidence of TD Inch and W Boyd, 1 November 1955).

[23] See PRO, HO345/7, CHP/36 and 345/16, CHP/ TRANS/62, PWC, evidence of W Rushforth and WP Kreamer, 10 April 1956. In 1956, the Clinic was staffed by five medically-qualified therapists and six lay therapists. Both medical and lay therapists underwent a period of training during which they themselves had to undergo 'a complete and successful personal analysis'. The Clinic employed a mixture of Freudian and Jungian techniques, with drugs used 'only exceptionally as an adjunct to treatment'. Its practice was heavily influenced by the work of Melanie Klein, the pioneering Viennese psychoanalyst. In evidence, it was claimed that the Clinic was the only 'analytical group' then operating in Scotland. The clinic accepted in the region of 100 new patients a year, of which about 10% were 'overt homosexuals', largely referred by the police, a Minister, or a GP. The lay therapists, who were unpaid during their training, were not formally recognised within the Edinburgh medical establishment or by the University.

[24] PRO, HO345/16, PWC, evidence of WP Kreamer, 10 April 1956.

not only the homosexual's sense of social isolation but also his sexual ego. As Dr Kreamer testified:

> I feel that if we make them into heroes and put them into prisons ... it is not really doing very much good, and it gives them a wrong idea of self-importance. ... [I]f you do that I feel it is bad for society and for the character of these men, too.[25]

In his view, many of such 'young heroes want[ed] to suck forbidden fruit' and prosecution often served to fuel a neurotic compulsion for punishment.

In his contribution to the BMA's evidence to the Wolfenden Committee, John Glaister, Regius Professor of Forensic Medicine in the University of Glasgow, also combined a somewhat pathological view of homosexuality with support for its limited decriminalisation. He was a vigorous supporter of coercive measures, including segregation in colonies, for 'the inveterate and degenerate sodomist, the debauchers of youth, and those who resort[ed] to violence to meet their desires'. Likewise, he endorsed a 'major attack by the law' on 'the confirmed invert and the male prostitute'. However, he did not feel that the incidence of homosexuality threatened the nation with 'racial decadence' and considered that consenting acts of adults in private (not including sodomy) were a matter 'of private ethics' and should be outwith the law. In his opinion, while society's disapproval was 'inevitable and desirable' and while homosexuality was certainly not something that should be encouraged, incarceration was not the answer in the majority of cases that involved minor offences. Glaister viewed prison as 'the last place for homosexual treatment'. On the contrary, he emphasised its propensity 'to incubate and foster homosexual tendencies'. Moreover, he also considered that the risk of prosecution often acted as an aphrodisiac for offenders. 'Many homosexuals', he averred, 'feel that to flout the law is fraught with adventure due to possible detection, and to their peculiar make-up this may tend to add a fillip to their sex life'.[26]

At the same time, much of the evidence presented on the effectiveness of existing medical treatments for homosexual conditions was far from compelling. The experience of the Scottish Home Department was that, within the prison population, only a minority of homosexual offenders, some 30 per cent, were suitable for medical treatment and only 11 per cent prepared fully to cooperate with a course of psychotherapy.[27] In particular, it was claimed that short-term prisoners proved reluctant to agree to a course of treatment that might be prolonged beyond the date of their release. Nor were the medical staff of the Scottish Prison and Borstal

---

[25] ibid.
[26] British Medical Association Archives, B/107/1/2, memo. by Professor John Glaister, 30 June 1955.
[27] The reasons listed for unsuitability for treatment were: not recommended by specialist (44.7%); too dull or inadequate character (23.4%); absence of any anxiety over sexual practices or of any real wish to change (8.5%); denial of tendency or tendency not apparent (17%); too old and unadaptable or practice too well established (4.3%); belief that conviction has cured offender (2.1%) (PRO, HO345/9, CHP/88, PWC, evidence of Scottish Home Department, 30 October 1955; PRO, CAB129/66, Cabinet Memorandum, Sexual Offences, Secretary of State for Scotland, 17 February 1954). For comparative data for England and Wales, see *RWC*, 66, para 197.

Services at all certain of the outcome of their therapies. They insisted that it was never their aim to try and change the sexual identity of a homosexual, which they regarded as 'expensive, dangerous' and, almost certainly, impossible. Dr W Boyd admitted that, although they might 're-direct' the energies of homosexuals and 'allow them to make a more adequate adjustment to their responsibilities', he did not for a moment suggest they could 'cure' homosexuality.[28] In his experience, it was not possible to treat homosexuals as sex offenders in prison and he recommended that hardened offenders should be treated in separate psychopathic institutes.[29] Even with the more limited aim of trying to reduce the levels of sexual urge and mental anxiety in homosexual offenders, the medical science was hazy. As Drs Inch and Boyd freely admitted, 'we do not know what may be happening so far as the endocrine treatment is concerned and what the ultimate result may be', and, although evidence suggested that in many cases it alleviated 'a most uncomfortable feeling of tension and guilt', and rendered patients more amenable to psychotherapy, they had never undertaken a controlled experiment 'to see whether aspirin would [have been] equally successful'.[30]

The evidence of the Davidson Clinic suggested that the scope for addressing homosexual behaviour by means of psychoanalysis was also limited. Although its staff claimed relatively high levels of success, this was clearly based on a relatively modest definition of 'success' and on extremely selective and long-term labour intensive therapy, exploring the patient's history right back into infancy and his/her earliest family relationships.[31] While it was argued that men in their late teens and twenties, who were still developing emotionally, might benefit from treatment, sexually active men who 'had extensively practised their perversion' were viewed as unsuited to analysis. For later age groups, the view of Rushforth and Kreamer was that 'if there had been little or no perverted behaviour', treatment might, at the most, free the patient from undue anxiety and enable him to find a less compulsive, and more 'discreet' and 'creative way of living' that was of value to himself and the community. In their opinion, a person who had been homosexual for any length of time, even if he adjusted by means of marriage, remained fundamentally homosexual. Moreover, the Davidson Clinic had found that homosexual patients referred by the police or social workers were especially unresponsive to

---

[28] Professor Glaister also considered the likelihood of cure for 'innate inverts' as utopian. He felt it likely that 'there will always be a nucleus in our midst, just as we have other groups of handicapped persons' (BMA Archives, B/107/1/2, memo. by Glaister, 30 June 1955).

[29] PRO, HO345/15, CHP/TRANS/42, PWC, evidence of W Boyd, 1 November 1955.

[30] PRO, HO345/15, CHP/TRANS/42, PWC, evidence of KM Hancock and TD Inch, 1 November 1955; evidence of W Boyd, 1 November 1955. Evidence on the outcome of treatment was also compromised by the lack of follow-up surveillance of released prisoners. Inch testified that: 'As regards the after effects, certainly none of them have yet come back to us but we do not know, and we have no means of knowing, whether they continue treatment afterwards or not. ... I am unfortunately quite unable to say what the permanent end result is.' (PRO, HO345/15, CHP/TRANS/42, PWC, evidence of KM Hancock and TD Inch, 1 November 1955; NAS, HH57/1288, Departmental minute, 5 December 1957).

[31] PRO, HO345/7; 345/16 PWC, evidence of W Rushforth and WP Kreamer, 10 April 1956.

psychotherapy.[32] Significantly, its analysts either would or could not furnish the Wolfenden Committee with any recorded case where sexual reorientation had been effected.[33]

Such uncertainties merely fuelled the scepticism surrounding the medical treatment of homosexuality within the Scottish judicial and penal systems.[34] Thus, in evidence to the Wolfenden Committee, several sheriffs argued that, in many instances, homosexuality was an issue of criminal wilfulness rather than medical dysfunction and should be addressed accordingly.[35] Insofar as they viewed it as a 'disease', they stressed its dysgenic impact upon the nation's health and demography and its essentially predatory and 'infectious' nature, with an initial sexual act engendering a cycle of addictive debauchery, often with ever-younger and more vulnerable partners.[36] Even where Scottish sheriffs and magistrates advocated greater recourse to medical treatment, they were insistent that it be part of normal criminal proceedings so that the element of deterrence remained and offenders could be compelled to comply with appropriate therapies.[37]

Significantly, the most influential attack on the 'medicalisation' of homosexuality came from James Adair, a member of the Wolfenden Committee, and former Procurator-fiscal. His virulent critique, which effectively amounted to a minority report, and which echoed the prejudices and concerns of many within the Scottish legal and political establishment,[38] was scathing of the tendency of psychiatrists to sentimentalise the problem of homosexuality and to downplay its paedophilic aspects and damage to physical health. In his opinion, much of the evidence presented by 'mental specialists' was 'quite inexplicable and in not a few cases manifestly indefensible'. He considered that homosexuality had become the latest disease 'fashion' or 'craze' of 'medical men', and highlighted the uncertainties of

---

[32] ibid. They anticipated that group psychotherapy might prove more effective but predicted that bringing together a group of homosexuals within the Clinic would provoke a public outcry.

[33] Indeed, Winifred Rushforth considered that the primary role of the Clinic was not to try and alter sexual orientation, but to facilitate the patient's understanding of his homosexual feelings and anxieties.

[34] Sir David Henderson attributed the failure of psychiatrists to 'gain the complete confidence of the legal profession' in homosexual cases to this lack of any clear evidence of a 'cure'. See DK Henderson, above n 5, 25. This disparity between medical and legal expectations also prevailed south of the Border. See Westwood, above n 14, 90.

[35] Thus, according to Sheriff Hamilton: 'It [was] fashionable to say that homosexual offenders [had] a "mental kink" and required[d] treatment but apart from the odd case of physical ailment such as prostate gland enlargement, the only "treatment" which [might] be beneficial [was] such as [would] strengthen the willpower to resist offending' (PRO, HO345/8, PWC, memorandum prepared by The Association of Sheriffs-Substitute, 1955).

[36] Thus Sheriff Substitute Middleton of Dumfermline and Kinross challenged the Committee as to whether there was ever a homosexual case 'where the relationship [was] confined to two individuals, and there [was] no danger to other members of society' (PRO, HO345/16, evidence on behalf of Association of Sheriffs-Substitute, 9 April 1956).

[37] PRO, HO345/8 and 16, CHP/44 and CHP/TRANS/60, PWC, evidence of Association of Sheriffs-Substitute, March 1955, 9 April 1956; PRO, HO345/16, PWC, evidence of Stipendary Magistrate, Glasgow, 9 April 1956.

[38] For a discussion of the broader debate over homosexuality in Scottish society, see Davidson and Davis, 'A Field for Private Members', above n 1, 174–201.

medical and mental science 'and the limited knowledge and powers of the medical profession under existing circumstances to deal with homosexual patients'. According to Adair, a significant proportion of homosexuals seeking treatment were only doing so in order to evade the due process of law and were merely using medical therapy as a smokescreen for their perversion. Many, he argued, were already too old at 18 for treatment, with their sexuality and behaviour 'for all practical purposes immutable'.[39] Adair was especially concerned to elicit from witnesses the physical damage done by sodomy and was adamant that it should be retained as a separate offence with heavy penalties.[40] Indeed, in some ways, he displayed an obsession with anal intercourse reminiscent of the medical discourses surrounding the prosecution of sodomy in late 19th-century Britain.[41]

The View from the High Courts

The extent to which the testimony submitted to the Wolfenden Committee accurately reflected the role of medical evidence in cases involving homosexual offences in Scotland in the 1950s, and the degree to which that role subsequently evolved, can in part be obtained from a study of court proceedings. A survey of cases brought in district courts under section 11 of the 1885 Criminal Law Amendment Act, and under byelaws relating to public conveniences, does reveal an increasing use by offenders of medical arguments in written pleas to the court. Some emphasised that they were already seeking referral for psychiatric treatment;[42] others, especially those accused of contravening byelaws, increasingly proffered medical excuses for their behaviour, including hypertension, epilepsy, alcohol addiction, and, most commonly, prostate and bladder problems.[43] However, in the lower courts, medical reports were rarely called for prior to formal summons or sentencing.[44] Limited and fragmentary evidence suggests that

---

[39] See esp, *RWC* 117-21; PRO, HO345/12 and /16, PWC, 15 October 1954, 10 April 1956; HO345/2, J Adair to WC Roberts, 4 October 1956; HO345/10, note on WC discussion meetings, 11 and 12 September 1956.

[40] See PRO, HO345/9, PWC, minutes of 21st Meeting, March 1956.

[41] See I Crozier, '"All the Appearances were Perfectly Natural": The Anus of the Sodomite in Nineteenth-Century Medical Discourse' in CE Forth and I Crozier (eds), *Body Parts: Critical Explorations in Corporeality* (Oxford, Lexington, 2005) 65–84.

[42] See eg Edinburgh City Archive, District Court Papers, case of WBA, letter of defendant to Clerk of Court, 25 May 1960. Significantly, some 36% of the patients attending the Jordanburn Nerve Hospital in the 1950s for problems relating to homosexuality, for whom medical correspondence survives, were referred either by solicitors or general practitioners in relation to criminal proceedings. (Lothian Health Services Archive, Edinburgh University Library, LHB7/CC1, Royal Edinburgh Hospital medical clinic and out-patient letters, 1950–58).

[43] Edinburgh City Archive, District Court Papers for 1960 and 1970.

[44] This lack of medical investigation was one of many criticisms of the judicial system levelled by the Scottish Minorities Group in their campaign for homosexual law reform (National Library of Scotland, miscellaneous pamphlets of the SMG, *The Case for Homosexual Law Reform in Scotland*, 1973).

medical reports were deployed more regularly within the Sheriffs Courts, but the absence of surviving case papers, coupled with issues of data protection, inhibits any systematic research in this area. This is the more disappointing in that it was before the sheriff courts that the bulk of prosecutions for 'homosexual offences' between consenting adults were tried.

What have been available to the author, under restricted access, are the psychiatric reports on defendants and convicted offenders submitted to the Scottish High Court and Court of Appeal over the period 1950–80 in all cases involving sodomy or contravention of the 1885 Criminal Law Amendment Act section 11. These reports form part of the judicial 'processes'; case papers in the proceedings before the court, including summonses, indictments and productions.[45] Inevitably, evidence drawn from such processes will be highly selective as the cases involved only the more serious crimes involving homosexual practices. Nonetheless, they do convey some impression of the weight attributed within the legal process to psychiatric opinion.

An examination of High Court cases relating to homosexual offences suggests that, over the period, there was, quite apart from routine medical inspection under the mental health act in respect of fitness to plead, and forensic investigations of 'anal interference' where minors were involved, an increasing recourse to psychiatric evidence, commissioned both by the Crown and defence lawyers. By the 1970s, some 30 per cent of cases involved such medical evidence. This appears to have been especially so where the accused was a professional man such as a teacher or where he was socially well-connected.[46]

Broadly speaking, there are four treatment strategies for homosexual offences that can be detected in the medical evidence to the Scottish High Court in the period 1950–80. First, there were isolated cases where homosexual offences were diagnosed as primarily a function of mental deficiency and where the offender was deemed a danger both to himself and society. In such cases, admission to an 'institution or colony for mental defectives'—typically Carstairs—was recommended.[47]

Secondly, there were a group of offenders for whom medical treatment (predominantly psychotherapy but sometimes supplementary hormone therapy) was recommended with the aim of changing the direction of their sexual preference. These were cases in which, typically, the offender was either under 25 or deemed to be psycho-sexually immature for reasons of up-bringing, social conditioning, or the impact of random sexual advances or homo-erotic experiences. These were offenders whose homosexuality was regarded, primarily within a Freudian perspective, as 'transitional' rather than innate, with restrictive home environments and sexual ignorance impeding normal heterosexual development and outlets.

---

[45] Although previously in the public domain, because of their sensitive nature, in accordance with the 1998 Data Protection Act, these records are now closed for 75 years unless special access is granted by the High Court of Justiciary.

[46] See, eg NAS, JC9/36, 38; JC26/1956/65, trial papers of HCM. On the correlation of class and medical evidence, see also, Higgins, above n 1, 160–61.

[47] See, eg NAS, JC9/37; JC26/1954/145, trial minutes and papers relating to JH.

However, even for this group, claims for the ability of medical treatment to secure a 'cure' or genuine sexual reorientation became more qualified as the period progressed. Thus, in the case of CWH, charged in Hawick in 1955 on two counts of contravening the 1885 Criminal Law Amendment Act, the Physician-Superintendent of Dingleton Hospital, Melrose, was adamant that there was a 'recognised cure' for homosexuality, that there were cases of successful treatment 'within [his] own purview' and that the panel's homosexual tendencies could be 'cured and eradicated'.[48] Such unconditional claims were seldom, if ever, heard in medical testimony in the 1960s and 1970s. It should be added that, during the period 1950–80, in medical evidence to the High Courts, aversion therapy using drugs or electric shocks was never explicitly recommended for this group of offenders.

Thirdly, there were offenders for whom medical treatment was recommended not to change their sexual orientation but to enable them to better adapt to their sexual problems and to life in general. Typically, these were cases where the accused was viewed as a latent homosexual who had successfully sublimated his urges over a long period but for whom an additional dysfunction such as alcoholism or marital stress had triggered overt homosexual behaviour, very often associated with acute anxiety and guilt. In such cases, 'latent homosexuality' was presented as 'an illness of the mind' and extensive psychotherapy, attached either to a probationary sentence or to admission to a psychiatric unit under section 55 of the Mental Health (Scotland) Act 1960 was often suggested as a means of enabling the offender to come to terms with his condition and to develop a self-awareness of social and other factors precipitating inappropriate urges and behaviours. A primary aim was to ensure that he did not remain socially isolated but was 'helped back into his place in society and to maintain his employment in the community'.[49]

Finally, there were medical offenders for whom medical treatment was advocated, often in association with a custodial sentence, as a means primarily of achieving greater continence and self-control. Typically, these were cases where homosexual behaviour was viewed as either obsessive and/or predatory. By the 1970s, group psychotherapy, such as that available at the Douglas Inch Centre in Glasgow, a forensic outpatient clinic in Glasgow specialising in psychodynamic therapy, was increasingly recommended for such offenders, but the predominant treatments advanced were aversion and sex-suppressant therapy. Thus, in the case of TP, tried before the High Court in Glasgow in 1968 for contravention of section 11 of the Criminal Law Amendment Act 1885, the Physician Superintendent of Dingleton Hospital recommended that, in addition to his prostate gland being investigated, the panel should be referred to the Royal Edinburgh Hospital for

---

[48] NAS, JC34/4/189, appeal papers relating to CWH, report of proceedings at Sheriff Court, Hawick. 'Panel' is a Scottish legal term meaning a prisoner arraigned for trial at the criminal court.
[49] See, eg NAS, JC26/1962/90, trial papers relating to JJT, report by Dr MAES, Eastern District Hospital Psychiatric Unit, 26 October 1962; NAS, JC26/1973/293, trial papers relating to JG.

aversion therapy. In his view: 'It might be that some kind of negative conditioning, like electric shocks, in relation to homosexual stimulation might turn him against this form of sexual activity'.[50] In other cases, such as that of AHL, tried for a series of offences against teenage boys in 1977, supervised drug therapy, such as the use of Anquil, designed 'to curb his sex drive', was recommended.[51]

In assessing the impact of psychiatric evidence on sentencing for homosexual offences in this period, the picture is complicated by the fact that many such offences were part of wider charges involving the sexual assault or corruption of young children. Indeed, one of the more notable features of such trials was the conflation of homosexual offences with what would now be regarded as paedophilia. Moreover, due to the severity of the charges brought in the High Court, its proceedings inevitably excluded many cases in which medical evidence may have contributed to more lenient, non-custodial sentences being passed.

In general, where an offence was deemed sufficiently serious as to warrant a prison sentence, the duration of such a sentence was not determined on therapeutic grounds. However, there was a small but increasing number of cases where medical evidence does appear to have elicited the use of section 3 of the Criminal Justice (Scotland) Act 1949 to impose probationary orders with associated psychiatric treatment.[52] In many such instances, the younger, the more self-reflective and cooperative the defendant, the less fixated his sexual behaviour, and the less protracted the recommended treatment,[53] the more likely it was that such evidence would affect sentencing.

Thus, in the case of HCM,[54] accused in 1953 of sodomy and lewd and libidinous practices with soldiers from Redford Barracks, medical testimony for the defence stressed the panel's self-awareness that there was 'something far wrong with him psychically' and his willingness to leave the country after treatment to go for further 'special' therapy in Denmark.[55] No treatment, it was alleged, would be forthcoming within the Scottish prison system.[56] It was also argued that, as a

---

[50] JC9/57; JC26/1968/216, trial minutes and papers relating to TP. For reference to the use of aversion therapy, see also JC26/1970/204, trial papers relating to RC. In such cases, aversion therapy was clearly perceived as suppressing anti-social behaviour rather than effecting a genuine reorientation of sexual preference.

[51] NAS, JC26/1977/386, trial papers relating to AHL. For the use of drug therapy, including oestrogen therapy, see also NAS, JC26/1956/65; JC26/1979/402; JC26/1979/200.

[52] In the view of two leading Scottish psychiatrists, Sir David Henderson and Ivor RC Batchelor, by 1962 improving relations between the medical and legal professions had 'led to a greater emphasis on treatment and rehabilitation rather than on an arbitrary prison sentence' (Henderson and Batchelor, above n 15, 194).

[53] Sir David Henderson, who had given evidence in Scottish trials over many decades, reported that, where psychoanalysis had been recommended, once its duration and uncertain outcome had been explained, the Court usually took the view that treatment should be undertaken only after a prison sentence had been served. (Henderson and Batchelor, above n 15, 206).

[54] NAS, JC9/36, JC9/38, JC26/1956/65, trial minutes and papers relating to HCM.

[55] Specifically, oestrogen treatment under Dr Christian Hamburger, the Danish endocrinologist. 'An institution in Ireland' was also recommended.

[56] Significantly, the Lord Justice General declined to have this point elaborated, interjecting that: 'I think I know the position in prison'. Evidence in other cases suggests that this was in fact the situation

'passive homosexual', in medical circles, the defendant would be viewed as having 'a definite constitutional disease' rather than the criminality often diagnostic of the 'active homosexual'.[57] In the event, HCM was sentenced to three years' probation on condition that he entered Moray Royal Institution at Perth for treatment for 12 months as a voluntary boarder.

In the case of TA, convicted in 1954 of eight charges of gross indecency and three of attempted sodomy in Hawick, under section 11 of the 1885 Criminal Law Amendment Act, the defence also requested a psychiatric report with a view to mitigating sentence.[58] Despite the involvement of males below the age of 21, again the willingness of the panel to 'have himself put right' and to cooperate in treatment was decisive, as was his awareness, in the view of the psychiatric witness, that homosexual relations would always be intrinsically unfulfilling and 'accompanied by feelings of shame and disgust'. TA was put on three years' probation, subject to spending 12 months in a mental hospital. Subsequently, a revised court order requiring attendance only as an outpatient was issued on the grounds of his responsiveness to oestrogen treatment and psychotherapy.

Similarly, in the case of RH, tried in 1956 at the High Court in Edinburgh on charges of sodomy and lewd and libidinous practices, mitigating evidence in favour of treatment as a voluntary boarder in a mental hospital was submitted both by Professor Sir David Henderson, Physician Superintendent of the Royal Edinburgh Hospital, and Dr William Boyd, Consultant Psychiatrist to the Scottish Prison Service. The panel was portrayed as the victim of predatory and precocious male teenagers, and not, given his previous heterosexual relationships, as a 'true homosexual'. His sexual proclivities were seen as a function of his deprived upbringing—sharing a bed throughout adolescence with his brother—and his dysfunctional relations with girls, rather than a deep-seated fixation, indicating a likely positive outcome for treatment. Accordingly, RH was remitted to Hawkshead Hospital for residential treatment for one year under a three year probationary order. As with TA, treatment proved so effective that this was duly revised in favour of outpatient therapy.[59]

---

in the 1950s. See, for example, evidence of CWFW, a habitual homosexual offender, to the effect that he was promised treatment but 'as soon as I have got into prison nobody has in any way been concerned with the matter except that I should serve the sentence. ... I have been compelled to be my own doctor in this matter.' (NAS, JC34/4/209, appeal papers relating to CWFW).

[57] Medical evidence for the defence was submitted by Dr AP Cawadias, an endocrinologist, author of *Hermaphroditos: The Human Intersex*, and former Vice-President of the Royal Society of Medicine. In practice, there is some evidence that law officers viewed the 'active' partner more leniently and perceived the 'passive' partner as the 'real' transgressor' in bringing another man to orgasm. See J Bancroft, *Human Sexuality and Its Problems*, 2nd edn (Edinburgh, Churchill Livingstone, 1989) 714. This viewpoint was undoubtedly reinforced by the medical discourse surrounding the increase in sexually transmitted diseases, which identified passive homosexuals as major 'reservoirs of infection'. See R Davidson, *Dangerous Liaisons: A Social History of Venereal Disease in Twentieth-Century Scotland* (Amsterdam, Rodopi, 2000) 251.

[58] NAS, JC9/37, trial minutes relating to TA.

[59] NAS, JC9/39; JC26/1956/122, trial minutes and papers relating to RH.

A fourth case illustrates that, by the end of the period, medical options were being deployed even in cases involving younger male adolescents. In the case of ISN, charged with sodomy and lewd and libidinous practices in 1979,[60] a number of considerations were advanced by a Consultant Psychiatrist of the Douglas Inch Centre; that the behaviour was immature rather than predatory; that a custodial sentence would not be in the long-term interests of society; that progress in therapeutic techniques had considerably increased the chances of effecting behaviour modification, and that such techniques were available at the Centre. Accordingly, sentence was deferred while the panel attended the Centre for group therapy and individual counselling. Although, after six months, psychiatric reports could not report any 'dramatic change in his personality [or] sexuality', the accused was eventually admonished and dismissed so as to enable him to 'continue to work on his problems and consolidate his gains'.[61]

However, such attitudes were often contested by psychiatric witnesses for the prosecution. In the case of HCM, after he had breached his probation order and re-offended, the Lord Justice Clerk endorsed the view of Sir David Henderson that 'lenient treatment' having failed, a 'stringent penalty of imprisonment' was called for. In his opinion, 'a little severity just for once might put him in a proper frame of mind' for benefiting thereafter from therapy. The defence counsel's plea that the panel should 'be allowed to leave the country in order to his undergoing treatment in a foreign clinic for his mental condition' was summarily dismissed.[62]

The medical case for the prosecution also prevailed in the case of JG, tried before the High Court in Edinburgh in 1973 for sodomy and attempted rape. The defence psychiatrist from Woodilee Hospital pressed for a sentence of compulsory admission to a psychiatric unit for two to three years under the 1960 Mental Health (Scotland) Act, on the grounds that his 'personality disorder, ... associated with sexual deviation of a homosexual nature', could be expected to respond to treatment. However, Dr HG, Consultant in Charge of Stobhill General Hospital and Clinical Lecturer in Psychological Medicine at the University of Glasgow, while conceding that homosexuality amounted to 'mental illness', did not regard the panel as a suitable case for treatment, given 'the long duration of his homosexual orientation'.[63] A sentence of four years' imprisonment was imposed. Similarly, in the case in of IN, the Consultant Psychiatrist giving evidence on behalf of the Procurator-fiscal was dismissive of any recourse to medical treatment in sentencing. While he conceded that the defendant's behaviour might be modified, he

---

[60] NAS, JC26/1979/194, trial papers relating to ISN.
[61] This is in marked contrast to the case of TF the same year, charged with similar offences before the High Court in Edinburgh. In this instance, psychiatric reports stressed that the panel had long-standing predatory paederastic tendencies, that he regarded his casual sexual acts with adolescent males as socially acceptable, and that, given his previous convictions, it was not considered that 'psychiatry ha[d] anything to offer as an alternative to imprisonment' (JC9/82; JC26/1979/402, trial minutes and papers relating to TF).
[62] NAS, JC26/1956/65, trial papers relating to HCM.
[63] NAS, JC26/1973/293, trial papers relating to JG.

considered it unlikely that his sexual orientation would be changed since 'he [was] not genuinely disposed to change it':

> He is talking of treatment at present because he wishes to avoid prison ... I do not think it would help his prospects of learning to conform to society's wishes if, having thoroughly broken the law because he believes it is a bad law, he were to be encouraged to view medical treatment as a means of escaping punishment. If convicted, he would do best to thole his assize and seek help at a later date out of a genuine wish to change.[64]

In a variety of other cases also, favourable psychiatric evidence signally failed to affect sentencing, especially where minors were involved. In the case of JB, tried before the High Court in Dundee in 1961 on charges of sodomy and lewd and libidinous practices, extensive psychiatric evidence was produced relating to the impact of his previous imprisonment in Japanese prisoner-of-war camps, his vulnerability to blackmail from adolescent boys, and his willingness to enter a mental hospital for treatment, but three years' imprisonment was imposed.[65]

Likewise, in the case of PC, charged at the High Court in Perth in 1965 with sodomy and lewd and libidinous practices, the presiding judge was not disposed to delay sentencing for a psychiatric report.[66] He rejected the argument of defence counsel that such a report might be useful in determining the effects of different terms of imprisonment, on the grounds that, in his opinion, the offender would receive treatment in prison anyway. A sentence of six years' imprisonment was duly delivered.[67]

A similar fate befell WTM, convicted in 1971 for a range of homosexual offences with males between the ages of 14 and 22. When the case had been initially heard before the Sheriff Court, strong evidence in favour of a non-custodial sentence, conditional on a two-year period of treatment, had been submitted by Dr HG. In his opinion, WTM's homosexuality was 'a mental illness' and 'require[d] and [was] susceptible to treatment', but did not justify detention under a hospital order. A further report from Dr JM of Riccatsbar Hospital, Paisley, was even more supportive of a probationary sentence. In his view, the fact that the panel was bisexual and had previously enjoyed satisfactory heterosexual relationships, that 'his basic personality' and 'motivation towards normal behaviour' was 'good', and that he was 'very willing to co-operate', made the prognosis for treatment very hopeful. However, when, because of the nature of the charges, the case was remitted to the High Court in Edinburgh, a sentence of three years' imprisonment was imposed.[68]

---

[64] NAS, JC26/1979/194, trial papers relating to IN. See also, JC/34/9/184, trial papers relating to JR; JC34/21/230, appeal papers relating to RMKW.

[65] NAS, JC26/1961/3, trial papers relating to JB.

[66] The possible conflict between the need for prompt sentencing and for adequate medical evidence was an issue that had been raised by the Wolfenden Committee. See *RWC*, 64.

[67] NAS, JC34/11/42, appeal papers relating to PC, transcript of trial in Sheriff Court. See also, NAS, JC26/1966/67, trial papers relating to CEJT.

[68] NAS, JC9/66; JC26/1971/344, minutes and trial papers relating to WTM.

The views of the judiciary with respect to psychiatric evidence were sometimes most clearly articulated during appeal proceedings. In the appeal by CWH in 1955 against conviction for contravention of section 11 of the Criminal Law Amendment Act 1885, the transcript of the original trial clearly reveals that, despite the evidence of the Physician-Superintendent of Dingleton Hospital that the panel's homosexuality was a mental disease with 'a pathological origin' and susceptible to treatment (including drug therapy), the Sheriff was disposed to view the offences as a function of a 'moral' rather than 'psychological' defect. He reported to the Appeal Court that he was not satisfied that the offender's mental condition was abnormal or that 'it required, or would be susceptible to, medical treatment'. The appeal against a one-year prison sentence was accordingly dismissed.[69]

Similar sentiments were expressed by the presiding judge in his report to the Court of Appeal in the case of AHL in 1977 against a seven-year prison sentence.[70] Psychiatric reports had emphasised that AHL's offences against young boys were due to his homosexual proclivities and could possibly be treated as a mental illness; preferably by attendance at a psychiatric clinic. In the view of Lord Wheatley, the priority was to take the offender 'out of circulation', whether or not effective treatment might be available in prison. He added a pointed postscript that the suggestion by psychiatrists that probationary treatment might be an option was wholly 'unrealistic' and merely served to raise 'unjustifiable hopes and corresponding disappointment'; something he recommended that psychiatrists submitting evidence in court should firmly take on board.[71] Although in this case the psychiatric reports were forwarded on to the prison authorities, application to appeal was refused.[72]

Conclusion

It is problematic to draw firm conclusions from this overview of merely two perspectives on the medical perception and treatment of homosexual offenders in Scotland in the period 1950–80. Evidence to the Wolfenden Committee was arguably driven as much by concern to justify departmental procedures as to capture an accurate picture of contemporary medical and legal practices. In addition, not only may the evidence from the High Court be far from typical, but also the use of trial processes and appeal papers, as with all legal records, pose a

---

[69] NAS, JC34/4/189 appeal papers relating to CWH.

[70] NAS, JC9/78; JC26/1977/386; JC34/26/300, minutes, trial papers and appeal papers relating to AHL.

[71] This very much echoed the views of the Wolfenden Report. See *RWC*, 61–2.

[72] Such a case resonated with earlier warnings by the psychiatrists, David Henderson and Ivor Batchelor, that a coordinated approach to cases involving sexual anomalies would 'never be accomplished so long as angry judges thunder[ed] moralistic platitudes from the Bench, and indiscreet psychiatrists indulge[d] in optimistic theorizing …'. See Henderson and Batchelor, above n 15, 207.

range of methodological challenges.[73] It could be argued, for example, that due to the closure of High Court precognitions, I have accorded the narratives derived from medical reports undue priority and lacked due regard to 'the multiple texts that make up a legal record'. Finally, the evidence presented here was very much shaped and informed by legal discourses and desiderata. The exploration of clinical records and of gay archives and recollections may well reveal alternative narratives of how law and medicine interacted over homosexual issues.

Nonetheless, some tentative conclusions can perhaps be drawn. First, it is clear that, in testimony to the Wolfenden Committee, the evidence of medical and legal witnesses from Scotland reflected the more general ambivalence towards medical strategies for homosexual offences articulated in its proceedings and final report. While many witnesses did embrace the need for the medical treatment and rehabilitation of offenders, and appear to have been increasingly sympathetic to more psychodynamic forms of psychotherapy, their mindset remained heavily rooted in taxonomies of deviance shaped by established notions of sexual pathology rather than in more progressive ideas of sexual expression and inclusion. Cure or sublimation, with their implications of self-rejection or self-denial, remained at the basis of therapy.

Secondly, an analysis of court records suggests that the impact of medical evidence on trial proceedings for homosexual offences was complex. From the 1950s, such evidence did play an increasing role in cases, and psychiatric reports figured ever more prominently in trial processes. However, medical testimony was by no means monopolised by the defence and could also be mobilised very effectively by the Crown Office. The evident lack of consensus over the aetiology of homosexuality and the efficacy of medical treatment further ensured that medical evidence was often marginalised within legal proceedings. Indeed, many cases reflected enduring tensions between medical conceptions of homosexual behaviour 'as a pathology or intrinsic condition' and judicial conceptions of it as embodying 'criminal sexual "acts" rather than identities'.[74] As a result, psychiatric issues continued to be framed within legal discourses that often reflected broader moral assumptions and concerns surrounding homosexuality within Scottish civil society, the very same assumptions and concerns that were to delay homosexual law reform north of the Border until 1980.[75]

---

[73] On these challenges, see esp, S Robertson, 'What's Law Got to Do with It? Legal Records and Sexual Histories', (2005) 14 *Journal of the History of Sexuality* 161.

[74] On this tension, see M Cook, 'Law' in HG Cocks and M Houlbrook (eds), *Modern History of Sexuality* (Basingstoke, Palgrave Macmillan, 2006) 79.

[75] The Sexual Offences Act 1967, which decriminalised male homosexual acts in private in England and Wales between consenting adults over the age of 21, did not apply to Scotland. Similar provisions for Scotland had to await the Criminal Justice (Scotland) Bill 1980. For details of the constraints operating in Scotland after 1967, see Davidson and Davis, 'Sexuality and the State', above n 1.

8

The Medical Community and Abortion Law Reform: Scotland in National Context, c 1960–1980

GAYLE DAVIS[*]

This chapter will focus on the 1967 Abortion Act, which arguably constituted one of the most significant and contentious medico-social legislative developments of the 20th century within the British context. This Act was the first piece of abortion-related legislation to cover Scotland, England and Wales collectively, and brought the British medical profession much more fully into the arena of termination of pregnancy. The Abortion Act made termination legal where the risk to the life of a pregnant woman, or injury to her physical or mental health, or to that of her existing children, was greater than the risks from abortion, or where there was a substantial risk that a baby would be born seriously handicapped.[1]

The history of abortion law reform has attracted fairly substantial academic attention. Broadly speaking, historians of sexuality have analysed the 1967 Act as part of the general programme of so-called 'permissive' measures introduced to Britain during the 1960s, including the partial decriminalisation of homosexuality and the easing of access to contraception, which redefined the relationship of the State to the moral domain of the private citizen.[2] Other commentators have focused on the social politics surrounding the genesis of the Abortion Act and subsequent attempts to restrict or overturn that legislation.[3] A final group has

---

[*] This research was undertaken with the generous financial support of the Wellcome Trust (Grant 061152/Z/OO/Z/JM/HH/SW) and the generous intellectual support of the grant holder, Professor Roger Davidson. I would also like to acknowledge with gratitude the archival assistance I received from Lesley Hall, Fiona Watson, and the staff of the National Archives of Scotland. Limited excerpts of this chapter appeared previously in G Davis and R Davidson, '"Big White Chief", "Pontius Pilate", and the "Plumber": The Impact of the 1967 Abortion Act on the Scottish Medical Community, c 1967–80' (2005) 18 *Social History of Medicine* 283–306.

[1] Full details of the Act can be found at *Public General Statutes* Eliz II, Ch 87.

[2] See, eg J Weeks, *Sex, Politics and Society: The Regulation of Sexuality since 1800*, 2nd edn (London, Longman, 1989); LA Hall, *Sex, Gender and Social Change in Britain since 1880* (Basingstoke, Macmillan, 2000).

[3] See, eg BL Brookes, *Abortion in England, 1900–1967* (London, Croom Helm, 1988); M Durham, *Sex and Politics: The Family and Morality in the Thatcher Years* (Basingstoke, Macmillan, 1991); J Lovenduski and J Outshoorn (eds), *The New Politics of Abortion* (London, Sage, 1986).

explored abortion within the gendered context of the politics of reproductive health.[4] However, this chapter locates itself with the relatively small body of scholars who have chosen to focus upon the role of the medical profession within the process of abortion law reform, and the degree to which that law has influenced, and been interpreted within, medical practice.[5] It is argued here that a consideration of the medical community's role is crucial in order fully to understand the workings and significance of the legislation, since the implementation of that legislation has been so dependent upon the ideologies and actions of doctors and nurses.

Furthermore, while the social and legal history of abortion policy and provision in Britain has received widespread attention from scholars, existing studies have centred mainly—either explicitly or implicitly—upon Whitehall and Westminster, and upon the English experience of this legislation. The fact that Scotland has been largely omitted to date is a particular shortcoming given that, as it will be argued here, the 1967 Act was to be substantially modelled on the distinctive legal and medical traditions found north of the Border, and quite particularly in the north-east area of Scotland, Aberdeenshire. It is therefore further intended that this chapter contribute both a regional and intra-regional dimension to this aspect of the history of sexuality in order to gain a more nuanced understanding of both the policy and practice surrounding later 20th-century abortion in Britain, and the interaction between medicine and the law in this sphere of reproductive health.

The first half of the chapter will begin by surveying abortion law and practice as it existed in Britain prior to 1967. It will address briefly the differing legal status of abortion in England and Scotland, and the inconsistencies in practice intra-regionally. It will then examine the personalities involved in the successful passing of the 1967 Act, particularly the political architect of the Medical Termination of Pregnancy Bill which became the Abortion Act, the Scottish politician David Steel, and his chief medical advisor, the Scottish gynaecologist Dugald Baird. The second half of the chapter will chart the impact of this legislation upon the medical profession and the problems which they perceived to have been created by it, as articulated by Scottish witnesses to the Lane Committee (1971–74)—the only thorough review of the working of the Act—through reports in the media, and through Scottish medical responses to a subsequent Abortion (Amendment) Bill put forward by a Scottish politician, John Corrie, in 1979. Finally, the chapter will explore how the Scottish medical community responded to the challenge of this new

---

[4] See, eg S Sheldon, *Beyond Control: Medical Power and Abortion Law* (London, Pluto, 1997); M Latham, *Regulating Reproduction: A Century of Conflict in Britain and France* (Manchester, Manchester University Press, 2002); L Hoggart, *Feminist Campaigns for Birth Control and Abortion Rights in Britain* (Lewiston, Edwin Mellen Press, 2003).

[5] See esp SJ MacIntyre, 'The Medical Profession and the 1967 Abortion Act in Britain' (1973) 7 *Social Science and Medicine* 121; J Keown, *Abortion, Doctors and the Law: Some Aspects of the Legal Regulation of Abortion in England from 1803 to 1982* (Cambridge, CUP, 1988); T Newburn, *Permission and Regulation: Law and Morals in Post-War Britain* (London, Routledge, 1992) ch 6.

responsibility, and review briefly the range of strategies employed by those who wished to minimise or devolve their role within the decision-making process.

Abortion Law and Practice Prior to 1967

Previous to the 1967 Abortion Act, English abortion legislation was derived from the Offences Against the Person Act of 1861, which made the procurement of a miscarriage a crime. This was subsequently modified by the Infant Life (Preservation) Act of 1929, which exempted those cases where abortion was deemed necessary to save the life of the mother; and by a 1938 judicial ruling, *R v Bourne*,[6] which interpreted the 1929 Act as permitting abortion where 'the probable consequences of the continuance of the pregnancy [were] to make the woman a physical or mental wreck', in relation to a particularly disturbing case where a 14-year-old girl was raped by a group of soldiers.[7]

However, none of the aforementioned applied in Scotland, where abortion law followed a somewhat different course. North of the Border, abortion constituted a common law offence without strictly defined limits, so that it was possible to interpret it more elastically than English statute law. Scottish legal textbooks recorded that abortion could be performed legally when certain medical criteria relating to the life and health of the mother were satisfied.[8] In short, it was possible for a medical practitioner to terminate pregnancy after a careful study of all the circumstances of the case, and when acting in 'good faith' in the interests of the health or welfare of his patient. Thus, abortion was only a crime in Scotland if 'criminal intent' could be proved, doctors otherwise having freedom to practice in accordance with their clinical judgement.

There were further peculiarities between the two countries with regard to the enforcement of these laws. Under English law, the offence of abortion was defined as an act intended to procure an abortion. There was no requirement that a foetus must actually have been aborted for a person to be convicted of the offence of abortion. Therefore, a person could be found guilty regardless of whether the woman on whom the abortion was performed was actually pregnant.[9] In contrast, conviction for attempted abortion in Scotland could be obtained only if it was proved that the woman concerned was or had been pregnant, because under Scots law the offence required a victim for the crime of abortion or attempted abortion, namely the potential child. Hence in Scotland, if there was no potential child there

---

[6] *R v Bourne* [1939] 1 KB 687.
[7] For further details of this case, see Keown, above n 5, 49–59.
[8] See, for instance, GH Gordon, *The Criminal Law of Scotland* (Edinburgh, W Green and Son, 1967).
[9] Wellcome Library for the History and Understanding of Medicine, London (WL), SA/ALR/C.119, R Ireland, 'Scottish Section of the Historical and International Appendix' (undated).

was no crime, whereas the existence of a victim or otherwise was irrelevant to the English offence.[10]

Furthermore, the mechanics of the law appear to have made prosecution more problematic in Scotland. A doctor who carried out an abortion in Scotland could not be charged with any crime unless a definite complaint was made against him, in which case the matter would be investigated privately by doctors nominated by the Crown Office, and if they were satisfied that the operation had been carried out in good faith and in a proper manner the case would simply be closed.[11] It was often said to be difficult to obtain sufficient evidence for a conviction under these circumstances, particularly since those involved would generally have a joint interest in concealment. In England, by contrast, all such matters were brought before either a magistrate's court or a coroner's court to decide whether there was a case, and a prosecution could be instituted by any of the innumerable local police forces, even if all proper professional procedures had been followed and there appeared to be clear medical grounds for the termination. Such police investigations were conducted openly and could seriously disrupt the clinical environment that was placed under scrutiny.[12]

Whilst, on paper, Scottish abortion law was more flexible and liberal than its English counterpart, and the number of prosecutions in Scotland minimal during the 1950s and early 1960s, it seems that the line between criminal and non-criminal abortion was just as indistinct in both countries. The differences between English and Scottish law were not made clear to medical students during these decades, so that graduates believed generally that performing an abortion was a crime unless the woman's life was in imminent danger. Indeed, textbooks such as John Glaister's *Medical Jurisprudence and Toxicology*, the 'medico-legal bible' for generations of doctors in Scotland, failed entirely to differentiate abortion law in the two countries.[13] Archival evidence and the oral testimony of retired Scottish medical practitioners suggests that the legal right to terminate pregnancy was not being exploited in the majority of Scottish cities, except for reasons of an emergency medical nature. This appears to have been for partly ethical reasons, and partly because most doctors believed erroneously that social and psychological grounds were illegal in the two decades before 1967.[14] Indeed, press

---

[10] This was founded on a 1928 ruling by a judge in Glasgow (*HM Advocate v Anderson* (1928) JC 1), who asserted that 'to attempt to do what is physically impossible can never … be a crime'.

[11] In the period between 1945 and 1966, not a single registered medical practitioner in Scotland was prosecuted with procuring an abortion where the defence argued that the abortion was in the interests of the life or health of the mother. See National Archives of Scotland, Edinburgh (NAS), AD63/759/1, House of Commons question, 19 July 1966. Prosecutions tended to involve cases where an 'amateur' person was performing abortions for private gain, or where health had been compromised through the use of improper methods.

[12] *The Observer* (Manchester, 6 February 1966).

[13] J Glaister, *Medical Jurisprudence and Toxicology*, 12th edn (Edinburgh, E and S Livingstone, 1966) 363–6.

[14] Interviews with retired general practitioners, gynaecologists and psychiatrists, April 2003–April 2004, which form part of a series of interviews conducted (and held privately) by Gayle Davis with retired general practitioners, gynaecologists and psychiatrists between April 2003 and August 2004.

correspondence suggests that some doctors—including a Director of Midwifery and Gynaecology in Glasgow—even believed that abortion 'in the interests of the patient's health' was liable to prosecution.[15] Thus, the services of illegal abortionists were in all likelihood as heavily used in Scotland as they were in England.[16] In fact, oral testimony indicates that some doctors positively valued the existence of competent local 'back-street' abortionists who were willing to help out desperate women with unwanted pregnancies at a time when doctors felt unable to assist.[17]

However, there was one exceptional geographical area with regard to the medical provision of abortion—Aberdeenshire—where doctors appear to have taken full advantage of the potential flexibility of Scottish abortion law in the decades before the 1967 Act, under the guidance of their chief gynaecologist, Dugald Baird (1899–1986). Born in Greenock and educated in Glasgow, Baird was employed initially as a gynaecology registrar at Glasgow Royal Infirmary. It was in this city, the most Catholic in Scotland,[18] that Baird witnessed excessive childbearing, high maternal mortality, and lack of family planning information, including highly restrictive access to abortion, the factors that were to shape his whole future career.

In an interview given shortly before his death, Baird told the story of a patient of his who required a termination because she had a severe kidney disease, and who agreed to the procedure until her priest came into the ward and 'interfered' while Baird's back was turned.[19] Baird claimed that, in abject disgust, he took the man by the back of the neck, marched him down the stairs and ejected him forcibly from the hospital. Whilst Baird believed abortion to be a reliable medical practice applicable in many different situations, abortion was a notoriously unpopular procedure among most Glaswegian doctors, due primarily to the relatively high proportion of Roman Catholics who resided there. In despair at the way his hands were tied by the Catholic administration in Glasgow, Baird began to look elsewhere for a post, and found it in 1936 when he was appointed to the Regius Chair of Midwifery at the University of Aberdeen.

Upon his arrival in Aberdeen, Baird found social conditions in some ways very similar to Glasgow, with both cities plagued by poverty and severe employment and housing shortages at this time. However, he accepted the Aberdeen appointment for various reasons, above all believing the city to be ideal for research into the factors needed for 'efficient' childbearing.[20] Aberdeen was

---

[15] *The Scotsman* (Edinburgh, 31 March 1966).

[16] See C Francome, *Abortion in the USA and the UK* (Aldershot, Ashgate, 2004) chs 8 and 9 for an account of pre-1967 abortion provision. The recent film about the illegal abortionist *Vera Drake* (2004) serves as a poignant reminder of the valuable social role that this figure could constitute in 1950s Britain.

[17] Interview with retired general practitioner and gynaecologist (12 April 2004).

[18] WL, SA/ALR/C.115, Note by D Baird (undated). One psychiatrist subsequently estimated the Roman Catholic proportion of Glasgow's population to be 30%, compared with 17% for Scotland as a whole and 8% for England and Wales. See NA Todd, 'Psychiatric Experience of the Abortion Act (1967)' (1971) 119 *British Journal of Psychiatry* 491.

[19] Aberdeen University Special Collections, MS3620/1/21–2, Interview with Sir Dugald Baird conducted by Elizabeth Olson, 3–4 April 1985.

[20] S MacIntyre and L MacAulay (eds), *Thirty Years and Still Going Strong*, Occasional Paper No 1 (Glasgow, MRC Medical Sociology Unit, 1996) 1.

of appropriate size for epidemiological research, the settled population and centralised medical service enabling the effective follow-up of women and their families.[21] The Medical Officer of Health during the 1950s and 1960s, Dr Ian MacQueen, also became instrumental in helping Baird to construct his maternal healthcare policies for the city, and ensured the backing of local health authorities; while Baird's wife, May, was a councillor who became Chairman of the Health Board, allowing Baird to exert significant influence upon subsequent policy and appointments. Finally, the Aberdonian community exhibited 'liberal' political attitudes and religious diversity in the post-war era, and provided an accepting environment for Baird's policies. As such, Aberdeen was able to offer administrative, medical and popular support to the progressive gynaecologist.

Baird took advantage of these circumstances to implement the sort of system he simply could not have obtained in Glasgow at this time. He was aware of the tenuous legal position of abortion when he arrived in Aberdeen. Indeed, in the late 1930s he sought the advice of Thomas Smith, Professor of Law at the University, for clarification on the issue. According to Baird, Smith explained that there was little likelihood of prosecution for terminating a pregnancy unless the authorities were convinced of 'criminal intent'.[22] Given such assurances, Baird and his colleagues adopted an active policy of 'therapeutic abortion', under which they recognised social as well as medical indications long before abortion practice had been liberalised in any other part of Scotland, and decades before the 1967 Act. With the support of the city's Local Health Authority, Baird also established a comprehensive preventive service that made family planning available free of charge from November 1966 onwards, making Aberdeen the first British city to do so.

In addition to his atypical clinical practice, Baird was unusual for his willingness to publicise his work and to become involved to an increasing extent in the 'politics' of abortion. By the 1960s, Baird had publicly dedicated himself to helping women achieve what he referred to in his classic lecture as the 'Fifth Freedom'—'freedom from the tyranny of excessive fertility'.[23] He began explicitly to discuss female rights within reproductive medicine, and to advocate free and effective contraception and abortion provision so that women could achieve autonomy over their bodies.

Meanwhile, Glasgow continued to lie at the other extreme in terms of Scottish abortion provision. This, the largest city in Scotland, had the lowest abortion rate of any Scottish city due mostly to the anti-abortion views of several of its leading gynaecologists, according to Baird. As with Aberdeen, an individual seems to have exerted considerable influence within the obstetrical community. Born in Cornwall and educated in Scotland and South Africa, Ian Donald (1910–87) returned to Glasgow in 1954 to accept the Regius Chair of Midwifery.

---

[21] D Baird, 'An Area Maternity Service' (1969) 293 *The Lancet* 515, 516.
[22] G Bhatia, 'Social Obstetrics, Maternal Health Care Policies and Reproductive Rights: The Role of Dugald Baird in Great Britain, 1937–65' (MPhil dissertation, University of Oxford, 1996) 59.
[23] D Baird, 'A Fifth Freedom?' (1965) 2(5471) *British Medical Journal* 1141.

An active member of the Scottish Episcopal Church, he was to become a committed opponent of termination of pregnancy for social reasons, a leading campaigner against the 1967 Abortion Act, and Dugald Baird's most outspoken critic. Consistently throughout his career, Donald refused to terminate a pregnancy unless the foetus was grossly deformed or the mother's life in serious danger, as he held the procedure to be 'fundamentally destructive'.[24] Just prior to the passing of the Abortion Act, the Glasgow-based gynaecologist claimed that one pregnancy in 50 was terminated in Aberdeen compared to one in 3,750 in Glasgow.[25] Whilst these two cities lay at the opposite extremes of Scottish abortion provision at this time, Aberdeen seems to have been the only city to have exploited the ambiguities of Scots law, and Baird remained an exception within the ranks of Scottish medicine until the mid-1960s.

The Medical Termination of Pregnancy Bill and the Input of the Scottish Medical Community

In Britain during the 1960s and 1970s, the private members' bill was the primary mechanism of reform in relation to such contentious matters as sexuality. Politicians deemed subjects like abortion a matter of individual conscience rather than party politics, leaving them to the private member 'lottery'. David Steel (1938–), a young Liberal MP from the Scottish Borders and the son of a Church of Scotland minister, became involved in the abortion issue at a time when public opinion was becoming more favourable to its liberalisation, although this was not his first choice for the subject of a private members' bill.[26] While Steel was subjected to advice and pressure from many sources during the drafting of his Medical Termination of Pregnancy Bill, not least the Abortion Law Reform Association (ALRA)—a group of articulate middle-class women, active in the fields of sex reform and socialist politics[27]—historians have, to a large extent, undervalued the role of the medical profession within this process.

It was in fact a Scottish doctor who was to prove one of the most influential individuals upon Steel. Dugald Baird was busy not only implementing his liberal abortion programme in Aberdeen but also taking an active interest in policy-making at the national level. He began to meet with politicians and publicly to

---

[24] I Donald, 'Abortion and the Obstetrician' (1971) 297 *The Lancet* 1233.
[25] *The Scotsman* (Edinburgh, 23 December 1966).
[26] The morally contentious subjects of homosexual law reform and abortion law reform were both suggested to Steel, for both of which private members' bills had already been passed in the House of Lords and awaited a champion in the Commons. Steel opted for abortion because Scottish opinion was noted to be adamantly opposed to homosexual law reform. See MD Kandiah and G Staerck (eds), *The Abortion Act, 1967* (London, Institute of Historical Research/Institute of Contemporary British History, 2002) 25; Newburn, above n 5, 142.
[27] Brookes, above n 3, 94–8.

support abortion law reform in his lectures and writings. In November 1966, Baird and Malcolm Millar, Professor of Mental Health in Aberdeen, lunched with Steel in Scotland. Baird voiced his interest in incorporating some kind of 'social' clause into the bill but also urged the MP not to separate social from medical factors as he did not view such a separation as good medical practice. Steel himself recognised the importance of this discussion, as he retrospectively claimed: 'I was greatly influenced by ... Baird, who persuaded me to accept amendments creating a single socio-medical clause rather than a series of individual categories'.[28]

Pressure groups also made use of Baird, particularly the ALRA, which publicised the support of such medical practitioners in order both to promote the passage of Steel's bill and to counteract competing anti-abortionist writings. Baird was also asked to persuade other gynaecologists to deliver statements to the local and national press in order to 'counteract [negative] publicity' engendered by opponents of reform.[29] Donald's ideology did not feed into policy debates as Baird's did, although his views were widely exploited by the Catholic Church and anti-abortion organisations in the later 1960s and beyond. Indeed, Donald became a founder member of the Society for the Protection of the Unborn Child (SPUC), established in January 1967 in opposition to Steel's bill and the ALRA. Steel claimed retrospectively that the 'real menace' of the SPUC was that it involved several major medical figures in its activities.[30] In this sense, both pressure groups were in agreement, finding that it was medical rhetoric that had the greatest potential in fighting their cause.

Although Baird and Donald reveal clearly the great diversity of medical responses to abortion in Scotland, and while policy makers noted that Scottish medical opinion 'embrace[d] all shades of attitude',[31] it should be noted that the vast majority of Scottish doctors were unwilling to involve themselves visibly in the politics of abortion at this time. While the major London-based medical bodies, in particular the British Medical Association (BMA) and Royal College of Obstetricians and Gynaecologists (RCOG), actively involved themselves in the shaping of the 1967 Act, neither the Scottish Council of the BMA nor the Scottish Standing Committee of the RCOG articulated a specifically Scottish view on the issue. In contrast, while the Royal College of Nursing refused to formulate a policy statement on termination of pregnancy on the grounds that the abortion decision-making process was a medical one and so beyond their remit, the Scottish Council of the Royal College of Midwives registered firm opposition to the bill on ethical grounds.[32] The attitude of general practitioners is more difficult to identify, but appears to have been broadly hostile, one family doctor likening

---

[28] D Steel, *Against Goliath: David Steel's Story* (London, Weidenfeld and Nicolson, 1989) 53.
[29] WL, SA/ALR/A.61, Letter from Vera Houghton to Dugald Baird, 4 November 1966.
[30] Kandiah and Staerck, above n 26, 42.
[31] NAS, HH41/1820, DJ Cowperthwaite to J Hogarth, Scottish Home and Health Department (SHHD), Edinburgh, 28 November 1966.
[32] 'Abortion Law Reform Bill' (1967) 80 *Midwives Chronicle* 70.

abortion to 'euthanasia and possibly even murder',[33] and another voicing his concern that the bill would enable abortion to be obtained on demand by any woman and leave the doctor in no position to refuse.[34]

In the event, Steel's bill was clearly underpinned by a strong Scottish tradition of medical autonomy, and appears to have been influenced by Dugald Baird in three key respects. First, in keeping with Baird's belief that the law should 'interfere as little as possible with clinical practice',[35] Steel opted to give doctors complete control of the decision-making process surrounding abortion, subject only to certain administrative formalities. Secondly, Baird's views appear to have had a decisive influence in relation to the desirability of social criteria for abortion, and that such social factors were inseparable from medical ones. While the ALRA felt strongly that the bill should contain a specific 'social clause' in order to allow abortion after rape, when a patient was aged under 16, or deemed to lack the capacity to be a mother, Steel was acutely aware of the opposition of the medical establishment to such a clause which, in the view of the BMA and RCOG, lay outside the medical realm of expertise. Upon advice from Baird, Steel amended his bill by widening the definition of 'social' and by adopting the idea of the mother's 'well being' and that of her existing children, thereby burying a social clause more subtly within the general grounds for termination.[36] Thus the Act referred in vague terms to 'injury to the physical or mental health of the pregnant woman or any existing children of her family', and stipulated that 'account [could] be taken of the pregnant woman's actual or reasonably foreseeable environment'.[37] Such wording allowed wider social and economic factors to be taken into account, but with such an assessment being entirely the responsibility of the doctors consulted, rather than the woman requesting a termination.

Thirdly, Baird's role was crucial in ensuring that the bill covered mainland Britain as a whole. During 1966 there appears to have been considerable doubt in the minds of Scottish politicians and administrators over the desirability of Scotland's inclusion in the bill, with 'no specific demand' for abortion law reform as they saw it, as well as practical difficulties perceived over variances between the legal systems of England and Scotland.[38] However, according to Steel, Baird made him aware that the situation in Aberdeen was very different from that in the other Scottish medical centres, and that he was 'the only person' taking advantage of Scots common law at this time.[39] Accordingly, Steel successfully orchestrated opposition to a series of amendments that threatened to delete Scotland from the bill.

---

[33] *The Scotsman* (Edinburgh, 31 December 1966).
[34] NAS, HH41/1820, Alan Orcharton, General Practitioner, Ayrshire, to Rt Hon W Ross, House of Commons, 3 May 1967.
[35] WL, SA/ALR/A.61, Dugald Baird to Vera Houghton, 12 March 1967.
[36] NAS, AD63/759/13, Policy file.
[37] See *Public General Statutes* Eliz II, Ch 87.
[38] See, eg NAS, AD63/759/1, Note by DJ Cowperthwaite, SHHD, 5 December 1966; HH41/1821, RA Lawrie, St Andrew's House, Edinburgh, to GI Mitchell, Lord Advocate's Chambers, 22 July 1967.
[39] Kandiah and Staerck, above n 26, 47.

The provisions of the 1967 Abortion Act came into operation on 27 April 1968. The legislation made termination legal where the risk to the life of a pregnant woman, or injury to her physical or mental health, or to that of her existing children, was greater than the risks from abortion, or where there was a substantial risk that a baby would be born seriously handicapped. Two doctors were required to certify that the indications for abortion existed, except in cases of medical emergency where one was deemed sufficient; and the operation was only to be performed in an NHS hospital or another officially approved location. No doctor had to administer such treatment if they conscientiously objected, except in cases of emergency. The Act was a victory for the ALRA, and more so for Dugald Baird, but not for the majority of Scottish doctors.[40]

The Medical Reception of the 1967 Abortion Act

The 1967 Abortion Act succeeded where six previous bills had failed, and yet criticism of both the terms of the Act and its operation began as soon as the legislation came into force. Nowhere were the Act's shortcomings said to be better demonstrated that in a disturbing case which occurred in a Glasgow hospital in January 1969. A doctor performed an abortion under the terms of the 1967 Act in the belief that the foetus's period of gestation was 26 weeks. However, as it was being taken to the hospital incinerator, the newly-aborted baby was discovered to be alive and whimpering. Resuscitation was applied but the infant lived only a few hours. Referred to in the press as the 'foetus which cried', a Fatal Accident Inquiry was conducted into the affair. The causes of death were judged to be prematurity, the absence of attempts to resuscitate the child in the period immediately after its birth, and subsequent exposure to cold. The jury unanimously recommended that, in all cases where an infant approaching viable age was being aborted, 'all facilities and resuscitatory measures applied in cases of ordinary birth should be adopted', and that legislation should be introduced which prohibited abortion when the foetus was approaching viability.[41]

In the summer of 1969, a brief flurry of parliamentary activity addressed the issue. Norman St John-Stevas, Conservative MP for Chelmsford and one of the foremost political opponents of the Medical Termination of Pregnancy Bill, argued that the Abortion Act created 'a climate of disregard for infant and foetal life, of which this case [was] a dramatic example', and that it was 'a symbol of a situation that had gone radically wrong'. He asked 'what was intended to be

---

[40] Despite the common legislation, certain legal anomalies remained between England and Scotland with regards to the provision of abortion. See G Davis and R Davidson, '"A Fifth Freedom" or "Hideous Atheistic Expediency"? The Medical Community and Abortion Law Reform in Scotland, c.1960–75' (2006) 50 *Medical History* 41–2.

[41] NAS, HH102/1389, Note by SHHD, 1 August 1969.

done to stop something like this happening again[?]', and suggested that the law required urgent modification through an appropriate private member's bill.[42] Given, however, that the 1967 Act already required doctors to 'take all reasonable and proper steps to preserve the life of the child irrespective of the duration of the pregnancy', the Secretary of State for Scotland, William Ross, under advice from the Lord Advocate, argued that no further legislation was necessary on this subject.[43]

Yet, the following year, in response to continuing Parliamentary, professional, and public pressure, the Government announced its decision to appoint a committee to review how the Abortion Act was operating.[44] Under the chairmanship of Justice Elizabeth Lane, the Committee on the Working of the Abortion Act (or Lane Committee) was assembled. It consisted of fifteen senior members from the fields of education, law, and medicine, and proceeded to take evidence from a variety of organisations and private individuals on their criticisms of the Act and suggestions for its improvement. The Committee published a three-volume report in April 1974 in which it suggested a variety of administrative measures to tighten the regulations and to improve the Act's effectiveness, but in which it also expressed unanimous confidence in the Act.[45]

The historian Ashley Wivel has provided an excellent overview of the composition and internal workings of this committee, as well as the evidence that it received.[46] However, if we come at this subject from a Scottish perspective, focusing purely upon the Scottish evidence submitted to the committee, we find a somewhat different list of main concerns north of the Border. Replies were received from some 30 medical bodies in Scotland, including the Health Boards, Royal Colleges, and University medical faculties. Although the Lane Report was generally well received by these bodies, their evidence to the Committee reveals that the dichotomy in medical opinion on abortion that Baird and Donald epitomised prior to the Act was still very much in evidence. As Professor McGirr, Dean of the Faculty of Medicine at the University of Glasgow, observed, there was a 'wide spectrum of opinion on the subject amongst medical teachers', which ranged from 'full agreement with the views expressed by the Committee' to the Act having constituted 'the most pagan in British parliamentary history' in its 'implied assumption of the utter disposability of life'.[47]

English critics of the Act focussed particularly on three issues: the role of the private sector, access by foreign women to British abortion services, and the advertising of British abortion services abroad. However, none of these issues

---

[42] *The Scotsman* (Edinburgh, 9 June 1969).
[43] NAS, HH102/1389, House of Commons written answer, 24 July 1969.
[44] NAS, HH61/1315, Draft memorandum by the Secretary of State for Social Services, 1970.
[45] *Report of the Committee on the Working of the Abortion Act* (Cmnd 5579, 1974) XVI.
[46] A Wivel, 'Abortion Policy and Politics on the Lane Committee of Enquiry, 1971–1974' (1998) 11 *Social History of Medicine* 109.
[47] NAS, HH102/1232, Prof EM McGirr, University of Glasgow, to Miss M Macdonald, SHHD (undated).

were felt to be particularly problematic within Scotland, not least because the vast majority of abortions were performed under the NHS, unlike in England. In 1973, for example, only 88 out of 7,498 abortions in Scotland were carried out in the private sector, and the number of abortions performed on foreign women in Scotland was only two in that year.[48] Instead, the majority of Scottish criticism focused broadly around four issues: the pressures that abortion work imposed on gynaecological services; geographical variations in the application of the Act; the statutory time limit for terminations; and the appropriateness of 'social' indications.[49]

By broadening previous criteria for abortion in making explicit reference to psychiatric grounds and in introducing a social dimension, the immediate effect of the 1967 Act was a striking increase in the number of women with unwanted pregnancies who attempted to obtain a legal abortion. As a result, the Scottish abortion rate rose sharply in the years immediately following the passage of the Act. The architect of the legislation, David Steel, welcomed this significant increase in women receiving safe and legal abortions rather than 'risking a back-street operation'.[50] However, the medical interpretation of this increase was rather less positive. Its detrimental impact upon existing hospital facilities and staffing was noted widely. As Lothian and Peebles Executive Council lamented, due to the limited number of consultants and because terminations required to be carried out as early as possible, many other gynaecological cases had to be deferred for unreasonable periods.[51] The Scottish Association of Executive Councils argued that 'if a choice ha[d] to be made between more terminations and a reduction in the gynaecological waiting list they would unreservedly choose the latter'.[52]

The geographical variation in abortion provision was a related concern expressed in evidence and, more widely, in the media. In the first year of the Act's operation, the Scottish abortion rate ranged from 4.9 per 1,000 women in the Northern Hospital Board Region to 1.6 per 1,000 in the Western Hospital Board Region.[53] The *Scottish Daily Record* was among those who deplored the fact that obtaining an NHS abortion was highly dependent on where you happened to live.[54] While in Glasgow, 'diehard pro- and anti-abortion forces' battled over the issue, abortions in Edinburgh 'seem[ed] to be left pretty much to the consciences of individual doctors', while in Dundee terminations appeared to be carried out

---

[48] NAS, HH101/2877, Note by SHHD, 4 February 1975.

[49] For a fuller consideration of Scottish evidence to the Lane Committee, see G Davis and R Davidson, '"Big White Chief", "Pontius Pilate", and the "Plumber": The Impact of the 1967 Abortion Act on the Scottish Medical Community, c 1967–80' (2005) 18 *Social History of Medicine* 285–95.

[50] WL, SA/ALR/G.69, David Steel MP, Speech to the AGM of the Abortion Law Reform Association, 'Abortion Act Vindicates 16 years of Effort', 19 October 1968.

[51] WL, SA/ALR/C.41, Proceedings of the Lane Committee (PLC), Submission of Lothian and Peebles Executive Council, 2 November 1971.

[52] WL, SA/ALR/C.27, PLC, Submission of A Smith, Scottish Association of Executive Councils, 20 December 1971.

[53] I MacGillivray, 'Correspondence' (1969) 1 *British Medical Journal* 167–8.

[54] *Scottish Daily Record* (Glasgow, 16 May 1973).

'almost on request'. As a result of this postcode inequality, and also in an attempt to protect their anonymity, significant numbers of Scottish women were reported to be obtaining abortions in England and Wales—as many as 7,500 abortions each year by 1972.[55]

The appropriate time limit for a termination also elicited significant concern from Scottish doctors and nurses, an aspect of the 1967 Act that has formed the basis of most of the subsequent reform attempts. While the legislation did not include a specific time limit, a 28-week limit was effectively read into it by the earlier Infant Life (Preservation) Act.[56] However, since this legislation had not applied to Scotland, there was effectively no time limit for terminations performed north of the Border. Scottish commentators warmly welcomed the Lane Committee's recommendation that the time limit be reduced to 24 weeks in order to safeguard the life of a viable foetus, and in light of the availability of 'modern support systems'.[57] Indeed, there was strong support for a reduction in the upper limit to 20 weeks, particularly from nursing and non-medical organisations, including the Royal College of Midwives and the Church of Scotland Moral Welfare Committee. At its most extreme, the Scottish Public Health Nursing Administrators and Tutors Group argued that abortion should not be performed after the twelfth week of pregnancy, due both to the higher rate of mortality and the increased distress felt by both patients and staff when a termination was performed at a later stage in the pregnancy.[58]

Finally, the medical community professed deep concern over the appropriateness of 'social' indications for termination and whether this was the province of the medical profession. Many perceived a fundamental conflict between the established role of doctors to save and preserve life and the more destructive implications of abortion, a conflict said to be felt particularly acutely by obstetricians and midwives whose prime responsibility was to 'preserve life in all its human forms' rather than to conduct a 'haemorrhagic exercise in destruction'.[59] Several commentators also complained about the 'technologically unchallenging' nature of the operation, suggesting that this was an issue of professional status as well as medical ethics.[60]

However, such concerns seem to have varied depending on the type of woman seeking a termination. In the early years of the Act, Dugald Baird observed a growing willingness among the Scottish medical profession to terminate pregnancy in married women who, while not suffering from serious physical illness, were tired

---

[55] H Homans (ed), *The Sexual Politics of Reproduction* (Aldershot, Ashgate, 1985) 84–5.
[56] 28 weeks was, historically, the point where the foetus was deemed to be 'viable', or capable of surviving outside of the womb.
[57] NAS, HH60/665, RP Fraser to GN Monro and Secretary of State for Scotland, 8 December 1973.
[58] NAS, HH102/1232, PLC, Submission of Royal College of Midwives (Scottish Council), 30 July 1974.
[59] Cited in MacIntyre, above n 5, 123.
[60] See, eg 'The Royal College of Psychiatrists' Memorandum on the Abortion Act in Practice' (1972) 120 *British Journal of Psychiatry* 449.

or depressed by their heavy workload and responsibilities. He contrasted this with the still pronounced reluctance to terminate in the case of single women, despite the fact that their socio-medical plight could be far more serious.[61] There is also evidence that the likelihood of a termination being recommended increased with the age of the patient.[62] In short, as Hamill and Ingram noted, young single women who were pregnant for the first time appeared to provoke the most censorious and moralistic response from the medical profession.[63] Yet, there also appears to have been a strong class dimension to such recommendations. The demand for abortion from the better-educated girl and her parents seems to have elicited a greater degree of sympathy from the Scottish medical profession. Many doctors acknowledged that for such patients, educated young women who were 'anxious that their future should not be imperilled by one mistake', abortion was the least damaging solution, and one which provided such respectable girls with 'a second chance'.[64]

The attitudes of the Scottish medical community towards termination of pregnancy at this time can be categorised broadly into three groups. First, there was a very select group of doctors who held abortion to be neither a medical nor a social decision, but a personal decision that the woman herself should make. Thus, Dugald Baird's solution to the disparities in abortion provision was that 'more weight should be given to the opinion of the woman herself' and that 'she should have the ultimate decision as to whether the pregnancy should continue or not'.[65] A comprehensive study of abortion in Aberdeen, which found that serious emotional disturbance in the aftermath of abortion was rare and that very few women regretted their decision when interviewed three months after a termination, was used to justify this most liberal application of the 1967 Act.[66] In addition, section 1(a) of the Act specified that an abortion could be legally performed where the risk to health by continuance of the pregnancy was greater than if the pregnancy was terminated. Since the danger of death as a consequence of legal abortion was lower than that of dying in childbirth, the Act could be read as legally justifying an abortion in every case presented.[67] Ironically, this clause

---

[61] D Baird, 'The Galton Lecture, 1970: The Obstetrician and Society' (1971) 3 *Journal of Biosocial Science* 110. See also Todd, above n 18, 491.

[62] The Glasgow-based psychiatrists Evelyn Hamill and Malcolm Ingram found that those patients recommended for termination had a mean age of 31 years, while those refused had a mean age of 24 years. See E Hamill and IM Ingram, 'Psychiatric and Social Factors in the Abortion Decision' (1974) 1 *British Medical Journal* 230.

[63] ibid 231.

[64] J Aitken-Swan, *Fertility Control and the Medical Profession* (London, Croom Helm, 1977) 11; D Baird, 'The Abortion Act 1967: the Advantages and Disadvantages' (1970) 90 *Royal Society of Health Journal* 293; D Baird, 'The Changing Pattern of Human Reproduction' (1975) 7 *Journal of Biosocial Science* 90.

[65] Baird, above n 61, 107–8.

[66] G Horobin (ed), *Experience with Abortion: A Case Study of North-East Scotland* (Cambridge, CUP, 1973).

[67] In the first year of the Abortion Act, 21 per 100,000 cases were recorded to have died as a consequence of legal abortion, and 24 per 100,000 to have died in childbirth. See 'The Royal College of Psychiatrists' Memorandum', above n 60, 449.

was added at the demand of anti-abortionists during the final stages of debate in the House of Lords, on the false assumption that an early termination was more dangerous than a full-term pregnancy.[68]

A second and much larger group of doctors accepted that there was some need for social as well as medical criteria, which generally included economic deprivation, emotional distress, contraceptive failure, and high parity,[69] but that promiscuity and inconvenience were unacceptable reasons to allow a termination. The success of the patient in obtaining an abortion in such cases depended on her ability to engage her particular doctor's sympathy. Finally, there were those who adopted the most narrow application of the Act, and who refused to terminate a pregnancy unless the foetus was grossly deformed or the mother's life in serious danger. This group rejected social indications outright and saw psychiatric indications rarely to exist. As one consultant surgeon from Greenock Royal Infirmary stated, psychiatric grounds for abortion were merely 'pandering to the social conscience of women who [were] not ready to accept parental responsibility'.[70]

Medical and Political Responses to the Act

Evidence to the Lane Committee can also be employed to gain access to the strategies that the medical community used in order to cope with this new and largely unwelcome area of responsibility. The three most significant appear to have been the exercising of the 'conscience clause' that was built into the Act, an attempt to reframe the abortion issue in terms of 'prevention' at a time when family planning was becoming more efficient and more widely available, and the exploitation of the psychiatric profession as a tool to make the Act workable in its very early years.

The 'conscience clause' stipulated that no doctor or nurse was required to participate in abortion work, except in emergency circumstances, should it contradict their own personal beliefs. Lane Committee testimony indicates that the clause was fairly heavily used by nursing staff and by doctors located in some Catholic areas of Scotland, despite the concern that this course of action could impair their career progression and was deterring 'good young doctors' from working in gynaecology.[71] Indeed, a mid-1970s survey of Glasgow-based nurses revealed that many were reluctant to withhold participation from the abortion procedure on the grounds of conscience 'through fear of occupying an unpopular role in the

---

[68] Kandiah and Staerck, above n 26, 50.
[69] 'Parity' is defined as the number of times a woman has given birth to a child of 24 weeks gestational age or older, which includes babies born alive and stillbirths.
[70] *Greenock Telegraph* (Greenock, 3 July 1969).
[71] NAS, HH102/1232, EM McGirr, Department of Medicine, University of Glasgow, to M Macdonald, SHHD, 30 July 1974.

treatment team', since opting-out would inevitably result in a greater work-load being placed on their colleagues.[72] The need to balance the right of the individual member of staff to conscientiously object with the broader NHS obligation to provide an abortion service appears to have proven highly problematic for senior clinicians seeking to staff their departments.

The concept of prevention was a second recurring theme in Scottish evidence to the Lane Committee. There was said to be 'massive support' for proposals relating to the education in family planning of both the public, especially the young, and those working in the abortion field, so that fewer women would require a termination.[73] It was argued by a number of bodies and individuals that abortion was no substitute for adequate contraception, and that contraceptive advice and facilities should be freely available in order to 'produce a more responsible attitude on the part of the community as a whole'.[74] The fact that therapeutic abortion was legal but local health authority provision of contraceptives merely optional was seen to be particularly unacceptable. While a number of local authorities were beginning to make arrangements for the provision of family planning services by this time—most notably, Aberdeen—it was only as a result of NHS reorganisation in the mid-1970s that contraceptives became freely and widely available throughout Scotland.

Finally, the psychiatric profession appears to have been used by the medical fraternity in order to facilitate the abortion decision-making process in the initial years of the Act. Prior to 1967, Scottish psychiatrists seem to have seen such patients only in cases of severe mental illness or a history of such.[75] However, statistics from the first year of the Act reveal that the vast majority of terminations performed in Scotland (84 per cent) were granted under section 1(b) of the Act, that is, a threat to the physical or mental health of the mother, and the majority of these appear to have been performed on mental rather than physical grounds.[76] This was despite the fact that only a small proportion of these patients were judged to be suffering from a major psychiatric illness or to have had any history of such.[77] It seems that psychiatrists played a key role in facilitating access to abortion in the first uncertain years of the Act, not because the impetus came from them, but because general practitioners and gynaecologists felt that strong

---

[72] AB Sclare and BP Geraghty, 'Termination of Pregnancy: The Nurse's Attitude' (London, 1975) 140 *Nursing Mirror* 60.

[73] NAS, HH102/1232, EUE Elliott-Binns, SHHD, to GG Hulme, Department of Health and Social Security, 10 December 1974.

[74] NAS, HH102/1232, FN Mitchell, Honorary Secretary of the Scottish Association of Nurse Administrators, to M Macdonald, SHHD, 3 July 1974.

[75] Interviews with retired psychiatrists, 30 January 2004 and 12 March 2004.

[76] 'The Abortion Act—Scotland 1968' (1969) 27 *Health Bulletin* 67–9; RG Priest, 'The British Candidate for Termination of Pregnancy: A Quantified Survey of Psychiatric Referrals' (1971) 118 *British Journal of Psychiatry* 579.

[77] Norman Todd, for example, found that only 13 per cent of abortion cases referred to his two psychiatric departments in Glasgow had any history of previous psychiatric illness. See Todd, above n 18, 490, 493.

health grounds, whether physical or mental, were necessary in order to justify termination, and exhibited a pronounced unease at the concept of purely 'social' indications. The psychiatric doctor was perceived to take a wider range of social and environmental factors into consideration when assessing the patient's state of health, and thus to adopt a broad interpretation of health and illness. Abortion patients were thus routinely sent to the psychiatric department in those cases where medical indications were lacking.[78]

This tendency to employ psychiatric diagnosis was strongly criticised in some quarters for facilitating an overly liberal application of the Act, and for allowing non-psychiatric doctors to 'shirk' their responsibilities.[79] However, this system only seems to have lasted during the very early years of the Act, a more discriminating pattern of psychiatric referral having supervened by the mid-1970s at the latest. There are two potential reasons for this phenomenon: either, as in the English context, gynaecologists found that the pressure of work exerted by the Abortion Act led to delays in psychiatric appointments, and thus began to save only 'problem patients' for psychiatric consideration;[80] or, as oral testimony suggests, doctors may have merely become more comfortable with the variety of 'acceptable' indications for termination, including broader 'social' grounds.[81] Either way, it seems that the involvement of the psychiatric profession 'dwindled sharply' during the life of the Lane Committee.[82]

It was during these few years of psychiatric 'exploitation' that a Scottish psychiatrist wrote one of the most damning medical indictments of the 1967 Abortion Act. In his controversial but widely cited *Lancet* article, 'Abortion Games', Malcolm Ingram, a psychiatrist based in Glasgow, considered the deeply problematic situation for women seeking abortion in the years immediately after the passing of the Act, and the dilemma for doctors involved in the abortion decision-making process.[83] Examining the working of the Act in terms of 'game theory',[84] Ingram argued that the legislation had 'created an arena for the development and multiplication of a variety of games', the concealed function of which was to 'abolish or minimise personal responsibility for decisions made for or against termination'.[85]

---

[78] Hamill and Ingram, above n 62, 229.

[79] See, eg WL, SA/ALR/C.35, PLC, Submission of Board of Management for Glasgow Royal Infirmary and Associated Hospitals, December 1971; SA/ALR/C.33, PLC, Submission of Royal College of Physicians and Surgeons of Glasgow, January 1972.

[80] A Hordern, *Legal Abortion: The English Experience* (Oxford, Pergamon Press, 1971) 115.

[81] One retired gynaecologist interviewee, for example, contrasted this later confidence in medically interpreting the Act with earlier 'feeling our way' concerns (interview conducted 12 July 2004).

[82] NAS, HH102/1232, GC Timbury, Honorary Divisional Secretary of the Royal College of Psychiatrists, Glasgow, to A Laurie, SHHD, 20 November 1974.

[83] IM Ingram, 'Abortion Games: An Inquiry into the Working of the Act' (1971) 2 *The Lancet* 969–70.

[84] Ingram employed the Canadian psychiatrist, Eric Berne's 'transactional analysis' as his interpretative framework. See E Berne, *Games People Play: The Psychology of Human Relationships* (London, A Deutsch, 1964).

[85] Ingram, above n 83, 969.

Three groups of doctors were involved in these 'games': general practitioners, gynaecologists, and psychiatrists.[86] The general practitioner might discourage the patient or refuse to refer her to a gynaecologist. More subtly, he could play 'Pontius Pilate' by referring the patient but writing a neutral letter that made no recommendation for or against the procedure, or 'Bounced Cheque' by apparently agreeing to an abortion request but then referring the patient to a specialist known to be antagonistic to termination, thereby evading a confrontation. Since most Scottish abortions were performed within the NHS, and since the general practitioner acted as gatekeeper within this system, family doctors could exercise a great deal of discretion in how the Abortion Act was interpreted.

At the specialist level, Ingram described more complicated games. Within gynaecology, those in positions of authority could play 'Big White Chief', imposing on their staff an extreme policy for or against termination, depending upon their particular social and medical ideology. As the general practitioner got to know the local consultant's views, he could refer or divert patients accordingly, leaving the 'Chief' to see only those patients he wished to see. His neighbouring colleagues might play a defensive corresponding game of 'Catchment Area' when they were seeing an influx of patients as a result of the 'Chief's' restrictive policy. A further popular game was said to be 'Plumber', in which the gynaecologist would claim to be a 'simple craftsman whose abilities [were] bounded by the female pelvis', and who deemed himself not competent to determine psychiatric and social factors, thus devolving responsibility to the general practitioner, social worker, or psychiatrist.[87]

Finally, Ingram did not absolve his own specialty. Indeed, he claimed that psychiatrists, with their 'specialist training', revealed 'more sophistication in their choice of gambits'.[88] The best documented of these was described as 'Sim's Position', through which the doctor adopted the blanket stance that reference to mental health in the Abortion Act meant purely the absence of psychotic illness. Since evidence suggested that the major psychoses were not worsened by pregnancy and that suicide was rare, he could justifiably refuse a termination to the vast majority of patients. Another psychiatric game involved an opposite reading of the Act's wording, the doctor interpreting mental health in the widest possible sense and maintaining that, if a woman was forced to bear an unwanted child, her mental health must suffer automatically.

Ingram's article made clear that the legal need for a woman to obtain the support of two physicians before she could have her unwanted pregnancy terminated was a not insignificant hurdle. While these 'games' clearly did not reflect well upon the British medical profession who held the responsibility for the Act's implementation, they were ultimately a damning indictment of the legislation itself. The inherent ambiguities of the 1967 Act, Ingram argued, were primarily to blame for the confusion and insecurities experienced by both doctors and patients, and

---

[86] For a fuller consideration of these games, see Davis and Davidson, above n 49, 301–4.
[87] Ingram, above n 83, 969.
[88] ibid 970.

the consequent inconsistencies in decision making. Doctors found themselves 'unwittingly' involved in game-playing due largely to the fact that most women who sought a termination were not ill in a strictly medical or psychiatric sense, which was forcing doctors to give opinions on matters that they considered to be non-medical, and asking them to take life when their natural feelings and training predisposed them to conserve it.[89]

Contemporaneous political developments in this sphere were substantial, the vast majority of such activity attempting to restrict the Abortion Act in some capacity. So-called 'pro-life' groups such as the SPUC and LIFE were established in the aftermath of the Act and engaged in vociferous, if ultimately unsuccessful, lobbying in an attempt to reverse the trend of liberalisation in the laws restricting abortion which was, by the mid-1970s, a fairly global phenomenon.[90] While the majority of political attempts to overturn or restrict the terms of the 1967 Act came from Conservative MPs, abortion remained an issue that refused to be confined to party political terms within the British context. However, geography continued to play a prominent role within the politics of abortion, with Scottish politicians in this case locating themselves at the forefront of attempts to restrict access to the procedure.

Whilst a number of parliamentary attempts to clarify and restrict the Abortion Act can be charted in the decade that followed the Lane Committee, there is general historiographical agreement that the two most significant efforts were the abortion amendment bills of 1975 and 1979.[91] Significantly, the architects of both of these bills were MPs serving Scottish constituencies: James White, Labour MP for Glasgow Pollok, and John Corrie, Conservative MP for Bute and North Ayrshire. White introduced his 1975 Abortion (Amendment) Bill in order to 'make the 1967 Abortion Act work as Parliament meant it to work, and to cut out current abuses'.[92] His bill sought to reduce the time limit to 20 weeks in most circumstances, and to allow abortion only where there was 'grave risk' to the woman's life or health.[93] Corrie's Abortion (Amendment) Bill of 1979 was similarly restrictive, and aimed to reduce the upper time limit to 20 weeks, to reduce the circumstances which merited a termination, to tighten licensing procedures, and to extend the 'conscience' clause so that doctors and nurses might opt out more easily.

---

[89] ibid 969.

[90] Indeed, many countries adopted a much more liberal form of abortion policy by allowing the procedure on the woman's request up to 12 weeks and beyond, thus obviating the need to involve the medical profession in many cases. However, as academic commentators like Sally Sheldon have argued, 'medicalisation' has been the 'greatest strength' as well as the 'greatest weakness' of British abortion law, since it has 'depoliticised the extension of women's access to abortion services' and 'defused political conflict' as well as leaving women dependent on the 'vagaries of medical discretion and good will'. See Sheldon, above n 4, 168.

[91] See, eg A Cohan, 'Abortion as a Marginal Issue: The Use of Peripheral Mechanisms in Britain and the United States' in Lovenduski and Outshoorn, above n 3, 41.

[92] *Glasgow Herald* (Glasgow, 9 June 1975).

[93] *The Scotsman* (Edinburgh, 28 November 1974).

By the mid-1970s, West of Scotland MPs in particular were said to be 'under heavy constituency pressure to reverse the liberalising effect of the 1967 Act'.[94] Certainly, pressure does not seem to have come from the medical community. During the autumn of 1979, once the second reading of Corrie's private member's bill had taken place, the Scottish Home and Health Department circulated the bill to all medical and nursing bodies in Scotland, amongst others, for their professional consideration.[95] The responses of the Scottish medical community allow us to chart medical attitudes towards abortion by 1980. In short, doctors and nurses appear to have been overwhelmingly in favour of retaining the status quo as governed by the 1967 Act. As one consultant obstetrician commented, most doctors by this time held the Act to be 'fundamentally correct' and to strike a good balance, since there could be 'no doubt' that it had been 'of considerable benefit' both to the woman who found herself in 'a distressing position' and to the doctors who had been 'protected both individually and as a group'.[96]

The vast majority of respondents expressed 'profound concern' for a reduction in the upper time limit to 20 weeks, which would 'create more problems than it would solve'[97] and did 'not seem really tolerable on humane or economic grounds'.[98] However, a number of bodies did support a reduction to 24 weeks as a result of recent advances in paediatric neonatal care, including the Scottish Executive Committee of the Royal College of Obstetricians and Gynaecologists, the Royal College of Physicians and Surgeons of Glasgow, and the Scottish Health Visitors' Association, whose General Secretary argued that this time limit 'would ensure that those women who delay[ed] attending for advice or examination for reasons of ignorance, apathy or fear' would not be disadvantaged.[99]

Corrie's attempt to restrict the qualifying criteria for a termination, for example by adding the word 'grave' before 'risk', met with similar criticism. There was wide concern that such vague wording was 'subjective and emotive, and could lead to attempted prosecution of practitioners acting in good faith by persons hostile to the Abortion Law'.[100] The Chairman of the Royal College of Psychiatrists expressed it most forcefully when he argued that Corrie's proposed amendments were

---

[94] D McKie, 'Talking Politics: The White Bill on Abortion' (1975) 1 *The Lancet* 388.
[95] NAS, HH102/1395, Circular letter from DA Bennet, SHHD, 24 August 1979.
[96] NAS, HH102/1395, Consultant Obstetrician, Western Isles Health Board, to SHHD, 18 September 1979.
[97] NAS, HH102/1395, Secretary of Forth Valley Health Board, Stirling, to SHHD, 1 October 1979; Honorary Secretary of Royal College of Physicians and Surgeons of Glasgow to SHHD, 17 September 1979.
[98] NAS, HH102/1395, Consultant Obstetrician, Western Isles Health Board, to SHHD, 18 September 1979.
[99] NAS, HH102/1395, General Secretary of The Scottish Health Visitors' Association to SHHD, 20 September 1979.
[100] NAS, HH102/1395, Moat Brae Nursing Home Ltd, Dumfries, to SHHD, 1 October 1979.

'retrograde and would lead to considerable distress and difficulty for pregnant women', and that this Amendment Bill would:

> set back the clock to the time that women seeking abortion would have to be judged as potentially suicidal or psychotic before their case could be supported on psychiatric grounds.[101]

Once again, however, the nursing bodies constituted the most conservative section of the medical community in Scotland. While the Central Midwives Board for Scotland argued that there was 'little evidence' that the 1967 Act was 'causing problems',[102] the Scottish Board of the Royal College of Midwives agreed with Corrie that the 28-week limit should be reduced to 20 weeks except in cases of severe handicap.[103] Indeed, the Chief Area Nursing Officer for the Western Isles Health Board described Steel's 1967 Act as having 'verge[d] on legalised murder' and argued that Corrie's suggested restrictions were 'not … going far enough'.[104] While both the White and Corrie bills received a large second reading majority, both failed through lacking in parliamentary time and being talked to death by their opponents.[105]

Conclusion

While, prior to 1967, Scottish abortion law could be interpreted more flexibly than could statutory provisions south of the Border, a review of practice reveals that most Scottish doctors were not in fact taking advantage of this flexibility because they were unaware of their legal right to terminate a pregnancy when acting in good faith in the interests of the health or welfare of their patient. This might explain the seeming irony that, after six failed attempts to liberalise access to abortion within Britain, it was a Scottish MP, David Steel, who successfully managed to negotiate such a bill through parliament. In fact, it seems that Aberdeen was the only city in Scotland to systematically exploit the potential liberality of Scottish abortion law prior to 1967, principally through the influence of the gynaecologist Dugald Baird, whose pioneering abortion work and willingness to publicise it were to prove crucial both to David Steel's drawing up of the 1966 bill and to the course of abortion law reform within Britain as a whole. The apparent

---

[101] NAS, HH102/1395, Chairman of The Royal College of Psychiatrists, Gartnavel Royal Hospital, Glasgow, to SHHD, 14 September 1979.
[102] NAS, HH102/1395, Secretary of Central Midwives Board for Scotland to SHHD, 21 September 1979.
[103] NAS, HH102/1395, Royal College of Midwives Scottish Board to SHHD, 19 September 1979.
[104] NAS, HH102/1395, Internal memorandum from Chief Area Nursing Officer to Secretary, Western Isles Health Board, 3 October 1979.
[105] A reduction in the time-limit to 24 weeks was, however, finally made law through the Human Fertilisation and Embryology Act of 1990, in view largely of the increasing sophistication of medical techniques and the consequently ever-improving viability of the foetus.

progressiveness of Scots law and local practice in Aberdeenshire thus contrasts markedly with the conservatism of opinion present more generally in Scottish medicine and civic society at this time. This dramatic contrast is perhaps best illustrated by the contrasting ideologies of Baird in Aberdeen and his medical counterpart in Glasgow, Ian Donald, who epitomised the powerful anti-abortion culture of the West of Scotland that was to mobilise political attempts to amend the 1967 Act in the following decade.

The ambivalence and hostility that characterised much Scottish medical input to the 1967 Act is an even more apparent feature of the early years of the Act's operation, as doctors and nurses attempted to reconcile themselves to this new duty, both practically and ethically. Evidence submitted to the Lane Committee reveals that, while the major English concerns were not voiced north of the Border, and although the Committee's three-volume endorsement of the 1967 Abortion Act was mostly well received, a range of anxieties continued to be aired by the medical community. Such concerns were strengthened as a result of the striking rise in the number of women seeking a termination as a direct consequence of this legislation. Medical personnel subsequently found creative ways in which to extricate themselves from, or at least limit their involvement with, fertility limitation.

By the early 1970s, while the medical profession in Scotland had clearly begun to come to terms with the provisions of the 1967 Act, and while there is substantial evidence that consultants were now stressing the need for medical control of the abortion procedure, such behaviour appears to have remained motivated largely by concerns over autonomy and professional status than any newly acquired ambition to dominate women's reproductive strategies. Moreover, a small but significant body of the medical community in Scotland—particularly the nursing staff—remained hostile to this procedure and continued to voice pronounced logistical and ethical concerns. Furthermore, politicians serving Scottish constituencies played a particularly active role in political attempts to restrict medical applications of the 1967 Act, but attempts that were ultimately unsuccessful, due in part to the overwhelming dissent of doctors.

As Ian Donald's much more liberal successor, Malcolm MacNaughton, argued in the early 1970s, there were two issues of over-riding importance in relation to abortion: the need to preserve 'the all important right of the doctor to decide his own position', and the need to protect the patient from 'having to accept the ethics of the doctor in her zone'.[106] In leaving access to abortion dependent upon medical discretion, the 1967 Abortion Act really only served the former of these. Certainly, clinical autonomy was the one aspect of abortion on which Scottish doctors were generally in agreement throughout these decades. It was also arguably the main reason why the medical profession obstructed further legislative

---

[106] MC MacNaughton, 'Termination of Pregnancy in the Unmarried' (1972) 17 *Scottish Medical Journal* 382.

activity in this field, since it was felt generally that 'any attempt to reduce or eliminate' the difficulties revealed by the Lane Committee could 'only succeed to the extent that it curtail[ed] the scope for individual clinical judgement'.[107] Thus, doctors and nurses opted to continue to be governed by the terms of the 1967 Act, a compromise measure that reflects the historical tension between a general public wish to liberalise access to abortion, Governmental reluctance to take responsibility within this sphere, and a medical profession whose support was crucial in order to make the Act work.

---

[107] NAS, HH102/1395, Internal memorandum from Treasurer to General Administrator of Western Isles Health Board, 17 September 1979.

9

Regulating Reproduction in the United Kingdom: Doctors' Voices, 1978–1985

IMOGEN GOOLD[*]

The birth of Louise Brown following conception by *in vitro* fertilisation on 25th July 1978 is a pivotal moment in the history of reproductive medicine.[1] It marks the beginning of a new phase in our capacity to direct reproduction, because for the first time a human baby was born live and healthy as a result of fertilisation that occurred outside her mother's body. Although artificial insemination had been practised for decades, and enjoyed reasonable public acceptance, the first successful use of IVF threw up a range of ethical issues that challenged ideas about families, parenting, reproductive choice and infertility.

From the early days of research in the 1960s and 1970s, IVF generated significant opposition due to concern about these issues.[2] In the lead up to Louise's birth, debate raged across the press—both popular and scientific—and it would take 12 years for the United Kingdom to agree on how to deal with this new capacity to enable reproduction, and the embryo research that attended it. But despite the early opposition to the new technologies, IVF and other assisted reproductive technologies (ART) now enjoy widespread community acceptance as a solution to the suffering many couples experience in being unable to have children.

---

[*] Acknowledgments: This research was funded by a Wellcome Trust studentship in biomedical ethics, and I would like to thank the Trust for its support. Much of the research behind this paper involved interviews with doctors, medical researchers, MPs and members of the Warnock committee. Some interviews have been anonymised at this stage of the research to ensure confidentiality. I would also like thank all those who consented to be interviewed, as the information they provided has been invaluable.

[1] IVF involves stimulating egg production in the woman through hormone injections to improve the chances of collecting a sufficient number of eggs. Eggs are then removed from the woman either using a laparoscope under general anaesthetic, or via a needle inserted through the vaginal wall under local anaesthetic. After a few hours maturation, the eggs are mixed with sperm in culture in the laboratory. If fertilisation occurs and the embryo appears normal, the resulting embryo is transferred into the woman's uterus through the cervix.

[2] See, generally M Mulkay, *The Embryo Research Debate: Science and the Politics of Reproduction* (Cambridge, CUP, 1997).

This chapter examines the ethical debate from the early 1970s through to the end of the first parliamentary debate on the Unborn Children (Protection) Bill in 1985, and explores the role doctors played in it. When new technologies emerge now, much of the exploration of the issues they raise occurs within the now well-established academic field of bioethics, as well as within medicine and science themselves. But in 1978, bioethics as a discipline was in its infancy and there were few people specifically trained in exploring the ethical dimensions of science and how it should be regulated. There was little expertise to help those needing guidance on how to proceed.[3] Yet, control was considered desperately necessary, either to prevent unethical research such as that which used human embryos, or to stave off developments that might be put to problematic uses like eugenic selection and surrogacy. At the time, scientists and doctors working in IVF and embryo research were characterised as unable to self-regulate, bent on pursuing their research goals regardless of the ethical objections to what they might achieve. However, in reality, many in the medical and scientific community both appreciated the ethical dilemmas their work presented, and welcomed regulation and guidance to help them deal with these problems. As a result, much of the debate about how IVF was to be controlled occurred within the medical profession, whose publicly voiced opinions in the science literature, news media and later as evidence to the Warnock Committee were highly influential. Doctors and researchers also made important contributions to the Parliamentary process that eventually led to the passage of legislation in 1990. This chapter brings this influence to the fore, and examines how doctors and medical researchers in this period bore very little resemblance to the mad scientists whose spectre was invoked by those who feared the worst.

Baby Steps: The Early Days of IVF Research and its Reception

> their imaginations have already been dramatically doom-lit and gaudily coloured by science-fiction fantasies and visions—fantasies of horror and disaster, and visions of white-coated, heartless men, breeding and rearing embryos in the laboratory to bring forth Frankenstein genetic monsters.[4]
>
> Robert Edwards on why people feared the uncontrolled scientist

On 15 February 1969, Robert Edwards, Barry Bavister and Patrick Steptoe published 'Early Stages of Fertilisation *in vitro* of Human Oocytes Matured *in vitro*' in leading science journal *Nature*.[5] They stated that the work may have

---

[3] This view was reflected in interview with Baroness Mary Warnock (London, 28 November 2005).
[4] R Edwards and P Steptoe, *A Matter of Life* (London, Sphere Books, 1981) 13.
[5] RG Edwards et al, 'Early Stages of Fertilisation *in vitro* of Human Oocytes Matured *in vitro*' (1969) 221 (15 February) *Nature* 632–635. The paper was published about year after the first fertilisation was observed.

some clinical and scientific uses—to produce a supply of embryos for research and to treat some forms of infertility, a statement Jack Challoner later called 'a wonderful understatement'.[6] They noted the possibility of abnormal development due to the fertilisation process: 'problems of embryonic development are likely to accompany the use of human oocytes matured and fertilised *in vitro*' but they felt that these problems might be solved when the conditions for maturation *in vitro* were better understood.[7] Edwards and Steptoe knew their work would face publicity and opposition, but even they under-estimated the magnitude of the response.[8] Challoner notes that they tried to reduce 'the inevitable pressure' that would come from public commentators by announcing their discovery only in the science press. Their efforts failed; upon publication of their paper in *Nature* in 1969 their work was reported across the national and international press.[9] Creating embryos outside the womb in laboratory was, and would remain, big news.

When their paper was reported in *The Times* that year, many of the future implications of the technology were difficult, if not impossible, to predict, but it was clear that if successful, IVF (and the embryo research it entailed) would raise serious ethical issues. There was a widespread sense that these ethical implications needed to be examined and that the science should not be allowed to develop without some external scrutiny. Edwards, in fact, repeatedly called for the ethics of their work to be explored. In 1968, he had already stated that

> [i]t is perfectly obvious to many people that the development of powerful new biological tools demands care and forethought in their application to medical and social practice. Responsible comment is therefore welcome and needed.[10]

He further pointed out that were there to be committees to assess the ethical concerns raised by new technologies, then the scientists who developed them would have to be included in these committees to explain the science itself.[11]

Edwards was not alone in offering views about the ethics of IVF and embryo research. News media and the scientific literature were two of the main forums for discussion of these future possibilities and their implications, and in these the views of prominent doctors and scientists were often cited. Headlines blazed with predictions of life being created in a test tube, the breeding of clone armies and that eugenic

---

[6] J Challoner, *The Baby Makers: The History of Artificial Conception* (London, Macmillan, 1999) 27.
[7] RG Edwards et al, 'Early Stages of Fertilisation *in vitro* of Human Oocytes Matured *in vitro*' (1969) 221 (15 February) Nature 632–635, 635.
[8] Challoner, above n 6, 87.
[9] Edwards and Steptoe, above n 4, 28.
[10] RG Edwards, 'Explosive Biology: *The Biological Time Bomb* by Gordon Rattray' (Book Review) (1968) 218 Nature 987.
[11] ibid.

reproduction was not far off.[12] In the pages of the papers (and the scientific literature from which many articles were drawn), doctors and scientists raised arguments for and against the use of IVF, should it ever become effective. When it came time to do so, many MPs who participated in the 1984–85 and 1989–90 Parliamentary debates followed the media coverage of the issues closely, and gained much of their knowledge of the technology and the ethical concerns from this source.[13]

One of the major early fears about IVF was that the children born using these new technologies would be afflicted with severe deformities or abnormalities, a concern that remained and indeed came to the fore when, in 1978, the world learned that Lesley Brown was carrying the first 'test tube baby'. The possibility that IVF babies would be born with disabilities or abnormalities was considered a real concern, and for many a good reason not to proceed with the research or the insertion of IVF embryos.[14] Scientists publicly attacked Edwards and Steptoe on this basis. One, Nobel Prize winner Max Perutz, argued in 1971 that Edwards' work could have 'horrifying' consequences and suggested the scale of abnormalities could match that caused by thalidomide.[15] The same year James Watson, who had some years earlier won the Nobel Prize in Physiology or Medicine for his joint discovery of the molecular structure of DNA, also attacked Edwards, stating 'you can only go ahead with your work if you accept the necessity of infanticide. There are going to be a lot of mistakes'.[16]

---

[12] Edwards later commented that 'what worried most commentators … were the implications, rather than the direct consequences' of the new breakthroughs in the science of reproduction. For example, the lead writer of *The Times* was, he noted, 'pre-occupied with the moral problems of selective breeding, of eugenics'. See Edwards and Steptoe, above n 4, 88. See also interview with B (Cambridge, 7 February 2006).

[13] See interview with Baroness Lockwood (London, 14 February 2006); interview with Baroness Masham (London, 14 December 2005); interview with Edwina Currie (Oxford, 16 December 2005); interview with James Couchman (Oxford, 14 February 2006); interview with Lady Saltoun (London, 1 February 2006); interview with Lord Carter (London, 8 February 2006); interview with Rev Martin Smyth (by written questionnaire, 17 January 2006); interview with Michael Meadowcroft (by telephone, 6 January 2006); interview with Patrick Nichols (Oxford, 24 February 2006); interview with Peter Thurnham (by telephone, 16 January 2006); interview with Robert Key (London, 18 January 2006); interview with Ian Lloyd (by written communication, 26 March 2006).

[14] Edwards himself had worried about deformities, particularly after reading a paper reporting abnormal development in mice born conceived using IVF. The mice were born with very small eyes, but Edwards noticed that only half were afflicted, suggesting Mendelian inheritance of a defective gene which, he discovered after contacting the author, turned out to be the case.

[15] 'Deformity Fears over Test-Tube Babies' *The Times* 20 October 1971, 2. The thalidomide tragedy was still fresh in the minds of those concerned about reproductive medicine, and the public generally, and coloured the views of many in relation to IVF.

[16] L Andrews, *The Clone Age: Adventures in the New World of Reproductive Technology* (New York, Henry Holt, 1999) 14. Watson's comments were made at a symposium in Washington. Edwards had already publicly addressed this concern in 1971. The problem of defects was met first because some defects, such as Down's syndrome, could be detected during pregnancy. The unwritten conclusion was that these defects were not problematic, because the pregnancy could be terminated. Other defects often resulted in miscarriage, the body naturally ending a pregnancy that would have resulted in a badly deformed child. Again, the problem was solved—teratogenic development should therefore 'not present undue difficulties'. See RG Edwards, 'Problems of Artificial Fertilisation' (1971) 233 *Nature* 23, and also RG Edwards and DJ Sharpe, 'Social Values and Research in Human Embryology' (1971) 231 *Nature* 87.

While some doctors expressed concern about abnormalities in public, others weighed in to support Edwards and Steptoe. In 1970, *The Times* quoted Dr Christiaan Barnard as saying he did not think 'test tube' baby research would lead to the creation of Frankenstein monsters.[17] Three years later, at a meeting of the British Medical Association in Hull, Professor Douglas Bevis of Leeds University suggested that the risk of abnormalities was likely to be small.[18] Leading embryologist Dr Anne McLaren, later a member of the Warnock Committee, also came out in support of Edwards and Steptoe's work that year, saying she thought the most likely handicap they would suffer would be publicity, rather than any medical problems.[19] Three years later she also told a meeting on social concern and biological advances at the British Association for the Advancement of Science at Stirling that animal work indicated that the risk of abnormalities in IVF pregnancies would be lower. She suggested that this was the case also because IVF pregnancies would be monitored so carefully.[20] Yet, when in 1983 Edwards proposed an international follow up study of children conceived through IVF, the idea was rejected by the Medical Research Council—they felt it might make the children feel different from others.[21] Concerns about potential defects would be a major theme of the later parliamentary debates.

Writers in the scientific press also seemed well aware that embryology research posed difficult ethical problems (an awareness noted by *The Times*[22]), but balanced these against the benefits. For example, a few months after the first announcement that early stage fertilisation had been achieved, *Nature* published an overview of the techniques and the science. This piece concluded with a discussion of some of the benefits. Using the 'awkward but inevitable phrase', 'test tube babies' conceived and gestated entirely *ex utero* as a future possibility were considered, citing two main possible 'benefits'. First, that women might achieve 'true and final emancipation' when able to delegate their child-bearing to 'a labour-saving machine'. The other perceived benefit was that 'greater selectivity in human births' would be possible 'by culling the disadvantaged embryos before

---

[17] '"Incubator Mothers" Forecast' *The Times* 26 February 1970, 1. Cardiac surgeon Barnard had performed the world's first successful human-to-human heart transplant in 1967 and was something of a celebrity.

[18] '"Test-Tube" Baby Alive and Well in Britain' *The Times* 16 July 1974, 1.

[19] P Wright, 'Less Risk of Test-Tube Baby Being Born with Brain Damage, Doctor Says' *The Times* 7 September 1974, 4. 24 years earlier, McLaren, with John Biggers, had achieved the first successful birth of mice that had been conceived and initially grown outside the mother's body, and her work was an important contribution to the perfecting of IVF. McLaren had also attended the meeting where Watson had denounced Edwards' work. She did express support for IVF, but also commented that in her view, Edwards and Steptoe were not ready and might proceed too soon. She was worried, she said, 'by the possibility that the desire to be first in the field will bias the judgement of those in a position to carry out egg transfer'. See above n 6, 33; n 4, 125.

[20] P Wright, 'Less Risk of Test-Tube Baby Being Born with Brain Damage, Doctor Says' *The Times* 7 September 1974, 4.

[21] See Challoner, above n 6, 49.

[22] 'Implications of the Test-Tube Embryo' *The Times* 15 February 1969, 8.

term'.[23] But far from arguing in favour or against these possible 'benefits', the piece noted:

> If these remote possibilities were to become feasible overnight they would certainly exceed what most people consider to be the ethical limits to improving on nature.[24]

It argued instead that such issues needed to be considered when they arose, and hence dealt with according to the morality of the day.[25]

Attention to the potential problems IVF would pose also came from interested medical professional bodies, such as Royal College of Obstetricians and Gynaecologists (RCOG), the British Medical Association (BMA), and the Medical Research Council (MRC). By February 1970, interest in official responses to the new technique had been growing. *The Times* reported that RCOG had had no official discussions of ethics of IVF at that stage,[26] but that the BMA was planning to discuss the technology.[27] The MRC, however, took a much stronger and more direct stance in refusing to fund Edwards and Steptoe's work. In April 1971, Edwards received a letter from the Council explaining that its rejection was based on its 'serious doubts about [the] ethical aspects of the proposed investigations in humans'. For the Council, the most significant concern was the implantation in women of oocytes fertilised *in vitro*, which it considered 'premature in view of the lack of preliminary studies on primates and the present deficiency of detailed knowledge of the possible hazards involved'.[28] Birth defects were clearly one concern, but more generally the Council questioned Edwards' methods, despite the fact that primate work was not at that time the best means to study human fertilisation—as Edwards noted some years later when commenting on the matter, it was impossible to fertilise monkey eggs *in vitro* and hence they were not a good model for research. The Council also questioned the safety of laparoscopy, the procedure Steptoe had established in the United Kingdom for acquiring eggs from the woman's fallopian tubes. Edwards responded to the Council's concerns, explaining the problems with primate research and pointing out that not a single death had resulted from the more than three thousand laparoscopies carried out at Oldham General Hospital where Steptoe was based. His explanation fell on deaf ears. No funding was to be available.

The Council's refusal did not prevent Edwards and Steptoe continuing with their work. The Oldham Area Health Authority gave them financial support and the use of some rooms at St Kershaw's Cottage Hospital, while Edwards also received funds from the Ford Foundation, an American research funding body.[29]

---

[23] 'Embryos Outside the Body' (1969) 223 *Nature* 1041, 1044.
[24] ibid 1044.
[25] ibid.
[26] J Roper, 'Difficult Ethical Problems Call for Careful Thought—BMA' *The Times* 25 February 1970, 10.
[27] ibid.
[28] Edwards and Steptoe, above n 4, 116–18. Edwards explains in detail in his memoir of these years the many reasons why mice, rather than monkeys, were a better model.
[29] The Ford Foundation was established in 1936 with a grant from Henry Ford's son Edsel to provide funding 'for scientific, educational and charitable purposes, all for the public welfare'.

Eight months after being refused MRC funding Steptoe transferred an embryo fertilised *in vitro* into a woman for the first time. But the lack of support did cause them difficulties, as they were not able to treat patients at Cambridge—Edwards had to continue driving across the country from Cambridge, where his research was carried out, to Oldham where Steptoe treated their patients. While their work was made more difficult, there was nothing to prevent them continuing if they could find the financial support they needed. Although the Medical Research Council, and the medical professionals who comprised it, had concerns about the ethics of a medical research project, they did not have the means to prevent it, only to hamper it.

Concerns about defects, though prominent, were not the only objection raised against the development of IVF. Religious groups were concerned that IVF separated the act of conception from the act of love, and was therefore against God's will.[30] Another early concern was that IVF would enable the mass production of people. In February 1969, the editor of *The Times* warned 'The cheapest and surest way for any small, impoverished country to improve its wealth and influence would be to concentrate on breeding a race of intellectual giants'.[31] Early the following year Dr Kit Pedlar made similar warnings on a BBC radio programme as reported in the pages of *The Times*, when it was reported that implantation of embryos might soon begin. Pedlar argued that were IVF techniques developed to a particular level and the technology made widely available,

> [t]hen you have a means … of mass-producing people without the advent of a mother at all. If you extend the experiment a little bit, it is a question of biological engineering. A general might order 100,000 troops to be produced. This can only be stopped by the public making some sort of objection.[32]

While debate continued in the news media and the scientific press, Edwards and Steptoe went on with their work, culminating finally in the summer of 1975 in their first successful pregnancy. Edwards' initial jubilation was soon to fade, however, when the pregnancy turned out to be ectopic and had to be terminated.[33] 'This was the sudden end of our high hopes', Edwards wrote, 'and how sad it was for our patient'.[34] The report of the pregnancy was published in *The Lancet* and sparked new debate, or as Challoner has put it, 'the work at Oldham once again became the subject of both interest and scorn'.[35] One particular voice from the medical profession emerged at this time in opposition to the work, a voice that

---

[30] See variously S Jessel, 'Views on Experiment Divided' *The Times* 15 February 1969, 8; J Roper, 'Difficult Ethical Problems Call for Careful Thought—BMA' *The Times* 25 February 1970, 10; MM Murry, '"Test Tube" Life' (Letter) *The Times* 27 February 1970, 9.
[31] 'Life in a Test Tube' (Editorial) *The Times* 15 February 1969, 9.
[32] P Wright, 'Progress towards "Test Tube Baby"' *The Times* 24 February 1970, 1.
[33] An ectopic pregnancy occurs when the embryo implants in one of the Fallopian tubes, rather than the womb. In this instance, the embryo had implanted in the stump of the fallopian tube that had been earlier removed.
[34] Edwards and Steptoe, above n 4, 143.
[35] Challoner, above n 6, 38.

would later become one of the most prominent and influential voices on the other side of the debate—that of Robert Winston.

Speaking on the BBC television programme *Horizon*, Winston doubted the value of Edwards and Steptoe's work, arguing that transplantation of fallopian tubes was a better means to treat infertility in women. Winston was not alone in his criticism; others considered that the team's work would give women false hope.[36] Years later Winston apologised, explaining that while he had seen the scientific importance of their work, it was not until 1980 that he began to see how IVF could have a clinical application.[37] For many, however, IVF was clearly going to have significant impact. Some worried about its effect on familial structures, others that it would facilitate surrogacy arrangements.

In 1978, after Steptoe and Edwards finally succeeded in producing a live, healthy baby through IVF, the time for speculation was over. When Louise was finally born, the news made front pages across the country, and later a film of parts of her birth was broadcast on BBC and ITN.[38] Patrick Steptoe and the Browns were splashed across the pages of every newspaper and were the daily subject of television news reports. The public reception of Louise was largely positive, and in much of the press the technology was presented as 'miraculous' and Steptoe as a heroic pioneer (Edwards received only rare attention). Only in a few stories were some concerns are raised, such as that the technique would not help all women, and Sir John Stallworthy's warning in one that test tube babies could present 'the worst problems since the invention of nuclear weapons'—these were far outweighed by the narrative of triumph and joy in which Brown's story was told.[39] Far from the fears of uncontrolled scientists that would permeate the Parliamentary debate that was to come, IVF was presented in the tabloid press as a miracle cure. In the science press, the response was also positive. In *Nature*, the birth of the first test tube baby was greeted with little but applause, with one editorial noting that the birth had been 'almost universally welcomed and hailed as an important advance in the treatment of some types of infertility'.[40]

The birth had been awaited as much to see if the technique would succeed as to see if the baby born as a result would be free from defects. To address these concerns, doctors at Oldham hospital published a report of the tests conducted on Louise soon after she was born, and reported no evidence of any major congenital abnormality.[41] Such focus was reflected in news reports. While most reports of a

---

[36] J Roper, 'Difficult Ethical Problems Call for Careful Thought—BMA' *The Times* 25 February 1970, 10.

[37] Above n 6, 38.

[38] 'Test-Tube Baby is a 5lb 12oz Girl' *The Times* 25 July 1978, 1; 'BBC and ITN to Show Birth of Test-Tube Baby' *The Times* 22 August 1978, 2.

[39] 'Our Miracle Baby' *The Daily Mail* (London, 12 July 1978) 1–2. This narrative is also evident in other *Daily Mail* pieces on the Browns: see 'Test-Tube Mother is "Fantastic"' *The Daily Mail* (London, 21 July 1978) 2; 'The Waiting Is Nearly Over for Historic Mother-to-Be' *The Daily Mail* (London, 24 July 1978) 1.

[40] 'Reproductive Technology: Whose Baby?' (1978) 274 (3 August) *Nature* 409–410, esp 409.

[41] D Hilson, RL Bruce and DG Sims, 'Successful Pregnancy Following *In Vitro* Fertilisation' (1978) 312 *The Lancet* 473.

child's birth give details of weight, of eye colour, and of general health, the early reports of Louise's birth had one other feature—they reported that she seemed 'normal'.[42] For example, on 25 August, 1978, *The Times* printed a picture of Louise captioned 'Test-tube baby "normal"', under which it recounted the results reported in *The Lancet*. The writer commented that 'the apparent normality of the infant should allay fears that the technique is fraught with dangers to the foetus, the report says.[43]

With this positive result, doctors and researchers were buoyed up to continue their work. IVF centres began to be established in Britain in the following few years, and by 1981 dozens of babies had been born following IVF. These numbers would only increase as the technique was further refined. By 1984, the term 'ice baby' was coined to refer to children born not just following IVF, but from embryos that had been created *in vitro*, frozen, and then thawed later for implantation. Clearly, the concerns raised in the early days were becoming more pressing as science and doctors forged ahead while the law failed to keep up. The need for regulation was keenly felt by both the science community and the public.

Regulation on the Way: The Warnock Committee and Others

As a result of these developments, by the early 1980s pressure for the government to act on IVF and embryo research was mounting. Labour member Leo Abse had been pressing for action to be taken since 1978, but his suggestions had been rejected by the government. Early in July 1978, he suggested to Shirley Williams, the then Secretary of State for Education and Science, that the Genetic Manipulation Advisory Committee (GMAC) should consider the ethical, legal and social issues raised by the new reproductive technologies. In his words, she turned him down flat, on the basis that the GMAC was not the appropriate body. She further pointed out that the MRC was unwilling to support research in this area without sufficient evidence from animal studies that the techniques were safe for human application. Abse has cast this refusal to consider the matter as an instance in which 'the sulking medical establishment had given encouragement to the Minister and her bureaucracy to sweep the problem under the carpet'.[44] With the birth of Louise, however, Abse argues that his request began to appear in a different light: 'The Minister's reply had barely been given when, doubtless to the embarrassment of the Medical

---

[42] 'Test-Tube Baby is a 5lb 12oz Girl' *The Times* 25 July 1978, 1.
[43] 'Test Tube Baby "Normal"' *The Times* 25 August 1978, 3.
[44] Leo Abse, 'The Politics of In Vitro Fertilisation in Britain' in S Fishel and EM Symonds (eds), *In Vitro Fertilisation: Past, Present and Future* (Oxford, IRL Press, 1986) 207–213, 208–9.

Research Council, the first British 'test-tube' baby was born, healthy and without blemish'.[45]

He and others finally succeeded in instigating a debate in the Commons in April 1982, which was followed three months later by the announcement that an inquiry into the issues would be held. The Inquiry into Human Fertilisation and Embryology was duly established in July 1982,[46] and its committee soon came to be known as the Warnock Committee, after its chairman Mary Warnock. Writing in 1986 about the background to the Warnock Committee, Malcolm MacNaughton explained that

> in the wake of these new methods [of assisted reproduction] it became evident that there were anxieties about where these new techniques might lead... Some members of the public viewed these new methods with relief and pleasure because they realised they that this meant, for some, that the unhappiness of infertility could be relieved and that they would be able to have children using these new methods. Others were very unhappy about these developments; at the apparently uncontrolled advance of science, the interference with creation and the possibilities for manipulating the very early stages of human development. It was against this background that the Warnock Committee was constituted.[47]

The committee comprised doctors, scientists, social workers and philosophers, and Warnock noted in the letter of submission at the front of the report that the Government 'rightly ... chose a membership which encompassed not only the many professions with a concern in these matters but the many religious traditions within society, so that as many viewpoints as possible could be brought to bear on the morally sensitive issues before us'.[48] After consulting over 200 organisations and individuals, and working for two years on the issues, the committee would eventually report its findings to Parliament in mid-1984.[49]

The Warnock Committee was not, however, the only group to consider how the new reproductive technologies should be regulated. Many doctors and researchers welcomed government action to help them deal with the ethical issues they were facing, but as the government dragged its heels, organisations within the medical profession felt it was time to take steps themselves towards producing regulation

---

[45] Of his ongoing push for an inquiry, Abse has commented: 'From then on for four years, I was to tread a lonely path making my demand. As late as February 1982 the Prime Minister gave me a dusty procrastinating reply when I urged the formation of a comprehensive interdepartmental interdisciplinary committee. I pressed the demand again in an adjournment debate in March 1982, and then for the first time the Government began to falter. Hesitatingly the Under Secretary of State for Health and Social Security admitted the need for some enquiry. In July 1982 the formation of the Warnock Committee was announced: four years had passed since I had first demanded it'. See ibid, 209.

[46] Department of Health and Social Security (United Kingdom), *Legislation on Human Infertility Services and Embryo Research: A Consultation Paper* (HMSO, 1986) 1.

[47] MC MacNaughton, 'The Current Status of the Warnock Report and Other International Reports' in S Fishel and EM Symonds (eds), *In Vitro Fertilisation: Past, Present and Future* (Oxford, IRL Press, 1986) 197–205, 197.

[48] Department of Health and Social Security, *Report of the Committee of Inquiry into Human Fertilisation and Embryology* (Cmnd 9314, 1984) iv.

[49] Baroness Mary Warnock, Prof Malcolm MacNaughton, Dr David Davies, Lord Justice Scott Baker, Prof John Marshall, Dr Anne McLaren, Mrs MM Carrilline, Mrs J Walker, Prof WG Irwin, Mr QS Anisuddin, Mrs NL Edwards, Mr DJ McNeil, Dame Josephine Barnes, Prof Anthony Dyson and Prof Ken Rawnsley.

or, at a minimum, ethical guidance. As the Warnock Committee worked on, collecting opinions and evidence from scientists, doctors, interest groups and the public, the MRC released its own guidelines on human fertilisation and embryology in November 1982. It had established an advisory group to review policy on IVF and embryo research some four years earlier, which had reported to the Council that scientifically sound research on IVF was acceptable, and that IVF should be treated as a therapeutic procedure regulated by the usual doctor/patient relationship.[50]

In May 1983, this group reconvened to again make recommendations to the MRC in light of new developments since the birth of Louise. The MRC accepted its conclusions, and issued a statement that it considered research into IVF that entailed fertilisation using human gametes was acceptable so long as no embryos resulting from such research were transferred into a woman's uterus. Throughout, the guidelines carefully avoided the term 'embryo', despite supporting research using 'fertilised ova' allowed to develop up to implantation stage—a clear euphemism.[51]

RCOG began work on its own report on IVF in 1982, and reported in May 1983. It supported the use of IVF and recommended that it be offered to couples in a stable relationship, though not necessarily married. It also approved of egg donation, embryo freezing and even embryo division, as well as endorsing the MRC's position on research, supporting a limit of 17 days' embryo development on research.[52]

Three months before the Warnock inquiry was announced, on 10 February 1982, the BMA's Central Ethical Committee had also discussed IVF and recommended that the BMA Council establish a working group to consider the ethics of the new technology, which had its first meeting on 30 April 1982.[53] At the time, the committee drew attention to the fact that it had, since 1978, endorsed guidelines on IVF that required informed consent to be obtained for the procedure and that research was acceptable provided its implications were kept under review.[54]

The BMA working group reported in April 1983 and its report was considered by the BMA Council in its May 1983 meeting and was released as interim guidelines that month. The group's recommendations were directed at doctors making decisions about IVF, and were largely in line with those of the MRC and RCOG,

---

[50] Medical Research Council, 'Research Related to Human Fertilisation and Embryology' (1982) 285 *British Medical Journal* 1480.

[51] ibid. The group was comprised almost entirely of medical researchers and doctors (including members of the Warnock Committee Anne McLaren and Malcolm MacNaughton), with addition of the Bishop of Durham, John Habgood, who had a background in science (particularly physiology) and held a doctoral degree, as well as having written on science and religion.

[52] 'Report of the Royal Society of Obstetricians and Gynaecologists on *In Vitro* Fertilisation and Embryo Replacement' (1983) 286 *British Medical Journal* 1519.

[53] 'In-Vitro Fertilisation: BMA Working Party Proposed' (1982) 284 *British Medical Journal* 609; 'In-Vitro Fertilisation: BMA's Working Group' (1982) 284 *British Medical Journal* 1356. The group included Anne McLaren and Josephine Barnes, both of whom would later become members of the Warnock Committee.

[54] 'In-Vitro Fertilisation: BMA Working Party Proposed' (1982) 284 *British Medical Journal* 609.

save on the issue of licensing—the BMA did not call, as those organisations did, for governmental oversight and licensing of premises where IVF was carried out.

At this time, the MRC and BMA guidelines together determined what could be done in all areas of IVF and embryo research. Some, however, did not welcome the plethora of guidelines being offered by various groups. One article in *Nature* criticised the moves by each society or group to produce guidelines, stating:

> the British medical establishment seems bent on making an unpalatable mess of its consideration of the ethical problems occasioned by recent developments in the treatment of human infertility ... whether or not physicians are enlightened by the work of the committees now hard at work, it is certain that the public will be confused.[55]

In the maelstrom of public and parliamentary debate that was soon to follow this would, however, be the least of medical and scientific communities' worries.

While Regulation is Coming, Doctors Voice Their Views

In 1983, Robert Edwards reviewed a new book on ethics and embryos: *Test-Tube Babies: A Guide to Moral Questions, Present Techniques and Future Possibilities*, edited by philosopher Peter Singer and gynaecologist William Walters. The book included chapters from philosophers, theologians and ethicists but where, Edwards asked, were the views of the doctors and scientists actually involved in the work? 'Surely', he wrote, 'those most clearly involved should have something to contribute, something others cannot'.[56] Edwards called for doctors and researchers working in the field to publicise their ethical attitudes and justify their work to avoid the implication of 'an uncaring, unfeeling science'.

The pages of the major British medical journals of this period are in fact filled with editorials, news pieces, articles and letters debating what was to be done about IVF and embryo research. Far from sitting back while others produced regulation or debated the ethics, doctors and scientists were deeply engaged with the issues raised by the new technology and much of the ethical debate in these pages was nuanced and considered. The *British Medical Journal*, *The Lancet* and *Nature*, amongst others, regularly printed opinion pieces on the ethical issues and the many letters that responded to them. Any doctor who read the medical press could not fail to be aware that the new reproductive technologies raised significant concerns. Indeed, some even lamented the lack of consideration of ethics in some articles—there was, it seems, an expectation that a discussion IVF or embryo research of any kind demanded some exploration of the ethical dimensions of the work.[57]

---

[55] 'Test-Tube Babies Pilloried Again' (1982) 295 *Nature* 445.
[56] R Edwards, 'Test-Tube Babies: A Guide to Moral Questions, Present Techniques and Future Possibilities (Book Review)' (1983) 302 *British Medical Journal* 775.
[57] See, eg B Frazer, 'Ethics and In-Vitro Fertilisation' (Letter) (1982) 285 *British Medical Journal* 1113.

Edwards' point, though, was for doctors and researchers to take their views to the public and to government, which over the ensuing seven years they did.

As will be discussed below, many involved themselves in the parliamentary process on either side of the debate, providing information about the science behind IVF and views on the nature of the embryo and the benefits or otherwise of research. Some also spoke to the press. For example, on the emerging issue of egg donation, where eggs from one woman are used to create an embryo which is carried to term by another woman, *The Times* presented the views of various doctors. Professor Ian Craft was quoted as being in favour of the technique, while another doctor reported that he was waiting on the Warnock decision before proceeding.[58] Another article in the same newspaper reported the following year that many doctors and scientists supported the Warnock recommendations, demonstrating their public voicing of views.[59]

Doctors and researchers also attempted to gauge views on embryo research themselves, with a number conducting surveys of IVF and sterilisation patients. In part, these efforts were about providing information to the public and regulators to help in deciding what to do about the new technology. Arguably, they were also attempting to inform themselves as a profession of what those they treated thought about what they did. In one survey, 50 women undergoing laparoscopic sterilisation were asked if they would donate ova for research, with 35 (70%) responding that they would do so. Of these, eight would have participated but for their unease about having to stop oral contraceptives for two months as required by the research.[60] In another study from Singapore, conducted in 1981 but submitted for publication in *The Lancet* in 1984, 113 patients at a sub-fertility clinic and 164 medical students were asked whether they considered IVF ethical. 73.5% of infertile patients did, as did 78.8% of students. Students were split roughly 50–50 on whether embryo research was ethical.[61]

Some issues were hotly debated by doctors and researchers in the science press. One was whether IVF should continue. Views were divided, although the balance seems to be in favour of the technique.[62] Regular note was made of the risk of deformities as something that must be considered and addressed.[63] Some doctors considered IVF itself abhorrent because of the dangers it presented. One example

---

[58] C Cookson, 'Fertility Clinics Hope to Use Donated Eggs' *The Times* 29 August 1983, 3.
[59] 'Pressure on for "Test Tube" Baby Legislation' *The Times* 18 June 1984, 3.
[60] AA Templeton et al, 'What Potential Ovum Donors Think' (1984) May 12 *The Lancet* 1081–82.
[61] See NS Chye and SS Ratnam, 'Ethics of Research on Embryos' (Letter) (1984) 28 July *The Lancet* 231. See also E Alder and AA Templeton, 'Patient Reaction to IVF Treatment' (1985) 19 January *The Lancet* 168.
[62] See, eg A Trounson and A Conti, 'Research in Human In-Vitro Fertilisation and Embryo Transfer' (1982) 285 *British Medical Journal* 244, and cf S Hayes, 'The Warnock Report' (1984) 289 *British Medical Journal* 1006.
[63] See, eg PK Smith, 'Ethics and In-Vitro Fertilisation' (Letter) (1982) 284 *British Medical Journal* 1287; J Scotson, 'Ethics and In-Vitro Fertilisation' (Letter) (1982) 284 *British Medical Journal* 1560; M Kaufman, 'Chromosome Abnormalities' (1983) 304 *Nature* 482. Some, as Edwards had, called for surveys to be done to track the outcomes of IVF. See, eg D Woolam, 'The Warnock Report' (Letter) (1984) 289 *British Medical Journal* 439, 440.

given was that it would cause the breakdown of marriages due to the separation of the act of love and of conception.[64] This assertion received a vigorous denial in response.[65] Doctors also argued about when IVF should be offered, with Edwards and Steptoe publicly criticising Australian IVF specialist Alan Trounson for fertilising eggs taken from a 42-year-old infertile woman for implantation. The two IVF pioneers asserted that there should be an age limit on donors due to the risk of abnormalities associated with the eggs of older women.[66]

Another crucial issue that would arise in the first parliamentary debates was the status of the embryo, and this was one question on which many doctors and researchers voiced an opinion. The question was regularly cast in the public, and later parliamentary, debate as one about when life began as a means to determine whether an embryo was a person, and hence whether it should be afforded the same rights and protections and children and adults. In both the Lords and Commons this would be a tremendously vexed question, as the next section demonstrates, but underpinning that debate was the belief—on both sides—that there was a definitive answer to the question. Either life began at the moment of conception (which many equated with the 'moment' of fertilisation) or it did not (it might occur later or gradually over time).

One might think that such a debate was only a matter for the lay person, that the medical profession could within itself arrive at an answer that most could agree upon. The debate on this issue that raged across the pages of the medical journals is evidence that this was anything but the case. Doctors and medical researchers, like everyone else, were split in their views on this question, a split that most likely supported the parliamentary split as medical experts provided their views MPs.[67] The Royal College of General Practitioners publicly declared that from the moment of fertilisation the embryo should be given the same rights and respect as children and adults, while other professional bodies such as RCOG supported research on living embryos. Looking through the arguments put on either side within the medical community demonstrates that there was no clear medical consensus on either the scientific question of when human life began, nor on the status of the embryo as a person.

---

[64] B Frazer, 'Ethics and In-Vitro Fertilisation' (Letter) (1982) 285 *British Medical Journal* 1113.

[65] S Pinkerton, 'In-Vitro Fertilisation' (Letter) (1982) 285 *British Medical Journal* 1355.

[66] T Beardsley, 'Human Embryo Experiments: Societies Urge a Softer Line' (1983) 302 *Nature* 739.

[67] See, eg B Frazer, 'Ethics and In-Vitro Fertilisation' (Letter) (1982) 285 *British Medical Journal* 1113; JR Baker, 'Human Conception' (Letter) (1982) 299 *Nature* 674; SJG Spencer, 'Human In Vitro Fertilisation and Embryo Replacement and Transfer' (Letter) (1983) 286 *British Medical Journal* 1822–23; MM Heley, 'The Warnock Report' (Letter) (1984) 289 *British Medical Journal* 440; GIM Swyer, 'The Warnock Report' (Letter) (1984) 289 *British Medical Journal* 694; DR Bromham, 'Progress In In Vitro Fertilisation?' (Letter) (1985) 291 *British Medical Journal* 1643; JR Ling, 'Human Embryos' (Letter) (1985) 313 *Nature* 262; JR Baker, 'Human Embryos' (Letter) (1985) 313 *Nature* 524; T Cavalier-Smith, 'When Does Life Begin?' (Letter) (1985) 314 *Nature* 492; S Lovell, 'When Does Life Begin?' (Letter) (1985) 314 *Nature* 492; JA Davis, 'Embryo Research (cont)' (Letter) (1985) 314 *Nature* 666; J Wolfe, 'The Embryo's Right to Protection' (Letter) (1985) 315 *Nature* 92; DA Darcy, 'Embryo Research' (Letter) (1985) 315 *Nature* 710; RL Hoult, 'The Meaning of 'Human Life'' (Letter) (1985) 316 *Nature* 480.

The third major issue was whether research on embryos should be undertaken, given its possible consequences as well as the implications for the embryos it would destroy. From letters and articles published in journals such as *Nature* and the *British Medical Journal*, it is evident that this issue concerned many in the profession.[68] While many were in favour of research, not all considered it acceptable.[69] There were a number of groups who worked to oppose embryo research and, to some degree, IVF. Organisations such as the World Federation of Doctors Who Respect Human Life were wholly opposed to IVF and embryo research and made submissions to this effect to the Warnock Committee. Margaret Heley, organiser of the LIFE Doctors Group (a pro-life organisation) wrote to *The Lancet* that the Warnock Report made alarming reading,

> providing as it does a vision of a bleak and nightmarish future—a future of cold, clinical conceptions, of silent stockpiles of frozen embryos, of test-tube adultery and 'do-it-yourself' sex selection kits, of a Brave New World where archetypal mad scientists create 'spare parts' from living human organisms.[70]

Others urged caution, with the author of one letter in the *British Medical Journal* urging 'that medical science should not feel impelled to all that it is capable of doing'.[71]

Evidently, the image of the mad scientist lived in the minds of doctors, as well as those outside the profession. This image had been apparent in some of the news coverage throughout the 1970s, and when the parliamentary debates began, it was clear that there was a deep-seated fear that scientists would proceed with research well beyond what many considered morally acceptable. In 1970, an editorial in *Nature* summed up the issue well. These were, it was considered,

> [d]ark atavistic fears … that scientists have usurped the created powers and should assume the moral responsibilities formerly attributed to gods.

Such an image, the editor argued, was false—'These are not perverted men in white coats doing nasty experiments on human beings, but reasonable scientists carrying out perfectly justifiable research'.[72] Despite this kind of defence in the scientific press, and the actions of doctors and researchers in explaining their work and calling for regulation, many MPs would express the view that regulation was needed because scientists were unable to control themselves.[73] For example, one Conservative MP commented in interview that 'scientists will always try to

---

[68] J Scotson, 'Ethics and In-Vitro Fertilisation' (Letter) (1982) 284 *British Medical Journal* 1560; S Browne, 'Ethics and In-Vitro Fertilisation' (Letter) (1982) 284 *British Medical Journal* 1950.

[69] In favour, see eg 'Human Reproduction: Regulated Progress or Damned Interference?' (editorial) (1984) 324 *The Lancet* 202. Against, see eg B Malloy, 'One Law for Conceptus, One for Abortus' (1984) 324 *The Lancet* 231.

[70] MM Heley, 'Mrs Warnock's Brave New World' (Letter) (1984) 4 August *The Lancet* 290.

[71] J Scotson, 'Ethics and In-Vitro Fertilisation' (Letter) (1982) 284 *British Medical Journal* 1560.

[72] 'Premature Birth of Test Tube Baby' (1970) 225 (7 March) *Nature* 886.

[73] Many of the MPs interviewed expressed this view. interview with Edwina Currie (Oxford, 16 December 2005); interview with Ann Widdecombe (London, 18 December 2005). See also

push the boundaries because they're curious ... one of the reasons why you can't control [science] is that people will always push limits'.[74] Another felt similarly, stating that 'scientists are going to push it further because that's the very nature of a scientist ... they are not self-limiting ... the very nature of being a scientist by their job is to keep pushing',[75] while one, himself a doctor as well as an MP, regarded fears about uncontrolled science (and scientists) as legitimate, because he did not think 'that you can let scientists, whether they be doctors or not, loose to muck around with genetic material without some sort of licensing or regulatory body overseeing what they are doing'.[76]

While largely eschewing the idea of the amoral, uncontrolled scientist, medical researchers and doctors did see the need for guidance. One, a member of the Warnock Committee, later commented that he knew himself, from being a researcher, 'how you get carried along by enthusiasm ... you can see an objective and you get swept along to some extent and don't always stop and check and think enough about the ethical issues enough'. For him, boundaries were pushed not for any 'malevolent' reason, but as a result of enthusiasm. However regardless of this, external control was still required to scrutinise the ethics of work to be done.[77]

For both this reason, and their own belief in the need to help in determining what to do, it is clear from the public expression of views by members of the profession that that doctors and medical researchers desired regulation of some kind. None advocated wholly uncontrolled research or argued for the exclusion of views and controls from outside the profession. Quite the opposite of this, the tone of the discussion between 1982 and 1985 suggests a real awareness of the ethical difficulties they were facing as doctors and researchers, and of their inability to deal with them on their own. Some railed against the destruction of human life when embryos were sacrificed to research into IVF, while others highlighted the misery of childlessness. Far from the unfeeling mad scientists depicted in the newspapers and coming Parliamentary debates, the emotion and concern felt by each writer is evident. A comment from Dr Robert Newell, in response to a previous letter referring to IVF as unethical and abhorrent, is telling:

> I did not know whether to be angry or sad that a gynaecologist, who presumably witnesses the tears of childless women, could be so totally lacking in compassion.[78]

The need for control was obviously recognised by profession's representatives as well, which the actions of the BMA, the MRC and RCOG, amongst others show.

---

interview with Dr Charles Goodson-Wickes (London, 8 February 2006); interview with James Couchman (Oxford, 14 February 2006); interview with Lady Saltoun (London, 1 February 2006).

[74] Interview with Ann Widdecombe (London, 18 December 2005).
[75] Interview with T (London, 19 January 2006).
[76] See also interview with Dr Charles Goodson-Wickes (London, 8 February 2006).
[77] Interview with Prof John Marshall (London, 14 December 2005).
[78] R Newell, 'Ethics and In Vitro Fertilisation' (1982) 285 *British Medical Journal* 1581.

Accompanying the worry that scientists would take their work beyond what was acceptable was the belief that scientists, unlike others, often lacked either the distance from their work, or the moral understanding, to recognise its problematic implications. According to one member of the Lords who participated in the first debate, scientists were not self-regulating about moral issues. For them, the pursuit of knowledge was 'paramount above all'.[79] Such views also came from medically trained MPs and medical researchers, as well as those outside the profession. As a physician and MP, one interviewee suggested that 'scientists are too close to what they are doing scientifically' to assess its moral dimension, they need 'the warning hand of somebody on their shoulders to say "this is not proper"'.[80] Again, the actions of the medical profession demonstrate that they knew they needed outside guidance, in their support of government steps to achieve this through regulation.[81] Very few demanded complete scientific freedom; the great majority called for help and guidance through the morass of ethical issues they faced.

Some also called for doctors and philosophers to allay public fears about research, commenting that in the past once the public had been informed about new technologies and allowed to consider the issues surrounding them, they had largely supported their practice (artificial insemination and recombinant DNA technology were two examples). Such an approach is evident in much of the medico-ethical literature of the time in the mainstream medical journals, notably once it appears that research might be prevented. Many doctors and researchers called for information to be provided and the issues considered by society, rather than bullishly demanding to be allowed to do as they saw fit. The gulf between the popular and political images of the doctors and researchers involved in IVF, and their own expressed views was wide indeed.

The Warnock Report and the First Debates: 1984–85

The Warnock Committee released its report in July 1984 to both criticism and praise. Robert Edwards said of the report that it 'lifted heavy ethical obligations from my shoulders. Before this, Patrick and I had stood first in the firing line, initiating and doing the work, and justifying it, and now Dame Mary would take that responsibility'.[82] In the science press, it was warmly received, while for the opponents of research it was a significant blow.

---

[79] Interview with Lady Saltoun (London, 1 February 2006).
[80] See also interview with Dr Charles Goodson-Wickes (London, 8 February 2006).
[81] See, eg J Cundy, 'In Vitro Fertilisation' (1984) 288 *British Medical Journal* 1918; GIM Swyer, 'The Warnock Report' (Letter) (1984) 289 *British Medical Journal* 694; M Hull, 'The Warnock Report' (1984) 289 *British Medical Journal* 694. See also the welcome given the Warnock report in the journals, such as 'A Welcome Report' (Editorial) (1984) 289 *British Medical Journal* 207.
[82] R Edwards, *Life Before Birth: Reflections on the Embryo Debate* (London, Hutchinson, 1989) 121.

The Committee recommended that IVF be permitted to continue, considering that the major argument in favour of IVF—its capacity to increase the chances of some fertile couples to have children—was more convincing than objections based on the production of excess embryos through super-ovulation and on resource allocation concerns.[83] Yet despite placing individual needs and concerns for the childless at the forefront of its reasoning, the Committee also recommended making IVF available only to heterosexual couples in stable relationships (although they need not have been married). It argued, in tune with its view that the interests of the child born following IVF were paramount, that as a general rule, 'it is better for children to be born into a two-parent family, with both father and mother'.[84]

By far the most influential (and controversial) contribution made by the report to the debate about ART and embryo research, and certainly its most famous, was the view that the embryo had a different status prior to 14 days' development. The Committee concluded that the embryo did have special status and should be afforded legal protections, however it recommended that prior to 14 days' development this protection extended only to ensuring that research using such 'pre-embryos' was subject to licensing. It justified the time limit it imposed on the basis that the 14-day point marks 'the beginning of individual development' of the embryo. The Report's recommendations were debated in the House of Lords in October 1984,[85] and three weeks later in the House of Commons.[86]

In the *British Medical Journal*, the Warnock report was greeted as 'a timely and thoughtful contribution to a difficult problem', which had come none too soon. According to the editorial, legislation was needed to reflect public concern but must be flexible enough to take account of new technology as it was developed. But the editor felt it should not be left solely to government to ensure practices in research and medicine were acceptable. Doctors, the editor wrote

> have a responsibility to ensure not only that they understand the scientific facts but also that they get to grips with the moral and ethical issues concerned in order to present their patients with a balanced and informed view.[87]

Yet, before the first debate on the Warnock Report in the House of Lords on 31 October 1984, most doctors and scientists did not believe that IVF would be prohibited and did not fully perceive the need to act.[88] One prominent embryologist of the time observed that the objections raised during that debate began to make scientists aware of how great the opposition to their work was.[89] Even Anne

---

[83] Department of Health and Social Security, *Report of the Committee of Inquiry into Human Fertilisation and Embryology* (Cmnd 9314, 1984), 31–32.
[84] ibid 11.
[85] Hansard HL vol 456 cols 524–93 (31 October 1984).
[86] Hansard HC vol 68 cols 547–90 (23 November 1984).
[87] 'A Welcome Report' (1984) 289 *British Medical Journal* 207–08.
[88] See, eg interview with Dr David Davies (by telephone, 21 January 2006).
[89] Interview with Prof Anne McLaren (Cambridge, 7 February 2006).

McLaren, who was at the time working in mammalian development and was a member of the Warnock Committee, had little conception of the uproar research into reproduction was causing, and was a self-described 'ethical illiterate'. In a letter to Mary Warnock sometime after the committee had reported, McLaren wrote

> I had led an ethically sheltered existence and it had never crossed my mind that fertilising frozen and thawed donated human eggs as part of a research project to help young women [to conceive] could equally well be described as 'creating in order to destroy'.[90]

Commenting on McLaren's response to concerns about the ethical issues raised by embryo research, one friend said 'she had no idea that she was going to end up being called a murderer and it came as a terrific surprise to her'.[91] This comment echoes many voiced throughout this period. James Drife observed in a *British Medical Journal* review of two television documentaries on IVF screened in late 1981 and early 1982 that television was able to demonstrate

> the streak of naiveté that seems to be a necessary part of a medical pioneer's character: now and again an eminent doctor or scientist appeared to be thinking about an ethical problem for the first time as the cameras rolled.[92]

The first debate in October 1984 saw the House of Lords in uproar. The debate focused on embryo research, although issues surrounding embryo use also applied to some aspects of IVF. Much of the debate in the Lords turned on the moral status of the embryo and concerns about playing God or unnatural processes. The anti-embryo research lobby within Parliament adopted as a basic principle that the embryo either had the potential for human life, or was in fact a human person. In either case, it followed from this argument that the embryo deserved protection and that research that used embryos was therefore morally wrong.[93] The majority of speakers in the House of Lords were strongly against the use of embryos for research purposes, and many also rejected surrogacy arrangements of most kinds.[94]

---

[90] M Warnock, *Making Babies: Is There a Right to Have Children?* (Oxford, OUP, 2002).
[91] Interview with Baroness Mary Warnock (London, 28 November 2005).
[92] JO Drife, 'Medicine and the Media' (1982) 284 *British Medical Journal* 487.
[93] For example, in the House of Commons, Sir Gerald Vaughan argued that that 'while the ovum and sperm have potential life, life begins at conception. It is unacceptable to bank fertilised ova and to experiment on human embryos'. See Hansard HC col 551 (November 1984).
[94] Many of the ideas raised in relation to IVF and embryo research, particularly the moral status of pre-born life, had already been hotly debated in relation to abortion. The reproductive medicine debates, following less than 20 years on, were deeply influenced by these debates. The ART and embryo research debates were also influenced by the actions of lobby groups, many of which were formed during the abortion debates. These groups included the Society for the Protection of Unborn Children (SPUC), formed in January 1967 and LIFE, formed in 1970, which worked to repeal the Abortion Act, and prevent 'destruction of pre-born life': (1995) 28 *LIFE News* 1 (the issue details the establishment of the organisation).

The notion of the embryo as deserving protection was not new. Edwards and Steptoe's work had been criticised on this basis since the late 1960s, with opponents viewing the destruction of embryos as akin to abortion and infanticide. The absolutists 'regard fertilisation', Edwards wrote in 1981, 'as a kind of holy event above the interference of man', but he pointed out that their views were not reflected in the consensus opinion of society nor the law. If embryos were people in the sense the absolutists regarded them, abortion would be illegal.

Others raised objections on the grounds that such experiments were an affront to human dignity and based on the risks this research might pose to humanity. The final major argument raised against embryo research was based on the uniqueness of human life, which demands special protection. Clear themes emerge from these views, most particularly an acceptance of the 'humanity' of embryos, and that this necessitated special treatment that other living things, such as animals (which of course were widely and legally used in scientific experimentation at that time) did not deserve. Considerable concern about assisted reproduction was expressed in the House of Lords, including the legal status of children conceived in this way, were also expressed.

Those on the pro-science side of the debate argued that that the therapeutic benefits that might flow from embryo research outweighed concerns about the use of embryos that have the potential to become human beings. This side of the debate was much better represented in the House of Commons debate, in which a larger proportion of members focused on the benefits of the science rather than concerns for the rights of embryos. Speakers in the Commons worked hard to demonstrate that the benefits of embryo research and IVF outweighed their problematic implications. Varying views about the moral status of the embryo were expressed within this side of the debate. Those in favour of allowing embryo research and IVF often also considered scientists capable of self-regulation.

Many of the Lords found 'slippery slope' arguments about the direction in which IVF and embryo research might go convincing.[95] Only a few examined utilitarian approaches in weighing the benefits of treating infertility or allowing research.[96] For the most part, however, the Lords relied on either their own sense of morality, rather than research data or academic philosophy to support their views, supplemented by religious views in many cases. In fact, far greater reference was made to religious teachings than any other basis for their views, particularly those of the Church of England and the Roman Catholic

---

[95] Hansard HL vol 456 col 544 (31 October 1984) (Lord Coleraine); col 550 (Viscount Hanworth); col 557 (The Earl of Halsbury); col 563 (Lady Saltoun); col 574 (Lord Tranmire); col 576 (Baroness Masham of Ilton).

[96] Hansard HL vol 456 col 529 (31 October 1984) (Lord Winstanley); col 539 (The Lord Bishop of Chelmsford).

Church.[97] Some also invoked the principle that as a person is created in the image of God, he or she has intrinsic value which should be respected.[98] Others criticised the Warnock report for its alleged failure to fully consider religious views or develop principles based on these views.[99]

Some also noted public opinion as a relevant input in determining the stance to be taken by Parliament on the ethical questions before it.[100] This appears to suggest that some of the Lords were prepared to accept that public or majority opinion were relevant to determining the answers to moral questions, however it should be noted that this approach was probably also motivated by a desire to represent the views of the electorate in resulting legislative measures. Little reference was made to the views of doctors or medical researchers in support of their views. Rather, a largely negative attitude towards the medical research profession was expressed in the Lords. Many voiced fears that research would lead to the manipulation of human characteristics, largely expressed as opposition to eugenics. References were made to the Nazi experiments, as well as to the story of Pandora, in a number of speeches.[101] In the Lords debate there was much reference to possible future developments in science, and in relation to these, two main premises appear to be accepted. The first was that scientists are incapable or unwilling to self-regulate by reference to ethical or moral concerns.[102] The second, based on slippery slope views, was that science is likely to develop uncontrolled, that is has a life of its own in some sense, and if progress is not restricted, it would move towards unacceptable developments such as trans-species fertilisation and eugenic creations.[103]

In the House of Commons debate three weeks later, the tenor of the debate was markedly different. Similar moral views on ART to those expressed in the Lords were given, such as repugnance at money exchanges in surrogacy

---

[97] For example, a number of the Lords referred to passages from the Old and New Testaments in support of the view that the embryo is a human being from the moment of conception. Hansard HL vol 456 col 527 (31 October 1984) (Lord Ennals); col 536 (The Marquess of Reading); col 551 (The Lord Bishop of Norwich); col 556 (Lord Rawlinson of Ewell); col 564 (The Earl of Lauderdale); col 577 (Baroness Masham of Ilton). See variously Hansard HL vol 456 col 536 (31 October 1984) (The Marquess of Reading); col 544 (Lord Coleraine); col 557 (The Earl of Halsbury).
[98] Hansard HL vol 456 col 536 (31 October 1984) (The Marquess of Reading).
[99] Hansard HL vol 456 col 551 (31 October 1984) (The Lord Bishop of Norwich); col 564 (The Earl of Lauderdale).
[100] Hansard HL vol 456 col 553 (31 October 1984) (The Lord Bishop of Norwich); col 567 (Lord Robertson of Oakridge); col 572 (Viscount Sidmouth).
[101] Hansard HL vol 456 col 546 (31 October 1984) (Lord Coleraine); col 550 (Viscount Hanworth); col 551 (The Lord Bishop of Norwich); col 576 (Baroness Masham of Ilton); col 579 (Lord Milverton); col 580 (Wiscount Buckmaster).
[102] Hansard HL vol 456 col 544 (31 October 1984) (Lord Coleraine); col 555 (Lord Rawlinson of Ewell); col 573 (Viscount Sidmouth); col 577 (Baroness Masham of Ilton).
[103] Hansard HL vol 456 col 549 (31 October 1984) (Lord Soper); col 550 (Viscount Hanworth); col 553 (The Lord Bishop of Norwich); col 556 (Lord Rawlinson of Ewell); col 563 (Lady Saltoun); col 563 (The Earl of Lauderdale).

arrangements;[104] beliefs that the embryo is a person from conception;[105] and the view that marriage and the nuclear family were the proper and ideal family model in which to raise a child.[106] Many concerns similar to those put in the Lords were also raised, such as worries about the possibility of eugenics.[107] Some degree of rights-based analysis also appeared in the Commons debates,[108] as did arguments based on the primacy of the welfare of children.[109] Religious sentiments as the basis for moral views were also often raised.[110] However, a number of other ethical and related arguments were raised that perhaps demonstrate a shift in attitude or a difference in approach between the Houses. For one, members attempted to present greater reasoning behind their conclusions, rather than declaring a technology or action 'abhorrent' or 'immoral'. As an example, Nicholas Winterton, the member for Macclesfield, drew on arguments against abortion to support an alternative to the use of ART, instead attacking ART on its face.[111] Considerably more evidence and argument was also put (or at least hinted at existing) in favour of positions, and challenged in return.[112] For example, evidence on the need for embryo research was given by both sides of the debate.[113]

More tellingly, many presented utilitarian-like arguments in favour of ART and embryo research, which were largely absent from the debate in the Lords.[114] In a similar approach, some argued that the benefits of these technologies could outweigh moral concerns about them, even where these concerns might be valid or at least reasonably held by some in the community.[115] For example, Leo Abse argued that the issues must be thought through in light of the benefits to infertile women and not solely by unalterable reference to moral views; that people should not 'in a spirit of moral censoriousness, believe that they should take a superior stance over those of us who … take a contrary view'.[116] Some, such as Michael

[104] Hansard HC vol 68 col 530 (23 November 1984) (Norman Fowler, The Secretary of State for Social Services).
[105] Hansard HC vol 68 col 531 (23 November 1984) (Harry Greenway); col 540 (Sir Bernard Braine, Castle Point); col 554 (Rev Ian Paisley); col 562 (Sir Hugh Rossi).
[106] Hansard HC vol 68 col 539 (23 November 1984) (Sir Bernard Braine).
[107] Hansard HC vol 68 col 539 (23 November 1984) (Sir Bernard Braine); col 553 (Mr Michael Meadowcroft).
[108] Hansard HC vol 68 col 529 (23 November 1984) (Norman Fowler, The Secretary of State for Social Services); col 534 (Michael Meacher); col 554 (Rev Ian Paisley).
[109] Hansard HC vol 68 col 529 (23 November 1984) (Norman Fowler, The Secretary of State for Social Services).
[110] Hansard HC vol 68 col 531 (23 November 1984) (Nicholas Winterton); col 540 (Sir Bernard Braine); col 554 (Rev Ian Paisley).
[111] Hansard HC vol 68 col 531 (23 November 1984) (Nicholas Winterton). On reasoning through of positions, see also col 549 (Leo Abse).
[112] Hansard HC vol 68 col 537–8 (23 November 1984) (Michael Meacher); col 541 (Sir Bernard Braine); col 553 (Michael Meadowcroft).
[113] Hansard HC vol 68 col 541 (23 November 1984) (Sir Bernard Braine, Castle Point); col 548 (Mr Leo Abse); col 557 (Renée Short).
[114] Hansard HC vol 68 col 532 (23 November 1984) col 532 (Norman Fowler, The Secretary of State for Social Services).
[115] Hansard HC vol 68 col 535 (23 November 1984) (Michael Meacher).
[116] Hansard HC vol 68 col 544 (23 November 1984) (Leo Abse).

Meacher, also suggested that such benefits might be a valid basis for determining how to deal with technologies in the face of uncertainty about the answers to the ethical questions they raised.[117] In response, some argued that benefits could not outweigh such moral objections.[118]

The House of Commons debate also demonstrated a shift towards a more forthright stance in favour of ART and embryo research, rather than the defence of it against moral objections evidenced in the Lords. While many (like the Lords) took the view that science (and scientists) should not continue uncontrolled, as they were incapable of self-regulating in line with ethical and moral principles,[119] other began to put the contrary case. For example, Abse in his speech shifted the onus onto those who objected to the technologies to justify their right to prevent others from enjoying their benefits.[120] A shift away from the general view in the Lords that scientists were amoral and uncontrolled towards praise for science and arguments based on its value and success were also in evidence in the Commons debate.[121] Some, such as Renée Short, argued that in fact scientific breakthroughs find acceptance once they have proved themselves, suggesting that it was incorrect to reject them on their face and instead they should be given time to demonstrate their safety and value.[122]

Opposition Builds

With the release of the permissive Warnock Report, opponents of embryo research saw the need to act immediately if they were to prevent a largely pro-research government from implementing its recommendations. The most important initial response after the statements against the Warnock Report was the Unborn Children (Protection) Bill, introduced as a private member's bill by Enoch Powell at the end of 1984. If passed, the bill would prohibit fertilisation *in vitro* of embryos for any purpose other than insertion into a woman's uterus to be carried to term. It created, as Michael Mulkay notes, 'the opportunity for a concerted attack on embryo research during the first half of 1985'.[123]

Powell's bill passed second reading in the British House of Commons on 22 February 1985 with an overwhelming majority, and suddenly the possibility that embryo research and IVF might be under threat became real. Numerous

---

[117] Hansard HC vol 68 col 536 (23 November 1984) (Michael Meacher).
[118] Hansard HC vol 68 col 541 (23 November 1984) (Sir Bernard Braine).
[119] Hansard HC vol 68 col 528 (23 November 1984) (Norman Fowler, The Secretary of State for Social Services); col 539 (Sir Bernard Braine); col 550 (Sir Gerald Vaughan); col 551 (Hugh Dykes); col 555 (Rev Ian Paisley).
[120] Hansard HC vol 68 col 547 (23 November 1984) (Leo Abse).
[121] Hansard HC vol 68 col 549–50 (23 November 1984) (Leo Abse).
[122] Hansard HC vol 68 col 557 (23 November 1984) (Renée Short).
[123] Mulkay, above n 2, 24.

opinion pieces and editorials in the *British Medical Journal*, *The Lancet* and *Nature* and others included scathing comments about the Powell bill, with headlines such as 'A Bill That Should be Stopped' and, when the bill failed, 'Powell Bites Dust'.[124] Scientists, such as Anne McLaren, spoke out publicly against attempts to prevent research. McLaren published a piece in *Nature* in 1985 explaining that if the bill were passed, many promising avenues of research would be blocked.[125] On learning of the bill clinical scientist Professor Peter Braude, who had just received a large MRC grant to fund work on human embryos, faced the stark realisation that were it to go through, his work would suddenly be illegal. He and others approached the head of the MRC who, appreciating the urgency and significance of the events, provided them with secretarial help and accommodation to gather likeminded scientists and clinicians. The group, later called PAGIGS (Professional Advisory Group for Genetic and Infertility Services), wrote briefing papers for MPs who opposed Powell's attempts, providing vital information to support the push to ensure IVF and embryo research were not prohibited.[126]

Having been brought as a private member's bill, the first Powell bill was vulnerable to being talked out. Such bills, as opposed to those presented by Government, are not allocated a specific time to be debated. Instead, five hours is given over to debating private members' bills 13 Fridays of the year. If a bill does not come to a vote, it will be tabled for the next session for private members' bills. This may occur if the bill is later on the list of bills for debate or if it is talked out. A bill is talked out when debate over it continues until the end of the session and a vote cannot be called in time, and MPs will use this technique to block bills which they do not want passed. A bill that has been talked out will face less chance of success each successive time it is re-tabled.

Doctors and medical researchers played a crucial role in talking out the first Powell bill. Having realised that there was now a real chance that embryo research could be prohibited, they responded by taking a much more active role in the parliamentary process.[127] Virginia Bolton, a scientist working in fertility recalled how she and others felt

> This was actually a very dangerous moment, and if we didn't do something now, the future of our research, and research nationwide could be changed forever.[128]

---

[124] 'A Bill That Should Be Stopped' (1985) 290 *British Medical Journal* 586; 'Powell Bites Dust' (1985) 314 *Nature* 568. The writer of the latter article stated 'The British government has done the decent (and courageous) thing by deciding that it will not lift a finger to save Mr Enoch Powell's bill on *in vitro* fertilisation from being lost in the procedural hazards of the House of Commons'.

[125] HJ Evans and A McLaren, 'Unborn Children (Protection) Bill' (1985) 314 *Nature* 127.

[126] Interview with Prof Peter Braude (London, 1 February 2006)

[127] It should be noted that there were also doctors and researchers working to push the Powell bill through. The most notable ally of the pro-life MPs was was Jérôme Lejeune, a paediatrician and geneticist who had discovered the cause of Down syndrome.

[128] Challoner, above n 6, 72.

Regulating Reproduction in the United Kingdom 191

According to the procedural rules of the House of Commons, speakers must restrict their speeches to topics relevant to the debate, and if they are unable to must cease to speak. With five hours to fill to talk the bill out, those who opposed it needed material to fill their speeches. One researcher laughingly recalled the bill being defeated

> by some of us sitting up through the night writing stuff for those dedicated parliamentarians to read out endlessly between four o'clock in the morning ... it was a real farce ... but it was all quite exciting ... they had no idea what they were reading, we gave them handbooks of obstetrics ...[129]

Information was fed to MPs such as Peter Thurnham, to read until the bill was talked out. He remembers:

> I was given a copy of the Hammersmith Hospital laboratory procedure notes for getting the test tubes clean, and I thought this was something that the committee should be aware of[!], so we had an all night sitting once and it took me about three hours to get through all of that. Enoch Powell sat through it all: quite extraordinary for a man of his age.[130]

The Powell bill was talked out at third reading on 3 May 1985, and its defeat was a turning point in the involvement of doctors and medical researchers. It marked the beginning of the integrated scientific campaign to prevent prohibition, a campaign in which the medical profession and MPs worked together towards a common goal. Following the general rejection of the Warnock report's conclusions in the initial Parliamentary debate, and the strong early response to the Unborn Children (Protection) Bill in 1985, those in support of ART and embryo research had begun to push back against the moves to prohibit them. As one MP commented

> The medical and scientific community became alarmed and those who came to sympathetic MPs for advice were quickly instructed that ... they must learn to defend themselves. There were not a few who learned with speed to shed their political innocence and come out of the laboratory and the gynaecology wards to join the battle in public debate. ... The Medical Research Council recanted and threw its full weight behind Warnock. The feminist movements and the traditional pro-abortionist lobbies infuriated by the coup of their old anti-abortionist enemies entered the fray with relish.[131]

One of the major steps by the medical community to deal with the issues, however, was the creation of its own regulatory body, the Voluntary Licensing Authority (VLA).

---

[129] Interview with Prof Anne McLaren (Cambridge, 7 February 2006).
[130] Challoner, above n 6, 73.
[131] Leo Abse, 'The Politics of In Vitro Fertilisation in Britain' in S Fishel and EM Symonds (eds), *In Vitro Fertilisation: Past, Present and Future* (Oxford, IRL Press, 1986) 212.

Voluntary Licensing Authority

The Warnock Committee had recommended the creation of a statutory licensing body to regulate research and the clinical provision of IVF. It would be seven years before the government established such a body in the form of the Human Fertilisation and Embryology Authority (HFEA).[132] The medical profession had supported the establishment of an oversight body for some time, but in early 1985 it became clear that the government did not intend to act swiftly on the matter. While Parliament debated the Warnock Report and the Powell bill, the medical profession chose to act. Concerned about the lack of oversight, and public unease about IVF and embryo research, it took matters into its own hands and established a voluntary body—the VLA—to carry out the same functions. For seven years until the establishment of the HFEA, the medical profession would self-regulate.

Some weeks before the Powell bill had its second reading, the MRC had published its response to the Warnock Report in which it proposed that a independent licensing body be set up to fill the legislative and regulatory void that surrounded IVF and embryo research. This void had become particularly problematic when the Government failed to implement the Warnock recommendations—at that point it became clear that far from being imminent, regulation might be some way off. Michael Mulkay, in his in-depth study of the embryo debates of the period, has commented that for some of those in favour of research setting up such a body seemed a means of heading off the looming threat of a moratorium posed by the Powell bill. In particular, he notes the sense of panic in the editorials of *Nature* criticising the Powell bill and calling for the licensing body to be created.[133]

RCOG and the MRC published the VLA's guidelines in June 1985, which were largely based on the Warnock recommendations but also required each research programme to be licensed and for projects to be individually considered. Its committee established, it began to oversee research from 1985 onwards until the establishment of the HFEA in 1990.[134] Under its guidelines, permitted research would focus on clinical problems through study of the processes and products of IVF. Fertilised ova were not to be cultured outside the body beyond 14 days. Committee members would visit research centres prior to deciding whether to grant a licence. Significantly, the VLA would also publish the details of all approved and unapproved research, a major step towards both transparency and alleviating public concerns about maverick scientists. Prior

---

[132] The HFEA was created under the Human Fertilisation and Embryology Act 1990 and began to function on 1 August 1991.

[133] Mulkay, above n 2, 25.

[134] The VLA was originally chaired by Dame Mary Donaldson, who had trained as a nurse and then gone into local politics. It also included three Warnock Commitee members—embryologist Anne McLaren, RCOG president Malcolm MacNaughton, and philosopher Gordon Dunstan. The VLA was later renamed the Interim Licensing Authority.

to its establishment, an opinion piece in *Nature* had made the point that this was exactly the way to 'nail the widespread supposition that laboratory people are just bursting to fashion Aldous Huxley's Brave New World'.[135] The VLA would in fact have an enormous influence in convincing MPs to allow embryo research and IVF to continue. As one commented

> the Voluntary Licensing Authority, although it had no legal teeth, managed to keep everything under control and each year it published its report with every research project listed, who was doing it, where it was being done and what it was for … [meant that] people realised that actually wicked scientists weren't making monsters behind closed doors.[136]

The Aftermath

Because significant majorities in both Houses opposed the Warnock Report's recommendations on embryo research, the Government was unable to use the Report's recommendations as the basis of legislation. This had been compounded the Powell bill bringing opposition to the research to the fore, opposition which would continue as further private members' bills were introduced in the following years, each of which attempted to prohibit the creation, storage or use of human embryos for purposes other than assisting a woman to achieve pregnancy.[137] The Government considered that further consultation was required before proposing legislation due to the 'strength and diversity of opinion' expressed on the matters before it.[138]

Consequently, in December 1986 the Government released a consultation document, and invited public responses.[139] This consultation period ended in June 1987, and the Government affirmed its intention to introduce legislation, indicating that it would release a White Paper describing the proposed legislation. The White Paper was released in November 1987.[140] Following the submission of a number of bills, reviews of these bills and considerable parliamentary debate in 1988 and 1989,[141] the Human Fertilisation and Embryology Act 1990 (UK) was passed.

The successful defeat of the Powell Bill was far from the end of attempts to prevent embryo research and IVF. Over the ensuing five years, as the government dragged

---

[135] 'Embryos Untouched' (1985) 313 *Nature* 612.
[136] Interview with C (by telephone, 25 January 2006).
[137] Enoch Powell submitted the first Unborn Children (Protection) Bill in 1985. After it was talked out, a failed attempt was made to re-introduce it that year. Further attempts were made to revive it in the following years.
[138] Department of Health and Social Security (United Kingdom), *Legislation on Human Infertility Services and Embryo Research: A Consultation Paper* (HMSO, 1986) 1.
[139] ibid.
[140] ibid.
[141] Hansard HL vol 491 cols 1450–1508 (15 January 1988); Hansard HL vol 504 cols 1538–80 (8 March 1989); Hansard HL vol 513 cols 1002–114 (7 December 1989); Hansard HL vol 515 cols 950–90 (8 February 1990); Hansard HC vol 126 cols 1202–61 (4 February 1988); Hansard HC vol 170 cols 914–90 (2 April 1990); Hansard HC vol 171 cols 31–133 (23 April 1990).

its feet on producing legislation, vehement attempts would be made to achieve legal prohibition by MPs and lobby groups. Those in favour of the technology galvanised themselves, and in November 1985 formed Progress, a group comprised of members of Parliament, doctors, researchers and philosophers, many of whom had helped to defeat the Powell bill. Progress formed the nucleus of the lobby in favour of permitting research.[142] The entry of doctors and medical researchers into the parliamentary process as lobbyists and educators ensured, Mulkay has suggested, that the debate would from that time on be less unequal that the initial debates.

Not all doctors supported embryo research, and nor did the profession present a wholly united front on all issues. But by taking on the role of advisors, coming to Westminster to provide scientific evidence to support arguments (on both sides) and clarify areas of confusion, they ensured that the debate was better informed. Misunderstandings and misrepresentations had dogged the debate about embryo research, and did so throughout. One of the main objections to embryo research and aspects of IVF rested on the view that embryos were human beings and, like children and adults, they deserved to be treated as having full human dignity and the rights that attend it. While there are arguments that support this view, some who held it had no sense what an embryo actually looked like. Others held this view with little understanding of the emotional and psychological implications infertility had for women and couples. Doctors and medical researchers did much to address these areas of confusion by offering MPs the chance to see the process first hand and decide for themselves by inviting them to their fertility clinics.[143] One researcher commented that 'we encouraged people to go to IVF clinics and ... look down a microscope to see a human embryo and see how carefully and scrupulously they were treated'.[144] For some, this experience had a profound impact on their views. One Lord later recalled:

> I think one single incident probably sort of crystallised the whole thing for me. I went to [Robert Winston's] clinic, at Hammersmith, to see what happened. And I met two women who had decided to have IVF, they were trying to get children—whether they ever did or not I don't know—they were both Catholics. And I talked it over with them and they'd been through agonies of conscience and the rest, and I thought this isn't right ... these were people whose purpose was wholly good—they wanted children, you know—and to be put through this, the torture chamber of conscience I thought was just wrong, you know. And that's why I took the view, rightly or wrongly the view ... that up to 14 days it was okay.[145]

---

[142] Progress later evolved into the Progress Educational Trust, a charity that seeks to facilitate 'balanced public and professional debate' on reproductive and genetic issues: Progress Educational Trust, 'About Progress Educational Trust' <http://www.progress.org.uk/About/Index.html> accessed 11 November 2008.
[143] See, eg interview with H (London, 9 February 2006); interview with Lady Saltoun (London, 1 February 2006).
[144] Interview with Prof Anne McLaren (Cambridge, 7 February 2006).
[145] Interview with Lord Carter (London, 8 February 2006). For others, however, they had little effect on their views: interview with Lady Saltoun (London, 1 February 2006).

It is unsurprising that Robert Winston is mentioned here. Post-Warnock, his presence in the debates would become all-pervasive.[146] Seemingly a constant presence in Parliament House in the lead up to the passing of the HFEA, Winston walked the halls talking to MPs, gave talks and explained not just the science, but his views on the ethics of IVF and embryo research to any who would listen. One MP commented that he 'collared the market', another that one 'couldn't walk through the Central Lobby without bumping into him'.[147] No-one had quite the impact Winston had.[148] Many MPs recalled him as an important source of information and views on reproductive technology, and for some their experience with him was significant.[149]

Conclusion

In 1990, with the passage of the Human Fertilisation and Embryology Act 1990, the pro-research lobby finally emerged victorious after seven years of political machinations, lobbying and heartfelt argument on both sides of the debate. Since that time, the United Kingdom has enjoyed both the fruits of embryo research and improvements in IVF technique, and of an effective regulatory structure that has done much to ensure the ethical conduct of research in this country. Much of the force behind this regulatory approach came from those who were to be regulated—the doctors who helped the infertile, and the researchers who made the breakthroughs that made it possible. Far from being either passive or unconcerned, these men and women were acutely aware of the problems their work posed, just as much as they knew and believed in its benefits. Their efforts to inform the public and government about the merits of their work, and to address their concerns were a fundamentally important force in ensuring IVF remained available in this country.

---

[146] Already an expert in human fertility during the 1970s, he was the World Health Organisation's scientific advisor on human reproduction from 1975–1977. One of his major achievements was the development of tubal microsurgery techniques for reversing sterilisation.

[147] Interview with Ann Widdecombe (London, 18 December 2005); interview with James Couchman (Oxford, 14 February 2006).

[148] Interview with X (London, 1 February 2006).

[149] ibid; interview with Lord Carter (London, 8 February 2006); interview with Robert Key (London, 18 January 2006). For other MPs, however, the way Winston and other doctors and researchers had influence on the pro-IVF and pro-research side was problematic. While accepting that Winston's influence derived in part from his legitimately trading on his eminence in the field to put forward his philosophical position, one MP argued that the media did not allow scientists on the other side of the debate to do the same. See interview with Ann Widdecombe (London, 18 December 2005).

10

Nobody's Thing? Human Tissue in Science, Ethics and the Law during the late 20th Century

DUNCAN WILSON

In July 2008, the science think-tank Newton's Apple issued a press release criticising the 'stifling' effect that the 2004 Human Tissue Act was having on biomedical research. Formulated in response to the non-consented retention of children's organs in certain British hospitals, which was exposed in 1999, the Act regulates the removal of human tissue—defined as 'material that has come from a human body and consists of, or includes, human cells'.[1] Newton's Apple stated that it was not regulation of post-mortem material which caused problems, but rather that the Act also encompassed the countless tissues that are removed from living patients, in surgical and diagnostic procedures. To obtain these samples, or data derived from them, researchers have to apply to the recently established Human Tissue Authority for a licence. Newton's Apple, and researchers it surveyed, portrayed this as a bureaucratic obstacle to a vital biomedical resource, which would severely hamper research into disease and drug development. The think-tank's director went so far as to describe the requirements for clinical samples as being like a 'sledgehammer to crack a nut'.[2]

Such criticism hinged on the fact that this stringent regulation was not only time-consuming, but was also unnecessary. Whilst Newton's Apple and the medical groups it surveyed conceded that the Act had aimed to assist researchers, by increasing public confidence in research that used human tissue, they claimed that lawyers and policymakers had fatally misjudged the public mood, and presumed popular opinion demanded stringent regulation. Instead, according to the vice-president of the Royal College of Physicians, the public did even not care what happened to tissue, biopsy or urine samples removed in the course of clinical treatment. Most patients, he told *The Guardian*, expected such material to be

---

[1] Newton's Apple Research Report, *Delivering Innovative Cancer Diagnostics and Treatments to Patients* (London, 2008) 9.
[2] J Randerson, 'Medical: Rules on the Use of Human Tissue Stifle Research, say Scientists', *The Guardian* 18 July 2008.

incinerated; and when approached to ask if they consented to its use in research, he stated that only about one in 50 objected.[3]

The deployment of public opinion to bolster an argument concerning the regulation of human tissue research is, as we shall see, a longstanding tactic. As this chapter demonstrates, throughout the 1980s and 1990s various bodies in Britain debated whether the hitherto unregulated acquisition of clinical tissues from living patients needed legal regulation—and arguments for or against such measures were regularly based on the ways these groups interpreted what counted as 'public opinion'. This, then, is not so much a narrative about how the requirements and limitations of legal regulation shape medical practice. Rather, it is more concerned with how the views and motivation of various stakeholders in biomedicine, the law, and bioethics, shaped debates about the legislation of professional practices.

Themes that appear throughout this volume are apparent here. For one, we see that legislation was regularly proposed as a means to reassure the public, and forestall possible litigation. Legal regulation has often served to assuage tangible, or seeming, popular anxiety at medical or scientific use of human material, from the Anatomy Act 1832, to the recent Human Tissue Act 2004. This has led several legal and ethical commentators to frame the history of human tissue research as marked by distinct dichotomy between the views of scientists and doctors, on the one hand, and the public on the other. In such accounts the history of research on human tissue is punctuated by a series of controversies that stem from, and further, 'a growing divide between scientific and social views of the body'—where scientists view human material as a commodity to be procured and researched upon, whilst a resistant public view it as the site of personal experience and social meaning.[4]

This chapter argues this approach is problematic. Rather, as I show, debates concerning human tissue in the 1980s and 1990s do not highlight the existence of a longstanding and deep-seated opposition to the biomedical use of such material; nor do they reveal a dichotomous gap between scientific and 'public' views (the 'human tissue' I cover here excludes only the sperm, eggs and embryos that are the subject of separate debates). Instead, where controversy arose, discord centred less on the acquisition and use of human tissue per se, but was used as a vehicle for the articulation and amplification of broader, historically contingent, standpoints. Arguments for the legislation of tissue research in the late 20th century were completely different from those that motivated legislative discussion during, say, the 19th century. The proposals I detail here embodied the growing late-20th century emphasis on choice in healthcare. Here, as authors like Nikolas Rose and Helen Busby note, bioethics and regulatory policy reframed patients less

---

[3] ibid.
[4] L Andrews and D Nelkin, 'Whose Body is it Anyway? Disputes over Body Tissue in a Biotechnology Age' (1998) 351 *The Lancet* 53. See also D Dickenson, *Body Shopping: The Economy Fuelled by Flesh and Blood* (Oxford, Oneworld Publications, 2008); L Andrews and D Nelkin, *Body Bazaar: The Market for Human Tissue in the Biotechnology Age* (London, Crown, 2002); A Kimbrell, *The Human Body Shop: The Cloning, Engineering and Marketing of Life* (Washington DC, Gateway, 1997).

as passive consumers and more as empowered agents—fully informed of practices and implications and thus free to make rational choices with respect to their participation in treatment or research.[5] Allowing a person to consent to, or forbid, the use of excised tissue in research seemed to many a laudable, and logical, extension of this ideology. The emphasis on informed consent that became the cornerstone of calls for regulation of tissue research was itself the product of a historical process. It was first emphasised in the immediate aftermath of the Second World War, after the exposure of Nazi medical crimes, and truly became a cornerstone of research ethics and professional policy in the late 1960s and 1970s, following evidence that researchers had failed to inform participants of inherent risks in several high-profile projects. At a more general (though no less relevant) level, the stress on individual autonomy sat amidst neo-liberal governmental practices during the last twenty-five years of the 20th century, where 'active' citizens were encouraged to engage with public sector services, including medicine.[6]

At the same time, when we look at who exactly proposed legislative tightening of tissue research, we move further away from a dichotomous separation between scientific and legal or public interests. During the 1980s and 1990s in Britain, some of the strongest advocates of new regulation based on patient consent were scientists. Conversely, some of its strongest opponents were lawyers and bioethicists. Neither social world held consensus on this matter and, as elsewhere in this volume, we see considerable interaction between scientific, legal and ethical standpoints. The human tissues we encounter here were clearly not repositories of static and simple values, then. As Bronwyn Parry and Cathy Gere suggest, we need to appreciate how they are

> made and remade in response to new technologies, new scientific expertise, public consultation, funding crises, institutional expansion and reform. This engagement alters the constitution of the artefacts themselves, their status and the conditions of their use.[7]

As I show, during the 1980s and 1990s the status and conditions of use of human tissues were indeed 'made and remade' in accordance with various scientific, legal and political values. Scientists who endorsed new regulation did so to maintain confidence in non-animal techniques and tools. For them, allowing patients to control the fate of tissue would promote the use of human material in research, which was seen as more clinically relevant and, in some quarters, as more ethically acceptable than non-human tissue. For others, including legal supporters of patient consent, allowing patients to consent to, or forbid, the use of tissue reflected an emphasis on individual autonomy. Legal or bioethical opponents

---

[5] N Rose, *The Politics of Life Itself* (Princeton, Princeton University Press, 2007); H Busby, 'Informed Consent: The Contradictory Ethical Safeguards in Pharmacogenetics' in R Tutton and O Corrigan (eds), *Genetic Databases: Socio-ethical Issues in the Collection and Use of DNA* (London, Routledge, 2004).

[6] N Rose and P Rabinow, 'Biopower Today' (2006) 1 *Biosocieties* 195; M Marinetto, 'Who Wants to be an Active Citizen? The Politics and Practice of Community Involvement' (2003) 37 *Sociology* 103.

[7] B Parry and C Gere, 'Contested Bodies: Property Models and the Commodification of Human Biological Artefacts' (2006) 15 *Science as Culture* 141, 153.

of new consent measures, meanwhile, argued that consent to treatment implied that patients abandoned their tissue—an approach that adhered to the body parts' common law status as *res nullius*, literally 'nobody's thing'. Moreover, this stance was justified by the claim that most patients were happy to abandon their tissue on its removal.[8] Importantly, as with the contemporary debates on the Human Tissue Act, all these arguments were justified as being truly representative of public opinion. All just happened to have different views of what this constituted.

Obtaining and Using Human Tissue for Research: Practices and Laws, 1907–80

The human body and its parts have always been an important resource in medicine and science. Their use in anatomical observation has been dated back to Ancient Greece, and is well-documented from early-modern to 19th century Britain.[9] Well-documented, too, is the controversy that the medical and scientific acquisition of human parts has intermittently caused. As historians such as Ruth Richardson have detailed, such scandals have occasioned legal regulation. The 1832 Anatomy Act, for instance, was passed in order to govern the supply of bodies to medical schools, which had hitherto circulated amidst a thriving and publicly contentious black-market. Although it had been long mooted in order to distance medical practice from its association with grave-robbing, the Act was hastily drawn up after the exposure of two rackets that committed murder in order to sell on human bodies, which inflamed popular anger towards anatomists and anatomy (though by permitting the procurement of 'unclaimed' workhouse bodies, the Act was no less contentious).[10]

During the late 19th century, and throughout the 20th century, new research techniques and medical practices increased the scientific and medical demand for human material. The growth and institutionalisation of biological disciplines such as embryology, pathology and biochemistry, the emergence of surgical transplant techniques, and the development of tissue and cell culture methods, ensured that a greater range of tissues became endowed with epistemological, practical and, latterly, economic values. Most of these new practices fell outside the purview of the Anatomy Act, which only governed the supply of bodies for medical demonstration. A battery of further acts were promulgated throughout the 20th century

---

[8] O O'Neill, 'Medical and Scientific Uses of Human Tissue' (1996) 22 *Journal of Medical Ethics* 5, 5.

[9] SC Lawrence, 'Beyond the Grave: The Use and Meaning of Human Body Parts—A Historical Introduction' in R Weir (ed), *Stored Tissue Samples: Ethical, Legal, and Public Policy Implications* (Iowa, OUP, 1998) 111.

[10] The best work on the origins and reception of the Anatomy Act 1832 remains R Richardson, *Death Dissection and the Destitute*, 2nd edn (London, Phoenix, 2001).

to regulate the new uses that were being made of human material—including, in Britain, the 1952 Corneal Grafting Act, the 1961 Human Tissue Act, and the 1989 Human Organ Transplants Act.[11]

But, despite this growing body of legislation, the acquisition and use in research of tissue that was removed from living patients, in the course of clinical treatment, remained unregulated. All the above Acts regulated the removal of tissue from cadavers, or regulated its use in therapeutic procedures. Whilst the removal of tissue in research was covered from the 1960s onwards by professional guidelines, or research ethics committees, none considered tissue that was removed in treatment.[12] These samples were the most commonly used human materials in the tissue culture techniques that I focus on here. 'Tissue culture' applies to the maintenance and growth of explanted human, animal and plant material in glass vessels (*in vitro*). It was first employed in 1907 by the Yale embryologist Ross Harrison, in order to settle a dispute regarding the mode of nerve outgrowth.[13] Harrison obtained his tissue from frog embryos, which were longstanding experimental models in embryology. The procurement and culture of human tissue did not begin until researchers at the Rockefeller Institute in New York, and elsewhere, attempted to fashion culture methods into a medical tool.

The first human tissue culture was recorded in 1910 by the Rockefeller surgeon Alexis Carrel, who explanted a section of a sarcomatuous tumour removed from a 35-year-old woman at the nearby Memorial Hospital.[14] During this period, Carrel and his assistant Montrose Burrows, as well as several other New York-based researchers, explanted a wide variety of material *in vitro* in order to ascertain the optimal conditions for tissue survival, investigating which species provided the best tissues. As part of this, a wide variety of human tissues were procured from the Memorial and neighbouring hospitals, including carcinomas from the lip and breasts, lymph glands, spleens and skin samples.[15] As this research continued it became clear that human tissue did not survive long *in vitro*, in contrast to certain non-human tissues (chick tissue was so hardy that many scientists believed than one particular culture was immortal).[16]

---

[11] J Herring, 'Giving, Selling and Sharing Bodies', in A Bainham et al (eds), *Body Lore and Laws* (Oxford, Hart, 2002) 43.

[12] See above n 9.

[13] On the origins of tissue culture see H Landecker, *Culturing Life: How Cells Became Technologies* (Cambridge, Mass, Harvard University Press, 2007).

[14] A Carrel and M Burrows, 'Human Sarcoma Cultivated Outside the Body' (1910) 55 *Journal of the American Medical Association* 1732.

[15] A Carrel and M Burrows, 'Cultivation In Vitro of Malignant Tumours' (1911) 13 *Journal of Experimental Medicine* 571; JR Losee and AH Ebeling, 'Cultivation of Human Tissue In Vitro' (1914) 19 *Journal of Experimental Medicine* 593.

[16] This supposedly 'immortal' culture also arose from Carrel's Rockefeller stable. Considerable speculation exists as to whether or not it was genuine, although its veracity was hardly called into question at the time and it was thought to have 'lived' for over twenty one years. See JA Witkowski, 'Dr Carrel's Immortal Cells' (1980) 24 *Medical History* 129.

Nevertheless, researchers persisted in obtaining and culturing human tissue. Though it had not yet provided any useful experimental data, they believed human tissue was the most clinically-relevant material. One researcher declared that he persisted with human tissue as any findings generated on it would be 'more clearly applicable to human beings'.[17] During these early efforts it also transpired that some human tissues survived better *in vitro* than others. Samples obtained from dead bodies were generally unviable, as exposure to the slightest decay or infection impaired a tissue's capacity to grow in culture (plus, the need for coroner approval posed an administrative obstacle and added further time delay). This narrowed potential material to that removed from living bodies in the course of clinical treatment.

With this in mind, what one later tissue culturist called the 'good offices' of helpful surgeons and pathologists quickly became crucial contacts in a network for obtaining human tissue.[18] These networks also facilitated the supply of tissue in Britain. Here, the first recorded human cultures were established in 1914, by David and John Gordon Thomson of the Marcus Beck Laboratory in London. Using tissue from nine separate operations the pair established over fifty cultures of human tissue; in each case, tissue was obtained from operations at the nearby Middlesex Hospital.[19] Both authors gratefully acknowledged the central role of the presiding surgeon, to whom they were 'much indebted'.[20] Scientists at the Strangeways Research Laboratory in Cambridge, a focal point of tissue culture research before the Second World War, similarly exploited contacts with local clinicians to obtain relevant material.[21] After being appraised by surgeons at the nearby Addenbrookes Hospital, Laboratory staff or technicians would often walk in and leave with as many samples as they deemed necessary.[22]

These arrangements were flexible and unregulated; as I have already noted, no legal or professional guidelines covered the scientific procurement of tissues that had been removed in the course of clinical or diagnostic procedures. This lack of regulatory control was compounded by the fact that excised human tissues were regarded as *res nullius* under English common law. A line of cases dating back to the 17th century supported the view that human body parts could not be owned—meaning, as Susan Lawrence argues, that no one had standing to bring a

---

[17] RA Lambert, 'Technique of Cultivating Human Tissues in Vitro' (1916) 24 *Journal of Experimental Medicine* 367.

[18] H Harris, *The Cells of the Body: A History of Somatic Cell Genetics* (Cold Spring Harbor, Cold Spring Harbor Laboratory, 1995) 58.

[19] D Thomson and JG Thomson, 'The Cultivation of Human Tumour Tissue *in Vitro*' (1913) 7 *Proceedings of the Royal Society of Medicine, London* 7.

[20] Above n 19, 8.

[21] The Strangeways Lab had been founded in 1912 by a University pathologist, keen to investigate the cellular and pathological basis of disease; after pressure from the UK Medical Research Council it concentrated on tissue culture methods after the First World War. See D Wilson, 'The Early History of Tissue Culture in Britain: The Interwar Years' (2005) 18 *Social History of Medicine* 225.

[22] H Fell to HT Laycock (27 September, 1939), Contemporary Medical Archives, Wellcome Trust Library for the History of Medicine. File number SA/SRL/H.4.

claim for damage or theft of human material, and nor could tissue be dealt with under the usual rules of inheritance or exchange.[23]

This position was, however, subject to an important exception, deriving from the Australian case of *Doodeward v Spence* (1908), in which Griffith CJ held:

> when a person has by lawful exercise of work or skill so dealt with a human body or part of a body in his lawful that it has acquired some attributes differentiating it from a mere corpse awaiting burial, he acquires a right to retain possession of it, at least against any person not entitled to have it delivered to him for the purpose of burial.[24]

Griffiths and the other judges in the case were dealing with a detinue claim over a two-headed foetus that had been displayed as a curio. The plaintiff, a showman, had been charged with indecent exhibition of a corpse, and the foetus had been confiscated. When he asked for its return, he received only the jar and spirits in which he preserved it. The court had to determine whether he had a permanent right of possession—and found that he did.

Griffith's approach reflected a Lockean approach to the notion of property, relying on the doctrine of work expenditure that stated an individual established a property right over natural material if he 'hath mixed his Labour with [it] and joined to something that is his own'.[25] Importantly, this judgement reflected the fact that the medical procurement and use of biological matter did not sit at odds with wider cultural norms. For Griffiths, its use, retention, and transformation into a novel object were both normal and acceptable. So it was, it seemed also, for patients and the public at large. Histories of embryology in the early 20th century reveal that patients similarly conceived of miscarried foetuses as waste material, and happily handed it over to doctors and scientists.[26] Similarly, the creation and use of human tissue cultures attracted little evident criticism throughout the early and mid-20th century. Though tissue culture was embroiled in several controversies in this period, these centred on the possible misuse of the technique, and not on its source material. Novels such as Aldous Huxley's 1932 *Brave New World*, for instance, darkly portrayed the way a dystopian regime might utilise the *in vitro* growth of human babies, but one finds no anxiety at the practical way tissues were collected and, as *The Times* reported, were grown 'outside the body of which they were once part'.[27]

When the collection of tissue for biomedical research did attract criticism, this was tied to broader political and social agendas. As Naomi Pfeffer and Julie Kent have detailed, during the 1970s the longstanding acquisition of foetal material for tissue culture began to attract criticism from opponents of recent abortion reforms, who alleged that researchers were encouraging abortions in order to

---

[23] Above n 9.
[24] *Doodeward v Spence* (1908) 6 CLR 406, 414.
[25] J Locke, *Two Treatises of Government* (Cambridge, CUP, 1988) 288.
[26] L Morgan, 'Properly Disposed Of: A History of Embryo Disposal and the Changing Claims on Foetal Remains' (2002) 21 *Medical Anthropology* 247.
[27] 'Progress in Study of Common Cold' *The Times* 5 September 1959.

acquire more research material.[28] Few, if any, equated this with a general 'public' opinion though. Many papers claimed, like the *Daily Express*, that the use of extant foetal tissues in tissue culture was essential to research and vaccine development and caused 'no concern' among the public at large.[29] This was echoed by a governmental review of the use of foetal tissue in research, chaired by the obstetrician John Peel, which stated that in view of 'the essential contribution that is made by this research to medicine' there was no justifiable reason to legislate the collection of foetal tissues.[30] There was hence 'no statutory requirement to obtain the parent's consent for research' once consent for an abortion had been acquired.[31] By consenting to an abortion, the parents abandoned any claim to the foetus or its tissues and had no say over their subsequent use.

In the United States though, there was more anxious debate regarding the collection and use of tissue for research. Here, following the liberalisation of abortion laws in *Roe v Wade* (1973) a more influential and extensive pro-life movement began to target the biomedical acquisition of tissue from abortions.[32] As the Princeton bioethicist Paul Ramsey noted, anti-abortion campaigners claimed that 'research on foetal tissue is as outrageous as research on the whole living foetal human being' and picketed laboratories that employed foetal tissue culture.[33] Perhaps more seriously, they managed to secure an indictment for graverobbing against researchers who procured an aborted foetus.[34] Keen to avoid further controversy, researchers who used foetal tissue in their work convened at symposia to discuss new practices and guidelines.

Attendees of these meetings heard that the collection of tissue in general was also coming under criticism from legal and bioethical perspectives, which, as a response to concerns about the rights of patients and experimental subjects, began to emphasise patient or research subject autonomy, and the need for full scientific disclosure of procedural risks.[35] It appeared that the previously unregulated collection and distribution of clinical tissue samples was now open to challenge. As Bernard Dickens argued in 1977, patients now had a 'justifiable interest in the use and disposition of their tissues'.[36] In *Browning v Norton Children's*

---

[28] N Pfeffer and J Kent, 'Framing Women, Framing Fetuses: How Britain Regulates Arrangements for the Collection and Use of Aborted Fetuses in Stem Cell Research and Therapies' (2007) 2 *Biosocieties* 429.

[29] H Stanhope, 'Live Foetuses Sold for Research-MP' *The Times* 16 May 1970; 'Unborn Babies: Now Doctors May Get New Code of Ethics' *Daily Express* (London, 18 May 1970).

[30] Department of Health and Social Security, Scottish Home and Health Department, Welsh Office, *The Use of Foetuses and Foetal Material for Research: Report of the Advisory Group* (HMSO, 1972) 8.

[31] Above n 30, 12.

[32] *Jane Roe at el v Henry Wade, District Attorney of Dallas County* (1973) 410 US 113 93 S Ct 705; 35 L Ed 2d 147.

[33] P Ramsey, *The Ethics of Fetal Research* (New Haven, Yale University Press, 1975).

[34] BJ Culliton, 'Graverobbing: The Charge Against Four from Boston City Hospital' (1974) 186 *Science* 420.

[35] See, eg RC Fox and JP Swazey, *Observing Bioethics* (Oxford, OUP, 2008).

[36] BM Dickens, 'The Control of Living Body Materials' (1977) 27 *University of Toronto Law Journal* 142, 183.

Hospital (1976), for instance, a patient with a pathological fear of fire brought an action against the surgeon and hospital for the mental anguish that, he alleged, he had suffered on learning that his recently amputated leg had been incinerated as surgical waste.[37] Similarly, in *Mokry v University of Texas Health Science Centre* (1975), an individual claimed to have suffered nervousness and mental anguish after his eyeball was accidentally lost down a plughole in the course of a pathological examination.[38]

Delegates at one meeting of biomedical researchers were accordingly urged by William J Winslade, from the University of California School of Medicine and Law, to seek the consent of patients before using tissue in research—either by approaching them directly or by distributing forms to the attending physician. Scrutiny of tissue culture practice was inevitable, Winslade stated, 'now that the legal establishment has begun to scrutinise the scientific community's research on human subjects'.[39] Informed consent, he continued, should be thus be adopted as a minimum requirement in a truly 'legally permissible and morally sensitive' method of acquiring and using human tissues.[40] To Winslade, it 'not only removes the taint of impropriety stemming from non-disclosure, but also gives a person an opportunity to express his/her desires and provide for the values, privacy and self-determination'.[41] Importantly, Winslade justified his proposal by evoking the effects it would have on a general public opinion. Once fully informed of the fate of excised tissue and the 'legitimate purpose of the research', he claimed it was likely that 'most human subjects … would freely consent to contribute their tissue'.[42]

Some scientists simply dismissed such suggestions as 'foolish restrictions on research'.[43] Others, notably, agreed that giving an individual the chance to control what was done to their body in treatment and research was a basic and laudable right, but dissented when it came to considering excised tissue in this way. As one delegate at a Tissue Culture Association meeting argued, whilst tissues may have originated as a part of a human being, removal from their corporeal source meant they were no longer 'properly speaking parts of persons'.[44] Introducing informed consent, which was a doctrine privileging control of one's body, thus seemed inappropriate. Some, too, envisaged a situation where patients or research subjects went so far as to claim ownership over excised tissue samples: demanding the right to control the future uses of tissue samples in research as well as, perhaps,

---

[37] *Browning v Norton Children's Hospital* (1974) 504 SW 2d 713 (Ky CA).
[38] *Mokry v University of Texas Health Center at Dallas* (1975) 325 So 2d 479 (Fla Dist Ct of App).
[39] WJ Winslade, 'An Overview of the Scientist's Responsibilities: Comments by an Attorney' (1977) 13 *In Vitro* 712, 714.
[40] Above n 36, 716.
[41] ibid.
[42] ibid 719.
[43] BD Davis, 'The Social Control of Science' in A Milunsky and G Annas (eds), *Genetics and the Law* (Plenum Press, New York, 1975) 301–314 (responding to AG Steinberg).
[44] T Hearn, 'The Ethical Responsibilities at Issue' (1977) 13 *In Vitro* 607 (responding to EM Adams).

being able to sell tissue to scientists. One Tissue Culture Association member stated in 1976 that it was 'quite unclear who has rights in cut hair, nail clippings and cells taken from human bodies ... that we are in a state of legal and moral confusion when questions are raised about whose permission is required for the use of material obtained in these ways'.[45] Whilst not endorsing patient ownership, several scientists certainly looked to lawyers for clarification of these questions.

Figures such as Winslade argued that an ownership-based market for tissue samples was not inconceivable, as blood had been considered personal property since the decision in *Perlmutter v Beth David Hospital* (1954), and was now the subject of a thriving market that also included 'urine, hair, fingernails, etc'.[46] Yet he also acknowledged that this commercial model raised more problems than it promised to solve. All the tissues currently sold were regenerative; different rules would be needed to prevent, or constrain, the sale of non-regenerative organs and tissues, as well as the exploitation of financially disadvantaged donors by third-party agents. In the meantime, new consent protocols remained essential.

It is clear that by the late 1970s, in the US at least, some researchers, bioethicists and legal academics were casting around for a means to better regulate how tissue was obtained and used, while the courts were being confronted with how to deal with problems that occurred when the medical or scientific treatment of human tissue was seen to challenge, or contravene, a growing emphasis on patient autonomy. As we shall see, the 1980s saw these questions become more pressing.

Commercialism, Litigation and Consent: the 1980s

One delegate at a 1976 meeting of lawyers, scientists and philosophers rather prophetically stated that whilst legal aspects of research on human tissue were not perceived as a truly significant problem at the time, 'some of my colleagues and myself have the sense [they] will become a significant problem over the longer term'.[47] Events in the 1980s vindicated this prediction. Questions regarding consent for, and even ownership of, tissue increased significantly during this decade. Lawyers, scientists and ethicists saw this upturn as a consequence of changes in what constituted patentable matter, which refigured human tissue as a raw material that now produced commercially lucrative inventions. As Barbara Culliton noted in the journal *Science* in 1984, though questions of consent and ownership had been posed in the 1970s, their time had truly come in 'this new era of commercialisation'.[48]

The newly commercial ethos in biomedical research sat amidst broad political encouragement of links between the public and private sectors at the turn of the

---

[45] Above n 41, 607.
[46] Above n 36, 717. *Perlmutter v Beth David Hospital* (1954) 123 NE 2d 792 (NYCA).
[47] Above n 36, 724.
[48] BJ Culliton, 'Patient Sues UCLA over Cell Line' (1984) 225 *Science* 1458.

1980s. Both the incoming Reagan and Thatcher administrations in the US and UK sought greater links between science and commerce, and began dismantling traditional boundaries between the public and private sectors. This ethos was crystallised by the 1980 Bayh-Dole Act, which granted US universities intellectual control over, and the right to commercially profit from, inventions that were the product of federally-funded research. In this changing environment, again in 1980, the United States Supreme Court was called upon to determine whether the legal definition of patentable inventions could be interpreted to include genetically modified microorganisms in the case *Diamond v Chakrabarty* (the advent of genetic engineering in the mid 1970s was perhaps the major contributory factor behind private interest in biotechnology).[49] The case saw the court dealing with the scientific view that these genetically modified organisms fell within the legal definition of a patentable invention that was discontinuous from its natural state. It held that patent legislation could be interpreted to include a modified organism or biological matter that was not a product of nature, but had been created through human ingenuity.[50]

Due to this ruling, which was emulated in EU countries, human tissue attained considerable financial potential. Contemporary sources noted that this had fostered a marked increase in its acquisition and use in research. In 1987, a US Office of Technology Assessment reported that the use of human tissue in US medical institutions in the four years after the Diamond case was 300 per cent greater than it had been in the four years preceding it. It also recorded that patents on products derived from human tissues amounted to one-fifth of the total patents medical schools filed between 1980 and 1984.[51]

But these changes raised significant problems. The notions of private exchange and profit that followed changes in patent law altered prior the habits of free and informal exchange of human tissue. Professional disputes over ownership of tissue samples, and the intellectual property that followed from research on them, reflected this.[52] But these remained intra-professional spats, whose coverage was confined to the biomedical press. Conflicts about the entitlement to tissue were not seen as overly pressing until 1984—when, in a high-profile case, a Seattle-based businessman named John Moore filed suit against the scientists who had converted his tissue into a commercially remunerative tool.

---

[49] *Diamond v Chakrabarty* 447 US 303, 100 S Ct 2204 US 1980. See also P Rabinow, *Making PCR: A Story of Biotechnology* (Chicago, University of Chicago Press, 1996). See also D Kevles, 'Diamond v Chakrabarty and Beyond: The Political Economy of Patenting Life' in A Thackray (ed), *Private Science: Biotechnology and the Rise of Molecular Sciences* (Philadelphia, University of Pennsylvania Press, 1998).

[50] *Diamond v Chakrabarty* 447 US 303, 100 S Ct 2204 US 1980.

[51] Office of Technology Assessment, United States Congress, *Ownership of Human Tissues and Cells* (New York, 1987) 45, 50–51.

[52] D Nelkin, *Science as Intellectual Property: Who Controls Research?* (New York, Macmillan, 1984). See also, M Sun, 'Scientists Settle Cell Line Dispute' (1983) 220 *Science* 393; N Wade, 'University and Drug Firm Battle Over Billion Dollar Gene' (1980) 209 *Science* 1492.

The central claim in this case, *John Moore v the Regents of the University of California*,[53] was the unauthorised conversion of a piece of the plaintiff's spleen, which had been removed in the course of leukaemia treatment and turned into a cell line, entitled Mo, without his knowledge or consent (a cell line is a tissue culture that divides indefinitely, generally due to its cancerous nature). 'Conversion' is a tort or civil wrong that occurs when a person deals with property that does not belong to them in a way that is inconsistent with the rights of the lawful owner. By charging staff at the University of California, Los Angeles (UCLA) in this way, Moore claimed a possessory right to his excised spleen cells. However, he wanted more than the return of the cells. He also argued that he had a propriety interest in any products made from them, including the cell line—fully aware that the researchers in question, realising the cell line produced a number of biologically-prised substances, had filed a patent and signed lucrative contracts with biotechnology firms.[54]

From the outset, scientists, lawyers and ethicists framed *Moore* as embodiment of the legal and ethical problems caused by the heightened commercialism in biomedical research.[55] In 1985, the Dean of Medicine at Yale University equated Moore's stance with that of a general 'public' and stated that:

> [t]he public cannot help but see that the goals of some scientists—clinical or basic—are different than in the past. No longer can the biological scientist simply be portrayed as a dedicated, noble, underpaid truth-seeker trying to unlock nature's secrets for humankind's benefit. The biotechnology revolution has moved us, literally or figuratively, from the class room to the board room and from the *New England Journal [of Medicine]* to the *Wall Street Journal*. ... Small wonder then that a patient who sees his or her tissues becoming commercially valuable might say 'why shouldn't I share in the profits. After all Dr. X wouldn't be getting rich without me.'[56]

All coverage pointed to *Moore*'s possible ramifications. Alan Otten in the *Wall Street Journal* nervously noted that granting patients ownership over tissue could derail much 'potentially valuable research'.[57] In this scenario scientists would have to spend time and money buying material from patients, and maybe even sharing profits. But, as Otten noted, research could just as likely be derailed by a growing public perception that patients whose tissue was unwittingly taken were being exploited by researchers, universities and companies. If this perception grew there was, he continued, a real danger that the public willingness to have tissue used in research would evaporate.

---

[53] *John Moore v the Regents of the University of California* (1990) 51 Cal 3d 120.
[54] BJ Culliton, 'Moore Case Has Its First Court Hearing' (1984) 226 *Science* 813.
[55] *Moore v Regents of University of California and Ors* (1990) 51 Cal 3d 120, 134 (Panelli J); above n 54, 813.
[56] LE Rosenberg, 'Using Patient Materials for Product Development: A Dean's Perspective' (1985) 33 *Clinical Research* 452, 453. This volume held the proceedings of an American Federation for Clinical Research symposium on 'The Legal, Ethical and Economic Impact of Patient Material Used for Product Development in the Biomedical Industry', held in Washington during 1985.
[57] AE Otten, 'Researchers' Use of Blood, Bodily Tissues Raises Question About Sharing Profits' *The Wall Street Journal* (New York, 29 January 1986).

Some scientists framed *Moore* as an 'outrageous' imposition into the vital practices that underpinned biomedical research.[58] This stance was illustrated by an article in *Nature*, which pictured an avaricious lawyer interrupting an operation to demand that the patient be granted full rights to his tumour (see Figure 1).[59] Others, however, endorsed some form of patient ownership in tissue. As an article in *Science* noted, 'several researchers contacted by *Science* see no reason why some sort of provision should not be made that would give patients rights in cases such as this'.[60] Ivor Royston, a researcher at the University of California, San Diego, stressed the need for 'new laws which delineate the rights, if any, of patients to commercial products of cell lines derived from their tissues'.[61] Royston suggested that, in cases where a patient was not known to an investigator, and where research on tissue did not identify the patient or lead to the development of commercial products, then it was sufficient to obtain their informed consent for research. However, when the patient or family was cognisant of the research being done with their tissue, which may in turn lead to development of commercial products, he suggested that consent forms be supplemented by an agreement that allowed the patient to waive their rights to the tissue and its downstream products.

Figure 1: ***Nature* represents *Moore* as an imposition into science. Note the contrasting portrayal of a humanitarian biomedical and a rapacious legal profession.**[62]

---

[58] Above n 54, 813.
[59] S Blake, 'Patient Sues for Title to Own Cells' (1984) 311 *Nature* 198.
[60] BJ Culliton, 'Patient Sues UCLA over Patent on Cell Line' (1984) 225 *Science* 1458.
[61] I Royston, 'Cells from Human Patients: Who Owns Them? A Case Report' (1985) 33 *Clinical Research* 443.
[62] Illustration, above n 59.
Reprinted by permission from Macmillan Publishers Ltd. *Nature* (Blake, 'Patient Sues UCLA') copyright (1984).

The lack of scientific consensus regarding *Moore* was mirrored by diverse legal and bioethical positions. Figures such as Lori Andrews, a *pro bono* member of John Moore's legal team, wrote in bioethics journal *The Hastings Center Report* in 1986 that patients 'should have the autonomy to treat their own parts as property'.[63] Framing *Moore* as synecdoche for a broader popular sentiment, she stated that legal recognition of this right was needed to acknowledge that 'people have an interest in what happens to their extracorporeal body parts'.[64] The extent to which *Moore* and other legal disputes over tissue reflected a broad popular opinion was questionable though: to support her argument that 'people' cared about the fate of body parts, Andrews cited an opinion poll where only 20 per cent of respondents expressed unease at the use of tissue in research.

Nevertheless, Andrews argued not only for the requirement of patient consent for research upon clinical samples, but also the adoption of a free-market approach to tissue research, where members of the public were considered the owners of tissue and able to sell it to scientists and doctors. She rejected the view that such a system would invariably lead to coercion and exploitation of the poor and vulnerable. Banning payment on these grounds, she claimed, overlooked the fact that 'to the person who needs money to feed his children or to purchase medical care for their parent, the option of not selling a body part is worse than the option of selling it'.[65] She also disputed the claim that granting patients title to tissue would burden scientists in negotiation and bartering. If a patient were reluctant to sell his or her tissues, she continued, the researcher could simply approach someone who was not.[66]

Bioethicist Arthur Caplan, however, rejected a free-market model, claiming that it would threaten traditional doctor-patient relations, and that the exorbitant prices individuals could charge might drastically reduce the amount of tissue available for research. Instead, he claimed that the solution to cases such as *Moore* lay in full scientific disclosure to patients of their interest in excised tissues. 'When research is the goal', he stated, 'whether for profit or not, those whose materials are to be used in research have a right to know'.[67] The ultimate judgment in *Moore* reflected Caplan's stance. In 1990 the California Supreme Court ruled that there was no basis for conversion, as the Mo cell line was 'factually and legally distinct from the cells taken' (this overturned a 1988 judgement by the California Court of Appeal, which ruled that Moore did have grounds for conversion).[68] The court did, though, hold that certain UCLA staff could be sued for breach of fiduciary duty since they failed to disclose an interest in producing a cell line from Moore's spleen, thus undermining any informed consent obtained.

---

[63] LB Andrews, 'My Body, My Property' (1986) *Hastings Center Report* 28, 37.
[64] ibid 29.
[65] ibid 32.
[66] ibid 29.
[67] AL Caplan, 'Blood, Sweat and Tears, and Profits: The Ethics of the Sale and Use of Patient Derived Materials in Biomedicine' (1985) 33 *Clinical Research* 448, 451.
[68] 'Outrageous Fortune: Selling Other People's Cells' in GJ Annas (ed), *Standard of Care: The Law of American Bioethics* (Oxford, OUP, 1993) 172.

William Curran, writing in the *New England Journal of Medicine*, greeted this decision warmly, stating it offered closure on the question of ownership.[69] This did not end legal or ethical interest in human tissues however. For one, *Moore* was only binding in California, so there was nothing to stop a similarly aggrieved patient bringing suit elsewhere. Consequently, a major theme in work published after *Moore* concerned whether plaintiff's stance reflected a broad popular opinion and, as a corollary, whether the case was to be the first of many. Several legal articles recommended that in order to prevent further controversy, the doctrine of informed consent should be extended to cover research on excised tissues.[70]

Britain: Debating Policy and Surveying Public Opinion in the 1980s and 1990s

The sense that *Moore* might encourage further litigation was not confined to the US. Writing in *The Lancet* in 1988, barrister Diana Brahams noted that given how widespread the procurement and use of tissue was, and given the absence of legislation covering this, there was a danger that British practices may be ruled as 'neither ethical nor lawful' if similarly challenged.[71] Excised tissue's status as *res nullius* seemed rather less tenable, Brahams wrote, now that 'DNA techniques [could] permit positive identification of the donor', linking people to excised parts. In light of this, it seemed 'unlikely that a patient being operated on can be said to have abandoned (and lost any rights in) his organs'—a statement backed up by recent convictions for theft of other supposedly 'abandoned' items, such as dustbin refuse and lost golf balls.[72] Brahams thus stated that a prospective plaintiff 'might well be entitled to all the proceeds produced by the cell line less the cost of developing and maintaining it'.[73]

To pre-empt such a scenario, British groups with a vested interest in human tissue culture called for the adoption of new practices, and even new legislation. Notably, as I stated at the outset, and as was sometimes the case in the US, these calls often came from scientists. For instance, one prominent tissue culture manual urged researchers to obtain the written consent of patients before they collected tissue.[74] Anti-vivisectionist charities that supported the use of non-animal models in biomedicine also called for adoption of new policies, to maintain public

---

[69] WJ Curran, 'Scientific and Commercial Development of Cell Lines: Issues of Property, Ethics and Conflict of Interest' (1991) 324 *New England Journal of Medicine* 998.

[70] See eg SN Perley, 'From Control Over One's Body to Control Over One's Parts: Extending the Doctrine of Informed Consent' (1992) 67 *New York University Law Review* 335; CA Tallerico, 'The Autonomy of the Human Body in the Age of Biotechnology' (1990) 61 *University of Colorado Law Review* 659; L Daniels, 'Commercialisation of Human Tissues: Has Biotechnology Created the Need for an Expanded Scope of Informed Consent?' (1990) 27 *California Western Law Review* 209.

[71] D Brahams, 'A Disputed Spleen' (1988) 332 *The Lancet* 1151.

[72] ibid 1152.

[73] ibid.

[74] RI Freshney, *Culture of Animal Cells: A Manual of Basic Technique* (Chichester, Willey, 1987) 112.

confidence in research and pre-empt a British equivalent to *Moore*. In 1987 one such group, the Fund for Replacement of Animals in Medical Experiments (FRAME), called for the promulgation of a 'sensible and widely adopted' professional policy to regulate the use of human tissue in biomedical research.[75] Formed in the late 1960s, FRAME lobbied for the uptake of alternatives to experimental animals, promoting human tissue cultures as tools that would render vivisection 'obsolete'.[76] Founded by a member of the public and a retired biologist, from the outset FRAME counted many scientists among its members; by the 1980s, it published its own journal, *Alternatives to Laboratory Animals*, and sponsored scientific work and conferences on the use of human tissue.

In order to determine what form this policy should take, FRAME commissioned a poll of public opinion in 1987. Such tactics, as Marilyn Strathern notes, were also tied to the contemporary neo-liberal 'rolling back' of centralised bureaucracy and management: instead of being passive recipients of policy, the views of 'the public' were increasingly sought as arbiter of what constituted ethical practice.[77] FRAME sent 1,000 copies of a questionnaire to names and addresses drawn from the electoral register. Recipients were questioned on whether they would consent to research on their own tissue; whether they preferred its use in medical, industrial, or cosmetic research; the sorts of tissue they would be willing to donate; and their views on animal experiments. Rather undermining the hope of clear policy guidance, the results were inconclusive: only 200 out of 1,000 people responded, whilst only 53 per cent supported use of their own tissue. FRAME questioned whether their respondents could even be figured as representative of broader opinion, as the responses suggested that replies mainly came from individuals with strong views on vivisection; and the 200 that replied were disproportionately young and female to represent the general population.[78]

The denial of Moore's claim to property rights in his tissue in 1990 did little to quell the sense of uncertainty amongst British researchers. As Brahams again noted in *The Lancet*, and as attendees at a FRAME conference on the use of human tissue attested, there remained an 'urgent requirement for legal guidelines on the recovery, distribution and use of human tissues, so that surgeons and researchers could be made aware of what was and was not allowed'.[79] Whilst Brahams called on the General Medical Council to draw up recommendations, FRAME members put forward their own advice to researchers.[80] Paramount in

---

[75] 'Human Tissue as an Alternative in Bio-Medical Research' (1987) 14 *Alternatives to Laboratory Animals* 375, 375.

[76] Fund for Replacement of Experimental Animals in Medical Experiments, *Is the Laboratory Animal Obsolete?* (1971).

[77] M Strathern, 'Robust Knowledge and Fragile Futures' in A Ong and S Collier (eds), *Global Assemblages: Technology, Politics and Ethics as Anthropological Problems* (Blackwell, Malden, 2005) 464–82.

[78] Above n 75, 376.

[79] JH Fentem, 'Conference Report: The Use of Human Tissues in *In Vitro* Toxicology' (1993) 21 *Alternatives to Laboratory Animals* 388, 389.

[80] D Brahams, 'Ownership of a spleen' (1990) 366 *The Lancet* 329.

this was the call to obtain patient consent before tissue was acquired—perhaps not surprising in light of the Supreme Court ruling that UCLA staff were liable for not getting Moore's permission to establish the cell line.[81] FRAME presented consent here as a means of safeguarding biomedical research and non-animal methods, by boosting public confidence and ensuring a ready supply of raw material. Consent offered patients 'reassurance that removal of tissues would be properly conducted', ensuring that the ambivalence encountered in the 1987 poll 'would be replaced by willingness to cooperate'.[82]

This recommendation, published in 1993, differed markedly from the conclusions of the recently established Nuffield Council on Bioethics. Created in December 1990, and funded by the charitable Nuffield Foundation, this Council, as Sheila Jasanoff notes, originated from scientific calls for ethical oversight and regulation, and was seen largely by scientists as a device for safeguarding research.[83] One of its first tasks was to undertake a thorough review of human tissue research—indicating just how uneasy the biomedical community was regarding the current lack of oversight and guidance. The Council's working party on human tissue was chaired by Dame Rosaline Hurley, a microbiologist, and counted among its membership several legal professionals, a philosopher, a marriage counsellor, and representatives of the Medical Research Council (MRC) and the Wellcome Trust.[84] Its terms of reference were, broadly, to survey and report current uses made of cells and tissues in biomedicine, and to scrutinise accompanying legal or ethical issues.

When it was published in 1995, the working party wrote that their report had its origins in the apparent 'public concern' raised by various biomedical uses of human material. *Moore*, described as something of a 'cause célèbre', was framed by the working party as evidence of the problems that accompanied the scientific and commercial exploitation of human material, also evident in growing reports of a black-market in human organs.[85] The issues cases like *Moore* raised were, they followed:

> both legal and ethical. For example, what relationship exists between the person who was source of the tissue and the tissue removed? Does tissue remain part of the person in any sense, whether symbolically or in some proprietary sense? Does the person retain any right of control over it or is the consent to removal [in operation] to be regarded as implying abandonment of the tissue?[86]

As we have seen, there was a clear demand for clarification of these issues, from both legal figures such as Brahams and from organisations such as FRAME. Little

---

[81] J Gurney and M Balls, 'Obtaining Human Tissues for Research and Testing: Practical Problems and Public Attitudes in Britain' in V Rogiers et al (eds), *Human Cells in In Vitro Pharmaco-Toxicology: Present Status Within Europe* (Brussels, VUB Press, 1993) 315.
[82] ibid 327.
[83] S Jasanoff, *Designs on Nature: Science and Democracy in Europe and the United States* (Princeton, Princeton University Press, 2005).
[84] 'Medical and Scientific Uses of Human Tissue' (1992) 20 *Alternatives to Laboratory Animals* 200.
[85] Nuffield Council on Bioethics, *Human Tissue: Legal and Ethical Issues* (London, 1995) 8–10, 55.
[86] ibid 11.

wonder, then, that the Council report, entitled *Human Tissue: Legal and Ethical Issues*, was widely reported. Most coverage in the biomedical press centred on the report's recommendations concerning patient consent and ownership. Here, as Richard Tutton has detailed, the Council drew heavily on Richard Titmuss' influential 1970 endorsement of blood donation in Britain as an altruistic expression of collective social relations. Like Titmuss, the authors of the *Human Tissue* report represented the biomedical use of human tissue as a similarly communal endeavour, 'in which researchers and research participants contribute to research that will benefit human health'.[87] Any policy that hinted at the commercialisation, or commodification, of body parts was anathema to this stance—and the report clearly recommended that patients were to be denied property rights in tissue samples, and hospitals were not to make a profit by selling such material either.[88]

The working party considered that patients whose tissue was removed in treatment should continue to be recognised as having abandoned it. To justify this recommendation, its report evoked a broad popular opinion, stating that 'in the general run of things a person from whom a tissue is removed has not the slightest interest in making any claim to it'.[89] The working party did not draw from any survey of opinion to justify this claim, but relied instead on the fact that 'the question of a claim over tissue' had not been tested in English law.[90] Though their report was expressly commissioned in the wake of a seeming 'public concern', the authors of *Human Tissue* clearly felt that this did not extend to research on tissue removed in clinical procedures. With this in mind, their report recommended that a patient's consent to the removal of tissue in diagnosis or surgery could still be construed as an act of abandonment, whereupon it attained the status of 'a *res* (a thing)'.[91]

Consequently, in 1996 the Royal College of Physicians stated that the long-standing use of 'discarded' tissue remained acceptable, even without the specific consent of patients.[92] Yet there was still no consensus on this within the biomedical community. Certain groups continued to urge scientists and doctors to obtain the express permission of patients before they used tissue. For example, an ad-hoc committee of researchers from the UK Co-ordinating Committee on Cancer Research (UKCCCR) produced a booklet that demanded researchers secure the informed consent of patients before creating tissue cultures or cell lines. These tissue sources were reframed here as 'donors', who might be legally entitled to sue implicated parties should it become apparent that tissue was used without

---

[87] R Tutton, 'Person, Property and Gift: Exploring the Languages of Tissue Donation' in R Tutton and O Corrigan (eds), *Genetic Databases: Socio-Ethical Issues in the Collection and Use of DNA* (London, Routledge, 2004) 19–39. See also R Titmuss, *The Gift Relationship: from Human Blood to Social Policy* (London, Allen and Unwin, 1970).

[88] Above n 85, 131. See also 'Working Party Speaks Out on the Use of Human Tissue' (1995) 310 *British Medical Journal* 1159; C Broadhead, 'Human Tissue: Ethical and Legal Issues' (1995) 23 *Alternatives to Laboratory Animals* 435.

[89] Above n 85, 68.

[90] ibid.

[91] ibid.

[92] As cited in M MacLean, 'Letting Go … Parents, Professionals and the Law in the Retention of Human Material after Post Mortem' in M Bainham et al, above n 11, 79.

their knowledge.[93] Notably, the Nuffield report had avoided the term 'donor' when discussing patients whose tissue was removed in therapy—since, as Council member Onora O'Neill stated, 'by definition, donors give tissue that *will not otherwise be removed from them*'.[94] The UKCCCR researchers justified their calls for consent as a means of avoiding litigation, and as recognition of a heightened patient demand for choice in healthcare. A tissue culture manual written by one UKCCCR member went so far as to include a sample consent form that researchers should distribute to patients before they obtained surgical or biopsy tissue (see figure 2).[95]

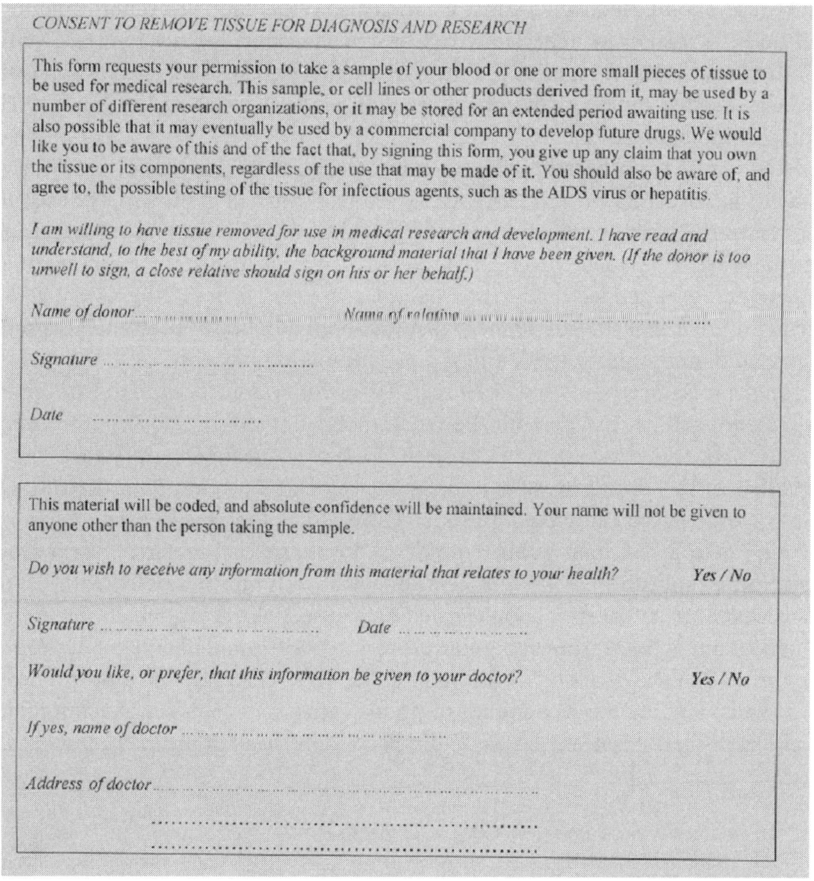

CONSENT TO REMOVE TISSUE FOR DIAGNOSIS AND RESEARCH

This form requests your permission to take a sample of your blood or one or more small pieces of tissue to be used for medical research. This sample, or cell lines or other products derived from it, may be used by a number of different research organizations, or it may be stored for an extended period awaiting use. It is also possible that it may eventually be used by a commercial company to develop future drugs. We would like you to be aware of this and of the fact that, by signing this form, you give up any claim that you own the tissue or its components, regardless of the use that may be made of it. You should also be aware of, and agree to, the possible testing of the tissue for infectious agents, such as the AIDS virus or hepatitis.

I am willing to have tissue removed for use in medical research and development. I have read and understand, to the best of my ability, the background material that I have been given. (If the donor is too unwell to sign, a close relative should sign on his or her behalf.)

Name of donor .... *Name of relative* ....

Signature ....

Date ....

This material will be coded, and absolute confidence will be maintained. Your name will not be given to anyone other than the person taking the sample.

Do you wish to receive any information from this material that relates to your health? *Yes / No*

Signature .... *Date* ....

Would you like, or prefer, that this information be given to your doctor? *Yes / No*

If yes, name of doctor ....

Address of doctor ....

....

....

Figure 2: Sample patient or 'donor' consent form drawn up by one UKCCCR member.

[93] United Kingdom Coordinating Committee for Cancer Research, *Guidelines for the Use of Cell Lines in Cancer Research* (UKCCCR, 1999).

[94] Above n 8, 6 (emphasis added.)

[95] RI Freshney, *Culture of Animal Cells: A Manual of Basic Technique*, 4th edn (New York, Wiley, 2000) 151.

The UKCCCR guidelines were largely dismissed by the biomedical community, in favour of the Nuffield review.[96] But, amidst the retained organ scandal that arose in 1999, scientific and medical practice was branded as unethical precisely because of the lack of control that patients or families had over human material; the parents involved in the organ scandal stated that the storage of and research on body parts was not the problem *per se*, but more the fact that they were not asked.[97] With belief in this strong popular sentiment paramount, the Department of Health drew up revised guidelines that ordered hospitals to obtain patient consent, without fail, for any retention or research on bodily material. In the same vein, a joint Medical Research Council and Wellcome Trust report on public attitudes to tissue research claimed: 'Consent is a crucial issue for [research's] continuing success ... especially in the current climate'.[98] Circumstances appeared to have quickly rendered the abandonment model supported by the Nuffield Council untenable.

However, it soon became clear that researchers were unwilling to approach patients to seek consent, and that this had led to a shortfall in the supply of tissues for research.[99] Some researchers argued that the emphasis on patient autonomy had now been pursued to unworkable ends, and called instead for consent to research to be appended onto existing surgical consent forms. Others went a step further, urging that the government instead adopt a policy of presumed consent, where all tissue could be used, unless a patient raised objection.

Amidst this uncertainty, a new Human Tissue Bill was introduced to Parliament in December 2003. In line with the recommendations of an inquiry into organ retention, the bill made the non-consensual use of tissue for any purpose a criminal offence. This clearly arose as a consequence of a perceived public demand for control over tissue samples: ministers claimed that the new consent measures were needed to maintain public confidence in biomedical research.[100] Far from welcoming ratification, however, the biomedical community reacted with barely concealed horror. Consternation centred on clause 1 of the bill, which stated that when obtaining tissue from living sources researchers should obtain the 'appropriate consent' of the patient.[101] Within days, the MRC responded in a press release and, whilst lauding the recognition of public concern, it criticised the ambiguity of the 'appropriate consent' clause. Colin Blakemore, head of the MRC, stated that

---

[96] RI Freshney, personal interview (Glasgow, 8 November 2004).
[97] Above n 13, 416.
[98] Cragg Ross Dawson, The Wellcome Trust and the Medical Research Council, *Public Perceptions of the Collection of Human Biological Samples* (London, Wellcome Trust and the MRC, 2000) 16.
[99] M Brindley, 'Research Hit by Organ Scandal', *Western Mail* (Cardiff, 17 December 2002).
[100] The final report of the Retained Organs Commission, *Remembering the Past, Looking to the Future* (London, Department of Health, 2004), delineates the Commission's overriding emphasis on consent, and its input into the Human Tissue Bill. For press and legal endorsement of patient consent, see J Wildgoose, 'Who Really Owns Our Bodies?' *The Guardian* 30 January 2001; JK Mason and GT Laurie, 'Consent or Property? Dealing with the Body and its Parts in the Shadow of Bristol and Alder Hey' (2001) 64 *Modern Law Review* 710.
[101] Human Tissue Bill (HMSO, 2004) 8.

scientists were likely to construe this as consent for each specific use of a tissue sample or derivative, and would have to re-contact sources every time tissue was used in different projects.[102]

Following these protests, the contentious 'appropriate consent' clause was removed from a new draft that was put to Parliament in June 2004. This redrafted bill implemented a policy of presumed consent. Now assuming, as in the Nuffield report, that patients did not generally care about the fate of excised tissues, the Human Tissue Bill allowed scientists to obtain material without consent, only prohibiting its use in research when a patient raised specific objection.[103] When it came to the acquisition and use of clinical tissue for research, policy had come full-circle.

Conclusions

Susan Lawrence has argued that the struggle over human tissue in the *Moore* case marks the 'beginning of a major transformation in Western culture of heretofore 'worthless' parts of the self and others'.[104] Whilst I do not dispute that the latter part of the 20th century saw increasing debate regarding the hitherto unproblematic scientific use of tissue, I have shown here that lawyers, scientists and ethicists had turned their attention to this subject before *Moore*. These debates arose due to historical trends that reshaped these 'worthless' tissues, and which feature prominently in, but were not started by the case: namely, the rising emphasis on patient autonomy in healthcare and, later, questions about commerce and exploitation in biotechnology. Similarly, I have shown that the need for legal clarification of tissue procurement was discussed in Britain prior to the organ retention scandal in the late 1990s and that, as in the US, calls for new measures often came from scientists.

Many of these scientific or medical calls for new regulation were similar to those made by some academic lawyers and bioethicists; scientists such as Ivor Royston, for example, supported the free-market system endorsed by Lori Andrews, or the extended consent measures endorsed by Arthur Caplan. We also see homology between these professional domains in the ways other scientists, ethicists and lawyers rejected calls for new regulation. Detailing how views on regulation, and specifically consent, varied within and overlapped between legal, ethical and scientific spheres demonstrates how these social worlds are interdependent and co-constitutive of each other.[105]

---

[102] C Blakemore, 'Human Tissue Bill: Views of the Medical Research Council', *MRC Press Release* (26 January 2004).
[103] G Hinscliffe and R McKie, 'Doctors Beat Curbs on Tissue Research' *The Observer* 6 June 2004.
[104] Above n 9, 131.
[105] S Jasanoff, *States of Knowledge: The Co-Production of Science and the Social Order* (London, Routledge, 2007); S Jasanoff, *Science at the Bar: Science and Technology in American Law* (Cambridge, Mass, Harvard University Press, 1997).

As I stated at the outset, these differing standpoints on the regulation of tissue research based their arguments on projections of 'public' opinion. Yet when efforts were actually made to survey this opinion, a complex and ambiguous picture emerged—as in the 1987 poll commissioned by FRAME.[106] How various individuals and groups interpreted this complexity depended on the regulatory model they were endorsing. The 20 per cent of respondents who claimed to be uneasy about use of body parts could be refigured by Lori Andrews as evidence that 'people' cared about what happened to extracorporeal parts. The Nuffield Council, by contrast, hinted that outright unease was marginal, and argued that 'in the general run of things' patients did not care what happened to tissue.

I would contend, also, that these seemingly divergent proposals are similar in other respects. Those that endorsed patient consent, those that refused it, and even those that endorsed patient ownership, shared a reluctance to ask how biologically-derived entities such as tissue culture fundamentally question the distinctions upon which common law, scientific practice, and patent regulation are based. To follow Klaus Hoeyer, perhaps the most interesting problem posed by such entities is not whether they can be classified as personal property or abandoned *res*, but the way they destabilise the distinction between these categories.[107] Tissue cultures and cell lines are not inert objects, but can grow and divide—and may thus be considered, as Catherine Waldby states, 'semi-living' entities.[108] Admittedly, they may only divide and grow thanks to scientific skill; but as Diana Brahams noted, they still contain genetic information that links them to their corporeal source—possibly undermining the tenet that a person can ever now be truly said to have 'abandoned' such material.[109] I would venture that the lack of consensus detailed in this chapter shows that tissue cultures confound basic legal and social principles of categorisation. They cannot be unproblematically made to fit legal conceptions of people, nor things; their collection and circulation in either free-market or communitarian models is no less contentious. Perhaps, then, the greater task ahead for scientists, lawyers and ethicists is not to force tools such as tissue culture into one of several established categories, but to ask how the creation and circulation of these raw-materials-turned-technologies has the potential to redefine them.

---

[106] See also R Tutton, 'Exploring the Languages of Tissue Donation' in R Tutton and O Corrigan (eds), *Genetic Databases: Socio-ethical Issues in the Collection and Use of DNA* (London, Routledge, 2004) 19–38.

[107] K Hoeyer, 'Person, Patent and Property: A Critique of the Commodification Hypothesis' (2007) 2 *Biosocieties* (2007) 327.

[108] C Waldby, *The Visible Human Project: Informatic Bodies and Posthuman Medicine* (London, Routledge, 2000).

[109] Above n 71, 1152.

INDEX

Abercromby, General Sir Ralph 21
Aberdeen, abortion provision 147–8, 149, 156
Abortion Act 1967, English/Scottish
   aspects 143–65
   background 143–5
   Bill *see* Medical Termination of Pregnancy Bill
   clarification restriction attempts 161–3
   conscience clause issues 157–8
   conclusion 163–5
   geographical variation in provision 154–5
   law/practice pre-1967 145–9
   medical reception 152–7
   prevention issues 158
   psychiatric issues 158–61
   risk to health issues 156–7
   social clause 151, 154
   termination concerns 155–6, 162
Abortion Amendment Bill (Corrie's) 161–3
Abortion Amendment Bill (Lane's) 161
Abortion Law Reform Association 149, 150, 151, 152
abortion notification 105–14
   confidentiality debate 107–9
   legal requirements 105–7
   therapeutic abortion 105, 158
Abse, Leo 175–6, 188, 189
Act for the Better Prevention of Offences 1851 76
acute mania 94
Adair, James 133–4
Adams, Sir William 27–31
Addenbrookes Hospital 202
Addington, Henry 20
Addison, Christopher 112–14
Anatomy Act 1832 4, 198, 200
Andrews, Lori 210, 218
anti-vivisectionists 211–12
Apothecaries Act 1815 4, 25–7
Armstrong, Annie 107
Army Medical Board
   Commissioners of Military Inquiry 25
   education/training 25–7
   ophthalmia disputes 28
assisted reproductive technologies 167
asylum surgeons/physicians 91–2, 95
automatons 89
aversion therapy 137
Avory, Horace 107–8, 109

Baird, Dugal 144, 147–52, 153, 154–6, 163–4
Baker, JH 69
Barlinnie prison 128
Barnard, Dr Christiaan 171
Bartlett, A 126
Bavister, Barry 168–9
Bayh-Dole Act 1980 207
Bennet, Mr HG 31
Berkeley, Admiral 20
Bethlem Hospital 95, 96
Bevis, Professor Douglas 171
bioethics 168, 213
Birkenhead, Earl of 112–14, 118, 119, 122
Black Act 1723 69
Blackstone, Sir William 69
Blakemore, Colin 216–17
Blane, Dr Gilbert 20–1, 36
Bolton, Virginia 190
Borstal system 128–9
Boyd, Dr William 127, 129, 132, 138
Bragge, Mr 22
Brahams, Diana 211, 212, 213, 218
brain fever 87
Braude, Peter 190
Brave New World (Huxley) 193, 203
British Association for the Advancement of Science 171
British Medical Association
   abortion law reform 117–22 *passim*
   IVF/embryo research 171, 172, 177–8, 182
   medical confidentiality 104, 107, 108–9, 110
Brown, Louise 167, 170, 174–6
Browning v Norton Children's Hospital 204–5
Burden Neurological Institute 129
Burney, I 4
Burrows, Montrose 201
bye laws, for the suppression of nuisances
   background 39–40
   Home Office *see* Home Office, bye law role
   as lay control 53–5
   municipal council influence 59
   as nuisance law 40–1
   sanitary nuisance on private land 44–5, 46–52, 53
   statutory background 41–5

Campbell, Archibald 72–3
Caplan, Arthur 210, 217
Carrel, Alexis 201
Carstairs (institution) 135
Cawthorn, E 3
Central Midwives Board of Scotland 163

Chadwicke, Edwin   40–1, 53
Challoner, Jack   169, 173
cholera epidemic   40, 46, 53–4
Christison, Robert   63–4, 71–2
Chudleigh, Elizabeth *see* Kingston, Duchess of
Church of Scotland Moral Welfare
   Committee   155
Clark, M   2, 5
Clarke, Sir Edward   107, 108, 109
Commissioners of Military Inquiry
   Army Medical System   25
common law
   nuisances of private property   47–8
   as regulation mechanism   41–2, 45, 57
concussion   87
confidentiality *see* medical confidentiality
Conolly, John   86
Contagious Diseases Acts 1860s   110
Corneal Grafting Act 1952   201
Corrie, John   144, 161–3
Coutts, Dr Francis   114, 115, 116–17
Coventry, Sir John   69
Coventry's Act   69, 73
Cox, Alfred   119
Crawford, C   2, 5, 101
Criminal Justice (Scotland) Act 1949   127, 130, 137
Criminal Law Amendment Act 1885   134–5, 136–7, 141
Culliton, Barbara   206
Curran, WJ   211

Davidson Clinic   130, 132–3
Dawson, Mr J   31
Dawson of Penn, Lord   121
delirium   80
delusion   79, 81, 84, 93, 97
Department of Health   216
   see also Ministry of Health
Derby   59
Diamond v Chakrabarty   207
Dickens, Bernard   204
Dingleton Hospital   136
divorce petitions   109–10, 111–12
DNA techniques   211
Donald, Ian   148–9, 150, 153, 164
Doodewood v Spence   203
doubled consciousness   80
Douglas Inch Centre   136, 139
Drife, James   185
Droitwich   50, 51, 54
Dundas, Sir David   27, 28
Dundee   154–5

East India Company   33
Edinburgh   154
Edwards, Robert   168–9, 170–5, 178, 180, 183, 186

Eigen, J   4
electro-convulsive therapy   129
Elliott, Dr John   114–19, 120, 122, 123
embryo research *see in vitro* fertilisation/
   embryo research
endocrine treatment   132
epilepsy   79–80, 87
   epileptic vertigo   86–7, 88, 89
Esquirol, Jean-Etienne-Dominique   84–5
ethical medicine *see* medical confidentiality
Evans, D   110
Evesham   51

family planning education   158
Ford Foundation   172
forensic psychiatry *see* psychiatric testimony
Foucault, M   101
French Revolutionary Wars   17, 36
Freudian concepts   90, 98, 130, 135
fumigation, nitrous   20, 21–4
Fund for Replacement of Animals in Medical
   Experiments   212–13, 218

Galen   84
Garner, Clara   111–112
Garner v Garner   111–12, 119, 121–2
General Medical Council   103, 212
Genetic Manipulation Advisory Committee   175
Gibson, Dr   117
Gibson, John Rowland   79
Gladstone, Dr William   36
Glaister, Professor John   106–7, 131, 146
Glasgow
   abortion provision   147–9, 154, 157–8, 159
   medical officer of health   104
   treatment of homosexuals   127
Glasgow Royal Infirmary   147
global delirium   81
Golla, FL   129
Goodwin, James   73
Grant, Mr JP   29
Greenock Royal Infirmary   157
Grenville, Lord   33
Grimes, Charles   79, 83
Guy, William   64, 67–8, 78
Gwyer, Sir Maurice Linford   113, 115, 116

Hadfield, James   81, 83, 96
Hale, Matthew   84
Hamill, E   156
Harrison, Ross   201
Harvey, Augustus John   102
Hastings   43
Hawkins, Caesar   102–3, 119, 121, 123–4
Hawkins, Henry   106, 109
Hawkshead Hospital   138
Heley, Margaret   181
Hempson, William   108–9

Henderson, Professor Sir David 138, 139
Hennock, EP 52
Henry IV 69
Hippocrates 84, 99
Hodgkiss, Annie 107
Hoeyer, K 218
Home Office, bye law role 55–9
    background 55–6
    central-local conflicts 56–7
    inconsistency 58–9
homicidal melancholia 94–5
homicidal monomania 94
homosexual offenders, in Scotland 125–42
    background 125–6
    conclusion 141–2
    psychiatric reports to High Court 134–41, 142
    Wolfenden Committee evidence 126–34, 141–2
homosexuality, latent/active 136, 138
Horridge, Justice 116, 117, 119
Human Fertilisation and Embryology Authority 192
Human Fertilization and Embryology Act 1990 193–5
Human Organs Transplants Act 1989 201
Human Tissue Act 1961 201
Human Tissue Act 2004 197, 198, 200, 216–17
Human Tissue Authority 197
Human Tissue Bill 2003 216–17
human tissue debates 197–218
    background 197–200
    in Britain 211–17
    commercialism 206–11
    conclusions 217–18
    practices/laws (1907–80) 200–6
Hume, Mr 36
Hurley, Dame Rosaline 213
Hurren, E 4
Hutchinson, General 21
Huxley, Aldous 193, 203
hypnotism 80

in vitro fertilisation/embryo research, regulation 167–95
    background 167–8
    conclusion 195
    early stages 168–75
    initiatives 175–8
    legislation 193–5
    medical opinion 178–83
    parliamentary debates (1984–1985) 183–9
    prohibitive legislation proposal 189–91, 193
    voluntary licensing 191, 192–3
Inch, Dr 128, 129, 132
Infant Life (Preservation) Act 1929 145, 155
Ingram, Michael 156, 159–61

Inquiry into Human Fertilisation and Embryology 171, 176–7, 179, 181
    aftermath 193–5
    licensing recommendation 192–3
    opposition to conclusions 189–91
    release/parliamentary debates on 183–9
insanity 80, 86–7
    moral 81, 85–6, 87–8, 93, 97
    partial 97
    puerperal 87, 88, 93
insensibility 81
inventions, rewards for 20
IVF see in vitro fertilisation/embryo research, regulation

Jackson, Sir John 33–4, 36
Jenner, Dr Edward 20

Kandinsky, Dr Salomon 111–12, 121–2
Kay, James Phillips 53–4
Keate, Thomas 20–1, 30
Keith, Admiral Lord 21
Kennedy, Hugh 73
Kent, Duke of 33
Kent, J 203–4
Keown, J 3
Kerr, D 68
Kidderminster 50, 58
King, M 126
Kingston, Duchess of 102–3, 119, 122, 123
Kitson, Linda 106
Kitson, Sir James 107
Kitson v Playfair 106, 108
Kraemer, WP 130–1

Lane Committee (on the Working of the Abortion Act) 144, 153, 157–9, 164
Lane, Elizabeth 153
Langbein, J 83
Lawrence, Susan 202–3, 217
legal medicine 2–6
legal regulation 1
LIFE Doctors Group 181
Lind, Dr James 22
Lind, Dr John 20, 22–3
Liverpool
    bye laws 47–8, 54, 58, 59
    local acts 46–7, 54
    medical officer of health 104
Lloyd, Honoratus 115, 116
local acts, as regulation mechanism 42–4
Local Government Board 120
London & Counties Medical Protection Society 116, 117
Lord Ellenborough's Act 70–2, 73–4
Lord Landsdown's Act 73–5
Lothian and Peebles Executive Council 154
Loudon, I 25

McCardie, Alfred   111–12, 119
McGirr, Professor EM   153
McGrigor, Sir James   28–9, 31
McLaren, Dr Anne   164–85, 171
Maclean, Charles   32–5
McMillan, Euphemia   72–3
McMurdo, Gilbert   91, 92, 96
McNaughtan, Daniel   80, 89
McNaughtan rules   80, 85, 87, 89, 91
MacNaughton, Malcolm   164, 176
MacQueen, Dr Ian   148
Malicious Shooting and Stabbing Act 1803   70–1
mania   84
  acute   94
manie sans délire   84
Mann, John Dixon   78
Mansfield, Lord   102
Marcus Beck Laboratory   202
Marshall, Dr Joseph   20–1
Matthews, Sir Charles   108–9
Maudsley, Henry   80
mayhem   69–70
Meacher, Michael   188–9
Medical Act 1858   103
medical confidentiality
  abortion *see* abortion notification
  challenges to   100–1
  current law   99*n*
  18th C precedent   102–3
  19th C professional changes   103–5, 123–4
  role   99–100
  VD *see* venereal disease (VD), confidentiality and
medical education, regulation   25–7
medical profession
  abortion and   150–1, 156–7, 162–3, 164–5
  changes   103–4, 123–4
  IVF/embryo research   178–83
Medical Research Council   171–7 *passim*, 182, 190, 192, 213–14, 216
Medical Termination of Pregnancy Bill   144, 149–52
  inclusion of Scotland   151
  social clause   151, 154
Medico-Legal Society   121
melancholia   81, 84–5, 89, 93–4
  homicidal linking   94–5
  utility   95–8
Mendelson, D   5
mental derangement, diagnosis   81–2
mesmerism   80
Middlesex Hospital   202
military medicine *see* select committees of inquiry, military medicine
Ministry of Health
  privilege, dispute/proposal   112–14, 114–19, 120–2
  see also Department of Health

Mokry v University of Texas Health Science Centre   205
Mond, Sir Alfred   118
monomania   84–5
  homicidal   94
Mooney, G   105
Moore (John) v the Regents of the University of California   207–10, 211, 212, 213, 217
moral insanity   81, 85–6, 87–8, 93, 97
Morrice, A   105, 110
Moseley, Dr   30
Mulkay, M   192
Municipal Reform Act 1835   39, 43
  as common law alternative   57
  municipal corporations and   45
Murder Act 1752   74
Murrow, Ann   74–5, 78

Napoleonic Wars   17, 36
narco-analysis   129
National Insurance/National Health Service   104–5
Needham v Needham   110, 115, 118, 122
New Poor Law   53
Newcastle   51, 59
Newell, Dr Robert   182
Newgate Gaol   79
Newman, Sir George   116–17
Newton's Apple   197
nitrous fumigation   20, 21–4
North, William   30
noxious trades   55
Nuffield Council of Bioethics   213, 218
nuisances *see* bye laws, for the suppression of nuisances

oestrogen treatment   129
Offences Against the Persons Act 1837   75–7
Offences Against the Persons Act 1861   63, 67, 68, 77–8, 105–6, 145
oil of vitriol   63
Oldham Area Health Authority   172
Oldham General Hospital   172, 174
ophthalmia   27–32
Otten, AE   208

Palmerston, Lord   26–7, 28–30, 32*n*
Parramore, Richard   79
Pedlar, Dr Kit   173
Perlmutter v Beth David Hospital   206
Perth prison   129
Perutz, Max   170
Pfeffer, N   203–4
Phillips, R   111
physicians
  asylum/prison   91–2, 95, 96–7
  professional changes   103–4, 123–4
Pinel, Philippe   84

plague, contagion 32–6
Playfair, William Smoult 106
Poor Law Commission 40, 53
Poppel, Henry Walter 94–5
Porter, R 83, 104
Powell, Enoch 189, 191
prisons
  psycho-therapeutic units 128–9
  surgeon/physicians 96–7
Professional Advisory Group for Genetic and Infertility Services 190
psychiatric testimony 79–98
  background 79–82
  1760–1843 82–5, 89
  1843–1876 85–8, 89
  1876–1900 88–90, 92–4
  evolution of terms 92–3
  social setting of diagnosis 90–2
  witness independence 95–7
  see also melancholia
psycho-therapeutic units (prison) 128–9
Public Health (Venereal Disease) Regulations 1916 110–11
puerperal mania/insanity 87, 88, 93
Pwllheli 51–2

quarantine regulations 34–5

R v Bourne 145
Ramsey, Paul 204
Reagan administration 207
Reagan, L 3
res nullius 202–3
Richardson, R 4
Robinson, Mr 33
Rockefeller Institute 201
Roe v Wade 204
Ross, William 153
Royal College of General Practitioners 180
Royal College of Midwives 150, 155, 163
Royal College of Nursing 150
Royal College of Obstetricions and Gynaecologists 150–1, 162, 172, 177, 180, 182, 192
Royal College of Physicians 26, 35–6, 107, 108, 117, 197–8, 214
Royal College of Physicians and Surgeons of Glasgow 162
Royal College of Psychiatrists 162–3
Royal College of Surgeons 117
Royal Commission on the Criminal Law 1836 75
Royal Commission on VD 120
Royal Edinburgh Hospital 138
Royston, Ivor 209, 217
Rushworth, Dr Winifred 130–1
Russell, Lord John 75
Ryan, Michael 64, 74

St John-Stevas, Norman 152–3
St Kershaw's Cottage Hospital 172
sanitary nuisance *see under* bye laws, for the suppression of nuisances
Saunby, Professor Robert 107, 108
Saunders, John Cunningham 27
scientific certainty 1
Scotland
  homosexuality *see* homosexual offenders, in Scotland
  vitriol throwing and 61–2, 71–3, 77
Scott, James 88–9, 96
Scottish Advisory Council on the Treatment and Rehabilitation of Offenders 128, 129–30
Scottish Association of Executive Councils 154
Scottish Health Visitors' Association 162
Scottish Home Department 128, 131, 162
Scottish Prison and Borstal Service 127, 128, 129, 131–2, 138
Scottish Prison Medical Officers 129
Scottish Public Health Nursing Administrators and Tutors Group 155
select committees of inquiry, military medicine 17–37
  army medical system 25
  background 17–18
  concerns 18–20
  conclusion 36–7
  expertise/make-up 31–2, 36–7
  function 18–19
  kinds of evidence 24–5
  medical education, regulation 25–7
  nitrous fumigation 20, 21–4
  ophthalmia inquiries 27–32
  plague, contagion 32–6
  rewards for inventions 20
  vaccine inoculation 20–1
semi-living entities 218
Short, Renée 189
Shorter, E 104
Simon, John 54
Singapore 179
Singer, Peter 178
sleepwalkers 89
Smith, Edgar 88–9
Smith, FE *see* Birkenhead, Earl of
Smith, G 126
Smith, Sydney 68
Smith, Thomas 148
Smyth, Dr James Carmichael 20, 21–4
Society for the Protection of the Unborn Child 150
sodomy (offence) 134, 138, 139, 140
somnambulism 80
Stallworthy, Sir John 174
Steel, David 144, 149–51, 163–4

Stephen, James Fitzjames 87
Steptoe, Patrick 168–9, 170–5, 180, 183, 186
Stockton
  byelaw 48–9, 59
  local act 43–4, 48
Stoddart, William 95–6
Strangeways Research Laboratory 202
Strathern, M 212
sulphuric acid 63–5
Sunderland 59
surgeons
  asylum/prison/gaol 91–2, 95, 96–7
  professional changes 103–4, 123–4
suspended consciousness 80, 87, 93–4
syphilis 105

Taunton 44
Taylor, Alfred Swaine 64, 66–7, 68, 78
Teesside 51
Terrorism Act 2000 77
test tube babies 171
Thatcher administration 207
therapeutic abortion 105, 158
Thompson, David 202
Thompson, John Gordon 202
Thurnham, Peter 191
tissue culture 201
Tissue Culture Association 205–6
Titmuss, Richard 214
Towns Improvement Clauses Act 1847 55
Trotter, Dr Thomas 22, 23–4
Trounson, Alan 180
Tyneside 51

UK Co-ordinating Committee on Cancer Research 214–16
Unborn Children (Protection) Bill 1984/5 168, 189–91, 193–4
unconsciousness 81, 87–8, 90, 93–4, 98
University of California, Los Angeles 208, 210
University of California, San Diego 209
University of California School of Medicine and Law 205
unwholesome food 54

vaccine inoculation 20–1
VD Treatment Regulations 1916 120
venereal disease (VD), confidentiality and 105, 109–22
  in divorce petitions 109–10, 111–12
  government policy on VD 110–11, 112–14
  medical developments 110–11

privilege case 114–19
  aftermath 119–22
  professional implications 123–4
  statutory priviledge proposal 112–14
vertique épileptique 81
Vetch, Dr John 29, 30, 31
vitriol throwing 61–78
  1861 onwards 77–8
  as felony/offences 61–2
  methodology of study 63
  mid-century 75–7
  as urban crime 64–5
  as wound *see* wounds/wounding
Voluntary Licensing Authority 191, 192–3

Wade, John 74–5
Wakefield prison 128
Waldby, Catherine 218
Walker, N 83
Walters, William 178
Ward, T 4
Warnock Committee, *see* Inquiry into Human Fertilisation and Embryology
Warnock, Mary, Baroness 176, 183, 185
Watson, James 170
Watson, K 4
Wecht, C 2–3
Wellcome Trust 213, 216
Western Isles Health Board 163
White, James 161
Williams, Shirley 175
Winslade, William J 205, 206
Winslow, Forbes 80
Winston, Robert 173–4, 194–5
Winterton, Nicholas 188
Wivel, A 153
Wolfenden Committee 126–34, 141–2
'women's problems' 87
Woods, Hugh 117, 118
Worcester
  bye law 50, 51, 54, 58
  local act 49–50
World Federation of Doctors Who Respect Human Life 181
Wormwood Scrubs prison 128
wounds/wounding
  burns and 65–9, 74, 77–8
  definition 61–2
  legal context 69–70
  Lord Ellenborough's Act and 70–1

Yale University 208
York 44